THE TRUMPET SHALL SOUND

Behold, I shew you a mystery; We shall not all sleep, but we shall all be changed,

In a moment, in the twinkling of an eye, at the last trump: for the trumpet shall sound, and the dead shall be raised incorruptible, and we shall all be changed.

St. Paul's First Epistle to the
Corinthians 15:51-52

THE TRUMPET
SHALL SOUND

A Study of 'Cargo' Cults in Melanesia

PETER WORSLEY

Second, Augmented Edition

SCHOCKEN BOOKS · NEW YORK

Published by arangement with MacGibbon & Kee, London

Copyright © 1968 by Peter Worsley

Library of Congress Catalog Card No. 67–26995
Manufactured in the United States of America

To

MY MOTHER

FATHER AND

SISTER

＝

Contents

Preface to the Second Edition

Cargo studies have now become so numerous that one cannot hope to review them all without writing another book, as, indeed, Professor Jarvie has done. I have therefore singled out for particular consideration in the new Introduction to this edition those works that seemed particularly important (mainly because of their theoretical content). Mr D. A. Heathcote's bibliography will guide those who wish to read further to the full range of available literature.

Since many of these works raise complex theoretical issues, the discussion of them in the Introduction may well not interest the non-specialist reader, though I hope it will probably interest any student of anthropology or sociology. The Introduction to the new edition, therefore, is oriented to colleagues and students, in sharp contrast to the aim expressed in the opening sentence of the original Introduction. The non-specialist reader, therefore, will probably prefer to start at the original Introduction, and by-pass the Introduction to the second edition.

My thanks are due to three people: firstly, to Wesley Sharrock, for his unstinted kindness in subjecting the new Introduction to searching and detailed criticism at a very high level of theoretical sophistication, as part of two years' intellectual interchange from which I think I have benefited more than he has; secondly, to Mr D. A. Heathcote, for allowing me to draw from his wider and, to my knowledge, quite exhaustive and authoritative bibliography of Cargo cults and allied movements in the whole of the South Pacific, which was designed to supplement Ida Leeson's earlier bibliography; and, finally, to Mrs Christine Hayes, who coped with the manuscript of the new Introduction with skill and exemplary patience under that most painful of pressures, a publisher's deadline. Finally, Mr Brian du Toit, of the Department of Anthropology, University of Florida, kindly allowed me to read and cite unpublished work.

PETER WORSLEY

Manchester
August, 1967

Introduction to the Second Edition:
Theoretical and Methodological
Considerations

The Concept of Charisma

One of the rewards of reading Marshall McLuhan is that it enables me to make my friend Horace Morris feel uneasy about not having read it, just as in the past I've made him feel very insecure for not understanding commitment and alienation, and not knowing what charisma was, and thinking that pop music was a bad thing after all the rest of us had realised it was a good thing.

The way the dissemination of ideas works around our way is that first my good friend Christopher Crumble gets to hear about them, and makes me feel insecure. Then I catch up and make Horace Morris feel insecure. By the time Horace had discovered the meaning and omnipresence of charisma, for example, I was right off it—no one seemed charismatic to me any more, not even Harold Wilson or David Frost. I was on to 'symbiosis'—and Christopher Crumble, the Speedy Gonzales of the intellect, was already out of 'symbiosis' and into 'I-Thou', or even 'freakout.'

(Michael Frayn, *The Observer*, June 18, 1967)

THIS RATHER FRIVOLOUS quotation from the work of a leading English humorist registers very well the extent to which the concept of charisma, once confined to narrow scholarly circles, has become by now one of the most popular pieces of coinage in the intellectual exchange market. One might well rejoice about this if the word summed up a new set of ideas previously inadequately clear; if there was some reasonable degree of consensus as to its meaning; and if there was, consequently, some overlap in the way it was used in actual research work. Given these conditions, communication of ideas would be improved: a concept previously restricted to the specialist academic world would have become available to a wider public, and more people enabled to think more clearly about social action.

It may be doubted, however, whether the concept of 'charisma' measures up to these requirements, whether in respect of clarity of meaning, or the novelty of the ideas it subsumes, or in terms of some common central meaning subscribed to by all users.

Charisma, according to Max Weber, who introduced it into the standard repertoire of concepts of modern sociology, refers to

> 'a certain quality of an individual personality by virtue of which he is set apart from ordinary men and treated as endowed with supernatural, superhuman, or at least specifically exceptional powers or qualities. These are not accessible to the ordinary person, but are regarded as of divine origin or as exemplary, and on the basis of them the individual concerned is treated as a leader.' [1]

The most common use of the term, in current fashionable use, however, seems to mean little more than 'personally popular,' or, alternatively, 'magnetic.' The rise of the term seems to be closely connected with the rise to the United States Presidency of John F. Kennedy, who was held by journalists to be peculiarly attractive to the general public, firstly, by virtue of certain personal attributes: his (and his wife's) handsomeness and youth, his familism and his intelligence (and intellectualism, as embodied both in the White House court-salon to which eminent academics, artists, etc., were invited, and in the ring of key advisers imported from the universities). His conquest—in the pursuit of the Presidency—of the handicap of Roman Catholicism for the first time in U.S. history, and his subsequent behaviour at the time of the Cuban missile crisis in December 1962, further consolidated the popularity established by virtue of primordial personality attributes: his charisma was now apparent in 'signs' and 'proofs,' to use Weberian terminology. It was now achieved, not simply ascribed; immanent attributes had become 'behaviours'; potentialities had become realized. In the process, a 'message' had been announced: the New Frontier.

Already, however, we can discern several empirical features which constitute dissociable and analytically problematic elements; the element of personal appeal; the fact that this appeal was not peculiarly the President's alone, but was shared, or contributed to, by the President's wife; the multiplex nature of this appeal, compounded as it is of personality attributes, acts, and a message; and finally, the existence of acts that constitute 'signs' or 'proofs' of charismatic claims and qualities.

[1] Max Weber, *The Theory of Social and Economic Organization* (New York: Free Press, 1947), pp. 358–59.

Given the subsequent tragic death of Kennedy, it is not hard to see why the specifically personal element he brought to the role of President should have registered sufficiently strongly with journalists to have caused them to search for a new word with which to describe it. 'Charisma,' we are told, was the 'O.K.-word' for 1963. 'Charismatic,' which in popular usage originally meant little more than 'personally popular,' came, in time, closer to Weber's original definition: at a time when two men appeared to hold the future continuation of the human species in their hands, it acquired additional overtones of the 'heroic' or even 'superhuman.' A martyr's death intensified this appeal.

The second major reason for the sudden fashionableness of this concept is ascribable to the rapid emergence of nationalist movements, mainly in Africa, in the 1960's. Since these were normally swift in their development, sudden and quick in their success, and were usually headed by a dominant leader commanding mass support, political scientists found the label 'charismatic' convenient. All too often, it became a substitute for the careful analysis of political organization and ideology. It has been, therefore, a concept of considerable ambiguity (and therefore dubious utility), more often, however, bandied about and used *en passant* and intermittently in empirical researches, than as a central concept around which whole theoretical schemes have been built. It has thus been a pervasive but elusive concept, a loose and imprecise shorthand term rather than a scientific concept with defined connotations. A few sociologists have used the concept more centrally in various studies of developing countries,[1] however, though not, to my mind, very convincingly or fruitfully.

As we find in the Kennedy case, a charismatic appeal, whether it depends upon attributes of personality and character or upon the performance of certain acts, or both, if it is to become the basis of collective social action, needs to be *perceived, invested with meaning*, and *acted upon* by significant others: those who respond to this charismatic appeal. The mere recognition that X displays unusual qualities is itself a complex social process, entailing the evaluation of X by others according to some value yardstick: such qualities must be positively registered and ap-

---

[1] E.g. Edward Shils, 'The Concentration and Dispersion of Charisma: Their Bearing on Economic Policy in Underdeveloped Countries,' *World Politics,* I, No. 1 (1958), 1–19; W. G. Runciman, 'Charismatic Legitimacy and One-Party Rule in Ghana,' *Archives Européennes de Sociologie,* IV, No. 1 (1963), 148–65; Immanuel Wallerstein, *The Politics of Independence* (New York: Vintage Books, 1961), chap. v.

praised, both cognitively and emotionally. To give rise to a charismatic movement or organization, however, to crystallize individual beliefs into a belief *system* and believers into a social collectivity, the perceptions must further generate a disposition to behave in socially meaningful and causally significant ways, and to do so in coordination with others in a goal-directed and normatively controlled fashion. The charismatic personality has to be 'recognized,' socially validated and accorded the *right*, firstly, to formulate policy (especially in markedly innovatory ways), and then to *command* support for that policy. In Weber's sociology, charisma is not mystically viewed as some inexpressible quality which we cannot comprehend. About its 'ultimate' authenticity, we are not, normally, as sociologists, concerned, for that is a matter for epistemological evaluation, and ultimately a matter of our reference-procedures for both arriving at value positions and relating these values to our scientific activities. The sociologist is not able to avoid being confronted with these problems, but normally by-passes them in his work, treating beliefs as elements in social interaction, insofar as, observably, some men believe that charisma is 'given off' by certain individuals and therefore act in special ways, both towards those individuals and towards others, because of that belief. To the sociologist, charisma—unless we ourselves believe in its authenticity—can only be that which is recognized, by believers and followers, as 'charismatic' in the behaviour of those they treat as charismatic. Charisma is thus a function of recognition: the prophet without honour cannot be a charismatic prophet. Charisma, therefore, sociologically viewed, is a social relationship, not an attribute of individual personality or a mystical quality. That people believe in it is a datum, not a confirmation of the ultimate validity of the belief. Charisma thus provides, for those who believe in it, more than an abstract ideological rationale or a special kind of legitimation. It is a legitimation grounded in a relationship of loyalty and identification, in which the leader is followed because he embodies values in which the followers have an 'interest.' Followers, that is, do not follow simply because of some abstracted 'mystical' quality: a leader is able to magnetize them because he evokes or plays upon some strand of intellectual or emotional predisposition, and because—more than this—he purports to offer the *realization* of certain values in action. But the promise has to be effected: an abstract programme is no lasting basis for a continuing and developing association-in-action. This is why 'signs,' 'proofs,' the behavioral acting out or demonstration of the abstract 'promise' are a *sine qua non* for the continuation of the movement. The charismatic leader, more than other kinds of ruler, whose leadership may repose on quite different bases—patronage, force, constitutional authority, traditional right to rule, etc.—is singularly dependent upon being accepted by his followers. Since he is unable to appeal to 'normal' sources of legitimacy, such as entrenched ideological values or reliance upon command over material resources (whether 'remunerative' or 'coercive' sanctions, to use Etzioni's terms [1]), he depends primarily upon faith, though in the longer run, not faith alone: 'signs' and 'proofs'—the acting out of the consequences of the charismatic belief in organizational and other behavioural terms—are needed for the faith to persist. (Though 'proofs,' one should note, need not necessarily take the forms of *successful* actions. Failure—e.g. martydom—is also a very suitable 'proof.') Friedland[2] has shown how the message and actions of the leader often require proof in the form of success, or the carrying out of *hazardous* tasks. (He uses as his case material Julius Nyerere's rise to leadership of the Tanzanian nationalist movement.)

The nature of the values held by the mass of followers is thus of prime significance in understanding how it is that charismatic leaders are able to mobilize support readily, or, in some cases, even to have support thrust upon them. Some charismatic prophets are obscure, often marginal, eccentric and unbalanced individuals, who are 'taken up.' Leaders are perceived and recognized, therefore, not merely as 'striking' personalities, expressive speakers, or the like. Such people are to be found at London's Hyde Park Corner every day of the week.[3] What these people lack, however, is a *relevant* message. It is not that they lack any message at all, for they often have quite definite messages, including some very radical ones. But they are, in fact, figures of entertainment, even fun, rather than serious potential leaders of movements or organizations, precisely because they possess only the technical trappings of personal leadership rather than the content, the communications techniques without anything acceptable to communicate, the medium without the message (which, *pace* Marshall McLuhan, may be quite separable). Without the message, there can be no serious content to the communication.

[1] Amitai Etzioni, *A Comparative Analysis of Complex Organizations: On Power, Involvement, and Their Correlates* (New York: Free Press, 1961), pp. 4–6.

[2] William H. Friedland, 'For a Sociological Concept of Charisma,' *Social Forces*, October, 1964, XLIII, No. 1, 23–24.

[3] See Heathcote Williams, *The Speakers* (Harmondsworth: Penguin Books, 1967).

And it cannot be *any* message: it must, firstly, speak to unsatisfied wants in the hearers, and, secondly, offer them some promise of eventual fulfilment. In the most radical variants, it offers very immediate achievement indeed: the imminent arrival of the Cargo, for example. As Friedland puts it:

> 'in sum, while there are plenty of people with messages, these must be *relevant to social groups* before they begin to be received and become the basis for action.' [1]

The followers, then, in a dialectical way, create, by selecting them out, the leaders, who in turn *command* on the basis of this newly-accorded legitimacy. The model is not a model of one-way traffic, as in Mills's famous description of 'mass society' as being typified, *inter alia,* by the fact that 'far fewer people express opinions than receive them'; by a communications system in which 'it is difficult or impossible for the individual to answer back immediately or with any effect'; by a state of affairs in which 'the realization of opinion in action' is controlled by 'the authorities who organize and control the channels of such action'; and in which 'agents of authority penetrate the mass.' [2]

A more valid model for the analysis of charismatic authority has to be interactionist: one in which followers with possibly utopian or at least diffuse and unrealized aspirations cleave to an appropriate leader because he articulates and consolidates their aspirations. He then specifies and narrows these aspirations, converting them both into more concrete and visible goals towards whose achievement collective action can be oriented and organized, and into *beliefs* which can be validated by reference to experience. This is normally done by so generalizing beliefs that virtually everything that happens in social life fulfils the prophecy.

The message, then, is the most important element: it is this that the followers or potential followers 'wish to know.' In her brilliant and over-modestly titled 'note critique,' the late Dr. Talmon indicated how the well-known phenomenon of the fissiparity of the movements is related to this primacy of the message.[3] To put it provocatively, the person of the prophet is

---

[1] *op. cit.,* p. 21 (my italics).

[2] C. Wright Mills, *The Power Elite* (New York: Oxford University Press, 1957), p. 304.

[3] Y. Talmon, 'Pursuit of the Millennium: The Relation between Religion and Social Change,' *Archives Européennes de Sociologie,* III, No. 1 (1962), 149–64.

commonly quite unimportant in the so-called 'charismatic' movement.

The extent to which the movement depends upon the personal innovatory initiative of the prophet is, at the least, highly variable, and cannot be assumed to be a constant; it requires empirical investigation to see what actually is the case. In some movements, the prophet is merely a 'vessel,' channel, instrument, or bearer of a message which he himself does not create, formulate, or even modify, but merely transmits. But other charismatic leaders tie the movement and the message to their coattails: *they* define what the message is, and their personal declaration is everything.

Lenin's arrival at the Finland Station in the famous sealed train in 1917 to announce a policy quite at variance with the official Bolshevik 'party line' is a classic case of this latter kind of charismatic 'annunciation.' The impact is beautifully caught in this pen-picture by a non-Bolshevik witness of the scene:

> 'I shall never forget that thunderlike speech, startling and amazing not only to me, a heretic accidentally present there, but also to the faithful, all of them. I assert that nobody there had expected anything of the kind. It seemed as if all the elements and the spirit of universal destruction had risen from their lairs, knowing neither barriers nor doubts, nor personal difficulties nor personal considerations, to hover . . . above the heads of the bewitched disciples.' [1]

Where leadership is not so closely focussed as this on the person of the outstanding prophet, but much more on the message 'borne' by him, it is indeed highly probable that a prophetic movement will generate not a centrally focussed, single authority-structure, but a fissiparous dispersion of leadership in the persons of numerous leaders, particularly where inspiration is open to all. Indeed, we find precisely this fissiparity in many cults, centralization in others. There is thus no single organizational pattern of 'charismatic authority,' certainly not always a single-focus structure.

But if the extent to which the movement allows the message to be formulated by the leader empirically varies, analytically the message has still to be acceptable, and those who do the accepting are the believers. They are thus not passive subjects, but partners in a relationship oriented to action. Lenin's impact was,

---

[1] Description by N. Sukhanov, cited in I. Deutscher, *Stalin: A Political Biography* (London and New York: Oxford University Press, 1949), p. 140.

of course, neither 'purely' personal-innovatory nor dependent
solely on his message. He had to formulate a message which,
however innovatory, was conceived within the context of established Marxist theory; his message had to be patently consonant
with assumptions shared by both himself and his audience. But
more than this, he was able to communicate such a message only
by virtue of his eminent position as Bolshevik leader, i.e., within
a highly bureaucratized structure. The weight placed upon the
leader in empirical instances and the analytical interaction
between leader, message, and followers are not fully enough distinguished in the following otherwise helpful passage of Talmon's. Noting that there are movements in which 'inspired and
energetic leaders' have played important parts in the genesis and
growth of the movement, she observes that in other cases:

> 'leaders function as a symbolic focus of identification rather than
> as sources of authority and initiative. In some regions, millenarism
> is an endemic force and when it reaches a flash-point it may seize
> upon *any available figure*. The initiative in such a case comes
> primarily from the community which sometimes almost imposes
> the leadership position on its leader. Some of its leaders are, in
> fact, insignificant and their elevation to such a position *seems to
> be accidental*—they happened to be there and fulfilled an urgent
> need for a mediator. That the function of leadership is sometimes
> primarily symbolic is clearly seen in the cases of movements with
> *absent leaders*. In some notable instances the influence of a leader
> and his integrating power have increased enormously after he left
> or was removed from the scene of operations. Death, imprison-
> ment or mysterious absence have increased their stature and en-
> hanced their authority. Only when absent did they begin to loom
> large as prophetic figures.'[1]

Charisma can thus be imputed retrospectively, or, as we shall
see, emerge *after* the assumption of power, not before.

Moreover, Talmon points out, 'often there is not just one
charismatic leader but a multiple leadership.' She then notes the
distinction between prophet and organizer suggested in the
present book, and adds the further point that 'the movements
are sometimes based on loyalty to leaders at the local level and
do not have an overall leadership.'

Far from being intensely focussed on the person of the leader,
then, we find movements which, empirically, are eminently millenarian, but in which the leader may be (a) absent; (b) not a
single person at all, but with leadership divided amongst several

[1] *op. cit.,* p. 134 (my italics).

people; (c) where the functions of prophet and organizer, at least, are separately embodied in two distinct persons; (d) where the leader is often one of a number of local leaders, rather than a single central figure (as Weber implies); (e) where the prophet is an insignificant person; (f) where the symbolic importance of the leader only becomes significant after his physical removal. Analytically, whatever the empirical case concerning the degree to which the component elements in the leadership syndrome are weighted, leadership still has to be comprehended as the meeting of social wants in potential followers in a given situation of unsatisfied aspirations. From this standpoint, all leadership, whatever the empirical facts, is primarily symbolic and relational, and only secondarily personal.

The contrast between this conception and Weber's own could not be sharper. 'Charismatic authority,' Weber remarks, refers to 'rule over men . . . to which the governed submit because of their belief in the extraordinary qualities of the specific person.' [1] Again, Parsons reiterates the point: 'As Weber treats charisma in the context of authority, its bearer is always an individual leader.' [2] How (or whether) Weber conceived of the 'person,' as distinct from the 'qualities' or 'powers' embodied in the charismatic leader's person, is extremely unclear, as is the status of the phrase 'specific person,' which could, of course, allow for the existence of multiple prophets. The fundamental ambiguity is expressed in Weber's own words elsewhere: 'A prophet is any man who by virtue of his *purely personal* charisma *and* by virtue of his *mission* proclaims a religious doctrine or a Divine command.' [3]

In any case, this emphasis on the importance of the personality of the leader distracts us, I would suggest, from focussing upon the social significance of the leader as symbol, catalyst, and message-bearer. (Of course, not 'any,' but only situationally appropriate and culturally/structurally-indicated and apposite persons are thrust into leadership.) Analytically, the charismatic leader must always be a symbolizer, and all movements, conversely, must always, intrinsically, be projected upon and organized around symbols, whether personalized ones or otherwise. Agents and message are thus ideal-type elements or aspects of

---

[1] *From Max Weber: Essays in Sociology*, H. H. Gerth and C. W. Mills (eds.) (London: Routledge & Kegan Paul; New York: Oxford University Press, 1948), p. 295.

[2] Talcott Parsons, in his introduction to Weber's *The Theory of Social and Economic Organization*, p. 65.

[3] Quoted from Reinhard Bendix, *Max Weber: An Intellectual Portrait* (New York: Doubleday, 1962), p. 89 (my italics).

leadership in movements which depend upon freely given consent for their legitimacy: the agent, personal or impersonal, is always attached to (whether as bearer or creator) a message; the message must always be communicated via agents. Any given movement will display these ineluctable ideal-type elements with different degrees of emphasis.

The message, as distinct from the 'theology'—Weber's 'ethic'—is also highly culturally conditioned itself. Hence, if we permit ourselves to focus our eyes exclusively or even primarily upon the leader element in the leader-follower relationship, our attention is distracted from what is sociologically more important, to wit, the relationship *between* the two elements. This is, at worst, to accept the ideological claims of the charismatic movement at their face value, as if the claims had ontological, and not simply sociological, status as truth. Charisma is not an *explanation* of behaviour: it is a datum, itself an element in sociological analysis—something that (some) people believe. This concentration on the person of the prophet is also a non-sociological view of organized behaviour, since it implicitly assumes that the leader-follower relationship is not reflexive, but unidirectional—from the top downwards. Initially, of course, there is not even any 'top' to what becomes a charismatic movement. To make the transition from being a *leader,* the prophet must, ultimately, be recognized and accepted, then invested with legitimacy and, ultimately, authority. Or to use the more traditional, but less nuanced, terminology of Weber himself, charismatic leadership becomes transformed into authority as the movement develops.[1]

To achieve this, the leader must, as we have seen, strike responsive chords in his audience. The charismatic leader, that is, is a catalytic personality. His catalytic function is to convert latent solidarities into active ritual and political action.

He has to do more than evoke private psychic responses, then, if he is to become a leader: he must generate modes of action and interaction; he must create an organization, or stimulate the creation of one. This is the second, profoundly social, phase in the genesis of this kind of social movement.

If the message, however, is what the followers basically 'wish to know,' its realization is what they wish to achieve. But the end of the world, in the nature of things, does not occur: what *can* be realized is the consolidation of a movement devoted to such chiliastic expectations, though even these must be deferred. At this point, in fact, the 'immediate' chiliastic cult usually undergoes a displacement of ends, or, to follow the kind of ter-

[1] Bendix, *op. cit.,* pp. 208–9.

minology used by Etzioni, there is goal displacement, goal succession, and goal modification: more briefly, the original goals are succeeded by others.[1]

Since the end of the world cannot be produced to order or on time, modifications of the original prophecy and explanations for its failure have to be produced. Short-term falsification is no serious problem, even for 'immediate' chiliasm. The classic study here is that by Festinger and his colleagues who studied a cult of flying-saucer enthusiasts in the United States.[2] Like so many of their chiliastic predecessors—and no doubt successors—they easily found 'reasons,' consonant with the basic ideological assumptions of the cult, for deferring the prophesied arrival of the Martians time after time. Such redefinition of prophecy is only seriously necessary where the prophecy is highly specific, however: where, for example, the arrival of the Martians (or the end of the world) is due on a certain date at a certain time in a certain place. Prophecies vary, however, from the highly precise to the extremely vague. 'Spongy' prophecies like those described for the Doomsday cult by Lofland [3] require no such manipulation, for both the macro-events at the international and national levels, as well as minor, local happenings to lesser mortals, were all seen as abundant 'confirmations' of the truth of the cult's basic, 'spongy' beliefs. All events are thus held to constitute fractional symbolic confirmations of the wider cosmic beliefs: particular wars, or local murders, as manifestations of the coming (or perhaps already present) 'Reign of the Beast': the belief is so vague, so ambiguous, so generalized, that no particular event can possibly constitute a falsification of it. Conversely, given a spongy enough style of prophecy, all events can be interpreted as positive confirmation of the prophecy.

More precise prophecies do face the serious problem, and prospect, of disconfirmation. It is not the case that experience confirms the truth of *any* ideological proposition, as some writers, in their sensitivity to the relativity of knowledge, appear to imply. *Dis*confirmation does take place. In Western Europe, one of the major cultural processes of the last century has been the loss of belief in Christian dogmas. The problem of redefining dogma—usually by so generalizing it that it thereafter becomes

---

[1] Amitai Etzioni, *Modern Organizations* (Englewood Cliffs, N. J.: Prentice-Hall), 1964, p. 13.

[2] Leon Festinger, Henry W. Riecken, and Stanley Schachter, *When Prophecy Fails* (New York: Harper & Row, 1966).

[3] John Lofland, *Doomsday Cult: A Study of Conversion, Proselytization and Maintenance of Faith* (Englewood Cliffs, N. J.: Prentice-Hall, 1966), Part III.

difficult to disprove—is common to all belief systems, whether Cargo cults, Christian denominations, or secular philosophies of history that involve statements about the future. Prophecy is most subject to disconfirmation when it is precise and testable, least vulnerable when most vague. But the *beliefs* underpinning prophecies (and especially religious beliefs)—as distinct from the prophecies themselves, whether these latter be precise or spongy—are always and necessarily general, and thus inherently capable of being stretched so as to cope with new or unexpected developments. Even so, long-term disconfirmation of the relevance of even basic beliefs does take place, as well as short-term falsification of immediate prophecy. The cult organized around 'immediate' chiliastic prophecies, therefore, since it is normally less elaborated and less developed and institutionalized over time than 'established' religions, is singularly vulnerable to disconfirmation, though its decline may still leave untouched diffuse yearnings for a messiah or regenerated world as the solution to felt discontents, for those can be culturally transmitted and persist in a minimally institutionalized way via the psyches of individuals for generations. But secondary elaboration of belief probably cannot sustain indefinitely those who anticipate and desperately hope for an immediate realization of the millennium: the immediacy must therefore be removed if the cult is to survive. So the chiliastic imminence is replaced, as we see from many instances in this book, by a more diffuse promise of the future Happening.

Those cults that have persisted, not just over years or decades but centuries, have done so by severely converting chiliastic immediacy into forms of remote, 'ultimate,' and usually otherworldly millenarism which cannot be easily falsified. In the extreme, the prophesied state will only be realized in the after-life, outside the quotidian, examinable world altogether. This kind of belief is indeed irrefutable in terms of any simple test of pragmatic experience, because its point of reference is transcendental and other-worldly. Hence it constitutes, together with Weber's famous 'meaninglessness,' one of the eternal founts of religious faith. It derives from psychic needs built into, informing, or underlying a whole range of types and cases of specific tenets of belief which, in consequence, are usually held with great tenacity and devotion.

But the failure of prophecy can be compensated for by much more radical tactics than the simple reshaping of the prophecy itself. It can be replaced by a quite different form of religious-philosophical system altogether. For chiliasm is only one way of providing hope and meaning, and channels of action. There are other religious and non-religious alternatives.

If the end of the world cannot be relied upon, at least the subjective state of the individual can be changed so that the world becomes a more tolerable place, or in such a way that events in the world are radically reinterpreted and given new meanings. In the extreme, the obdurate, continued existence of the world can be overcome by withdrawing from it, as in ascetic mysticism, monasticism, or religious utopian communities (if the world permits). Thenceforward, what goes on in the world is of minimal concern to the believer (or may be of subsidiary concern, since many such communities are not entirely world-renouncing; they perform good works, send members out to work in the outside world, etc.).

Religion as a Category

Weber's 'other-worldly' and 'this-worldly' orientations thus remain useful analytical categories, as long as we realize that they are constructed with reference to the mental orientation of an actor, who still has to establish some operational balance between, on the one hand, his physical and social existence in this world, and, on the other, his primary subjective orientation to the other, or next, world, or to a wider, more inclusive cosmic universe.

The relationship of this world to the other or next world may be variously conceived by the believer:

(a) *part-to-whole:* this life is a mere speck of dust in a cosmos which may be conceived of as more or less shapeless, timeless, and directionless, or highly structured; (b) *reflectional:* this life is the counterpart of an other-worldly existence, as in those primitive heavens where life is the same as on earth, only 'spiritualized'; (c) *emanational:* this life is a dependent variable of the Idea, as in Hegel; (d) *contingent:* this life is a forerunner of another, 'higher,' existence, a sequentially necessary passage through the 'vale of tears,' during which the soul undergoes tests of moral-spiritual virtue, is ultimately judged, punished or rewarded, either at one blow (e.g., the Day of Judgment) or phased intervals (e.g., successive reincarnations), with the successful examinee either reaching the highest hierarchical grades or losing his personality and humanity—i.e., sin, defects, fleshly commitments—and becoming absorbed into timeless eternity. The moral-ethical component is commonly found, since even the most transcendental religions usually recognize the world to the extent of recommending some, even if minimal, ways of behaving in this world, and towards one's fellow men, and not just towards God or in terms of orientation to the ultimate life. Religions thus concern themselves, in varying mixes, with ethical, cosmological, and eschatological problems, but by no means in the same way or with the same weight or place of emphasis; indeed, any of these concerns may be virtually omitted. As Macbeath has clearly shown,[1] there are, for example, religions which are profoundly cosmological—in that they are very much concerned with the relationship of this world to the rest of the cosmos—but which are not all eschatological. Indeed, the Christian notion of eschatology, as being concerned with 'last things,' itself needs to be broken into its constituent elements. It is, in any case, only one particular cultural conception of what the 'last things' are, and therefore a particular and parochial 'historical individual,' rather than an analytical category.

The Christian 'last things' conventionally include death, judgment, heaven and hell. But the notion of judgment at or after death is by no means universally linked to conceptions of an after-life; the belief in heaven and hell is even more parochial. Indeed, great world religions have been quite uneschatological and amoral, insofar as they have no place for such conceptions as that of judgment in the after-life, and/or insofar as they do not necessarily tie their cosmological conceptions to any system of ethical prescriptions and moral injunctions about behaviour on this earth *at all*. The extreme case is the antinomian 'heresy,' where the believer holds that this world is *only* a low-order, precursory phase of existence. To him, the demands of Caesar or of one's fellow men are as nothing, mere conceits and distractions— if not intrinsically sinful—which the truly spiritual man pays no heed to in his incessant orientation towards the true path, which he can only follow by emancipating himself from the demands on this earth *at all*. The extreme case is the antinomian 'heresy,' earthly order is concerned, because the earth's definition of sin is an arbitrary or irrelevant thing of Caesar's, or at best an invalid definition. The true believer can only sin within the framework of his own *religious* value system and relational system. The source of morality and, therefore, its requirements of man are other-worldly. Man's primary relationship is to God, not to man; the latter relationship is quite irrelevant, or, at best, secondary and derivative. (There is, of course, an eternal, immanent tension as far as the 'practical' implications of religious

[1] A. Macbeath, *Experiments in Living* (London: Macmillan, 1952).

belief for action in the world are concerned, since a prime orientation to the other world always invites the criticism that institutionalized religion is deaf to the claims of justice. Conversely, what one might call relational or 'moral' religions—which insist that one must act out the implications of belief in one's relations with one's fellow men—tend to become embroiled in the partisan conflicts of this earth, and cannot, like transcendental religions, appeal to all and rise above the secular political battle.) The dissociation between this world and the other one may take the form of inversion, whereby the price of sanctity is not simply the flouting or by-passing of earthly rules in a 'neutral' fashion, as being 'of no consequence,' but a crusading, militant, deliberate and systematic, sometimes nihilist, destruction and defiance of them.

The assumption that ethical values and moral behaviour on earth are always interwoven with religion, or that cosmology and eschatology are both necessary and related parts of religious world-systems, is erroneous. It is empirically falsifiable from our knowledge of those religions that do not postulate an other-worldly source of moral rules and do not, for example, endeavour to enforce conformity to those rules by applying 'mystical' sanctions (in the anthropologist's sense of 'mystical' as 'pertaining to sacred things,' to use a Durkheimianism). To assume otherwise is merely to substitute religion for sociology, to universalize, more or less unwittingly or arrogantly, the parochial values of the Judaeo-Christian-Islamic and certain other religious systems, with their particular combination of moral eschatology; an anthropomorphized Deity; the moralization of earthly life and the connecting of this to the after-life; the conception of supernatural intervention or involvedness in human affairs; a judgmental model of the relationship of this world to the next; and a single-lifetime, temporal framework—a 'one-shot' conception of judgment.

Nadel's description of the religious outlook and institutions of the Nupe, to take one outstandingly well-studied instance alone,[1] shows us a religion in which the link between the extrahuman realm and this earth is lightly emphasized, both in terms of mystical sanctions for this-worldly behaviour and in terms of the relative unimportance of religion as an exhaustive, overarching cosmological system. The 'otiose' High Gods of Africa may provide an *ultimate* 'mythological charter' for the cosmos and for man-on-earth within the cosmos, but just as 'long runs never come,' so 'ultimate explanations' are rarely required or

[1] S. F. Nadel, *Nupe Religion* (London: Routledge & Kegan Paul, 1954).

resorted to in day-to-day human affairs. More proximate entities, such as earth- or ancestor-spirits, or agents of magic and
witchcraft, positive and negative, are the common manifestations
of the other world.

Writers on religion all too often fail to make such distinctions
in their eagerness to demonstrate the interrelatedness of beliefs,
and the closeness of fit of these belief systems to the 'structure'
(i.e., usually, the formal morphological units) of the society.
Only in rare cases, like Evans-Pritchard's study of the Azande,[1]
are particular beliefs fully set in their particular situational context. Hence, all too often we find an exaggerated unity of belief
systems, as well as the imputation of exaggerated importance to
such systems, or parts of them, sometimes implicit in the very
process of presenting them *in abstracto* as 'the religion' or 'the
cosmology' of a given people. (I pass over, as a separate issue, the
functionalist mode of analysis in which it is assumed that the 'fit'
between belief system and social structure is virtually one-to-one
—or, at least, that the degree of congruence is non-problematic.)

Sequential presentation alone often implies a logic of priority
in the thought of the people that may be quite illegitimate, certainly as far as everyday 'operational' behaviour (as distinct from
situations where people are consciously enunciating a 'philosophy') is concerned.

It is necessary always to distinguish who 'they' are, who says
what in what situation, and what the 'task orientation' of the
various actors in the situation is, for 'religion'—in the form of
esoteric ritual lore and theology—is differentially distributed
throughout a society, or elements of it will be differentially distributed, or occur only in specific situations, contexts, and 'niches,'
or be available differentially to different actors. I studied an
Australian aboriginal tribe where the knowledge of the beliefs
and rituals of 'their' culture on the part of most members was
abysmal: as elementary and confused as that of the average
Church of England congregation member. Only the ritual specialists and leaders (and a few sceptics) possessed esoteric lore or
thought about its meaning. V. W. Turner has shown how
the key informant is often a man who, in our society, would be
a professor of theology.[2] Yet we would not, as sociologists, regard
the verbalizations of a professor of theology as an adequate repre-

---

[1] E. E. Evans-Pritchard, *Witchcraft, Oracles and Magic Among the Azande*
(Oxford and New York: Oxford University Press, 1937).

[2] 'Muchona the Hornet, Interpreter of Religion,' in J. B. Casagrande (ed.).
In the Company of Man: Twenty Portraits by Anthropologists (New York:
Harper & Row, 1960), pp. 333–55.

sentation of even the 'religious' in our societies. A spurious unity is projected onto other people's belief systems by outside observers—sociologists and anthropologists—even though they are often familiar with that kind of sociological theory which relates exaggerated awareness of the compulsions of social norms to the observer's 'external' position.[1] They do not, however, always apply these insights to themselves as research workers observing other people's behaviour from outside. This over-systematization of belief is commonly accompanied by a spurious ontological 'priority' or hierarchy: the assumption that general cosmological, philosophical, etc., beliefs are somehow 'primary' or 'higher' (and must therefore be discussed first in any academic analysis). This is a natural disease of academics, a consequence, again, of their specialized role in the social division of labour as dealers in ideas. This proclivity is evident even in such an excellent set of studies as *African Worlds.*[2] Douglas, for example, begins (p. 9) by discussing 'Spiritual Beings: God,' yet has virtually nothing to say of Him, but talks rather about humans, animals, and spirits. Wagner opens (p. 28) with 'Cosmogonic and Cosmological Ideas': the idea of God, he says, is a 'very firmly established belief and of basic significance for the whole world view of the Abaluyia,' though they were 'rather vague' about the Creation process. The Kriges specifically emphasize the disinterest of the Lovedu: 'speculation about first beginnings of final causes . . . origins of the cosmic order and wonders of celestial phenomena do not exercise the Lovedu mind' (p. 59). Little remarks that 'the Mende have an essentially "practical" attitude to life,' are uninterested in metaphysics, and are equally 'practical' vis-à-vis 'what we should term the supernatural world.' Yet he *begins* his analysis with a discussion of 'Beliefs in a Supreme Being and in Spirits' (pp. 112, 113). One could go on. True, there are indeed cultures, like that of the Dogon,[3] that not only display elaborate riots of imagery and imagination in their religious beliefs (to which religion lends itself, potentially, since it is least con-

---

[1] C. F. Merton's point that norms and values of non-membership groups are more visible than the actual behaviour within these groups, so that the non-member sees the official norms as more effectively binding than they are, and idealizes those who conform as 'the norm,' etc. Hence the familiar phenomenon of the rigidity and zealousness of the recent convert. (R. K. Merton, *Social Theory and Social Structure* [New York: Free Press, 1963], pp. 341–53.)

[2] *African Worlds: Studies in the Cosmological Ideas and Social Values of African Peoples,* Daryll Forde (ed.) (New York: Oxford University Press, 1954).

[3] See Marcel Griaule and Germaine Dieterlen, 'The Dogon of the French Sudan,' in *African Worlds,* pp. 83–110.

trolled by mundane structural and cultural constraints), but the relationship of these complex elaborations of belief—usually recorded on collective ritual occasions from specialists—to the general stream of everyday life, and especially the life of those who are not ritual specialists, is not apparent from the literature.[1]

The most common distinction made by social anthropologists in their discussions of primitive thought is, firstly, that of 'primitive thought' itself as a separate kind of thought, a distinction attacked by Evans-Pritchard.[2] The second major distinction is that between 'mystical' and 'empirical' action. 'Mystical' is a particularly unfortunate term, because of the special connotations, which it carries over from European and Asian religions, of individual, gnostic, or ecstatic experience. But the distinction itself is even more unfortunate if it implies that there is a discrete type of actions that are distinguishable from 'mundane' action by the actors themselves. Primitive people accept that the world around them exists, and that it has its regularities, its appropriate rules and operations. But these norms are not solely technical ones, any more than we operate in a totally technical manner. We, too, are influenced by jealousy, lust, magical notions, status seeking, generosity, etc., even in our most scientific moments. For primitive cultures, the area of the extratechnical is wider and often more supernatural simply because the volume of scientific knowledge is smaller. But there is no basic difference in principle between the intrusion of quite non-technical considerations into technical situations demanding primarily technical responses in our lives, and the presence of magic in the activities of the primitive. Moreover, there are no non-social acts that are 'purely' technical: one cannot conceive of them. Drilling a hole in a piece of metal is done for some purpose, under someone's direction; to the worker, it means far more than the act of drilling alone: it may mean money, security, resentment of authority, pride in dexterity, etc., etc. Similarly, the world, for the primitive, is not a special, sealed-off, technical world, in which purely technical norms obtain. Nor does he even conceive of two distinct worlds at all: this world is not a separate realm, insulated from the other world in which 'mystical' actions are appropriate. (Indeed, in primitive heavens, people carry on doing

---

[1] R. M. Berndt, *Kunapipi: A Study of an Australian Aboriginal Religious Cult* (Melbourne: F. W. Cheshire, 1951); and *Djanggawul: An Aboriginal Religious Cult of North-Eastern Arnhem Lane* (London: Routledge & Kegan Paul, 1952).

[2] E. E. Evans-Pritchard, *Theories of Primitive Religion* (Oxford and New York: Oxford University Press, 1965), especially chap. iv.

quite mundane things: hunting, fighting, etc.) This earth, in fact, is not the same demysticized world that White men think of it as being—when they think about it 'scientifically,' that is, for most of the time we also explain events by reference to 'luck,' 'accident,' etc., and even when we behave technically there are non-technical implications to, and dimensions of, our behaviour.

Similarly, to the man in a primitive culture, goals that we (in our 'scientific' capacities) label 'empirical'—planting potatoes, defecating, or drinking beer—have to be achieved by performing both what we call 'ritual' actions as well as 'empirical' ones. But it is common for the same word—often, in Melanesian tongues, the term for 'work'—to be used to describe both kinds of action. In other words, the distinctions we draw, they do not.

Of course, though we may not necessarily invest quotidian actions with *supernatural* connotations as often, we, like 'primitive' peoples, never perform technical acts 'in themselves.' We do invest them with all sorts of other social meanings, which are not extraneous to the technical act, but are always to be found and integral to it. The concept of pure technical action, therefore, can only be an ideal type, a dimension of concrete behaviour which includes many other dimensions. Even the scientist in his laboratory conducts his experiments in a social context: the laboratory itself is a complex social sub-system with its norms of behaviour, both those directly intrinsic to the performance of the work-task and other social norms. Thus, the scientist's white coat may have far more to do with status than hygiene. To this degree, our 'technical' acts are thoroughly invested with other complex, non-technical, social meanings.

The two kinds of activity—which we analyse out into two separate compartments—are thus abstractions from the social behaviour of men, which is of a piece until analytically broken down by the observer (or by the actor, who is then an observer of his own behaviour, a Me to his I). What we call 'ritual' action is therefore quite as 'empirical' as sleeping with one's wife, an act laden with social, including, in some cultures, ritual meanings.[1] There is no impermeable membrane between the 'mundane' and the 'magical,' for the primitive is not a dualist, operating with a model of 'two worlds,' nor a schizophrenic operating with different principles—empirical and mystical—in different situations.

Instead, he conceives of a single order of reality, in which man

[1] For a similar analysis of the apparently purely physical act of (literal) sleep, see Vilhelm Aubert, 'Sleep: A Sociological Interpretation,' in *The Hidden Society* (Totowa, N. J.: Bedminster Press, 1965), pp. 168–200.

has only restricted powers, and access only to limited areas, but, through ritual, has some contact with and influence (often via mediating agents: the ancestors, etc.) over powers of a more far-reaching and compulsive kind. The activities of the ancestors are therefore quite 'empirical.' Indeed, by canons of evidence available to people with limited technical knowledge—and one must insist that they do seriously examine experience (and dreams, for instance, are real experiences)—there is ample confirmation of the existence of the ancestors and of their interest and intervention in human affairs. The spirits are at work in our real world, and, equally incontrovertibly, men go to the spirit world and return.[1]

Therefore, although empirical acts are performed, what we call ritual acts are also integral, necessary, and effective dimensions of social action. The actions we classify as 'ritual' may be more or less elaborated in certain situations, e.g., danger, uncertainty, unpredictability, etc., as Malinowski and others have shown. But this does not mean that the actors see these situations as calling for a special *type* of activity; they are simply situations calling for a *lot* of activity, and since one soon exhausts the limits of what technical means are available, further activity must inevitably be primarily non-technical, i.e., our 'ritual.' But, to them, they are all appropriate behaviours geared and oriented to achieving given ends, *tout court,* not empirical or ritual respectively as quite distinct types of action.

Thus, though the magic and ritual may connect with a 'background' theology, cosmology, or philosophy, these remain very much unexamined and usually quite latent. What is uppermost, most dominant and prominent in everyday interaction, is magico-religious practice.[2]

There is thus some truth in Marett's statement that religion in primitive society is as much 'danced out as thought out,' even though the saying does undervalue the cognitive content of these religions.

[1] Schwartz (see below) even witnessed a 'resurrection' on Manus.

[2] Anthropologists are quite right to reject the old-fashioned distinction between 'magic' and 'religion,' where the former was conceived of as control via the supernatural, and the latter as the domain of extrahuman powers beyond human reach. These distinctions can easily be dismissed: magical actions necessarily imply some theory of the gods, spirits, 'life-force,' etc.; and religion is not just abstract theology; it is something acted out, i.e., it is usually most manifest as 'magic'! Even less is religion necessarily concerned with remote and inaccessible gods or spirits—the latter, indeed, are usually anthropomorphic: the living in another guise or phase of existence. (See Raymond Firth, *Human Types* [London: Thomas Nelson, 1945], chap. vi.)

Magic and ritual thus depend upon some wider theory of the world, of agency, of man, etc., but ethical, cosmological, and eschatological beliefs are normally embedded in behaviour, not abstractly formulated. But if religion is not simply a set of beliefs,[1] neither is it simply a mode of group coherence, a system of ordering one's relations with groups and categories of one's fellow men and with 'Nature,' as both the older structuralism-functionalism of, e.g., Radcliffe-Brown and the newer structuralism of Lévi-Strauss so often have it. It is, rather, a cluster of beliefs which are *used* in day-to-day social activities, with (variously) some of one's fellow men (not some abstract fellow man) in the contexts of changing situations focussed on a diversity of social activities. Religion, then, is a stream of processes, not just an ideal operation in the soul, heart, or intellect, or the ritual dance of puppets determined by the morphology of their social structure.

Because religion is intrinsically unbounded in its field of operation, because it is *ideal* as well as social, it is always potentially innovatory, and like all innovation, potentially hurtful to established interests. But religion, it ought to be said, is neither intrinsically conservative nor revolutionary. It can be infused with any kind of social content, notably political; there are both the religions of the oppressed discussed in this book, and the kinds of religion that have been summed up in the label given to the Church of England as 'the Conservative Party at prayer.' The relationship of religious beliefs, let alone movements and organizations, to the established power-system thus varies, and is not a matter for metaphysical pronouncement disguised as sociological generalization. It requires empirical investigation to see what the case is. We cannot know a priori (except to the extent that one can predict, e.g., that such-and-such a type of religion is appropriate to this or that social group).

Where religious movements are dissident or revolutionary, their innovatory potential can be held in check by the use of countervailing powers. Heretics can be burned at the stake. Powerful as this kind of deterrence can be, it is much more difficult, as has often been observed, to burn ideas, and burning people often only creates martyrs. Since men will continue to search for answers to eternal as well as novel problems, religion provides a channel of creative innovation. (I am not concerned

[1] See Evans-Pritchard's classic castigation of the nineteenth-century 'Intellectualists', in 'The Intellectualist (English) Interpretation of Magic,' *Bulletin of the Faculty of Arts*, I, No. 2 (1934) (Imprimerie de l'Institut Français d'Archéologie Orientale, Cairo).

here with the separate issue of whether such creativity and innovation is 'illusory' or otherwise, positive or negative, 'false'
consciousness or 'real,' etc.) Ultimately, too, the locus of religious
experience is in the individual psyche, not in some Spencerian
'social sensorium,' so that control over religious deviation from
orthodoxy is singularly difficult to police, even with modern
techniques of thought-control and brainwashing.

Functionalist schemata cannot, naturally, find a meaningful
place for these dynamic and subjective aspects of religion. Not
even Nadel, in his brilliant and rather ignored *Nupe Religion,*
has entirely escaped the determinism of functionalist analyses
of religion. He does, on the other hand, clearly specify (a) the
major 'competences' of religion; (b) the distinctiveness of the
religious experience and of religious relationships within the context of all the other dimensions of religion as an *institution;*
(c) the location of religious experience in the psyche of the
actor; (d) the link, and distinction, between the meaning of the
action to the individual actor and the consequences of this
action for society, as well as the 'conditioning' of the religious
experience and practice by society.

Nadel thus avoids many familiar and quite deadly traps. He
speaks of four major 'competences' of religion:

'(i) the capacity of religion to furnish certain supplements to [the]
view of the world of experience which intelligence is driven
to demand;
(ii) its capacity to announce and maintain moral values, or, more
generally, an "economic ethic," that is, its competence to guide
"the practical impulses for action";
(iii) its competence to hold together societies and sustain their
structure; and
(iv) its competence to furnish individuals with specific experiences
and stimulations.' [1]

The use of the word 'competence,' rather than 'function,' appears to be deliberate, so as to avoid any implication that religion is some kind of inherent 'functional requisite,' fulfilling
specifiable 'functions.' Instead, it can (or commonly does, or potentially may—i.e., is 'competent' to) do various things which
may, however, be done by other 'competential alternatives,' to
paraphrase Merton. By using the term 'competences,' Nadel
avoids the assumption too often hidden in the word 'function'
that religion is somehow *peculiarly* or *necessarily* fitted to fulfil
these 'requirements' of sociation. Furthermore, Nadel distin-

[1] *op. cit.,* pp. 259–60.

guishes between the first three competences, which 'refer to the nexus between religion and other, autonomous spheres of inter- est—the understanding of the universe; morality; maintenance of the given society.' (Analytically autonomous, presumably, not empirically. But, even so, a mistaken emphasis, since religion is not a separate 'province,' separate from other provinces, as we have seen.) 'Maintenance of the given society' is a rather unfor- tunate functionalist backsliding, too, insofar as it clearly cannot embrace the radical and revolutionary religions of the disinher- ited.[1] The label could perhaps be rephrased more adequately to refer to 'maintenance (and expansion) of the *collectivity of be- lievers.*' A 'collectivity of believers' could be, at different ex- tremes, members of an established church (in which case their solidarity *would* support, and be congruent with, the stability of the whole polity), or it could be a revolutionary micro-sect, in which case its 'sub-cultural' solidarity would be intrinsically dysfunctional for the wider polity, as Merton and most deviance theory have suggested.

But Nadel rightly observes that to analyse the links between religion and 'other autonomous spheres of interest—the under- standing of the universe; morality; maintenance of the given society'—does not help us distinguish just *what religion is.* An- thropologists and sociologists constantly show us its 'functions,' 'competences,' connections, etc.; i.e., they concentrate, as they properly should as the central part of their task, on tracing out the effects of religion on the behaviour of collectivities (and vice versa) and the ways in which religious institutions condition the behaviour of individuals. They not only tend to eschew, notably, the philosophical problem of the meaning of religion, but even sometimes neglect the meaning of religion to the actor; the former problem they leave to the philosopher or the theologian, the latter to the psychologist. In the process, a serious overly- sociological distortion emerges: by omitting to examine the mean- ing of religion to the actor, the group tends to be represented, in a reified way, as 'thinking,' 'believing,' or 'feeling.' A sociology that incorporates social action theory, however—as the older anthropological functionalism does not—cannot accept that the meaning of religious behaviour to the actor can be omitted, or taken as given, in any valid analysis of the cultural significance of religion. Collectivities do not think, or undergo religious ex- periences; men do. Even Durkheim's occasions of collective ritual

---

[1] See Vittorio Lanternari, *The Religions of the Oppressed: A Study of Modern Messianic Cults* (London: MacGibbon and Kee, 1965; New York: Alfred A. Knopf, 1963).

are situations in which men respond to the situation. Their behaviour is, to be sure, profoundly and directly conditioned by
the presence of many others, but not just by this: rather by the
presence of many others who act and require one to act *in
culturally prescribed ways*. Even so, the required or resultant
religious behaviour is still mediated through and only meaningful within the individual psyche. There is no group psyche. Conversely, individual mystical experience is a highly social form of
behaviour, conditioned usually by the internalization of sophisticated and culturally-given theological notions embedded in a
complex of values and beliefs about man, society, God, the
cosmos, morality, etc.

Nadel, therefore, quite rightly points out that the first of three
'competences' are *not* somehow functionally necessarily and immanently tied to religion alone. Understanding of the universe,
he points out, can be satisfactorily provided by science, for example; civic or political aims provide perfectly effective modes
of handling the problem of social order; and 'ethical tenets
would be just these and no more.' Empirically, and not a priori,
man need not be religious to be moral, to order his thinking
about the world, or to order his relations with his fellow men.
Some metaphysicians and religious people, of course, hold otherwise, particularly with regard to the unanswerable, ultimate
questions of creation, destiny, and the significance of human
life. The agnostic usually replies, in the face of these claims,
that he does not know, but will not fill the gap by mytho-
poeic 'explanations,' preferring instead the nobility—and agony
—of permanently suspended judgment about such ultimacies,[1]
much as Laplace, when asked by Napoleon what place there was
for God in his intellectual map of the cosmos, replied 'Sire, I
have no need of that hypothesis.'

The 'understanding of the universe' that is supplied by religion,
then, is often of a very different order from that supplied by
vulgar 'materialist' empiricism or by science; something else is
involved. Again, the kind of morality that is part of a theological system of belief is of a different order from that of the
agnostic: it derives its 'logic,' its legitimation, its charter, its
validation, from quite different sources. The social order buttressed by a dominant or established religion displays an overlapping of institutional orders, an extra dimension of congruence,

---

[1] Cf. Max Weber: 'it seems to me dubious whether the dignity of purely
human and communal relations is enhanced by . . . religious interpretations.'
(*From Max Weber*, p. 155.)

that the secular polity lacks. Religious *Weltbilden,* religious ethics, religiously validated polities differ in kind, quite simply, from those in which this dimension is lacking. (It is important to repeat that it may be lacking—religion has 'competences,' not 'functions.')

The meaning of the action to the actor necessarily involves, then, some ideal-type specification of what religious, as distinct from non-religious, behaviour is. This is' very simple and well known, though rarely stated in the sociological literature, which always tells us what religion does, or analyses its structural 'elements' (those which Nadel, following Durkheim, adequately identifies as 'doctrine,' 'congregation,' and 'observances'). Such writers may be correct, as sociologists, to avoid the metaphysical-philosophical questions of what religion is, in the sense of the truthfulness, or 'requiredness' or immanence of religion. What they cannot avoid as a fundamental sociological issue is giving consideration not only to the effects of religious commitment—the way in which religious commitment has consequences for one's relations to one's fellow men—but also to the way in which (a) the process of internalization in the psyche of the individual, (b) conceptions of what we call the supernatural and man's relationship to it, and (c) the content of belief are all culturally derived and socially prescribed.

Spiro has recently defined religion as 'beliefs in superhuman beings and in their power to assist or harm man. . . . This belief . . . is the core variable which ought to be included in any definition of religion . . . [and] approaches universal distribution.' [1]

It would be better to speak, however, of a superhuman 'realm' or of 'powers.' (Superhuman, that is, from our analytical point of view; not necessarily in the believers' own conceptual schema, for they may not distinguish their 'religious' beliefs from their other beliefs in the way that we do *for* them. They may have no conception at all of a 'natural' order as distinct from something called the *'super*natural': *we* have, and in using the distinction are supplying categories that depend upon our scientific distinctions, not necessarily the categories of the believers.) Moreover, Tylorian 'beings' may not be believed in, nor their intervention in human affairs. And in many religions 'power' of this kind can be mobilized: man is not confined, as

---

[1] Melford E. Spiro, 'Religion: Problems of Definition and Explanation,' in *Anthropological Approaches to the Study of Religion,* M. Banton (ed.) (London: Tavistock, 1964; New York: Frederick A. Praeger, 1966), p. 94.

far as his own action is concerned, to supplication. Otherwise, Spiro's emphasis upon the superhuman is useful, and forms a corrective to Nadel.

Nadel's fourth 'competence'—the *especially* religious—focusses upon the subjective emotional-psychic meaning of the religious experience to the actor, and is thus a quite different kind of analytical category from that we have used, which depends not on the actor's own categories, but on those of *our* scientific culture.

It is doubtful, however, that such experience is very common. The problem of eliciting the meaning of social action to the actor is a cardinal one in all sociology, of course, but it is particularly problematic where religious experience is concerned, since religious experiences may be held, both by the religious and the non-religious, to be 'inexpressible' (though even mystics seem to be able to communicate the substance, if not the 'reality,' of their experiences, and, unless we believe that something mystical *is* involved, the psychic impact of the mystical experience does not seem so remote from other dimensions of experience as to suggest that it is any more impenetrable to imaginative empathy than someone else's sex experience).

Nadel suggests that two elements seem to be discernible: 'something in the nature of an emotional state or a psycho-physical stimulation' and 'a more or less articulate assurance.' [1]

Both the experience of the religious 'thrill' and of the 'assurance' are highly socialized and institutionalized events, even if they (obviously) occur to the individual and within his psyche. Even the 'individual' experience, that is, is a highly social phenomenon.

Most of the religious experiences undergone by Cargo cult believers are far more immediately and visibly 'social' than the experiences of the mystic face-to-face with God. 'Possession,' individual enough to be sure, commonly takes place in a state of social stimulation via chants, songs, dancing, etc., in which people become possessed by 'contagion,' imitating directly behavioural norms of the possession-state, which are both culturally institutionalized generally, and under their very eyes immediately. Whole groups may participate via prayer or in ritual as congregations: indeed, nothing is more structured and culturally prescribed than the style of what is held by believers to be individual, unpredictable, and inspirational, however randomly the lightning strikes.

The point, however, is not simply the social nature of in-

[1] *op. cit.,* p. 260.

dividual mystical experience or of the experience of possession. It is that these are *special* forms of religious experience: that such ecstatic personal experience is rare, or foreign to many religions, or disdained or disapproved. It is, then, by no means a universal attribute of religion, and cannot be an irreducible part of the analytic definition of religion. But as the other three elements are only competential, and not necessarily found, what does religion consist of as distinct from other kinds of behaviour? In searching for the 'religious,' Nadel arrives at individual sensation: James's famous 'thrill.' But most religious people probably never, or only rarely, experience it. Such experience may be encountered, but most religions do not, as cultural systems, encourage, require, expect or induce people to do so: for some 'church' religions, this kind of experience would be satanic, not holy—an individualistic sin of hubris, something to be severely discouraged.

It seems much wiser, then, not to build into any definition this element of personal sensation, but rather to follow Spiro and simply observe that what distinguishes religious belief from other kinds of social belief is that, in some way or other (and that way may be oblique, remote, or tenuous), it refers to, and looks for validation in, a dimension beyond the empirical-technical realm of action. (This is, as we saw above, an analytical distinction *not* necessarily present in the minds of the believers themselves.) But for most believers, most of the time, the other competences of religion may be quite predominant, and are not necessarily anything to do with the supernatural specifically. Hence, alternatives may be found for ethical codes of particular religions: morality can be detached from religion. But reference to what lies beyond man's knowledge, experience, and control cannot.

The Cult: Process and Structure

We have already had cause to criticize approaches to the study of religion which are over-intellectualized (concentrating primarily upon the ordering of *belief*) or over-'affectualized' (concentrating primarily upon the 'thrill' as the kernel of the religious experience). We have also pointed to the charismatic leader, in relational terms, as a catalyst, and as partner in a relationship in which his message enshrines the interests and values of his followers. Further, we stressed the importance of the action context, not just abstract beliefs, in the development of the charismatic relationship. We now turn more directly to the question of the charismatic cult, and the progression—not necessarily always empirically found as a complete typological sequence—through which an _audience_ becomes a _following,_ then a _movement,_ and finally an _organization:_ the very process Weber himself was centrally interested in: firstly, the transformation of leadership into authority, and, more widely, the 'routinization of charisma.'

The validity of the prophet's message is proved (or disproved) by events, or, more strictly, the interpretation of events. But the prophet proves himself, and the truth of his message, not simply by passively awaiting confirmatory events, but by _creating_ events —by acting himself and getting his followers to act, notably by representing the interests of his converted and potential followers against their opponents in political conflict situations in which their interests are opposed to other interest aggregates. Even the simple fact of organization as a cult, for quite religious purposes, carries with it the built-in inevitability of political action, insofar as any organization, be it the most world-renouncing of sects, must stand in relationship to the world and ask of it something, even if it is only to be left alone in peace to worship God—a demand the world seems to find singularly hard to grant, as Jehovah's Witnesses, Doukhobors, Hutterites, and other religious sects have discovered in countries with political cultures as diverse as those of East Germany and Canada.[1] A movement, that is, must always, objectively, be _politico-religious,_ whatever its actors' willed purposes and conception of their movement and its ends.

The actor's 'definition of the situation,' that is, defines the situation _for him,_ in his consciousness. This, it is true, does have social implications for others also, both because his behaviour is guided by his own definition of the situation, and because others try to interpret the meaning of his behaviour to him as an actor and act accordingly themselves. But the actor's definition of the situation, though it has real consequences, does not define the situation totally; many of the consequences may be quite unintended, for other actors, too, define it their way, and possibly have greater powers to structure it their way. Whether the behaviour of the believer is subjectively oriented to purely spiritual ends or not, then, his behaviour, insofar as he acts with, or in relation to, other men, will have effects upon and consequences for them. Insofar as the believer acts at all, and not only where he tries deliberately to influence others, he

[1] See, for instance, H. B. Hawthorn (ed.), _The Doukhobors of British Columbia_ (London: J. M. Dent, 1955).

is acting politically, not just religiously. Insofar as he does deliberately seek to influence others, he acts 'politically,' whether he is propagating his religious beliefs as theology or challenging the secular authority of the State. No matter how spiritual his goals, he will produce political action simply through acting, even if as unintended consequences. Political action is thus an immanent dimension or aspect of all social action, whether the ends of this action, as far as the actor is concerned, are the worship of God, earning one's bread, caring for one's children, etc.[1] But there are those religious movements that aim specifically not only at other-worldly targets but also at altering arrangements on this earth, whether by vigorous proselytization, or via other modes of pursuing the cult's religious purposes, which may include changing the power-structure of the society. These cults then come up against institutionalized authority in many shapes, from that of other churches to that of the State.

One possible way of coping with an unfriendly world is to withdraw from it, though it is a course that activistic movements reject. But this option, in any case, is more often logically possible rather than socially feasible. The opportunity to withdraw is not always available or permitted. The creation of wholly segregated utopian communities is not easily effected, and is usually only possible in 'open,' permissive cultures, or on the margins of society altogether, classically, for example, in the 'frontier' situation.

More normally, the sect has to be involved in the world, and its mere existence as a separate entity and its rejection of conventional values (which are usually those of politically dominant groups) ensure for it the ready hostility of those—more numerous, entrenched, and powerful—it rejects. In this situation, the movement that sets out to live in harmony with God ends up by fighting the State (just as Weber's Calvinist set out to worship God, but produced capitalism). The existing ideological support accorded the charismatic leader is now greatly strengthened. He is a political as well as a religious leader, heading an organization and not simply an unstructured 'movement,' and one that, since it rejects the existing order, is likely to construct its own organizational categories, and not merely give off a mirror-like reflection of the existing orthodox order—as we have seen in the case of the Cargo cults with their 'unifying' tendencies.

The millenarian cult, then, normally goes through phases of development: change is intrinsic to it, since it looks to an order

[1] See my 'The Distribution of Power in Industrial Society,' *Sociological Review Monograph No. 8* (1964), pp. 15–34.

of things different from that which exists at present and makes demands of the world that cannot be granted. To the extent that it does succeed—e.g., in establishing a flourishing organization—it has to develop new forms and norms of sociation. Weber was right, then, to conceive of the charismatic phenomenon as a process. He develops the notion of charisma, indeed, precisely as part of a philosophy of history. His discussion of the 'transformation of charisma,' therefore, is much more developed than is the definition of the nature of charismatic authority itself, as Friedland notes, adding that it 'provided him with what Bendix calls "a sociology of innovation." ' [1] Nevertheless, he had scarcely anything to say—beyond vague references to times of trouble—about the conditions under which charismatic movements emerge: an omission which seems to the writer sociologically profoundly deficient.

From a sociological point of view, too, one would expect attention to be devoted to study of the milieu from which the prophet emerges, to the social groups that receive it readily (and those that resist it), and, as we have seen, to the message and its content, since this is the nexus linking leader and follower in one relationship.

None of these issues is seriously tackled by Weber. In contemporary sociology, too, the 'emergency,' crisis, conditions, and the 'challenging' quality of charismatic leadership are too often taken as given, and, if not as inexplicable, at least are not explained. The discussion stops short of examination of the situation out of which leadership emerges, and of the social support for the prophet, when this is exactly one of the most crucial features demanding explanation. The discussion remains, by default, implicitly at the archaic intellectual level of heroes and geniuses, and, in this respect, Weber's own treatment of the charismatic leader is a bad precedent, for—while accepting Bendix's qualifications noted above—I agree with Gerth and

[1] *op. cit.*, p. 19. Bendix, in fact, seems to me quite clearly to reject the notion that, for Weber, the concept of charisma is uniquely the source of innovation: 'he did not identify all positive and dynamic historical forces with "charisma" and all negative and retrogressive forces with "routinization" ' (Bendix, *op. cit.*, p. 327). Innovation takes place via legal rationality also, and charisma declines as a long-term secular process. But it is still an 'omnipresent possibility,' and one of the potential sources of innovation, so important in Weber's view that he argued for the introduction of the direct election of the President, as 'an aim for young and untried "charismatic leadership." ' It was presidential reserve power that destroyed the Weimar Republic. (See J. P. Mayer, *Max Weber and German Politics: A Study in Political Sociology* [London: Faber & Faber; New York: Hillary House, 1943], pp. 101–2, 152).

Mills that his conception of the charismatic leader 'is a continuation of a "philosophy of history" which, after Carlyle's *Heroes and Hero-Worship*, influenced a great deal of nineteenth-century history writing. In such an emphasis, the monumentalised individual becomes the sovereign of history.' [1]

Millenarism in Recent Theoretical Discussions

In the light of these pre-sociological shortcomings, both in the classic writings of Weber and in some contemporary research and theorizing, it is perhaps worth emphasizing, obvious though it might seem to be, that these kinds of movements do normally arise among the 'oppressed,' as this view has, indeed, been queried, notably by Cohn and Shepperson. Cohn, for example, notes that the Free Spirit heresy flourished in small sects that collectively formed an 'underground,' but 'with this peculiarity, that they disseminated [their doctrines] chiefly amongst unmarried women and widows in the upper strata of urban society.' The adepts of the Free Spirit were not, he points out, social revolutionaries 'and did not normally seek followers among the poor.' But they did

'conserve the one thoroughly revolutionary social doctrine known to the middle ages . . . that human beings had at first lived as a community of equals holding all things in common and knowing nothing of "Mine" and "Thine." ' . . . During the great social upheavals which accompanied the close of the middle ages various extremist groups were inspired by the conviction that at any moment the egalitarian, communistic Millennium would be established by the direct intervention of God.

It was always in the midst of some great revolt or revolution that the revolutionary millenarian group first emerged into daylight. . . .

What is seldom realised—and what Marxist and right-wing historians have united in concealing—is how little these groups had in common with the mass uprisings which they tried to exploit.' [2]

There are several points to be noted here. Firstly, that some sects do originate and flourish in upper-class milieux, not among the 'oppressed': Cohn later cites (p. 41) the transformation of

---

[1] Gerth and Mills, *op. cit.*, p. 53.

[2] Norman Cohn, 'Medieval Millenarism,' in *Millennial Dreams in Action: Essays in Comparative Study*, Sylvia L. Thrupp (ed.) (The Hague: Mouton; New York: Humanities Press, 1962), pp. 37–38.

Saint-Simonianism under Enfantin after Saint-Simon's death, and Boullan's sect in the 1880's (p. 41). Shepperson, in another essay in the same volume,[1] refers to various nineteenth-century millenarian sects among the middle and upper classes in Britain and the United States. No one, of course, denies that such cults can and do occur among the middle and upper strata. There are indeed the 'miseries of the rich,' and particular categories of even the rich are likely to experience frustrations that, though by no means unconnected with property relations and the class culture, are not the same direct and naked conflicts of interest that are generated by conflict of class interest within the production context as, for example, between peasant and lord, or worker and employer. Women, in particular, are likely to experience the pains of patriarchalism; the susceptibility of widows in such cultures to inspirational movements of this kind needs no elaborate explanations either. The main feature that one needs to note about these cults, however, is that they lack either the mass characteristics or the intransigence towards the orthodox world that is typical of the kind of sect we are concerned with, or both of these. Sociologically—whatever their resemblances in terms of belief—their differences in respect of their structures, ends, membership, recruitment style, scale, individualism, and absence of radicalism mark them off as quite different phenomena: they are *coteries,* not *movements.* Of course, ladies in polite circles have, we well know, been susceptible to all kinds of romantic and ecstatic fads and cults, and have swooned before attractive religious leaders even within the doctrinal and organizational confines of quite orthodox variants of Christianity. Rasputin, after all, flourished in the Orthodox culture of the Czarist royal circles. Such coterie-cults, however, have little in common with the movements of Thomas Münzer, Jan of Leyden, or the movements described in this book.

The aims, and the focus of interest, of the upper-class millenarist are normally anything but revolutionary. But the doctrines, by definition, do deviate from orthodoxy, as does the sect form of organization, which is that of a minority group within civil society. Naturally, then, particularly when alternative radical ideologies are lacking, these quite unrevolutionary creeds can be invested with quite different meaning and can come to possess a different social and sociological significance when taken up by radicalized masses, whatever the initial mildness of the doctrines, and however non-revolutionary the original progen-

[1] George Shepperson, 'The Comparative Study of Millenarian Movements,' *ibid.,* pp. 44–52.

itors. Indeed, Cohn himself notes that it is the revolutionary *situation* that calls the hitherto obscure millenarian groups and their doctrines into the daylight. The doctrines (usually modified) now become the charter of mass activist movements and the millenarist 'pioneer' sectaries the kernel, leaders, catalysts, or cadres, energizers or ideological specialists of the mass movement (or they may be simply swallowed up in it). The historical role of these initial, 'underground' micro-sects is thus the cultural transmission of doctrines that become absorbed into quite different mass and socially-radical movements, whatever the intentions and orientations of their original 'carriers.'

If the doctrines do remain locked in their original milieu, they undergo no such reinterpretation, no transmutation into an 'ethic' of mass action, but remain the property of micro-sects of no historical significance. In Melanesia, on the contrary, Cargo cults have been central, not marginal. Indeed, I undertook the study of them, not out of some interest in the bizarre, the marginal or the archaic—as from the point of view of their contemporary social importance, millenarian, fundamentalist, salvationist, and other cognate micro-sects in developed countries such as Britain are [1]—but because the opposite was true of Melanesian millenarian movements, which were precisely the most important, widespread, and pervasive manifestations of the self-expression of the peoples of Melanesia at that time.

There is nothing strange or difficult to explain about the phenomenon of the genesis, flowering, and maintenance of an ideology in one social stratum, group, or milieu, and its subsequent transmission to, and adoption by, another stratum, group, or milieu. This is a normal part of the process of cultural transmission and, far from constituting a difficult problem for sociological analysis, is a very simple manifestation of that well-known phenomenon, the social division of labour. More particularly, the production and elaboration of ideas is normally (and quite naturally) carried on by those with the cultural facilities—money, leisure, and education, in the main—that make it possible for them to sit and think or to do research. Most ideologies, historically, whether conservative or revolutionary, have been created by people from the privileged strata. But whereas some ideologies are readily acceptable to those who dominate the social order ('ideologies' in Mannheim's special sense of the term), others appeal more to the less fortunate

---

[1] E.g., those studied by Bryan Wilson in his *Sects and Society: A Sociological Study of Three Religious Groups in Britain* (London: Heinemann, 1961; Berkeley: University of California Press, 1960).

(Mannheim's 'utopias'). Empirically, the social background of the creators or formulators of the ideology is normally quite different from the social milieu into which the message is absorbed. The examination of the background of the recipients, too, is more important, for sociological analysis, than that of the ideology producers.

I am quite unrepentant, therefore, about cleaving to my basic assumption that *the millenarian movements that have been historically important* (and which include the cults discussed in this book) are movements of the disinherited. Indeed, there is almost an element of tautology in having to say this: the movements are normally important because they mobilize masses; therefore non-mass movements are unlikely to be important (unless they have other sources of power than mere numbers provide). Other sects, such as those mentioned by Cohn, are of quite marginal significance, however interesting from other standpoints. I cannot, therefore, accept Shepperson's judgment that Cohn's rejection of attempts to interpret millenarian movements as movements of the 'disinherited' is 'particularly important.' It seems to me, rather, obfuscating as well as wrong, and invites us to discard a very useful analytical framework, because it fails to make the crucial distinction between millenarian movements as large-scale social phenomena and 'millenarism' as the belief systems of small-scale micro-sects among coteries. If Cohn is simply saying that millenarian *ideas* can be created or emerge in a variety of milieux, the proposition is quite unexceptionable. If he is saying that millenarian movements and organizations are as common, or as important in terms of their consequences for the wider society, among the privileged as among the underprivileged, he is, empirically, wrong. Shepperson also challenges my conclusion that 'the future of the millenarian movement is to play a passive rather than an active role in contemporary politics,' and denies any such 'simple progression,' yet in the next sentence speaks of 'survivals of *once militant* groups, bravely carrying on the battle, or else quietly *withdrawing* into positions of *passive contemplation.*' [1]

One further point is developed by Shepperson: that activistic millenarism is not necessarily replaced or succeeded by secular, non-religious political movements (whether revolutionary or otherwise), as the present writer has suggested at the end of this book. Hobsbawm [2] and myself are cited as deserving of criticism

---

[1] *op. cit.,* pp. 46–47 (my italics).

[2] See E. J. Hobsbawm, *Primitive Rebels: Studies in Archaic Forms of Social Movements* (Manchester: Manchester University Press, 1959; New York: Frederick A. Praeger, 1963), p. 65.

on this point. In support of this criticism, Shepperson then cites Cohn's observation that medieval millenarian movements 'appeared when an organised insurrection of a decidedly realistic kind was already under way.' As to the validity of this view, I can only urge the reader to consider the historical evidence, much of which has been assembled for primitive societies by Professor Lanternari and Dr. Mühlmann,[1] since I cannot hope to undertake such a comparative study myself.

Millenarian or messianic movements and secular movements of protest can coexist chronologically; secular movements of protest have certainly preceded religious ones, in given historical instances; and millenarian cults can persist long after secular forms of protest have become uppermost. My point was a much more evolutionist one, concerning not the historical or chronological, but the typological, succession: that as the *dominant* form of protest, millenarism always gives way to secularized forms, and thenceforward becomes marginal, and usually more pacific and other-worldly. The type of millenarian cult can persist long after it has ceased to be, in evolutionary terms, the *dominant* type. Birds and fish share the British Isles with men, with whom they coexist, chronologically and historically, but the former are no longer (as they formerly, at different times, respectively, were) the dominant species.[2]

Millenarian and cognate religious cults (e.g., separatist sects) have thus persisted markedly in, e.g., the recent history of South Africa, the Congo, and Melanesia, to name no other regions and periods.[3] But they have quite changed their content, as we show

---

[1] W. E. Mühlmann *et al.*, *Chiliasmus und Naturismus: Studien zur Psychologie, Soziologie und historischen Kasuistik der Umsturzbewegungen* (Berlin: Reimer, 1961).

[2] See Marshall A. Sahlins and Elman R. Service, *Evolution and Culture* (Ann Arbor: University of Michigan Press, 1960), and the points made in my review of this work, in *Science and Society*, XXVI, No. 3 (1962), 365–69. The evolutionist view of the process of millenarian development is expressed by Robert Kaufman in his book on the African Watch Tower movement. In Melanesia and Africa, he remarks, the cult movements are '*une forme embryonnaire de nationalisme . . . la première forme efficace de lutte contre la puissance colonialiste,*' but '*une phase transitoire,*' and one destined either to give way to '*parti politique progressiste*' or '*se cristalliser en secte et servir de refuge à des elements qui se crispent dans une opposition inconditionelle.*' (*Millénarisme et Acculturation* [Brussels: Editions de l'Institut de Sociologie de l'Université Libre de Bruxelles, 1964], p. 108.) See also A. J. F. Köbben, 'Prophetic Movements as an Expression of Social Protest,' *International Archives of Ethnography*, XLIX, No. 1 (1960), 117–64.

[3] Latin America, too, promises to yield a rich harvest of such cults to the researcher, as Maurício Vinhas de Queiroz' *Messianismo e Conflito Social: A Guerra Sertaneja do Contestado: 1912–1916* (Rio de Janeiro, Editora Civilização Brasileira, 1966) indicates. For a survey of other literature, see Maria

below, have very little concern with the power-structures of the world in which they flourish, and are primarily vehicles for individual achievement and self-expression and the solution of problems predominantly at the level of the individual (Turner's 'religions of the afflicted'). Moreover, they have become quite secondary in importance—i.e., in terms of their present and potential impact on national developments—as compared to (for South Africa) the African National Congress or the Pan African Congress, or (for the Congo) the Lumumbist, military, 'rebel,' or other political factions. In India, millenarian sects, Fuchs shows, are mostly found only among semi-tribal groups or among low-caste or untouchable Hindus. In general they occur among strata and groups with the most 'archaic,' to use Hobsbawm's term, consciousness. They will decline with the modernization of even these social groupings: they will persist the more culturally and socially backward a social region.

Since I have been accused of something like conspiracy theory, and of finding evidence of 'underground' and secretive organization that the facts did not support, David Attenborough's material [1] and the fact that the Schwartzes had the Paliau Second Cult's existence completely hidden from them for eight months (when it was all around them) are worth noting:

> 'We learned abruptly that the village in which we had been living since June 1953, in the belief that we had excellent rapport and that we had a fairly good picture of all that was really important in its present life and culture, was in the throes of the greatest crisis of its eight-year history.'

By a series of accidents they gained access to the cult, but were provided by the cultists day and night with a guard equipped with pressure-lamps, since the cultists believed that the Austra-

---

Insuara Pereira de Queiroz' 'Messiahs in Brazil,' *Past and Present*, July 31, 1965, pp. 62–86. Recent research, too, has thrown up a goodly number of such cults from a cultural region—India—for which there had hitherto been little recorded. See S. Fuchs, *Rebellious Prophets: A Study of Messianic Movements in Indian Religions* (Bombay: Asia Publishing House, 1965).

[1] Besides this film on the John Frum cult, see 'The Cargo Cult and the Great God Frum,' *Sunday Times* (London), April 24, 1960, p. 5. The appendix to E. Andersson's *Messianic Popular Movements in the Lower Congo* (Uppsala, Studia Ethnographica Uppsaliensia XIV, 1958) further demonstrates cult hostility and secrecy.

The only other film publicly available of Cargo movements is Jacopetti's characteristically misanthropic interpretation of a New Guinea cult as pure irrationality in *Il Mondo Cane*.

lians had sent a man to kill the Schwartzes because they were now 'inside' with the natives.[1]

Certainly, however, one does not have to postulate deliberate concealment in every case. Berndt notes that the missionaries on Elcho Island were 'unaware of the implications' of a large cult shrine, in which sacred *rangga,* normally concealed from view, were set on a concrete base next door to the mission church: the missionaries thought it 'a memorial of some sort.' [2]

And they do persist, in Melanesia, remarkably: the recent movement on the island of New Hanover in which the islanders first tried to vote for President Johnson in the local elections, and then, when assured that he was not standing in those elections, collected money with which to buy President Johnson, shows powerfully the extent to which the Cargo belief flourishes and readapts to situations of failure. (This is, of course, only one of the more recent appearances of the 'Americanism' syndrome, earlier variants of which are described in this book.) At present, indeed, it is no doubt still the case that Cargo ideology has far more purchase on the minds of more Melanesians than have orthodox political and religious beliefs and organizations.

The evidence available on this point is rarely very satisfactory, either in terms of its depth and quality, or in terms of its systematic range and coverage. We often have nothing better than such a vivid piece of reportage as David Attenborough's television film of the John Frum cult, which, however, vividly communicates the 'underground' atmosphere of secrecy, hostility, and suspicion on the part of the cultists vis-à-vis the White man.

So pervasive, commonly, is the atmosphere of the Cargo Cult belief, and so thin the distribution of White men, that cults must often, whether deliberately concealed or not, spring up and disappear quite unperceived by White men. The literature probably underestimates their incidence both in time and space, and their extent and intensity. The contingent nature of the emergence of many cults was indicated in a recent *New Yorker* account of Japanese stragglers stranded after World War II on remote islands of the South Pacific. One of these unfortunate men, finally forced out of hiding in the bush by desperation, screwed up his courage and entered a New Guinea village. To his surprise, he found himself greeted not with fear or suspicion,

---

[1] Theodore Schwartz, *The Paliau Movement in the Admiralty Islands, 1946–1954 (Anthropological Papers,* XLIX, No. 2 [New York: American Museum of Natural History, 1962]), pp. 217, 292–94.

[2] Ronald M. Berndt, *An Adjustment Movement in Northern Arnhem Land, Northern Territory of Australia* (Paris: Mouton, 1962), pp. 84, 23.

but swiftly adopted as the harbinger of the return of the Cargo; he soon became the focus of a flourishing cult. To the villagers, this pale-skinned being from the unknown was a returned spirit of the dead ancestors.[1]

A better-documented instance of the continuity of Cargo cultism in New Guinea is provided by Brian du Toit's recent paper on the east-central New Guinea Highlands.[2] Cargo belief has already incorporated successive technological innovations: the Cargo was originally to come by sea—firstly, by canoe, then by ship—and later by aeroplane. The belief has now been adapted to incorporate the most recent instrument of delivery: the space-rocket. The disturbing news of these large 'flying houses,' flying much higher than aeroplanes, fortuitously coincided with the announcement by government officials that there would shortly occur an eclipse of the sun (*tudark* in Neo-Melanesian: 'pidgin English'). By further coincidence, du Toit went by Land Rover to stock up with two months' supplies on the precise day before the eclipse.

The area was one which had 'long [been] a hotbed for Cargo movements.' Little wonder that, on his return, he was asked why he was stocking up with food and kerosene, and why—if not because they were scared of the *tudark*—'the Americans were going to the moon in large flying houses.'

The situation was clearly ripe for a new Cargo phase. That it never jelled in a form appropriate to this conjunction of eclipse, first revelation of the space age, and the visible preparations of the Whites for the events seems entirely due to the prior elaborate explanations and the personal imperturbability at the moment of the eclipse that du Toit displayed when he, together with his wife and daughter, stood in the village square while the villagers stayed close to their houses. Here, then, is another recent instance both of the continuity of Cargo belief, and of its flexibility and capacity to develop new dimensions and adapt to new situations, and to re-emerge, given appropriate 'triggers,' 'cues,' and stimuli. In other nearby villages, indeed, where no one was available to provide the alternative interpretation and the demonstrative leadership du Toit provided in his village (for not every village, like the 'average Hopi family' of legend, can

---

[1] Referred to in my 'Progress and Cults in Melanesia,' *New Society*, I, No. 3 (1962), 16–17.

[2] Brian M. du Toit, 'Misconstructions and Problems in Communication: A New Guinea Case' (paper read at the annual meeting of the American Folklore Society, Toronto, November 18, 1967).

hope to have its resident anthropologist), the people did actually build ceremonial houses in which they congregated.

Cargo belief and ritual is thus very far from dead. Even so, it is to the new legislature of Papua-New Guinea, and to the emergence, for example, of a political party opposed to Papua-New Guinea's becoming an Australian state, that we need to look for an outline of the future shape of politics in New Guinea—not to Cargo cultism, no matter how strong its purchase may still be in many areas.

That it will persist for a very long time—though no doubt with changes of emphasis and on a reduced scale—we need not doubt. Indeed, the Congo provides more than one example of the way in which messianisms persist, but become incorporated within the wider framework of national politics. At this point, the millenarian cult becomes a sect within a much wider civil society, an interest- and pressure-group much like any other sect, or even any entity that can be mobilized or itself acts politically. If the sect is influential, the new political parties try to enlist its support, just as political parties anywhere go after 'the religious vote.' Thus the Kimbangist movement played 'an open political role allied to Abako, the Bakongo nationalist party,'[1] and Abbé Fulbert Youlou drew support from the Matswaist movement in Congo-Brazzaville.

If it is very much a minority and localized movement, and especially if it maintains a posture of immediate chiliasm, the movement is likely to come into conflict with the new State, just as it came into conflict with the colonial State. The most striking and violent of these cases was the battle by Zambian Army forces against the stockaded villages of the adherents of the Lumpa sect of Alice Lenshina's followers in the Northern Province of Zambia in 1964. At this point, the evolutionary displacement of millenarism as the vehicle for vigorous mass nationalism is abundantly clear: proto-nationalism couched in religious idiom is no longer required in an era when a full-fledged, wider and more inclusive, quite secular, nationalism has emerged. The millenarian sect now becomes an enclave within the new State, either accommodating to it—and thus becomes yet another denomination—or, by persisting with militant goals of its own, comes into conflict with the new polity and the new politics.

Those sects that do remain activist are usually no longer mass movements. They are also likely to invite attack and to encounter suppression if they do continue to insist on immediate

[1] Michael Banton, 'African Prophets,' *Race*, V, No. 1 (1963), 44.

millenarism. More usually, they become passive minority enclaves within a secular society. They become, in fact, more specifically 'religious' in that their concern is now primarily other-worldly: the other 'competences' of religion are removed and taken over by secular agencies.

Charisma without Religion

The ambiguities we have examined so far are only some of the many with which the concept of charisma is saturated. Most of them are built into Weber's own original usages, and are not simply the fault of imperceptive or loose-thinking epigones. Let us now move to examine some of these other ambiguities. One central quality Weber appears to be trying to emphasize is that of innovation, not simply that of leadership, as some users of the term seem to imply: the charismatic leader enjoins a *new* and different ethic ('it is written, but I say unto you . . .'), new modes of the orientation of behaviour and organization at the personal level and beyond. Charismatically inspired behaviour is specifically different from *alltäglich* behaviour: the charismatic ethic and practice have that differential quality precisely in contrast to habitual or conventional behaviour. It is non-routine behaviour par excellence.

Since this innovatory behaviour does not form part of established culture, it tends to be ascribed, in the effort to legitimize it, to extrasocial areas altogether: in the extreme, to non-empirical realms. Hence Weber's use of the word 'super-human,' equivalent perhaps to 'transcendental' (as his further use of the epithet *heilig* [sacred] also suggests). More widely, *all* values—not just those cherished by specifically charismatic movements, but even the values informing the most rational of systems of authority—lie in realms of faith beyond scientific scrutiny, and are thus ultimately charismatic, whether any specific reference to the supernatural occurs or not.[1]

Charisma is thus a multi-meaning concept, an ideal type with a differentiable profile of component elements: an element of personal leadership, itself compounded of two elements—personality and leadership; an element of autonomy; an element of innovation; an element of the transcendental or 'ultimate'; and, of course, an element of the 'affectual' (as opposed to rational or habitual action).

[1] See Talcott Parsons, *The Structure of Social Action* (New York: Free Press, 1949), pp. 661, 668.

Little wonder that subsequent commentators have seized upon different elements in this complicated ideal type and each perceived and developed his particular chosen element as *the* concept of charisma in ways strikingly different from his fellows.

The concept, moreover, has been used to analyse social relations in general, and not merely religious behaviour, notably by students of authority-structures. Thus it is used by Etzioni, in one of his studies of organizations, as meaning 'the ability of an actor to exercise diffuse and intense influence over the normative orientations of other actors,' [1] a defintion that I find so vague and ambiguous as to be virtually meaningless. Insofar as it would appear to lay the weight on personal power, it would invite the kinds of criticism developed earlier vis-à-vis Weber, but Etzioni goes on (more fruitfully) to emphasize that charisma is a 'relational property,' and then makes the Weberian distinction between personal charisma and charisma of office.

Weber himself, as we have seen, used the concept in the context of development, as part of a philosophy of history (in which one can discern both cyclical or oscillatory, and secular-linear models of development, just as the concept, when used by Weber *outside* the context of development, may refer, variously, either to particular types of legitimate authority-systems or to ideal-type elements of action in general). He emphasized, too, that charisma was intrinsically resistant to institutionalization:

> 'If [it] is not to remain a purely transitory phenomenon, but to take on the character of a permanent relationship . . . it is necessary for the character of charismatic authority to become radically changed. *Indeed, in its pure form charismatic authority may be said to exist only in the process of originating.*' [2]

Yet, having said that charisma must be 'radically changed' if it becomes institutionalized and depersonalized, Weber, unfortunately, goes on to use the same word for the two phases—albeit with qualifiers. Yet strictly, charisma cannot, by definition, become routinized. It can be transformed, but then becomes something else. What it does become is *tradition,* insofar as the movement, once it persists long enough to pass from the hands of those directly designated by the prophet as his successors, now refers to the tradition established by the original leader. The prophet's message, glosses, additions to the message, his life-actions, all become, as in Islam (the Koran and the *hadith,* for

[1] *A Comparative Analysis of Complex Organizations,* p. 203.
[2] *The Theory of Social and Economic Organizations,* p. 364 (my italics).

example), sources of legitimation and guides to action. But by this stage, the movement is strictly neither charismatic nor a movement. It has become a 'church' with a *charismatic tradition of origin.* Charisma, now, is merely what Malinowski called a 'mythological charter.' If such is the case, should we not use Malinowski's well-established and much clearer terminology, rather than the confused and illogical concept 'charisma of office'?

If by 'charisma of office,' alternatively, we mean the prestige attached to office, why not use the word 'prestige'? (We will certainly have to avoid the word 'status,' which is used to designate both a position and the social evaluation of that position. 'Statuses' in the first sense are thus accorded 'status' in the second.[1]) If we mean that occupying office gives the opportunity —even within the confines of the formal rules of the organization—to exhibit personal qualities and to develop 'informal' relations, then let us use the familiar distinctions between person and office, or status/role and occupant/actor, or even the older 'personal equation.' The distinction is not even very difficult or refined, and scarcely merits the invention of new terms: even non-sociologists are quite accustomed to appreciating that the kingship is prestigious even if a fool reigns; the emperorship even if defiled by Caligula; or that voters vote for their party ticket even if, as the folklore has it, 'they put a monkey up as candidate.'

It is not a question of terminological parsimony versus terminological neophily. It is a question of clarity versus the use of sponge-words.

When we find students of organizations using the term to make important analytical points that are in fact quite *different* analytical points which ought to be kept separate, the term has clearly come only to confuse, not clarify. Etzioni, for example, discerns a 'charismatic' element in offices at the apex of decision-making, power-wielding hierarchies.[2] He rightly observes that the man at the apex of even the most rational-bureaucratic organizations is not bound by the rules that subject those lower down, which restrict their range of personal actions and which inhibit personal innovation and deviation (since everything they do [ideal-typically] is done with reference to defined rules, and is inspected and policed to prevent deviation). Not so the man

---

[1] N. C. Gross, W. S. Mason, and A. W. McEachern, *Explorations in Role-Analysis: Studies of the School Superintendent's Role* (New York: Wiley & Sons, 1966).

[2] *Modern Organizations*, pp. 54–55.

at the top, who can change the rules, and interpret them his way, and who is not subject to the overriding sanction of superior authority—because there is no superior authority. (This is not to say, of course, that he is free from any kinds of constraints: these are many, and come both from his peers, if any; from those below him in the organization hierarchy; and from the world outside it.) In this usage, Etzioni is close to the 'innovatory,' 'autonomous,' and 'sacred' elements in the charisma complex.

In another book, on the other hand, Etzioni develops a different point, following one strand in Weber. When Weber talks of the 'charismatic' nature of the source of even the most 'rational' values, he is not categorizing 'charisma' and 'rationality' as two discrete types of social action. Nor is he merely pointing, empirically, to dimensions, aspects, or elements of the concrete behaviour of 'historical individuals,' e.g., a given cult organization in which certain features can be labelled more or less 'charismatic,' and others 'rational.' Rather, the point about the 'charismatic' source of *all* values, in even the most rational structures, is that, in this crucial respect, *charisma is intrinsic to all social action*. It is not just a special and separate kind of action, e.g., a label for certain kinds of authority-systems. (Further development of his theory, however, distinguishes between T-Structures in which charisma is concentrated in *top* positions, e.g. Ford Motor Company under the direction of Henry Ford; L-Structures in which all *line* positions are filled by charismatics, e.g. the hierarchy of the Roman Catholic Church; and R-Structures in which charisma is limited to one or more *ranks* other than the top one, e.g. doctors in hospitals—and other organizations, e.g. prisons, where no organizations or positions require charisma.)

Thus, starting from either of these points—the empirical intermingling of the charismatic and the rational (and/or the traditional) in any concrete piece of social action, or the general immanently 'charismatic' nature of values—we find that charisma is not confined to certain special kinds of social action, but is an omnipresent dimension of all social action.

By this point, Etzioni has moved from using 'charisma' to refer to the 'non-bureaucratic *head*' to using it to describe elements of *'any* social status.' [1]

It seems to me that, in the process, he has drawn attention (very usefully) to the autonomy of the non-bureaucratic head, on the one hand, and to the quite separate distinction between

[1] *A Comparative Analysis of Complex Organizations*, p. 204 (my italics).

office and person, on the other, and then confused the discussion by calling them the same thing—charisma.

But just as there will always be personal elements in 'rational' organizations (since persons fill statuses, and social control can never be absolute), so too the purely rational organization is only an ideal-type construct. Empirically, what are often labelled 'charismatic' movements are anything but charismatic in their organizational structure or economy. They commonly possess an administrative staff and organization, and mobilize and allocate resources on lines that exhibit a careful calculation of due order and economy in relating means to ends. These are scarcely the 'non-rational' methods of the pure charismatic movement, which recruits its administrative staff according to the evidence of their devotion to the leader, and acquires resources in *ad hoc* and arbitrary ways: sporadic gifts, booty, etc. But no movements are more tightly organized on quite such rational-bureaucratic lines—and from such an early stage in their development as to constitute a fundamental attribute *ab initio* (rather than a 'becoming' process of 'routinization')—than some of those movements for which the label 'charismatic' has been freely used. We have drawn attention in this book to the separability of the functions of prophet and organizer or—to put it more abstractly —of instrumental and expressive roles. (This was brilliantly depicted in the film *Viva Zapata,* where the heroic peasant leader was, throughout, flanked by the impersonal 'grey eminence' who was the cold, efficient organizer of the revolt. Certainly, the 'expressive' functions of the prophet *personally* are not needed beyond a certain point—he can die, and his person be replaced by disciples, as in the case of Christ. Or there can be 'mystical,' mediated, or gnostic, contact with him.) The separability of 'expressive' functions from organizational ones is also visible in the phenomenon Etzioni[1] has drawn attention to: the emergence of qualities of personal 'charisma' *after* the assumption of office within an otherwise quite formally rational-legal system. He mentions, for example, the success of Queen Victoria in transforming an unpopular monarchy into a popular personal cult focussed on herself. (Pope John XXIII provides a striking recent instance.) In this kind of situation, the rational-legal (and traditional) organization *pre-exists* and is independent of the charismatic element.

The building up of a personality cult around Stalin, after he had reached power through manipulation of the bureaucratic Party *apparat* (rather than as a result of any striking personal

[1] *loc. cit.*

appeal or leadership qualities), is a modern instance not only of the 'post-office' nature of some charisma, but also of the way in which 'charismatic' qualities can be developed by manipulation of the mass media: the leader may not even need to possess such qualities. 'Expressive' qualities can be fabricated through control of the machinery of expression.

At this point, we now see that what has been called charisma is not necessarily even innovatory; it is quite compatible with stability and traditionalism, especially since the leader so often registers or expresses what his followers want, or only arrives at power through established structures. The term charisma can thus obscure even the crucial difference between innovation and conservation.

At the lowest level, it tends to lure us into a psychologistic concern with personality attributes to the neglect of the sociological analysis of leadership in the context of the situation of action.

It is unwise, therefore, to talk of movements like Nkrumah's, for example, as 'charismatic.' Apart from the use of patronage, force, manipulation by propaganda, etc., there was a quite complex organizational machinery for the mobilization and control of the masses, including Party organization down to cell level, plus the organization of trade unions and work brigades, farmers', youth, and women's organizations, etc., etc. (however inefficiently and in a quite untotalitarian way these were actually run). The inadequacy of this kind of analysis is clearly shown in the collapse of such régimes, when the masses have revealed a remarkable indifference to the elimination of the postulated hero.

I suggest that there is little hope that we will get far in our efforts to develop and enrich sociological theory with such a blunt instrument as the concept of charisma as part of our theoretical tool-kit.

Had the concept not become, by now, all too often a substitute for serious research, and a barrier to thinking equalled by few other sponge-words of our time—notably 'alienation'—it would scarcely be worth devoting so much space to it. Thinking about its ambiguities, however, may help us clarify our minds.

The best recent writing on Cargo cults, certainly, has had little need of the concept of charisma.

Recent Cargo Studies

The literature published on Cargo cults since the first edition of this work has included some very important theoretical and comparative studies, notably I. C. Jarvie's superb polemic, *The Revolution in Anthropology*[1]; the same author's 'Theories of Cargo Cults: A Critical Analysis'[2]; W. E. H. Stanner, 'On the Interpretation of Cargo Cults'[3]; and two contributions by Judy Inglis.[4]

We have also had two field studies of major theoretical importance, by Burridge[5] and Lawrence[6] respectively; plus Maher's account of the Tommy Kabu movement,[7] Margaret Mead's book on the Paliau movement,[8] and Schwartz's more extended study of this movement.[9] Other contributions are noted in the supplementary bibliography to this work, compiled by Mr. D. A. Heathcote (pp. 289–93).

We have already mentioned the discussions of millenarism in general by Talmon and Aberle. In her article, Talmon develops the Mertonian theme of the 'uneven relation between expectations and the means of their satisfaction' further than I did originally (see pp. 227–43). Where I emphasized how the traditional Melanesian concept of rights in the *property* of their fellows was extended to that of White men, and thus produced intensified frustration, Talmon, more widely and more satisfactorily, emphasizes the gulf between inflated expectations and wants *in general* and the inadequate means for their satisfaction.

David Aberle, similarly, in the symposium to which Cohn and

---

[1] London: Routledge & Kegan Paul; New York: Humanities Press, 1964.

[2] *Oceania*, XXXIV, Nos. 1 and 2 (1963), 1–31 and 108–36.

[3] *Oceania*, XXIX, No. 1 (1958), 1–25.

[4] 'Cargo Cults: The Problem of Explanation,' *Oceania*, XXVII, No. 4 (1957), 249–63, and 'Interpretation of Cargo Cults: A Comment,' *Oceania*, XXX, No. 4 (1959), 155–58.

[5] K. O. L. Burridge, *Mambu: A Melanesian Millennium* (London: Methuen; New York: Humanities Press, 1960).

[6] Peter Lawrence, *Road Belong Cargo: A Study of the Cargo Movement in the Southern Madang District, New Guinea* (Manchester: Manchester University Press; New York: Humanities Press, 1964).

[7] Robert F. Maher, *New Men of Papua: A Study in Culture Change* (Madison: University of Wisconsin Press, 1961).

[8] Margaret Mead, *New Lives for Old: Cultural Transformation, Manus, 1928–1953* (London: Victor Gollancz; New York: William Morrow, 1956). See my review article 'Margaret Mead: Science or Science Fiction,' *Science and Society*, XXI, No. 2 (1957), 122–34.

[9] *op. cit.*

Shepperson contributed, takes my original note that 'material loss' was not the only source of deprivation much further, by spelling out the Mertonian concept of 'relative deprivation,'[1] which, he says, may be generated by (a) comparing the present to the past; (b) comparing present to future; (c) comparing self with others. This approach helps us to include *all* kinds of wants within our theoretical framework and helps explain, too, the interplay between the use of quite traditional modes of thought for explaining the new and the strange, and, at the same time, the very interest in what is new and strange. Any actor, of course, must relate himself, in some fashion, both to the past and to some envisaged future, and must have an image of his own society as against others. He must always be both 'forward-looking' and 'backward-looking,' both 'self'- and 'other'-oriented. No movement can purely divest itself of the past: even rejection is a response to a known and disvalued past. The debate about 'future-orientation' and 'past-orientation' has thus involved a lot of talking past one another, since the referents of these terms have not been clearly specified. It might be helpful if we observe that men locate themselves meaningfully in time in a cognitive *fashion,* but that they also *evaluate* time and its divisions, and, too, respond 'cathetically' to these. The orientation of behaviour includes all three dimensions. 'Future-orientation' and 'past-orientation' are thus both intrinsic frameworks of action. Lawrence, for example, categorizes the Madang Cargo movements as 'primarily forward-looking,' though his whole analysis shows how traditional categories and values were employed in interpreting and responding to the European order. Burridge shows how the Tangu, in seeking to create a new man and a new society, appeal to the 'primal' myth, in which traditional values and social relationships are embodied. But having identified the sources from which abstract ideas and values are derived, and with reference to which action is legitimated, we need to relate these ideas and values to new *institutional* arrangements, e.g., in production, village organization, family and kinship relations, etc., etc.—whether these are older patterns reintroduced, or quite new patterns. But the cults, whether they embody ancient or modern elements, are *introduced* and energetically pursued: they are activistic 'revitalizations,' to use Wallace's term,[2] mobilizing the individual into organizations, even

[1] 'A Note on Relative Deprivation Theory as applied to Millenarian and othr Cult Movements,' in *Millennial Dreams in Action*, pp. 209–14.

[2] A. F. C. Wallace, 'Revitalization Movements,' *American Anthropologist*, LVIII, No. 2 (1956), 264–81.

if the activities of the organization are only the gathering in of the faithful to wait and pray for the Cargo. We thus need to specify which of these numerous aspects we are referring to when we use terms like 'activistic'/'passive,' or 'future'-/'past-oriented.'

This 'Janus-faced,' two-way orientation, and the ambivalence of the Melanesians both towards their traditional culture and towards that of the Whites (despising and admiring elements in both), deserved much more emphasis than I gave it, particularly as these have consequences in terms of the internalization of social conflicts within the individual psyche, and are thus relevant to any social-psychological explanation of 'hysteria,' possession, etc.

I now turn to specific criticisms of the present book. In evaluating the state of Cargo studies ten years later, one's own work inevitably bears the stamp of time. I have no desire to defend positions I no longer hold, or to apologize either for having held them or for having changed my mind. I would hope that one develops, and knows better as time goes on. Certainly, whatever the individual's own personal intellectual development, the collective development of social science has made it richer and more theoretically sophisticated than a decade ago. To completely rewrite every book every decade would prevent one from undertaking anything fresh, but I agree also with Jarvie that we need more re-evaluation. It seems more rewarding, and economical of scarce resources (one's lifetime), to comment, briefly at least, on the inadequacies, major and minor, in one's work, and to take into account published criticism.

Much of this has been justified and helpful; some not, and I feel it necessary to deal with some of the unjustified criticism. Jarvie, for example, seems to find a deterministic assertion of 'social necessity' (*his* phrase) of Cargo cults in my discussion of their unifying effect in acephalous societies.[1] Yet I remarked that millenarian beliefs are neither 'inherently revolutionary' nor 'escapist'/'passivist,' nor 'inevitably or automatically produced in a given situation. . . . Protest can take numerous forms.' Though accepting the legitimacy of the charge of determinism for other places in the text, this is not one of them.

More particularly, I am accused not simply of determinism, but of *economic* determinism: 'Worsley . . . sees Cargo cults as the products of the economic forces acting on the Melanesians.'[2] Mair only just succeeds in keeping within the conventional limits of academic debate and ordinary civility. 'The reader,' she re-

---

[1] 'Theories of Cargo Cults: A Critical Analysis,' pp. 129–30.

[2] Jarvie, *The Revolution in Anthropology,* p. 91.

marks, 'begins to wonder whether he is to be told that the cults dramatize the natives' intuitive recognition of the theory of surplus value,' but charitably notes that 'it never comes to that though.' [1] 'Stanner, on the other hand, more accurately quotes my judgment that 'the movements represent desperate searchings for more and more effective ways of understanding and modifying the environment.' [2]

My book does not, of course, suggest that Melanesians appreciated the theory of surplus value (though they might be considered to possess a 'folk' variant of that theory). What it does state is that Melanesians were profoundly disturbed by the impact of the European economy and its effects on their indigenous economic arrangements—a view that I document, and still adhere to, especially as I find it strikingly confirmed in recent research, including research that is not focussed on cult movements.[3]

Of course, islanders who have never encountered the Europeans physically at all, like the New Guinea Highlands people studied by Salisbury, can hardly be said to have been *directly* affected by the coming of Whites, let alone by their economic activities in particular, since face-to-face social relationships have not been established. But we now know, from Salisbury's and other studies, that very widespread economic and other social changes did, in fact, take place before the White man actually arrived, simply—among other factors—as a result of the introduction of steel axes into the 'uncontrolled' areas along traditional trade routes. Moreover, rumours, accurate and inaccurate, about the White man and his doings circulated freely, and, most importantly, so did the Cargo *belief,* which was also partly imported.[4] Along with the European contact came a ready-made explanatory system, geared, too, to indigenous religious conceptions. Ideas, as well as material objects, flowed into the Highlands like pressure-waves thrown out ahead of the main body of the White advance. The extent of the diffusion of such ideas,

[1] Lucy Mair, 'The Millennium in Melanesia,' *British Journal of Sociology,* IX, No. 2 (1958), 178–79.

[2] *op. cit.,* p. 19.

[3] Particularly R. F. Salisbury's *From Stone to Steel: Economic Consequences of a Technological Change in New Guinea* (Melbourne: Melbourne University Press, 1962).

[4] See Salisbury, *op. cit.,* pp. 114, 121. Lauriston Sharp's 'Steel Axes for Stone Age Australians,' in E. H. Spicer (ed.), *Human Problems in Technological Change* (New York: Russell Sage Foundation, 1952), shows vividly the profound changes resulting from this technological substitution in one Australian tribe.

as compared with the generation of Cargo beliefs within the society, without any outside stimulus, varies. Given the kind of world view described by Lawrence, people can and do generate Cargo beliefs without outside assistance.

Once contact is directly established, economic relationships are by no means subsidiary, and returning labourers like Paliau are crucial mediators. His autobiographical sketch is most illuminating: property, work, exploitation, mobilization of economic resources, concern about the claims of kin, organization to avoid the gaoling of natives for failure to pay taxes are all key elements in his story [1] and central concerns in his programme of action. I have already pointed to certain formulations that are narrowly and 'economistically' put, but equally I wrote of people 'wishing to dissociate themselves spiritually . . . from the authority of their rulers' (though, after Burridge, one should say 'or wishing to demand equality from them'). When I wrote of 'people desperate for some explanation of the irrational and unjust world in which they lived, desperate for a solution to their problems and for a faith to steer by,' I meant (and thought I had clearly said) a lot more than that men had 'economic' motivations. And the conclusion of the book, with a dozen pages on 'the *idea* of the millennium,' on the moral codes, the symbolism, the emotionality, and the regenerative ideology of the cults, is surely far removed from economic determinism.

According to Jarvie, the sin of reification is added to that of determinism. I am held to attribute the development of the integrative cults to 'social forces' (p. 130). Rather than reifying 'social forces,' indeed, I observed, in the very passage he draws attention to, that

> 'since *the people* have developed new common political interests where previously they had none, so *they* must create political forms of organization to give expression to this new-found unity' (p. 228, my italics).

The last sin is that of resorting to conspiracy theory. My distinction between the prophet and the organizer (p. 271) is cited by Jarvie, on one page of his book (p. 65), as an assertion that there may be a figure 'behind' the prophet (though I only referred to a 'division of labour'); five pages later, this has become 'Worsley's conjecture that each prophet *always* has a sort of Machiavelli-figure behind him' (p. 70, my italics); by p. 85, it

---

[1] See Schwartz, *op. cit.*, pp. 239–44, and Schwartz's own comment on this issue at p. 264.

has become 'Worsley's theory . . . that there is *nearly always* a powerful figure in the shadow of the front man,' and by p. 86 a 'prophet-conspiracy [sic] view . . . of the shadowy figure behind the prophet.' With these critical standards and procedures, one can make a determinist out of anybody.

One is reluctant to have to debate these points because one does not wish to appear merely that defensive and wicked animal which defends itself when attacked (after ten years). But one does reply because one shares Professor Jarvie's view of the fruitfulness of both debate and reanalysis. Nevertheless, when one uncovers this kind of distortion and selectiveness, one is led to ask why this is so. I am led to conclude that these writers have a quarrel with Marx which they are conducting via my work. It seems difficult to explain, otherwise, why it is legitimate, apparently, for Professor Guiart to refer to 'European cheating, abuse, kidnapping, disease and weapon-bearing' on Tanna, and to mission and settler shortcomings, or for Professor Jarvie to refer virulently to mission activity, but for myself to be flippantly dismissed when I refer to such matters: 'the cult did not break out . . . until 1940, and when it did there were the following oppressors: one District Agent and four merchants, one of whom doubled as Assistant District Agent.' [1]

Having suggested an hypothesis to explain these invalid criticisms, let us unhesitatingly recognize the excellence of Jarvie's contribution in other, and by far the most important, respects. His book is primarily, of course, as he says, 'a book about methodology . . . not a treatise on the cargo cult' (pp. xviii-xix), but, being methodologically sophisticated, it does greatly contribute to the analysis of the cults even if as a by-product.

His invitation to build into our analytical framework the natives' 'horizon of expectations' is methodologically unimpeachable, but inadequately achieved in my book, which concentrates on the colonial situation and pays insufficient attention to the source of the beliefs which inform the dominant responses to that situation.

This was indeed largely due to a Marxist orientation in which there were elements of determinism that were discordant with other theoretical strands in the book. From these I now dissent, and would similarly dissociate myself from the historicist tendency of my earlier discussion of the concepts of 'law' and 'prediction' without subscribing to Jarvie's wholesale rejection of the notion of prediction (*Revolution,* pp. 198–207).

Jarvie's positive recommendations are more important than

[1] Jarvie, 'Theories of Cargo Cults,' pp. 134, 129.

his negative criticisms, however. In explaining why Cargo cults
(and not other reactions) eventuated, the factors mentioned
above—deprivation, rapid transformation, indeterminacy, discrepancy between inflated wants and available means, etc.—do
not constitute adequate explanations of the emergence of this
kind of belief. To explain that, we need to know about the
indigenous 'horizon of expectations.'

It is this knowledge, precisely, that Burridge and Lawrence
have given us. Lawrence's opening chapter is surely a *locus clas-
sicus* of social anthropology, in that he shows us authoritatively
and definitively how Madang religion is fundamentally *anthro-
pocentric* (and not other-worldly), *materialistic,* and *'technological'* (insofar as the gods—the originators of human culture—are
manipulable by man). But I feel less happy about the presentation of the cosmic order as timeless and complete, in which all
appears immutable and known. It seems difficult to understand
how a cosmological system as closed, complete, and certain as
that depicted could so effectively handle the radical problems of
change presented by the coming of the Europeans, unless traditional categories of thought had a greater capacity for dealing
with the novel and contingent, and unless there was greater flexibility in the native handling of these categories. While accepting his major point that the Garia 'accepted myths as the sole and
unquestionable source of all important truth' (p. 30), one feels
that his account of the cosmological system is overly systematic,
not as an *account* of this set of ideas (for that *should* be systematic), but—as we suggested in the discussion of *African
Worlds* above—in imputing such a degree of system to the body
of ideas itself. As we shall see, these ideas are notably manipulated by cultists and others alike: they are, to use an Americanism, a 'resource,' not an all-determining strait jacket. If they
were impervious to experience, if they were not potentially
amenable to, and exposed to, critical scrutiny, they could never
be altered or displaced. But the study of the very movements
shows that they were constantly scrutinized, tested, and manipulated, and were capable, too, of giving rise to quite different
variants of ideology and of organization and action.

Lawrence, like Burridge, is at pains to emphasize that the
acquisition of Cargo is more than a consumer itch. It is a search
for self-respect, identity, and meaning in life, though he has less
to say about 'renewal' than Burridge, and emphasizes rather more
insistently the persistence of traditional modes of thought. One
cannot be certain whether these differences of emphasis are differences between Burridge's Tangu and Lawrence's Madang peo-

ples, or differences between the two authors. Burridge's book, to me, seems infused, for example, by a fine Christian humanism, but it does mean that one finds it difficult at times to disentangle the interpretation from the indigenous beliefs. Again, Lawrence tends to overemphasize the pragmatic, unintellectualized and essentially non-rational nature of native thought: Yali is said to act 'not by . . . reference to [convictions or principles]' (p. 165), 'not on the grounds of rational belief but . . . [because of] fear of being accused of stealing other people's secrets' (p. 184). At times, it almost suggests mindless behaviour. Yet the moral content of his behaviour is clear: he exhibits moral scrupulosity in his relations with the women of Sigi (p. 127), 'wished to be treated by Europeans as an equal . . . ,' struggles intellectually, etc., etc.

Perhaps this is mainly a matter of tone and emphasis, but it does seem to relate to differences in attitude between Burridge and Lawrence, the former with his almost rhapsodic celebration of brotherhood, and Lawrence's identification with Administration policies ('which alone can give the native the higher standard of living, unity, and liberty they demand'). His own picture of White society is, in fact, at variance with this formal declaration, for he depicts not a 'rational' Administration confronted with a non-rational population, but a society in which there is scarcely any common language, so that both major parties, Whites and islanders, talk past and misunderstand each other. This is not just because the parties have different norms and interests: the ones that prevail are institutionally sanctioned and are those of the most powerful party, the Administration. There is, therefore, conflict and not simply anomie. From the villager's point of view the White order is singularly unsatisfactory: 'well over 75 per cent of disputes are settled in the villages because traditional means of negotiation are more satisfactory than European decisions' (p. 210).

An adequate account of Melanesian religion should, desirably, have stood at the head of my analysis: until Burridge and Lawrence, however, it was simply not available. Reo Fortune's *Manus Religion* [1] was the only substantial modern study of Melanesian religion, but its relevance for other cultures was uncertain. I was also banned by the Australian Government from conducting first-hand field research in New Guinea itself, so could not personally fill the gap. The chronological/typological-developmental approach I used, in combination with the treatment of the material by region—an extraordinarily difficult operation (later

[1] Philadelphia: American Philosophical Society, 1935.

paralleled by Schwartz's treatment of a single, but highly complex, cult)—in order to marshal and make sense of masses of disparate material, pushed the most modern anthropological analyses (notably Lawrence's and Burridge's early articles) into the end of the book. Moreover, the political consequences, implications, and forms of Cargo cultism were my primary focus of attention, not the beliefs themselves. There is, of course, no single 'problem' of Cargo cults, only those the researchers ask of their material. My concern, simply, was different from that of others. But even so, I was in error to conceive of 'the situation' as something in which 'beliefs' exist, as if these latter floated around in some kind of container. The belief is itself *an element of* the situation, an important definitional component of what the situation is.

Burridge's *Mambu*—surely one of the most humane anthropological works every written—explores a further set of problems: the moral and emotional, as distinct from the simple cognitive, dimensions of indigenous mental life, and relates all these to one another as aspects of a total mental universe. The crisis to which Melanesians have to adapt does not demand, solely, a cognitive explanation, or a 'cathectic' response, or dilemmas of economic, political and other kinds of choice and action, but a whole moral and relational crisis, which subsumes all these dimensions. (It is, perhaps, this 'totality' that underlies what Stanner speaks of as the 'inordinate' value placed on the Cargo: its 'total preference for cargo over any traditional wealth'—though, as we shall see, the valuation is not, as he thinks, irrational.)

'The most significant theme in the Cargo seems to be moral regeneration: the creation of a new man, the creation of new unities, the creation of a new society. . . . Moral regeneration and political independence which are subsumed in the new man and the new society, and a desire for material wealth together with a latent opposition between governors and governed, combine and meet in the advent of a hero through whom the conflict implied in these factors will be eclipsed.'[1]

The Tangu, who feel themselves to be 'dogs,' not men, strain to make 'new men' of themselves, and of the White man whose blows and punishments frustrate their own humanity. The cardinal values and interpretative categories available to the Tangu are embodied in the 'myth-dream,' in which a 'cultural idiom of brotherhood' is anchored in a relationship between men and the

[1] Burridge, *op. cit.*, pp. 247, 29.

divine; this relationship is flouted only at the expense of a deep sense of guilt, generating a desire to overcome the consequence of such deviation from the morally ideal by the re-establishment of a 'new and different relationship with the divine which, by inducing atonement, expiation of guilt, will imply an end to the consequences flowing from the disobedience.' [1]

Cargo phenomena are placed firmly in the context of social life as a whole: they are not treated separately from the analysis of the family, mythology, or the Tangu 'managerial' ideal. But the location within this cultural context is not functionalist. The opening roundly announces that 'there exists a basic situation of conflict' and 'to argue from a presumption of stability in Tangu during the last century and a half would be most ill-advised.' Gone is the timeless, often idyllic, world of the 'ethnographic present,' for Burridge writes historically. Tangu society came into existence in the 1880's or 1890's. It was then thoroughly disrupted by the advent of White men who established a régime of direct rule based upon a coconut-plantation economy and a few *idées fixes* about sanitation. As a result, the Japanese invasion was welcomed as a brief intermission of 'freedom.'

The Cargo cult he sees 'not so much [as] the protest of the oppressed against the oppressor—though these are the terms which a political leader finds most advantageous, and which an investigator could find most appropriate, because familiar, for purposes of analysis.' It is rather 'a protest against the disnomy' (p. 281). This passage is not without its ambiguities. If the political leader finds it 'advantageous' to use the language of 'protest against the oppressor,' is this not because his followers perceive it that way? If the categories are used by the investigator merely because they are 'familiar,' they are, scientifically speaking, *not* 'appropriate' at all, but quite inappropriate; though perhaps appropriate for the mental comfort of the inflexible investigator unable to adapt himself to unfamiliar cultural situations, or subject his concepts to reappraisal.

But he does correctly warn us against assuming a simple and universal conflict model for the cults: they are evidently not always a rejection of the White man, but may include or primarily emphasize a claim to human equality and community with him in the same society. (The problem is exactly visible in the diversity of attitudes vis-à-vis the White men in United States society among American Negroes, ranging from 'Black Power' to coexistence with equality. It is a repertory of choices and positions encountered by all radical minority movements within a

[1] *ibid.*, pp. 279–80.

society that subjects them to severe disadvantage.) It seems better, then, to operate with sets of ideal types, against the common background of a situation of intensified relative deprivation, inadequacy of means, and within a context of expanded horizons and inflated wants. Given this background, the existing situation can be defined, at one extreme, as one of oppressors versus oppressed; at the other, in terms of a disturbed ('disnomic,' in Burridge's terminology) moral order. The second pair of types concerns the course of action required to put these unsatisfactory conditions right: these can be either the destruction of the existing order so as to eliminate the Whites (whether by supernatural cataclysm, physical killing, or by withdrawing from their presence, expelling them, etc.), or the remaking of civil society on the basis of a new relationship of equality. The latter emphasis seems dominant among the Tangu: the establishment of a moral order in which Blacks and Whites meet in community, 'characterised by . . . prestation, reciprocity, obligation, and constraint' (p. 281). But it would seem that, empirically, movements differ in the degree to which these ideal-type emphases are combined and weighted, and they can be combined in many ways. 'Oppressors,' for example, can be remade into 'new men'; they need not be destroyed. Undoubtedly, movements vary in these respects; reform, restoration, and revolution are intertwined in complex ways. Moreover, there is running debate and experiment, in which groups and individuals constantly shift their views, tactics, aims, choice of means, etc. Now that we have the 'inside' accounts by Schwartz, Lawrence, and Burridge, this fluidity and experimentation are abundantly visible. Whereas formerly we had only external, overcoherent accounts of different movements by outside observers who foisted a spurious uniformity and consistency on them, we can now only be impressed by the successive shifts they undergo; the manipulation and furthering of private aims within the general context of the movement; the coexistence of many different strands at one and the same time, not only between individuals and groups but within the psyche of the individual; the situational contingency of many developments; the oscillations and the constant redefinitions of action as a result of the interaction of all these elements in the social field of force.

The cults are, then, not simply systems of thought, nor are they unitary systems of thought which contain no internal problems of interpretation and choice. In addition, they are institutional innovations, and highly flexible ones at that. A whole spectrum of organizational choices and alternatives presents it-

self, therefore, and, empirically, this is just what the best accounts we have show. According to these studies, there is not a
unitary cult, with a single, internally consistent, and unequivocal
body of belief, but whole sets and series of diverse and often
competing attempts to institutionalize particular ways of acting
out what different interpreters of the beliefs read as the implications of these beliefs for action. The empirical accounts we have
thus make us dubious of the postulated systematism and closure
of thought-systems, and of the related functionalist assumption
that these fit congruently and neatly with some 'appropriate' institutional, equivalent patterns of organizing men's activities.

Thus Schwartz takes us painstakingly through the various
phases of the First and Second Paliau *Cults* (and the 'noise'
and the *guria* within them), and shows how they paralleled,
constantly met, and sometimes merged with, the less chiliastic *Movement,* and carefully traces local sequences and variations. Lawrence, similarly, shows us no less than five waves of
Cargo activity in the Madang District and paints a moving portrait of Yali, the chief leader, not only as he wrestles agonizingly
with the intellectual problems posed by his effort to organize his
experience and to relate indigenous and European modes of
thought,[1] but also as he wrestles for leadership with much more
unambiguously chiliastic rivals. Clearly, these cults, and their
parallel rival movements, are neither 'purely' chiliastic nor secular, and need, as we suggested earlier, to be analysed as rational
attempts to comprehend and organize the world, given a cosmic
view which does not separate the natural from the 'super'-natural.

For all their personal importance—and Burridge is happy to
refer to Mambu as a 'charismatic' figure—the movements emerge
as vastly more complex than any simple leader-determined structures. The Paliau movement is by no means Paliau; Yali is an
element—albeit of very great influence—in a very complex context of shifting thought and action, which fluctuates in content
as well as in time and space.

With these studies, then, whole new dimensions have been
added to our understanding of the cults. I have not examined
the work of other writers so closely, because, since Jarvie, this
would be a work of supererogation. To express dissent from his
judgments on minor matters seems an unprofitable exercise. It is

---

[1] See the moving account of Yali's ingenious explanation of European culture, in which he brings together within the theoretical framework of traditional totemistic categories, zoos, pets, prehistoric remains, and other features
of European culture such as evolutionary ideas and myths of the Creation:
a Melanesian Lévi-Strauss? (*op. cit.,* pp. 173–75.)

his major attack on the confusions surrounding the word 'rationality' that we should pay attention to, and be thankful for. It enables him to reject Firth's description of Cargo thought as 'fantasy' or 'illusion,' since he holds, with Belshaw, that 'within the native frame of reference cargo myths are not illusions but attempts to solve certain problems in native terms.' [1]

The label 'irrationality' often contains the assumption that magico-religious explanations are not valid explanations, since they do not jibe with the knowledge we possess via modern science. But the Melanesian does not share this knowledge with us. In whatever way he thinks, no account, or evaluation, of his behaviour is relevant that measures his action in the light of knowledge and techniques unavailable to him. He can be called (relatively) ignorant, but not accused of misusing something he has to possess before he can misuse it.

This confusion underlies so many of the discussions Jarvie examines: Mair thinks explanations based on religious beliefs are 'non-rational'; Stanner designates the valuation of Cargo as 'inordinate,' 'hyperbole,' 'exaggerated,' 'one-sided,' 'factitious,' 'misjudgments of significance,' etc., because, as an educated man, he knows that the dream is unrealistic. But given the extent of knowledge, and the categories of magico-religious belief available for use as explanatory categories, it is reasonable to explain the European economy in terms of the activities of the ancestors, and a rational orientation of action to seek to encourage its coming by performing ritual acts.

Moreover, even given an awareness that one's knowledge is inadequate—and our knowledge is never adequate to achieve all our social purposes, even in societies with developed science and technology—one still has to act in the world. And it is not simply knowledge in the abstract that is lacking, but also the instrumentalities through which knowledge can be applied: they, and we, lack the techniques, too, with which to satisfy our wants. So they have to fall back on what is available. The alternative is to innovate by producing more adequate theoretical accounts of the world, as well as by creating the technical devices through which that body of theory can be turned into action. But this is not easy to do, and even scientists can demolish theories without being able to suggest better ones, let alone produce better techniques as well as better theories. Melanesians have this problem in acute form. They have their sceptics indeed, but Ein-

[1] 'Theories of Cargo Cults,' p. 27. Cf. Burridge, p. 273, for a similar observation.

steins and Marconis are as thin on the ground for them as they are for us.

One use of the term 'irrational,' which I introduced, needs mentioning here: my reference to the capitalist market as 'irrational.' This, of course, is another use, better kept separate, and it refers to the absence of human agency—and thereby the potentiality of more effective (though never 'absolute') control—in relating means to ends. It does not, therefore, describe an actor's subjective orientation to goals, but to discordance within a *system* (insofar as there is no structured mode of relating production to human wants). The classic word 'anarchy' might be better here. One should note that the Melanesian, however, cannot have that degree of knowledge of the working of the capitalist market that would enable him to evaluate it as 'anarchic'; indeed, using his own categories, he posits that the system *is* structured, and involves agents, since he develops an explanation that depends upon assuming the agency of spirits, on the one hand, and malevolent White men on the other.

Most writers, however, are not talking about *system* irrationality, but of the way in which means are related to ends in the action situation of the individual actor. Thus Jarvie's model of a 'rational actor' assumes (a) that he has a 'critical attitude towards knowledge' (p. 128); (b) that his behaviour is purposeful ('goal-directed activity').

Here, after a most valuable clarification of one set of problems posed by using this word to mean quite distinct things, we are back to another confusion. If 'rationality' merely refers to the 'goal-directed' quality of action, then all social action except that which is random, habitual, or affectual is rational. Goal directedness is characteristic of most action, and at least a dimension of all of it. In this use of the word, it is sometimes assumed that, given knowledge of the end, we can describe that action which is most 'appropriate' (or 'economical,' or 'optimal,' or 'elegant,' or 'fit') as being 'rational' action: where the means are 'best' adapted to achieving the end. But our yardsticks for determining what is 'appropriate' and what is not are singularly elastic. Indeed, we have to interpret and evaluate action and judge its 'fitness' according to standards of evaluation that are themselves relative, and therefore vary. Not only can ends be achieved perfectly satisfactorily by using 'uneconomic' or 'expensive' means, and not necessarily the optimal means, but just what 'optimal' is is inherently indefinite. I find this use of the term, fundamental to Weber's sociology, quite unilluminating, and think we had better dispense with it altogether. The second use is that which Jarvie points to: 'rational' refers to *modes of explanation,* and involves criticality.

So, when assumptions are protected from inspection and refutation, we speak, paradoxically, of 'rationalization.' By this we mean insulation of primary beliefs from critical scrutiny, and the elaboration of 'secondary explanations' so that the secondary explanations fit the primary beliefs, depend upon them, and protect the primary beliefs from scrutiny. The latter are held to be self-evidently true and unquestionable. (It should be noted that in evaluating the 'fitness' of means for achieving given ends —a use of the term 'rationality' we have rejected—we may be operating on the basis of precisely such unscrutinized primary beliefs about what constitutes 'optimal' means.)

This use of rationality is different from the 'goal-directed' implication. Yet if we use it, we must grant that Melanesians are as rational as we are, and as irrational.

Now Melanesians do subject belief to scrutiny: they do not simply 'hold' beliefs, they use and test them. Hence, notably, the shifts and phases of the movements. They develop new ideas and abandon others. But not always, and their primary ideas are not so easily displaced. They *do* fall back on 'unbreachable' assumptions [1] and 'cult doctrines are unlikely, if the prophets or the believers have anything to do with it, to be allowed to be put to the critical test for the simple reason that *the critical attitude does not prevail among them*' (p. 18, my italics); in the face of disconfirmatory evidence, too, they 'tend to invent *ad hoc* explanations, as would bad scientists' (p. 28).

Jarvie's argument needs extending to allow an explicit place for the 'non-rational,' both in general and in the particular context of the analysis of Melanesian behaviour. At the widest level, an ideal type of rational behaviour at least implies a conception of non-rational action by contrast: and there is plenty of 'uncritical' behaviour both at home and abroad.[2] Assuredly, Jarvie did not mean to invert the nineteenth-century imputation of 'prelogical mentality' to savages by reserving that kind of thought for Europeans, so it seems sensible to recognize the uncritical as well as the critical aspects of Cargo cult thought. But it would seem a

---

[1] Jarvie's word, 'Theories of Cargo Cults,' p. 7.

[2] Melanesians have observed some of our inconsistencies, unexamined assumptions, and matters taken on trust: White men, they observe, dismiss sorcerers as quacks, yet they prosecute them for sorcery. They are themselves terrified of small, invisible creatures called *jerms.*

good deal healthier all around if we dropped the use of this now sadly confused word, together with 'charisma.'

As far as future Cargo research is concerned, we seriously need depth studies of the kind carried out by Lofland for the Doomsday Cult; obviously, access is the problem. We know all too little about the situation of action and the processes of interaction: about the mode of recruitment and the kinds of people recruited, both as leaders and followers; about the competitive situation in which the cult comes into being, and within which it has to compete with rival organizations; about the competing variants of policy advocated by different rival individuals and factions, in ever-shifting situations; about the activities undertaken by the cults; about the leadership given, and the resolutions of choice arrived at in the aftermath of failure; about the way in which the cult beliefs are derived, received, developed, maintained, modified, and spread; about the reaction of non-cultists in the social field of the cult (including non-believing members of one's own society, and those Melanesians who are cultural outsiders, as well as the White agents in the situation); about the factors precipitating the cult, and the causes of its decline; and about the periodic experiments made with alternative courses of action (such as joining the mission, cooperating in Government development schemes, etc.). It would seem that it is in these areas, about which we know least, that the most valuable advances could be made, which could supplement the clarification that has been achieved in the area of the analysis of belief and its relationship to action.

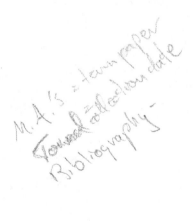

Maps

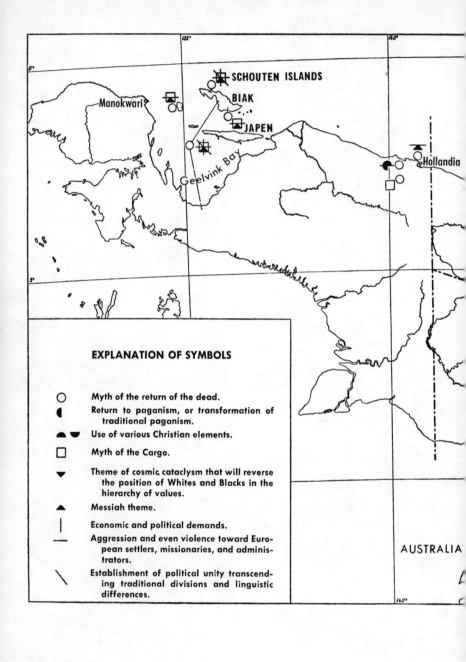

SCHOUTEN ISLANDS

Manokwari

BIAK

JAPEN

Geelvink Bay

Hollandia

EXPLANATION OF SYMBOLS

○   Myth of the return of the dead.

◖   Return to paganism, or transformation of traditional paganism.

◒ ◓   Use of various Christian elements.

☐   Myth of the Cargo.

▼   Theme of cosmic cataclysm that will reverse the position of Whites and Blacks in the hierarchy of values.

▲   Messiah theme.

| Economic and political demands.

—   Aggression and even violence toward European settlers, missionaries, and administrators.

\   Establishment of political unity transcending traditional divisions and linguistic differences.

AUSTRALIA

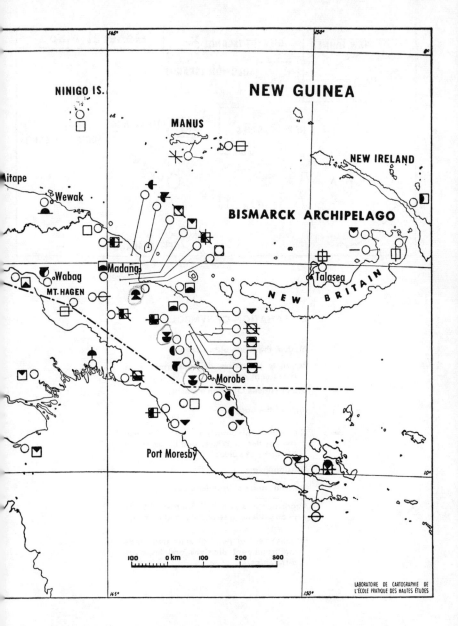

These maps appeared in Jean Guiart and Peter Worsley, 'La répartition des movements millénaristes en Mélanésie,' *Archives de Sociologie des Religions*, III, No. 5. Reprinted by permission of Editions du Centre National de la Recherche Scientifique.

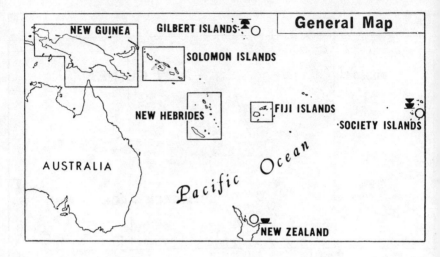

General Map

EXPLANATION OF SYMBOLS

○   Myth of the return of the dead.

◖   Return to paganism, or transformation of traditional paganism.

▲ ▼   Use of various Christian elements.

□   Myth of the Cargo.

▼   Theme of cosmic cataclysm that will reverse the position of Whites and Blacks in the hierarchy of values.

▲   Messiah theme.

| Economic and political demands.

—   Aggression and even violence toward European settlers, missionaries, and administrators.

\   Establishment of political unity transcending traditional divisions and linguistic differences.

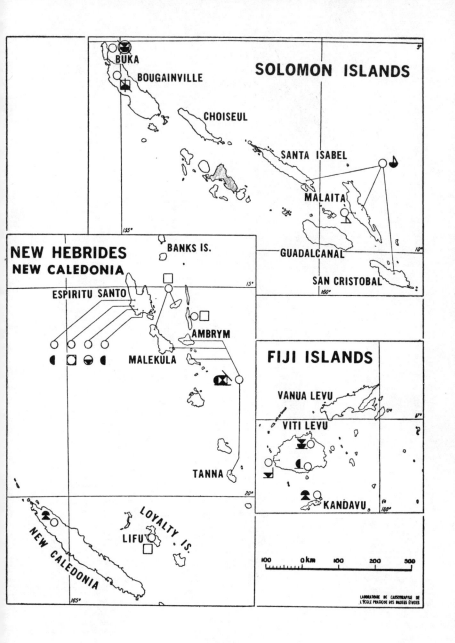

ABBREVIATIONS

The following abbreviations are used throughout:

Ann. Rpt.   Annual Report
Col. Off.   Colonial Office
TNG   Mandated (later Trust) Territory of New Guinea
BSIP   British Solomon Islands Protectorate
NMB   Neuendettelsauer Missionsblatt
PIM   Pacific Islands Monthly

Preface to the First Edition

MY THANKS are due to many colleagues who have helped me in this study. Anyone who has worked with Professor Max Gluckman must be permanently indebted to him for his deep interest in his colleagues' work and for the wealth of ideas which he pours forth inexhaustibly. He has also been of great practical assistance in making the writing of the book possible. Clifford Slaughter has read his way through a mountain of drafts and has always produced most illuminating criticisms. Discussions with Dr Eric Hobsbawm and Professor Norman Cohn on related movements which they have studied have been of enormous value.

I am indebted also to Dr Phyllis Kaberry and Mrs E. M. Chilver who made many useful suggestions about sources of material, to Mr John Saville, to Miss Ethel Drus and Messrs C. H. Allan, J. R. Wrightson and G. B. Sharp who read chapters touching on their special fields.

Dr V. W. Turner, Dr Tibor Bodrogi, Mr G. S. Parsonson and Professor Anthony Wallace helped me in various ways; and Professor Raymond Firth, M. Jean Guiart, Dr F. G. Bailey and the Rev. Rudolf Inselmann kindly allowed me to consult unpublished material. Drs Peter Lawrence and K. O. L. Burridge provided me with photographs, but, more importantly, helped me by discussions of their first-hand experience of Cargo cults in New Guinea.

The interpretation of the events described in this book is my own, however, and is not necessarily endorsed by the colleagues I have mentioned.

Without the facilities and practical assistance made available by the University of Manchester my task would have been much more difficult. To Mr P. W. van Milaan, Librarian at the Central Library of the Royal Tropical Institute in Amsterdam, to M. René Varin, Cultural Attaché at the French Embassy in London, and to the Editor of *Pacific Islands Monthly* I am deeply indebted for assistance in acquiring various publications and photographs.

9

Special thanks are due to Miss Audrey Barker and Mrs E. Jump, who typed much of the manuscript with extraordinary patience and interpretative skill.

I also wish to thank the following for their co-operation: The Editor of *Oceania* for permission to reproduce the three verses from *What Ancestral Wealth and Knowledge?* by A. P. Allan Natachee on page 32; and Messrs Routledge & Kegan Paul Ltd. for permission to reproduce the four verses from H. Ian Hogbin's *Transformation Scene* on page 195.

Introduction to the First Edition

THIS BOOK IS WRITTEN in the firm belief that anthropology can be interesting to the non-specialist. If its practitioners have not always made it so, one must acknowledge that some aspects of the subject are more attractive than others. It is difficult, for example, for the layman to derive much satisfaction from the algebraic intricacies of Australian aboriginal kinship.

The subject matter of this book, however, is not so esoteric, though it is certainly bizarre. It deals with the rise of a large number of strange religious movements in the South Pacific during the last few decades. In these movements, a prophet announces the imminence of the end of the world in a cataclysm which will destroy everything. Then the ancestors will return, or God, or some other liberating power, will appear, bringing all the goods the people desire, and ushering in a reign of eternal bliss.

The people therefore prepare themselves for the Day by setting up cult organizations, and by building storehouses, jetties, and so on to receive the goods, known as 'cargo' in the local pidgin English. Often, also, they abandon their gardens, kill off their livestock, eat all their food, and throw away their money.

Just what these events mean, and why they occur in particular areas at particular times, I hope to clarify in these pages. For, as we will see, similar movements have occurred throughout the world, even in the history of Europe, and are by no means peculiar to remote peoples and lands. So plentiful is the literature on these movements that no one person can hope to survey it all: only intensive team-work can make possible the disinterment of even a part of the material on movements which have occurred over centuries in many parts of the world, and which are often only described in unpublished documents in many different tongues.

I have therefore taken one region and subjected it to more intensive analysis. It is in Melanesia, that island region to the north and east of Australia, that the millenarian cult has become not merely a matter of theoretical importance to anthropologists, but also a matter of practical concern to governments.

I use the term 'millenarian' to describe those movements in which there is an expectation of, and preparation for, the coming of a period of supernatural bliss. I do not narrowly confine this term to the classical belief that the period will be one of 1,000 years. The term, in my use, includes both those movements which anticipate that the millennium will occur solely as a result of supernatural intervention, and those which envisage that the action of human beings will be necessary. I do not use the labels 'messianic' or 'prophetic' because, as I hope to show, the activities of messiahs or prophets are not the most important features of such movements.

A far more important distinction is that between movements which expect the millennium to occur in the near future and those which regard the millennium as a remote event. Modern orthodox Christianity itself, of course, falls in the latter category; the Christianity of the time of Christ falls into the former. Most of those movements which expect the millennium to occur soon are, in fact, what I call 'activist' movements, in which the people busy themselves with preparations for the Day; most of those which regard the millennium as a remote event are usually passive in character: people resign themselves to their present lot and look for salvation in the next world. Here, we are concerned primarily with the first type.

* * *

Though Polynesia has become a familiar name to many people—perhaps because of its varied associations with the Maori, 'Hawaiian' music and the Kon-Tiki expedition—the name Melanesia is probably less familiar to most. The Melanesian islands are bounded by Australia to the south, with the islands of Polynesia to the east, Indonesia to the west, and the coral atolls of Micronesia—of which Bikini is the best known—to the north.

It is typical of the general obscurity surrounding Melanesia that the region contains the largest island in the world, but one which is very little known: New Guinea, where even today considerable populations in the mountainous centre have yet to be brought under government control. The western half of New Guinea is administered by the Netherlands, which is spending money lavishly to develop and strengthen the Dutch title to this extremely backward territory, the only remnant of the former Dutch East Indies. It is this territory which Indonesia calls Irian, and to which she is pressing her claims.

Eastern New Guinea is divided into a northern and a southern part. The northern portion, which also includes the large islands of New Britain, New Ireland, and Buka, was formerly German New Guinea. After World War I it became an Australian Mandate, and since World War II has been a United Nations Trust Territory, administered by Australia. The southern part of eastern New Guinea is the Australian territory of Papua.

Eastwards from New Guinea are the Solomon Islands, where such bitter battles were fought in World War II. Except for Buka, these islands are governed by Britain as the British Solomon Islands Protectorate.

Further to the south-east lie the New Hebrides, jointly administered by Britain and France under a queer system which has provided the political scientists of the Pacific with a little light relief. Besides the separate courts which each Government maintains, there is also a Joint Court, whose first President was appointed by the King of Spain. As Oliver remarks: 'he was truly neutral, having understood little French, less English, and no Melanesian; but this was no particular handicap, because he was also deaf.'[1]

At the southern end of this long chain, we find the French territory of New Caledonia, and on the Polynesian 'border', the Fiji Islands. New Caledonia is no 'untouched South Sea Island': it is a major exporter of nickel, chrome and cobalt, and not so long ago was the world's leading exporter of these important ores. Its native population has been reduced from some 100,000 people in Captain Cook's day to about 24,000 today, but an influx of deported criminals and political prisoners—Communards, Arab nationalists, etc.—and free French settlers, gave New Caledonia an additional population of 17,000 by 1939. Most of the hard work in the mines was done by thousands of Javanese and Tonkinese contract-labourers.

Fiji, too, as we shall see, soon became a valuable economic asset by virtue of its rich sugar fields, gold mines and coconut plantations. Thousands of Indians were brought in to provide the unskilled labour in Fiji's sugar plantations; today Indians bid fair to outnumber the native Fijians.

[1] *Oliver*, p. 178.

But these territories are exceptional. Most of the other islands are very backward economically, and for the most part are inhabited by people whose traditional social organization was much less complex than that of Fiji and New Caledonia. This is reflected in the low population figures: there are only about one million people in the enormous Australian territories of Papua-New Guinea, for example—some five or six people to the square mile.

The name Melanesia—'black islands'—refers to the black-skinned inhabitants who belong to three different racial stocks: a few frizzy-haired pygmies, a Negroid population, and a 'Papuan' population, probably the latest to arrive. These divisions fit to some degree, but not at all neatly, with the division into two major language-groups, the 'Melanesian' * and the 'Papuan'. 'Melanesian' languages are related to the Malayo-Polynesian family, but 'Papuan' really means little more than 'not Melanesian'. There is a truly fantastic diversity of tongues: at one extreme, the speakers of some languages are numbered only in scores; even at the other, they rarely exceed 70,000.

Part of the explanation of this small-scale diversity suggests itself when we look at the topography of the region. Most islands are mountainous, with a high central interior, and are often covered by range after range of sharply-folded hills covered with heavy growth. In such country, the people commonly live on the razor-edged hilltops, and a journey of a few miles in a day can be excellent going.

The mountains in Central Papua-New Guinea, for example, rise to 15,000 feet and for years constituted a barrier to exploration that only the advent of the aeroplane finally overcame. Here cold mists are quite normal, in sharp contrast to the hot, steamy swamplands formed by great rivers like the Sepik, the Fly or the Digul, which drain out of the Highlands.

One of the marked features of the region is the dichotomy between 'bush' people on the one hand, and coast dwellers on the other. The latter are often of later immigrant stock, and their lives are more centred upon fishing, sea trading and sea communications.

Certain fertile areas support larger populations. The great valleys of the New Guinea Highlands, for example, contain an

---

* I use 'Melanesian' in this book to refer to the people of the entire region, not merely to speakers of these 'Melanesian' tongues.

estimated half million people; in the Sepik region, villages of one or more thousand are not unknown. But less than 200 people go to make up a village in most parts. The people live by cultivating basic staples: root vegetables such as taro or yams, sago in the lowlands, or sweet potatoes in the Highlands. Formerly, they only used stone, wooden or shell tools. This does not mean that Melanesians always lived near the starvation-line. Indeed, the problem in Melanesia was frequently what to do with the huge surpluses. Although there was some individual specialization, and although some whole communities traded objects—pots, baskets, feathers, even songs and dances—in whose production they specialized, for the most part every man cultivated his own garden, and the limited technological equipment inhibited the development of specialization and trade.

Under these circumstances, surpluses could not be stored, they could not be used to extend trade, or to acquire capital equipment; instead they were used as means of acquiring prestige. A man's personal material wants in perishable commodities like yams and taro were soon satisfied; he therefore gave his surplus away in feasts. But he gave it away in a manner which created an obligation on the part of those who participated in the feasts to render him respect, service or some return in the future. Feasting was thus the avenue to political success and even to religious authority; it was the means by which one humbled one's rivals.

The elaborate political organization of the Trobriand Islands, with its Paramount Chieftainship, has become widely known from Malinowski's descriptions. Unfortunately, this society is not quite typical of Melanesia. Normally, there were no hereditary political authorities, not even hereditary ranks or statuses. A man could, by virtue of his diligence in the gardens, his skill in warfare or trade, or his personality, quickly acquire high social status. He would then use his wealth to mobilize people for activities such as building a club-house, which would reinforce his importance, or he would organize trade expeditions or war parties. If his son was a man of few parts, he would be unlikely to benefit much from his father's material and social power, as there was often no real material wealth in permanent form to be handed down. It was largely open to any man to advance himself socially by his own endeavours. In such societies, status differences were often marked. Thus one finds elaborate secret societies with membership in several grades, access to which can only be gained through the possession of wealth, e.g. by slaughtering pigs for a feast. But at the same time, society was so unspecialized that there were no formal courts, police officials, etc.—political and legal security depended upon support by relatives and kin, and the impermanent authority of the 'big men'. Self-help was therefore a normal procedure; in more serious cases, one could only appeal to one's kin, since one could not appeal to the Law or the State. Cases thus had to be settled ultimately by mutual agreement.

It was societies of this kind that the early traders, recruiters, missionaries and officials encountered as the occupation of the region proceeded. How the occupation took place in different areas we shall see; suffice to say here that England, Germany, France, Holland and Australia had divided out the whole of the region in the rush that took place after 1880, partly with economic potentialities in view, but also with a view to establishing strategic bases. The effects of this European impact on indigenous society were often devastating, though it was a long time before control was extended beyond the coastal fringes.

From the earliest days, strange cults were reported wherever the white man penetrated. New movements are still being reported today from areas where men who are still using stone tools, and who only yesterday had never seen a white man, have stepped straight into a world of radios and aeroplanes, Government and mission, plantations and settlers.

But let us look first of all at one of the earliest reported cult movements, one which took place before the turn of the century in Fiji.

THE TRUMPET SHALL SOUND

CHAPTER I

The Tuka Movement of Fiji

Endua na kuvea na mbula?
Sa na kunei mai Mburoto Kula.

Where shall we find the life?
It is to be found in the Glorious Paradise.

(from a Tuka chant)

THE FIRST EUROPEANS to visit the islands of the Fiji Group were sporadic explorers: Tasman in 1643, Cook in 1774 and Bligh in 1792. After the turn of the nineteenth century, however, contacts between the natives of Fiji and Europeans became more frequent. Many of the Europeans were sandalwooders looking for this fragrant timber in order to supply China with the raw material for joss-sticks, incense and other objects used in religious observances. By about 1813, the Fijian supply of trees had been virtually cut out. Later European visitors concentrated on fishing for trepang (*bêche-de-mer*), a sea-slug which was cured and sold in China where it was greatly prized for its believed restorative properties. Whaling was also carried on extensively in Fijian waters by Europeans.

The methods employed by these entrepreneurs were not always very respectable, but they were much more respectable than the activities of the other major category of Europeans: beachcombers, castaways, escaped convicts and the like, who found Fiji a convenient and profitable haven.

Some of these men offered their services to the heads of rival native kingdoms. They were often employed as craftsmen, but their skills in handling muskets salvaged from wrecks and in casting bullets were especially prized. At the turn of the century, the islands of Fiji were not politically unified. There were small coastal kingdoms in the south-east of Viti Levu, the largest island, and on Vanua Levu, the second island, but the hilly interiors were occupied by independent peoples who had not developed a state organization.

The framework of Fijian social organisation was a system of agnatic descent-groups, of which the largest was the *yavusa*.* Through the breakdown and merging of numbers of these *yavusa*, there arose confederations, and later unified kingdoms. But even those *yavusa* which lacked such political unity under a king or paramount chief were still highly stratified by a ranking system which grouped people into six grades, ranging from serf and commoner to high chief.

Most European economic activity was carried on along the coasts, and it was here also that the castaways and beachcombers established themselves. Before long, those small local kingdoms which had acquired European arms began to expand at the expense of their neighbours. The castaways and beachcombers played a decisive part in these wars as skilled technicians, and, above all, as invincible slaughterers. The most famous of them was Charles Savage, a Swede who escaped from the wreck of the brig *Eliza* in 1808, and offered his services to Naulivou, chief of Mbau. Savage would stand out of range of indigenous weapons, picking off the enemy by musket-fire with complete impunity. To make the job safer, he had a portable protective enclosure of coconut fibre made in which he was carried to within firing range and then began his work. He soon formed a company of Europeans: with their aid, Mbau shortly became the dominant power in south-eastern Viti Levu.

As a result of these innovations, there was a great increase in the scale and cruelty of warfare. Fiji, indeed, became known as the 'Cannibal Isles', though one old chief of Mbau remarked in 1847 that 'all the old people, and especially his own father, used to tell him that these bloody wars, and this eating of one another upon the present enlarged scale, sprang up in their days, and did not obtain to such an extent in the generation before them'.[1]

Around the middle of the century, the Christianized Tongan immigrants in eastern Fiji began to extend the scope of their rule, and a complex struggle developed between several of the major kingdoms. Ultimately, the struggle narrowed down to two major contenders: Thakombau, King of Mbau in south-east Viti Levu,

* In parts of Fiji, descent and inheritance were determined through the male line, in others through the female line. The former system, introduced from Polynesia, was gradually displacing the earlier Melanesian matrilineal system (*Derrick*, pp. 7-9).

[1] *Lawry*, p. 95.

and Ma'afu, the Tongan leader in eastern Fiji. This struggle was complicated by a large influx of White settlers in the late sixties. Some were merchants, planters and traders, others layabouts and rogues, and many a mixture of both. The upshot was the growth of the notorious 'blackbirding' labour traffic to provide plantation workers; the growing indebtedness of Thakombau's kingdom; native resentment over the cession and sale of land; and lawlessness and chaos, especially amongst the White community, which the Fijian authorities were unable to control.

Native society was severely disrupted by war, by catastrophic epidemics of European diseases, by the introduction of alcohol, by the devastation of generations of warfare, and by the depredations of the labour recruiters. To put a stop to this chaos, both Fijian and European political leaders attempted to arrange the cession of the islands to one of the Great Powers. For long, Great Britain resisted this manoeuvre, regarding colonies as undesirable burdens, but the coming to power of Disraeli in 1874 led to a change in policy. In that year, Fiji was ceded to a now willing Britain.

The hill regions of Viti Levu were not directly affected by these events to any great degree. Even Thakombau's writ had never run there. Although the hill peoples gave an oath of allegiance to the new Government in 1875, a rising in the hills of Tholo Province had to be suppressed in the following year: all military resistance either from the kingdoms or from the hill peoples now seemed to have come to an end.

By this time, the active proselytization of Wesleyan missionaries had led to the triumph of Christianity in those areas long under European influence. The population, even to the old men, were nominally Christian, and had renounced their old religion. Regular village services by Wesleyan native 'teachers' had replaced the older worship, and the heathen temples had been demolished. But just when the Wesleyan mission was celebrating its fiftieth anniversary, alarming news was reported from the backward hill regions of Viti Levu, where there were still no European missionaries or planters, and where the first European government official had only just been appointed. Yet the advent of Christianity, carried by native enthusiasts and evangelists, and the impact of Government, soon produced a reaction in native society.

Native unrest, stimulated by a religious cult, had been noted in Ra Province as early as 1877. But it was not until 1885 that the administration became really disturbed: then they heard that parties of men with blackened faces, and clothed in robes of native cloth, were carrying out military drill on the upper reaches of the Rewa River.[1]

Investigations revealed that the new movement was led by men who had moved into Tholo Province from the adjoining province of Ra. They were well organized, though they had few guns and were mainly armed with clubs and spears. The rank-and-file, known as 'soldiers' were commanded by 'sergeants', *rokos* and *mbulis*, and 'scribes'—titles which were taken from those of native officials, from Armed Constabulary ranks, and from the Bible; high officers were called 'destroying angels'. The new cult, it transpired, was known as the Tuka cult.* Its leader, Ndugumoi, claimed prophetic, miraculous and occult powers, and his spirit was said to leave his body and move around the country. He had announced that the order of the world was very shortly to be reversed. Whites were to serve natives and chiefs were to be inferior to commoners.

This was not the first cult outbreak of this kind. Ndugumoi's father, indeed, had been involved in cult activities of this kind many years before, and had been flogged for his pains at Thakombau's order.[2] As early as 1873, Ndugumoi himself had been deported from Ndrau-ni-ivi, his home village, to the Lau Islands for sedition, but was freed in 1882 and returned to Ra. Ndugumoi was an hereditary priest, and is said to have worked for Europeans on Taveuni Island at one period in his life.[3] On his return, he announced that he had escaped from the foreigners who still believed him to be in Tonga, though, in fact, Ndugumoi had not been in Tonga. He had left only his body in Tonga, he claimed, and had reached Fiji once more by ship, escaping whilst off Nakauvandra, the sacred mountain, in spite of attempts to kill him by tying an anchor round his neck and throwing him overboard. Being charmed, he swam ashore unharmed and unnoticed.[4] The Government thus had no power to kill or hurt him.

Ndugumoi now took upon himself the title Navosavakandua, a

* Brewster suggests that the name is a compound of *tu*: to stand upright, and *ka*: a thing, i.e., that which stands for ever, that which is immortal.

[1] *Sutherland*, p. 51.

[2] Information kindly supplied by Miss Ethel Drus.

[3] *Thompson*, 1940a, p. 117.   [4] *Thomson, B.*, 1894, p. 357.

title applied by the natives to the Chief Justice of Fiji. This title—meaning 'he who speaks once'—symbolized the power over life and death possessed by that official. But Navosavakandua claimed far greater powers than those of a mere Chief Justice. It had been mystically revealed to him that the ancestors were shortly to return to Fiji. When they did, the millennium would begin: the faithful would enter the *Mburoto Kula*, the Glorious Paradise, and the ancient lands and independence of the past would be restored. Eternal life and eternal pleasure were to be the lot of the faithful. For the aged, youth would be renewed and desire would return. The shops would be jammed with calico, tinned salmon and other goods for the faithful, but unbelievers would die, or be condemned to everlasting hell-fire, or become the slaves and servants of believers. Navosavakandua's message was also directed against the Whites: government officials, missionaries and traders were to be driven into the sea.[1]

This doctrine incorporated many traditional elements intertwined with elements derived from the Bible. The Fijian Creation myth tells of three brothers who survived a great Flood at the beginning of time. The most important of these was Ndengei, the snake-god who lived in a cavern in the Nakauvandra mountains, the Fijian Olympus, where his movements caused the thunder to roar, and where, so the prophet said, the flames of hell might be seen by anyone brave enough to enter. One of the other brothers, Rokola, the carpenter-god, married a princess who bore him twin sons, Nathirikaumoli and Nakausambaria. These twins quarrelled with Ndengei and made war on him, but were defeated and forced to sail away into exile.

Now, Navosavakandua announced, the divine Twins were about to return. The false Europeans were only too aware of this. They pretended to be surveying the reef through instruments, but they were really scanning the horizon for the vessels in which the Twins were returning with the ancestors. The prophet said that he had been afraid when the two gods first appeared to him, but they had told him to listen and said that he would acquire great spiritual power as a result. Thus was the new doctrine revealed to him. In other visions he saw clouds full of flying chariots: this was eagerly recounted as a sign of divine inspiration by followers who had no conception of what a chariot was.

[1] *Thomson, B.*, 1908, p. 142.

The facility with which the prophet and his followers combined Christianity and indigenous mythology may be seen in the version of the myth of Creation retailed by one old man who declared that the carpenter-god Rokola was no other than Noah.

In the beginning, there had been two gods, he said, Jehovah and Ndengei. Jehovah challenged Ndengei to make a man from clay but the latter failed. Jehovah, however, did make a man, and later a woman, and brought them to life. He then drove the vanquished Ndengei away, and peopled the earth. He told the people to build a house to reach as high as heaven itself, from which immortality could be brought to the earth. The house was built, each contributing those articles in whose manufacture he was skilled, and the people then named the goods, thus giving rise to the present diversity of languages. When the house was completed, a huge feast was held of yams, taro and plantains which sprang up on the spot. Then Jehovah said 'Go! spread through the land!' and the people went, bearing with them plants after which they named themselves—a taro, a plantain, a kind of yam, etc.—and populated the islands, the commoners first, then the chiefs.

This is clearly a blending of indigenous totemic origin-myths and myths validating existing statuses and occupations (chiefs, craftsmen, etc.) with the story of Genesis. There is an added connotation of White-Black differences, and even antagonisms, in the defeat of Ndengei. This mythological self-validation appears again in the claim that the Fijians had always known Jehovah and that He had *not* been introduced by the missionaries. There was controversy as to whether Ndengei was to be equated with God or with Satan: most preferred the latter since he was also a serpent. The Glorious Paradise was similarly identified with the Christian Paradise. Navosavakandua now renamed the days of the week after figures in the Flood legend, and renamed places around his village Roma (Rome), Ijipita (Egypt), Kolosa (Colossians) and similar names.

But the prophet did more than merely recognize the Black-White division in his teaching. He made his doctrine specifically anti-White. He preached that the Whites had deliberately deceived them. When the divine Twins had sailed away, they had arrived at the land of the Whites, where the Bible was written about them, but the names Jehovah and Jesus Christ were substituted for the names of the Twins.

To spread his creed, the prophet carried out an intensive campaign and set up an elaborate organization. His lieutenants travelled far and wide urging people to abandon everything and become followers of Navosavakandua.

Believers were trained in a drill compounded of native dances and of Armed Constabulary drill, with imitations of the words of command, for amongst Tuka enthusiasts there were numerous ex-members of the Constabulary. The military salute was given to Navosavakandua himself. To enter the movement, and to obtain the bottle of holy water drawn from the Fountain of Life which conferred immortality, adherents paid from 10/- to £2. The prophet's success may be gauged by the extent of the wealth he accumulated; at one feast alone he presented 400 whales' teeth, a king's ransom in Fiji. In the cult temples, he performed 'miracles': God could be heard descending with a low whistling sound behind a curtain where priests and attendant women sat. In these temples, his lieutenants, mainly selected men of the hereditary priestly caste with their female attendants (*Yalewa Ranandi*), combined the traditional kava-drinking* ritual with dances, prayers, presentations of property and military drill, especially on the Sabbath. The people were called upon to renounce sin and to pray, and as a foretaste of future bliss, a cult house of sleep and pleasant dreams was built in Nakauvandra country.

The Administration soon became uneasy. In 1885 Brewster feared that the trial of a native headman on charges of desertion and adultery might spark off trouble in a predominantly Tuka area.[1] The fattening of a white pig—believed to symbolize the Whites—in preparation for its sacrifice to the ancestors on the Day, created great alarm. And native enemies of the movement began to attack it. Parents whose daughters were taken into the ranks of the Yalewa Ranandi informed the police of the prophet's sexual relations with these girls, who, he promised, would remain perpetual virgins as long as they drank the holy water.

Matters were brought to a head when the prophet fixed the day of the millennium, and issued mysterious threats to Government and mission. He and some of his 'destroying angels' were quickly

* Kava is the Polynesian term for the narcotic called *yanggona* in Fiji, It is a drink prepared from the root of the shrub *piper methysticum*, to the accompaniment of elaborate ritual, and is drunk on ceremonial occasions, those of highest rank drinking first.

[1] *Brewster*, p. 237.

23

arrested by outside police despite some resistance, after local village police who were sympathetic to him had failed to arrest him. Many of the female attendants with him complained that they were tired of having to prepare kava for him.

He turned out to be a 'sooty-skinned, hairy little man of middle age', with eyes bleary from excessive kava-drinking. Though he would not speak to his White captors, he pleaded with the Fijian warders not to undo his work by preventing the return of the Twins. If this were done, he said, Ndengei's evil power would continue.

Navosavakandua expected the death sentence. When he received only one year's hard labour he was both amazed and relieved. Legends now began to multiply on the basis of this unexpected sentence. According to native rumour, the gaoler had tried to crop his hair, but the scissor-blades had bent backwards and refused to cut the seat of spiritual power. He had not been sentenced to death, it was said, because Government could not kill him.

Later he was banished for ten years to Rotuma Island, three hundred miles to the north, where he got married, and died when already released and on his way home. But legend had it that Government had tried, and failed, to kill him, firstly by dropping him in the huge rollers of a sugar-mill, and later by dropping him down the funnel of a steamer. He had merely passed through both the flames of the furnace and the furnace doors.

The announcement of his death was therefore disbelieved, and in 1892 one of his lieutenants professed to have received letters from the prophet which had fluttered down from the sky to fall on a bayonet point while he was in the forest. (Navosavakandua, in fact, could not write.) The sale of holy water now began afresh; military drilling commenced once more and the end of British rule was forecast. The time the Government razed Navosavakandua's village of Ndrau-ni-ivi to the ground, and deported its people to Kandavu island. A force of Armed Constabulary was stationed in the country. Only after ten years of constant petitioning were the exiles finally allowed to return.

Even so, the last had not been heard of Tuka, for a disciple, Sailose Ratu, revived the movement once more. Sailose appears to have been mentally unbalanced. He described himself as a *voula*, an archaic name for a seer. He once came into a government office and announced that he had had a revelation of the death of Queen Victoria on the day before (though she did not die until two years later). He said that he was the shrine of a spirit and that, if the spirit so willed, he would kill anyone he was told to kill. He was put in an asylum for twelve years and later released—in his opinion, because the Government now admitted that he had been right about the Queen's death! Then towards the end of World War I he called a big meeting and announced that his spirit had told him that Great Britain had surrendered to Germany, that the Governor was deposed, and the people were now free and need no longer pay taxes. Taken back to the asylum, he later died.

Sailose had spent much time compiling the 'Tuka Gazette', a copybook full of records of the visions and prayers of the Prophet, together with appearances of the Prophet to Sailose even after Navosavakandua's death.

The occult, cabbalistic signs, mystic pass-words, cryptic writing, etc. of the earlier stages of the movement were freely elaborated by Sailose. Similar phrases had been used by even earlier Tuka adherents, e.g. '*Lilifai poliseni oliva ka virimbaita*': *virimbaita* means 'to hedge in' and *oliva* may derive from Olive, a local Commandant of the Armed Constabulary, but *in toto* the sentence is said to have no meaning.[1] Much of this esoteric ritual appears to derive from Freemasonry, and some from Roman Catholic missals.

It was many years before Tuka beliefs died. Even Brewster's right-hand man, a sergeant in the service of the judicial administration of Ra province, died a firm believer in Tuka, as did the head constable of Tholo North, a 'most revered official' who was at the same time one of the 'destroying angels' of the Tuka cult.

The Tuka movement has been attributed by Brewster partly to contact with Maori sailors on whaling ships who brought stories of the millenarian Hau Hau movement in New Zealand to Fiji, especially to the dockers in the small ports of Fiji. Even at this time some natives from inland sought employment at the coast. But it is doubtful if there was any such connection, or, if it existed, if it was important. The important factor is the receptivity of the people and their predisposition to accept new ideas. But we should not scout the possibility of such contacts entirely. Apart from modern media of communication, indigenous channels were surprisingly efficient and far-reaching. For example, Tongan expeditions to Eromanga in the Solomons for the purpose of 'trade' (which often meant the overwhelming of the native inhabitants)

---

[1] *Thomson, B.*, 1908, p. 140.

resulted in the establishment of an Eromangan community in Tonga itself as early as the 1830's.[1]

Thus the reaction of the hill people of Fiji to the coming of British administration differed considerably from that of the inhabitants of the coastal kingdoms. Foreign rule had been welcomed in Mbau and elsewhere where social life was menaced by the oppression of their rulers and the lawlessness of the Whites. In the hills, however, British domination meant the end of ancient independence, and the full extent of British power was not apparent to people who only saw the occasional administrator or a few policemen. Thomson remarks how the hill men chafed at the restrictions of British administration, at the slowness of the courts, at new property laws, and especially at the obligation to pay taxes to a Government which had never conquered them: they 'would welcome the worst anarchy so it were their own and not a foreigner's,' he remarks.[2] One of the last minor flare-ups of revolt was the Seanggangga Revolt in Mathuata Province, Vanua Levu, in 1894—also in the hills. To the hill people, Tuka represented a doctrine of resistance and hope. And they were led by a section of the society which had suffered particularly in loss of power and authority through the complete victory of Christianity—the hereditary priests. That the movement was not merely a religion was recognized by Thomson, who urged that it be put down 'with the same energy that they would employ against dangerous conspiracies of a political nature'.[3]

A movement which existed side-by-side with the Tuka, and which combined with it in some areas, was the Luve-ni-wai: the Water Babies, or Children of the Water. Though non-millenarian and less anti-White in content, this cult also represented a reaction, particularly on the part of the younger people, to radical social changes. It was first noted by Wesleyan missionaries, and was led by the *vu-ni-nduva* magicians, who astonished their followers by 'making' food and performing other sleight of hand tricks. Although adherents used occult signs and performed strange ceremonies, the Luve-ni-wai was regarded at first as merely a 'sort of junior republic', 'a pastime for young people'.[4] But since it expressed the restlessness of young people and of minor chiefs excluded from high positions in the traditional here-

[1] *Erskine*, p. 143.
[2] *Thomson, B.*, 1894, p. 359.
[3] *loc. cit.*
[4] *Brewster*, p. 222.

ditary power-structure, it became an alternative focus of discontent to the Tuka, with which it alternated or combined in Tholo Province. It soon became a channel for the expression of anti-White feeling, and as it showed signs of developing a programme of violence, the missionaries persuaded Government to ban it, and several chiefs were deposed for supporting it.[1]

The name of the cult was taken from the fairy-like 'fauns' who were believed to people the forests and waters, miniature men with large bushy heads of hair in the traditional style and very handsome withal. Men claimed to have met these friendly sprites in the forests and to have learnt songs and dances from them. Where they had met, 'fairy rings' were kept swept and magically protected and cleaned and decorated with flowers.

To join the movement, a man had to acquire his own personal guardian spirit from amongst these forest creatures. He would pray in the bush, offering kava, and wait until a spirit entered his body. Then he would take a new name, usually that of a flower. By 1884 the movement was said to be getting out of hand in Serea, the largest village in Tholo East. A government officer found all the young men and boys assembled in the temple in the presence of their elders. When they resisted arrest, forty-four were seized, including Pita, their leader, taken to Vunindawa and flogged.

For six years, nothing more was heard of Luve-ni-wai in this area. Then, in 1890, the local government representative went away for eight months. On his return, he found both the Luve-ni-wai and Tuka movements rampant. A number of youths were tried and sentenced to three months' hard labour.[2]

The activities of the Luve-ni-wai in later years appear to have been mainly confined to certain islands. It was concerned with propitiating the guardian spirits through ceremonies based on traditional rites such as kava-drinking, but with much prayer and song and dancing and violent possession by spirits, which often led to fights. In these ceremonies, *mana* was acquired from the spirits; on each island the leader was the man with the most *mana*, a qualification in which he could be challenged by aspiring leaders.[3] It thus provided a channel for the energies of youths aspiring upwards to social mobility and the acquisition of power.

The early phase of the movement was quite innocuous: '. . . in

---

[1] *Sutherland*, p. 56.   [2] *Brewster*, p. 229.
[3] *Thompson*, 1940a, pp. 114 ff., and 1940b, pp. 116-19.

my opinion, it was not really seditious, it led the boys to be cheeky and insubordinate, and to a certain amount of larceny. I think there is not much harm in it so long as the votaries refrain from picking and stealing, and are duly respectful to their elders, and there is certainly a fair element of romance and poetry about it.'[1]

Brewster himself attempted to provide an alternative form of social activity for the Fijians. He decided to start cricket clubs. At this period, theories which attributed native discontent to 'boredom', 'lack of interest in life', and which preached the necessity of some harmless, preferably creative *recreations* and pastimes to replace the old ceremonies, dances, etc., were very popular. But Brewster's cricket clubs became somewhat different bodies from those that he had envisaged. They multiplied rapidly, and became highly organized, with great stress upon rank. Besides captains (known as 'elders of the guild') there were the conventional secretaries, treasurers, and so on. But the offices of 'chief of the outer circle' and 'chief of the inner circle' were discovered to be more equivalent to 'Home Secretary' and 'Secretary of State for Foreign Affairs' than to president or even wicket-keeper or groundsman! Indeed there was one rank which could best be translated as 'Lord High Admiral'. Accompanying this structure of leadership was a great stress on books, registers, codes of signals and other organizational mechanisms.

When one club elected a Governor, a Chief Justice and a Chief Secretary, its leaders were gaoled, for it was felt that some of the clubs had become merely a cloak for the 'Water Babies', concerned more with obtaining freedom from foreign rule than with victories on the playing-field.*

After World War I, Fiji entered upon a period of development, particularly in the fields of sugar, gold, and copra production, which not only made her an important and valued economic possession in a region of very poor islands, but which also transformed the internal social structure.

Large-scale Indian immigration supplied the skilled or semi-

---

* The expression of political interests through the medium of cricket and football matches has been noted several times in Melanesia in the less dangerous form of inter-village competitions (with, however, no anti-White implications), e.g. in Dr H. A. Powell's *Cricket in Kiriwina* and Dr Peter Lawrence's unpublished Ph.D. thesis on the Garia of New Guinea.

[1] *Brewster*, pp. 116-17.

skilled labour for the expanding sugar industry, which exported £14M worth of sugar in 1939. It also provided Fijians with a new set of social problems. But Fijians still supplied the bulk of the unskilled labour as in other industries; as the second largest copra-producing territory in Oceania in 1938, and a gold-producing country employing some 2,000 unskilled natives alone by 1939, Fiji soon outpaced the other Melanesian territories, except for New Caledonia.[1] And the people soon found more familiar and orthodox forms for the expression of their political and economic demands as they rapidly acquired knowledge and experience of the White man's society.

There were only one or two flickers of millenarism after World War I. A man named Apolosi started a semi-religious anti-White and anti-Indian movement in 1914 for which he was banished to Rotuma in 1917. After seven years' exile, he returned and again preached his religion. He claimed to be King of Fiji and to possess supernatural powers, and offered freedom from disease; his authority derived from his possession of a sacred box from the original canoe of the mythical ancestors of all the Fijians. A brilliant organizer, with a magnetic personality, Apolosi was, however, strongly resisted by chiefs who saw in his cult a threat to their position. Banished again in 1930, he returned in 1940 and after another short spell received a third term of ten years.

Government's view of him is expressed by Sir Harry Luke, who called him the 'Rasputin of the Pacific'. He accuses him of 'intrigue, sedition, and lechery and debauchery on an heroic scale, ranging from drunken orgies to rape and incest' and stresses his 'genius for subversive intrigue, his quasi-religious influence over his dupes, his utter lack of scruple, his abnormally developed and sustained sexual appetites and the ease with which he secures the victims of his lust'.[2]

Apolosi's movement was evidently quite different from the Tuka. But true vestiges of the Tuka movement appeared in a cult recorded *after* World War II on Nakausele island[3] in the Kandavu sub-group, to which, as we saw, the population of the Tuka stronghold of Ndrau-ni-ivi village had been deported for several years.

This cult, led by one Kelevi, did not anticipate any cataclysmic change, but incorporated into its doctrine old Tuka notions. The locally-dominant Methodist church, Kelevi said, was not the true

[1] *Stanner*, passim.   [2] *Luke*, p. 140.   [3] *Cato*, passim.

29

church. 'Our Methodist God', he declared, 'is the Snake.' The Snake he meant was none other than Ndengei: prayers were offered up to Ndengei and the Divine Twins. Though non-millenarian in itself, Kelevi's movement stimulated millenarian beliefs. Kandavu medicine men claimed to have had news of the imminent return of the Twins who had been living in Germany and other European countries, giving *mana* and wisdom to their inhabitants.

Kelevi's doctrine itself stressed the achievement of eternal life in a new world, the Kingdom of Christ on this earth. He also claimed to have visited Heaven and to have supernatural powers, but his message was essentially passive and non-apocalyptic. And though specifically dissociating his church from Methodism, Kelevi was not violently opposed to the Europeans or to their church. Nevertheless he came into conflict with authority through countermanding the orders of the *de jure* chief, and through sleeping with his female attendants whom he organized into a body called the Roses of Life, just as Navosavakandua had organized his *Yalewa Ranandi* and Apolosi his *Leweni Ruve* (Flock of Doves). Finally, in 1947, the police invaded the cult community.

Kelevi's movement, in fact, was another of those many separatist native sects thrown up in colonial situations, notably in South Africa and the southern states of the USA, where the people wish to dissociate themselves spiritually—often the only way open to them —from the authority of their rulers. Where other channels of leadership and self-expression are blocked, energetic men frequently become prophets of these sects. Heavy emphasis is placed upon direct communication between the faithful and the Lord, upon inspiration, possession, visions, trances, faith-healing, speaking with tongues, etc., and the doctrine itself is a syncretic mixture of Christianity and other beliefs. Sects including more or less of these elements have also appeared amongst the Tahitians, Tongans, Hawaiians, and the Maori.[1] Some are 'respectable' movements for self-determination within the framework of Europe-based Christian churches; these are usually peaceful and mystical. Others, especially when persecuted, become apocalyptic and rebellious. Though they often overlap with the movements we are describing, on the whole they are passive movements which put the millennium off to a remote future date, and thus differ from the

[1] *Keesing*, pp. 78, 235-8.

specifically millenarian and activist movements: they will therefore only be considered incidentally in this book.

The real stream of activist millenarian thought was to flourish, not in the advanced ranked societies of Fiji and New Caledonia, but amongst the more primitive peoples of Melanesia, on islands where European trade and government reached the people much later on the whole.

CHAPTER II

Millenarism and Social Change

O stone-age child, why do you lie dreaming,
Of dreams and thoughts of your ancestor?
Why? Oh why do you continue clinging,
To way of life of your ancestor?

What sort of wealth did he possess for you,
And his knowledge of ability?
None but worthless heathen rubbish for sure,
Is now the cause of stupidity.

Leave all your heathen rubbish and behold,
An atomic-age and restless man,
Has come from land unknown just to unfold,
Way of life not as child but as man.

(excerpt from the poem 'WHAT ANCESTRAL
WEALTH AND KNOWLEDGE?' by A. P. Allan
Natachee, a Mekeo of Papua, *Oceania*, Vol.
XXII, 1951-2, p. 150)

━━━━

Copra, Gold and Rubber

IN CONTRAST to the more complex societies of Fiji, or of New
Caledonia (where resistance to European rule resulted in several
secular revolts), most of the islands of Melanesia were occupied by
people whose social organization and culture were of the simple
types described in our Introduction. Whilst not minimizing the
significant differences, there was considerable similarity between
the social organization and culture of these peoples, and the impact
of the Whites, too, generally took place in a limited number of
ways.

The documentation necessary for a broad picture of the general
effects of European rule on the whole of the Melanesian region is
sadly deficient; it is least bad for Papua-New Guinea. We will
therefore take this area, large enough in all conscience, as a representative area, before examining these social changes at the
village level.

It must be observed initially that the problem of a large White
minority, so important in many colonial territories, was not present

in this region. Consequently, land alienation on the scale familiar, for example, in Kenya did not occur. In New Guinea, 59.3 million acres out of a total of 60 million remained unalienated by 1940: 158,000 of these were actually leased. But such crude figures, of course, obscure the fact that 'much of the best economic land had passed out of native possession'.[1] Many of the limited areas of good soil were alienated; the areas most suitable for copra production were particularly subject to alienation. And, as Mair notes, although much land remained unalienated, this was small consolation to natives in those areas where most land had been lost, and for whom there was in practice no land actually available locally.[2] In land purchases the protection of native interests before sale was often neglected on the grounds of 'the wider interests of the territory'.[3]

Developments in this region were largely determined by the nature of European enterprise. Of these, undoubtedly the most important—at least in the initial stages—was plantation agriculture of a few major crops, mainly of coconuts for export as copra. In 1923, the Director of Agriculture for the Mandated Territory referred to the territory as 'labouring mentally under the desolating blight of an obsession of coconut planting'.[4] The effort put into coconut-plantation economy brought the copra exports of the Territory up from 2,000 tons in 1883 (when there was a White population of only thirty) to over 70,000 tons in 1939. In 1925, copra exports produced over 95% of export values, but gold soon came to outstrip copra as the major export. The initial major discovery was made in 1926, but it was only after 1936 that intensive mining really began, raising the share of gold in export values from 66% of the total to 86% in 1941, while the share of copra declined from 30% to 8%.

A basically similar situation obtained in Papua. Here rubber was added to copra and gold as a third major export, gold remaining a fairly constant third of export values from 1936 to 1941, rubber increasing from 25% to 35%, and copra again declining from 28% to 12%.

The Vagaries of the European Economy

Although copra production continued to rise fairly steadily right up to the outbreak of war, fluctuations of world economy reduced

---

[1] *Stanner*, p. 33.　　[2] *Mair*, p. 97.　　[3] *ibid.*, p. 95.　　[4] *ibid.*, p. 98.

33

its value considerably. Indeed, this area would have been in a desperate situation had gold not come to the rescue. Thus economic and social changes were by no means determined by internal developments alone. The following graph shows the movements of world copra prices:

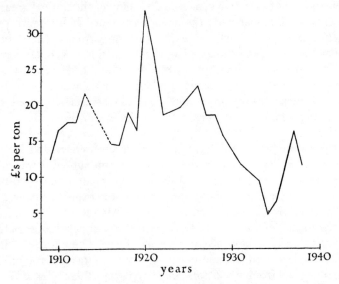

AVERAGE PRICE PER TON OF NEW GUINEA COPRA, 1909-1938
(*Australian Pounds*)

(Figures from *Reed*, p. 194; original source: R. E. P. Dwyer, 'A Survey of the Coconut Industry in the Mandated Territory of New Guinea', *New Guinea Agricultural Gazette*, Vol. 2, 1936, p. 2.)

Belshaw writes of a wider period, 'the price of copra . . . has fluctuated from £70/12/6 per ton to £2, and from £30 to £8 in a year'.[1] Well over £100 per ton was being offered by Canadian buyers in 1951.[2] Besides these fluctuations, and similar fluctuations in the prices of trade goods, the economy of this region was not strengthened by rising values of exports, since 'heavy repatriations of profits lessened, and equipment imports narrowed, the spread of local benefits'.[3] This meant that the continual favourable trade balances did not make for viability, since the profits transferred to external territories, particularly Australia, con-

---

[1] *Belshaw*, 1950a, pp. 40-41.   [2] *Stanner*, p. 121.
[3] *ibid.*, p. 37.

stantly drained the country of capital needed for development.[1]

The social implications of these dry figures are not far to seek. Constant changes in the price of trade goods, fluctuations in the price paid for primary products, the great copra slump of the early thirties with its ruination of the majority of small planters and their absorption by a few large enterprises, and the lack of visible return for the great values exported, made White society appear more mysterious and irrational to the islander than it had been even in periods of comparative economic stability. In the New Hebrides, natives considered that local merchants were responsible for these price variations.[2]

Many writers have drawn attention to important features of European society which must appear to be beyond rational explanation to the Melanesian with his limited knowledge. The processes of production of European goods, the nature of the tools used, the workers using those tools, and the relations between them and their employers, etc.—all these remain closed books to most islanders. Thus many visitors to colonial areas have found it difficult to persuade natives that the goods they see are made by White men, and it is even more difficult to persuade them that menial tasks are performed by Whites. The White men we see, the natives say, do not work thus. But these obvious gaps in knowledge are still matters which can be readily explained and appreciated. Not so readily explained and appreciated are the significance of boom and slump, the closing of plantations, experimental stations and other government and private enterprise which appears to be flourishing, the pressure on natives to produce cash crops which realize progressively less from year to year. And these violent swings affected not merely the small native producer, but also the vast numbers of migrant labourers. Hogbin notes, for the Solomons, how a minimum wage of £1 per month fell to 10/- in the depression year of 1934.[3]

This underlying irrationality of European society not only created great hardships; it undermined confidence in rational activity, it created frustrations, and it sapped morale more than mere ignorance of productive processes could do. For ignorance of these latter is a constant, not necessarily disturbing the social order. The vagaries of the economy are unpredictable, devastating and, for the most of the inter-war period, cumulatively worsening. They are also collective, and not merely individual, disasters. As Stanner,

<hr>

[1] *loc. cit.*   [2] *Guiart*, 1957.   [3] *Hogbin*, 1939, p. 161.

one of the few anthropologists who has pointed to this feature, remarks: 'Two factors which, probably, have had much more to do with native disenchantment with European economy than is realized are the colonial terms of trade and the repatriation of savings and net profits by European enterprise. A simple calculation of New Guinea imports as a proportion of the value of exports shows a marked *downward* trend between 1920-40.'[1]

There is evidently no close correlation between economic fluctuations and specific cult outbreaks. However, it is clear that the labelling of the cults as 'irrational' begs the question. Indeed, a Melanesian might make out a good case for flinging the label of 'madness' which has often been applied to these cults back at us, and asking whether his people, given the knowledge they possessed, have not made quite logical criticisms and interpretations of our own unpredictable and irrational society.

This instability and uncertainty strengthened such beliefs as the widely-held notion that the Australian Government itself was merely a transient phenomenon: just as the Germans had gone, so would the Australians. As the years passed, this idea weakened, but it received a sudden lease of life as World War II loomed on the horizon. The belief, of course, was to prove correct. How far it was stimulated by pro-Nazi elements amongst German missionaries, who numbered over half the missionaries in the Mandated Territory, is now difficult to say.

The Drive for Labour

The particular characteristic of this economy which was to make such great inroads upon indigenous social organization was its insatiable demand for ever-increasing supplies of unskilled labour, both for the plantations and the mines. Labour was for the most part obtained by indenture, and by 1938 nearly 42,000 indentured labourers were at work in the Mandated Territory, and some 10,000 in Papua. Mandated Territory labourers signed on for three years in the first instance, with a theoretical maximum of four years' continuous employment; in Papua the maximum was eighteen months' to three years' continuous service. But many served for much longer terms.

In addition to the pull of new wants, a powerful incentive to wage labour was the introduction of native taxation. In his report

[1] *Stanner, op. cit.,* p. 73.

on 'native affairs' in New Guinea for 1924, Col. Ainsworth stated that 'the primary object of the head tax was not to collect revenue but to create among the natives a need for money, which would make labour for Europeans desirable and would force the natives to accept employment'.[1] Since, in Papua, adult male natives in employment paid only 10/- instead of £1 tax, and in New Guinea the 10/- tax was not payable by indentured labourers, the pressure upon natives to 'offer' for work was clear, especially since alternative sources of cash were rarely available.*

Natives went to great lengths to avoid paying their taxes. On Karkar Island a tax collector was met by a crowd of women dressed in mourning garb and wailing. All the men, they said, had died, and they led him to fresh graves which had been made in the bush. The sceptical official, however, insisted on one of the graves being opened for inspection: it proved to be empty.[2]

The indentured labourers were not necessarily men of mature age, for boys of twelve were recruited until 1935, when the minimum age was raised to fourteen though the employment of boys of twelve was still permitted for domestic work; girls of ten were recruited before 1933, when the minimum age was raised to fourteen also.[3] However, the number of such young people recruited was not great. The natives were persuaded to sign on by professional recruiters; being under indenture, they were subject to penal sanctions if they infringed the conditions of their contract. In German times, these sanctions included floggings, administered by employers; this right was taken away only in August 1915, and 'Field Punishment No. 1' (hanging by the wrists) introduced by the British Military Administration in January 1920. Not until May 1919 was flogging for minor offences and labour offences stopped; Field Punishment No. 1 and flogging were legally abolished in 1922. In Papua, fines and imprisonment had been the normal sanctions. As Mair remarks of the Mandated Territory: 'It was in this period, during which most of the German employers

---

* The cost of an indentured labourer was estimated at £26 8/- for an unskilled plantation labourer, £33 16/- for miners and other heavy workers, and in some areas up to £70. 'Employers . . . pay less for labor than do employers in any of the other Pacific mandates' (*Decker*, p. 190). Recruiters received from £3-£20 per head; 'flagrant widespread illegalities' occurred during such periods as the gold-rushes (*Mair*, p. 153).

[1] *Decker*, p. 167. *Mair*, p. 63, gives a contrary opinion.
[2] *Flierl, J.*, p. 107.　　　　　　　　[3] *Decker*, p. 174.

were carrying on their normal business, that many of the Australians who later joined the public service or took up land in New Guinea acquired their first ideas on the treatment of native labour.'[1]

Equally, one might observe, it was during this period that the natives of the Territory formed their opinions of the new régime. Desertions were common, because of 'dissatisfaction with their employers or the conditions . . . [of] work' and brought sharp criticisms of the system from the Permanent Mandates Commission.[2] Offences against the labour code accounted for a very large proportion of all native convictions, which rose steadily 'while convictions of Europeans and Asiatics fell in at least the same proportion. . . . [This] reinforces the impression . . . that social conditions among the indentured labourers were bad'.[3] The indenture system and the great mobility of workers made for high turnover and instability of the labour force.

Unskilled New Guinea natives received 5/- per month; in Papua, 10/- was paid, wages which Decker described as 'exceptionally low even for native labour in Pacific dependencies'.

Without examining labour conditions in further detail, it can be seen that the experience of natives who signed on was likely to be highly unsettling under the conditions of barrack life, and destructive of confidence in the trustworthiness and honesty of the Whites. In New Guinea, in particular, a tradition of Black-White hostility and of the violent enforcement of European domination persisted into the Australian era.* Reed, in a detailed treatment of the question of Black-White relations characterized the situation as 'paternalistic peonage', whilst Stanner, who constantly stresses the practical difficulties facing the Whites, acknowledges that 'it was simple for the critics to list fact after fact that, given even without comment, were an affront to the sense of compassion and social justice'.

* Relations between Germans and natives had often been very bitter. Fifty-five Whites were killed in the first twenty-five years of European rule; the White population was only 230 in 1910. For the killing of three Whites by Duke of York Islanders, for example, 750 troops were landed; villages were shelled for disciplinary reasons (*Reed*, pp. 133-7). German punitive expeditions have been vividly described by Lajos Bíró, particularly his description of the shelling of Deslacs Island by a German battleship. After the bombardment, New Ireland natives armed with spears and European weapons were put ashore; no child under the age of ten was left alive (*Bodrogi*, 1951, p. 284; cf. also *Reed*, p. 118).

[1] *op. cit.* p. 141.   [2] *Decker*, p. 184.   [3] *Stanner*, p. 27-28.

But the young native now signed on for work, not solely because he was driven by such spurs as the tax, though these were important, especially in the period of the creation of the labour force. Now he was caught up in a new web of social relations; he wished to acquire the White man's goods, to buy clothing, lamps, food and a hundred and one objects for himself and his kin. To obtain these he needed cash and, to get cash, he had no choice but to seek employment with the Whites, except in those small areas where access to markets permitted the sale of cash crops. Once this new labour force had been brought into existence, all these new wants attracted an ever-growing army of recruits more effectively than any crude methods of compulsion. The native was now pulled both ways. Torn by his dislike of leaving home to work for the Whites, he was yet attracted by the hope of obtaining a portion of their riches, and by the fascination of many aspects of town, plantation and mine life. Attracted by education and medical aid offered by Christian missions, the native nevertheless found a contradiction between mission teaching and the lives led by the White men he met. In a hundred and one ways, he found himself reacting strongly against White domination, but ever more strongly drawn —and often willingly—into closer and closer relations with the Whites.

Far from satisfying his new-found wants, he acquired yet further wants during his period of service. He also found himself in peculiar social surroundings, living in 'barracks' where his companions were entirely male. The social stresses and strains arising from this situation, manifest in gambling, homosexuality and prostitution, are well known.

Such experience ill qualified the returning labourer for the resumption of the comparatively dull routine of the village. The absence of the menfolk at work for years on end had serious effects not merely on the men themselves, but on the villages they left. In 1937 'over 22% of the enumerated adult male population in the Territory were indentured labourers, and, if allowance be made for cripples, the aged and others who would not be eligible for recruitment, the percentage . . . would be still higher.'[1] Again, the incidence of recruiting did not fall evenly, since certain areas supplied the bulk of the labour. Thus the Sepik region supplied one quarter of indentured labour in the Mandated Territory in

[1] *Decker*, p. 169.

39

1940. Even 'uncontrolled' areas were recruited, and optimistic official estimates of the numbers which might be recruited without endangering community life in the villages were illegally exceeded.* In villages which had lost most of their adult males the bulk of the horticultural work fell upon women, old men and boys; there were less people to provide for the needs of the old, the sick and the young; ritual activities were abandoned since insufficient numbers of participants were available. Returning migrants flouted the authority of their elders, since they knew that real political power now lay with the Whites. They were no longer content to play a subordinate role to old men who knew nothing of the 'world', and many youths looked forward to migrant labour as an exciting liberation from parental and gerontocratic control. Then they would become economically and socially independent; if they remained in the villages, it might take years to accumulàte wealth with which to marry and with which to advance to more senior status in the community through feast-giving, etc. And there was always the tax to be met.

It did not take many years before the first signs of strain in some of the village economies were reported. 'In 1920 for the first time comes the significant comment that a dearth of native foodstuffs in the Baniara villages was due to the absence of many of the men as labourers.'[1]

It seems not unlikely that much of the stress in cult movements upon the maintenance of fertility and good crops may relate to this growing concern with diminishing production, or, at the least, with the increased effort required to maintain existing levels. Such an hypothesis to be fully validated would require detailed production records which do not exist. As we shall see for the Taro cult, horticulture, the central economic activity of the people, acquires a special symbolic significance as epitomizing the maintenance of the well-being and viability of the society as a whole. In Melanesia, the major ritual performances of most societies thus centre upon the display and consumption of large quantities of staple foods— yams, taro, pigs, etc.

---

* There seems much internal evidence to suggest that the aggressive, violent characteristics attributed to the Mundugumor of the Sepik region by Mead are largely a product of 'over-recruiting' in an area only recently brought under administrative control (*Mead*, 1935, Part Two).

[1] *Mair*, p. 86.

Mission and Government

Other important forces of change were Government and mission. Government in New Guinea has always been a direct form of administration. In Papua, 'the principle of coercion . . . covered almost every field of native development'[1]; in the Mandated Territory, the German tradition set the tone of future administrative developments. In these territories, native officials appointed in the villages were 'constitutionally mere mouthpieces of the Government',[2] as village elders are always telling the people. Since these individuals bore the brunt of official wrath during patrol officers' visits (estimated at two hours per year for most villages), and often had to receive 'indignities and blows', it is not surprising that the real indigenous authorities frequently stayed in the background, thrusting forward some luckless individual to be government *luluai* or *tultul*.[3] This divorce between native 'representatives' and the people resulted in the co-existence of two almost entirely separate authority-systems at village level, that recognized by the people, and that created by Government. Hogbin quotes these remarks of a Solomon Islander to a native official: 'You think you're a leader just because the District Officer made you an Elder? . . . Remember *he* chose you, *we* didn't. Who are you, anyway? Are you different from me? Of course you aren't. You never gave a feast in your life. If you want our respect you'd better start giving them quick.'[4] And of the Native Courts another native remarked 'The Court doesn't belong to us: we never had Courts before: it's a government affair.' This does not mean that government officials were necessarily passive incumbents of office; Bumbu, *luluai* of Busama, for example, used his position to terrorize the people under his rule.[5] Amongst a few detribalized communities near Rabaul, Talasea and Madang, native councils were set up just before World War II, but they had no powers of enforcing decisions and no money to expend.

[1] *Mair*, p. 45.　　　　　　　　　　　　　　　[2] *ibid.*, p. 48.

[3] The senior village official was called either *luluai* or *kukerai*; the *tultul* was supposed to assist with interpreting, and the third official, the 'doctor boy', with medical problems. In fact, these duties were not clearly understood, nor were the individuals properly qualified: more often, they merely formed a village triumvirate of officials, not necessarily powerful.

[4] *Hogbin*, 1944, p. 265. cf. e.g. *Blackwood*, pp. 48-50, where hereditary aristocrats on Buka referred to the Government-appointed *kukerai* as 'a nobody'.

[5] *Hogbin*, 1951, pp. 151-63, etc.

Government was particularly active in enforcing regulations about village hygiene, the maintenance of roads, etc., but the Courts were largely occupied by cases arising from the control of labour contracts. Together with the Armed Constabulary, the Courts, the native officials and the District Officers represented the most obvious manifestations of 'Government' to the people. Attempts at enforcing the regulations, however, were often met with passive resistance. The compulsory planting of specified plants (coconuts, rice, coffee, etc.), for example, seems to have been met with solid lack of enthusiasm even when penal sanctions for 'failure to plant' were applied. Plantations owned jointly by Government and village were established in some areas: only two still exist. 'Spontaneous' native production of cash crops remained at a low level, restricted by the loss of adult workers, the absence of local markets, and discouraged by price fluctuations and price discrimination against native growers.

The resources at the disposal of Government were so small as to make social improvement insignificant. It is not surprising that the Mandated Territory Government, whose financial resources were swallowed up by administrative salaries and 'normal' departmental contingencies to the extent of between 73% and 85% of the budget in pre-war years, were only too glad to hand over responsibility for such services to other bodies. Education remained predominantly in the hands of missions, with government financial assistance, so much so that no ordinary government native schools existed in Papua before the war. New Guinea was criticized before the Permanent Mandates Commission as the Mandate in which education had shown least progress.

The role of the missions in education had profound social repercussions. Over 15% of the Europeans in the Mandated Territory were missionaries, and their activity had been considerable since the establishment of the first mission in 1875. By 1940, the eleven missionary societies in the Territory could report the existence of 2,500 schools of various kinds, 3,354 'native workers' and a nominal following of nearly half a million natives. All but a few of the schools were village schools; the remarks of one anthropologist about the character of some of these schools are a typical evaluation by a non-missionary: 'The education given by the Mission is largely an adjunct of its primary aim to secure converts to the Christian faith . . . the instruction received aims little higher than a sufficient literacy to increase the pupils' understanding of the Scriptures.'[1]

As we shall see, Melanesians became so convinced that real education was being withheld from them that they placed special emphasis in their cult programmes upon obtaining the 'Secret' which the White man was concealing. This Secret was sometimes declared to be the first page of the Bible which the Europeans had torn out of the Bibles they gave the islanders. Knowledge was inevitably seen as religious knowledge, for nearly all education was mission education.

The theoretical stress laid upon religion in mission education is paralleled, in native experience, by practical evidence of the worldly power and importance of the missions. Not only are the missionaries numerically strong, but they also possess mission stations, buildings, land, goods, money and food. They are treated with respect by Government, given official assistance, are of the same ethnic stock as officials, and have been given hundreds of pieces of land for mission sites. In addition, they became large employers of labour and own coconut and other plantations 'and in general followed the patterns of European exploitation'.[2] This situation of combined spiritual and material power is perhaps best paralleled by the position of the Church in medieval Europe.

But there is one important difference from the medieval Church. There were eleven competing mission societies in the pre-war Mandate. 'Spheres of influence' were gradually worked out (although not in other parts of Melanesia), but 'native adherents' of rival sects in interstitial areas frequently became 'engaged in acrimonious disputes as to which sect [had] the right to proselytize in new regions'.[3]

In the very extreme, violence and the burning of rival adherents' huts occurred.

Such divergence between varieties of exposition of the Gospel have not merely introduced new, and often bitter, social divisions into native communities; they have introduced moral and religious uncertainty into an already unstable situation. This is exacerbated by the divergence natives note between Christian doctrines of equality and brotherly love, and actual practice. As one native of Tanna remarked: 'Which way Missionary e no stop with em you

[1] *Read*, 1952, p. 233.   [2] *Reed*, p. 237.   [3] *ibid.*, p. 236.

long one table? Him e preach Jesus e say love one another, e preach, e no do it.'*

On top of the peculiarity of the European economy, in addition to the instability of political régimes, and added to the new sectarian divisions, came an equivocal teaching. Said to be basically the same religion, it had numerous opposed representatives and sections. This moral difficulty was intensified by the open atheism and anti-mission sentiments and activities of many planters, traders, recruiters and officials.

The stage was truly set, then, for the development of independent native movements, and for the casting of social and economic aspirations in religious form. The form of these movements in Melanesia, therefore, can in no way be attributed to any inherent mysticism or religiosity of the Melanesians themselves.

The hysterical phenomena found in most of the cults, equally, do not derive from any peculiar inherent psychological characteristics of Melanesians. They are the product of the ambivalent attitudes and feelings of men torn between hatred of the White people who had destroyed the old way of life and who now dominated them by force, and the desire to obtain for themselves the possessions of these very Whites.

Some writers have seen in the cults nothing more than an atavistic rejection of European culture. In fact, Melanesians by no means rejected European culture *in toto*: they wanted the White man's power and riches, but they did not want the perpetuation of his rule. The myth of a Cargo, rightly theirs, but usurped by the Whites, expressed their political mood neatly.

In the absence of knowledge of the material reality of European society, in the belief that Europeans apparently did no work for the goods they obtained, and under the influence of all-pervading mission education, the Melanesians concluded that secret magical power was the key to the wealth of the Europeans. This power they were determined to obtain.

Their desperation is mirrored in the powerful emotionality of the cults with their compulsive physical twitching, in the sudden rejection of ancient customs and the radical reordering of life. It was a desperation growing out of their ambivalent attitude toward

* 'Why doesn't the missionary sit at the same table as us? He preaches that Jesus told us to love one another. He preaches this, but he doesn't practise it' (*Guiart*, 1957).

European culture, their confusion at the queer fluctuations of the European-imposed order, and the frustration of their growing wants at a time when higher production and harder work often brought only diminishing returns.

As we shall see, millenarian movements spread over most of Melanesia within a very short time. Some areas were subject to repeated outbreaks, and the cults were found both in areas where European influence had been strong for generations and in areas only recently brought under control. Only the small urban areas were free from cult movements. Here movements of protest took more orthodox forms—strikes, independent native organizations, etc.—but they were few between the wars.

Many planters, recruiters and commercial interests began to express uneasiness about the extent and continuity of the movements in the rural areas. Some of them blamed the missionaries, who exercised great influence over the rural population and whose teachings had provided much of the cult ideology. Public controversy between settler and missionary soon broke out.[1]

No very clear solution emerged from these altercations, for the answer did not lie in blaming any one section of the European community. The cults arose from the overall effects of the European impact on native society.

Other Forms of Native Organization

Social change did not take place at the same rate over the whole of Melanesia. It was very uneven, and the range of political and social variation was considerable: at one pole were the 'uncontrolled' regions, and at the other, the urbanized native residents of Rabaul and Port Moresby. In between was a wide range of diversity: the native communities of the Highlands, only discovered in the 'thirties; areas long under government control, where migrant labour was long established; and areas such as that round Rabaul where European goods, native trade-stores and other minor commercial enterprise, production for the market, and casual day-labouring were all to be found.

This variety of structure, and the varying degrees of dissolution of the traditional social relations under the impact of the new economy and Government, resulted in differential incidence of

[1] e.g. Thomas Gordon, 'A Plea for better Regulation of Mission Activities in New Guinea', *PIM*, 20th November 1935, pp. 25-26.

millenarian and other such movements. But the village economy, in which periodic migrant labour was as characteristic a feature as traditional hand horticulture, was typical of all but a very few spots. Millenarian movements appeared in such widely separated areas as New Ireland, the Rai Coast, the Gulf Division and the Mekeo District, because the fundamental economic and political pattern in all these areas was basically similar.

But significant differences also existed, and they had significant social results. It would be distorting the picture of political developments in this part of the world if we isolated millenarian movements, and ignored other forms of social expression. The different historical experiences of peoples in different areas also resulted in varying attitudes towards the Whites and varying forms of native organization. In those remote areas where the Germans had never penetrated, or only slightly, the old régime was often idealized; those communities which had known German rule at first hand, as at Blanche Bay, Kavieng, Namatanai and Madang, had quite different memories.[1] Of the non-millenarian forms of resistance, armed self-defence and attacks upon Whites, so characteristic of German times, now principally occurred in the semi-controlled and uncontrolled areas. But there were other non-millenarian forms of expression of native dissatisfaction in the controlled areas. Strikes, for example, showed a gradual increase over the years. Even the native police force was not free from disturbances, some of them violent. Three Europeans and a Chinese had been killed in a revolt of police at Astrolabe Bay as far back as 1900; with the advent of the Japanese, a rising of native constables was to take place at Madang, and, on the Sepik, an 'amok' of police in which one Chinese and four Whites were killed.[2]

Although frequently expressed, unrest amongst indentured plantation labourers rarely led to any stable native organization because they were a migrant population, constantly changing and moving. It was therefore amongst the growing body of casual labourers that strike action was more common, though even here it was limited. At the outbreak of war some 9,000 indentured natives were employed in such capacities as stevedores, lorry-drivers, messengers, porters, etc., but an increasing number of natives near the townships worked at daily (and higher) rates of pay.

Some authorities stress that the urban areas were training-

[1] *Reed*, pp. 153-5.   [2] *PIM*, November 1946.

grounds for agitators who later returned to the villages. Secret night-time meetings were held near Rabaul, and three mysterious beings predicted the coming of a new epoch in which Whites would serve natives.[1]

It was at Rabaul, capital of the Mandated Territory and the centre of the principal area of European plantations, that the most important strike of the inter-war period took place in 1929. Here, practically all the native labourers, including the 'boss-boys' and the great majority of the police, suddenly left town and gathered at the Methodist and Catholic mission-stations nearby. The 3,000 strikers were apparently influenced by foreign seamen (variously described as 'West Indians', 'White', 'Samoan', 'Samarai' and 'American Negroes') who jeered at them for accepting such low wages: 5/- per month for a labourer, with an average earning of 6/-. Led by the native master of a schooner and a Sergeant-Major of Police, and by the 'boss-boys' and the police, the entire operation was conducted in complete secrecy and disciplined order. Partly through lack of food, but also because expectations of concessions of £1 per month were not forthcoming, the strike ended without violence, apart from some turbulence amongst the 'Catholic' group.

The rage of the Europeans knew no bounds. Demands for the removal of the Acting Government Secretary and the Inspector of Police were made, a 'Citizens' Association' was formed in opposition to the 'pro-native' Government, and sanctions against corporal punishment were temporarily suspended as employers thrashed their workers. 200 of the 217 police had struck; the leaders of the police were given two to three years' hard labour; the rest received lesser sentences. In the subsequent inquiry, carried out against a background of White rage, the board of inquiry poured scorn upon the idea that any 'more deep seated and more involved' questions were involved than the foolishness of sheep-like natives under bad leadership. The board urged the imposition of a *maximum* limit to wages, denied that there was any 'general demand for higher wages', and suggested the removal of the labour lines farther out of Rabaul and the introduction of curfew passes.[2] Evidently, the European had learnt little from the strike; but the native had learnt a good deal, for in 1937

[1] see *O'Reilly*, 1937, passim, and *Eckert*, 1940, p. 33.
[2] *TNG, Ann. Rpt.*, 1928-9, pp. 19-20, 107-9.

another strike occurred in which a doubling of existing wage-levels was demanded.

Later, just before the Japanese arrival, the 'Dog' movement was set up in the nearby Duke of York Islands and Kokopo, its objective being the purchase of land and the building of schools for native use. The name is said to reflect the native view of the way they were treated by Whites. As it began to reveal signs of becoming a strong organization with 'seditious' tendencies, it was broken up by the arrest of the militants. Despite this unintelligent repression, the official who himself prosecuted these leaders recorded his sympathy with the aims of the movement.

The urban and adjoining areas of long settlement, then, on the whole found other forms of political expression than millenarism, and the casual labourers, peri-urban workers and small entrepreneurs had begun to develop orthodox political, economic and social organizations before World War II. This divergence was to become more marked in the post-war period as social differentiation increased and as the differences in levels of development between urban and rival areas became more sharply emphasized. But in order to see how this process took place, we must start at the beginning by examining early reactions to the European impact upon simple stateless societies.

CHAPTER III

Early Movements in New Guinea

*They shall hunger no more, neither thirst any more;
neither shall the sun light on them, nor any heat.
For the Lamb which is in the midst of the throne shall
feed them, and shall lead them unto living fountains of
waters: and God shall wipe away all tears from their eyes.*

Revelation 7:16-17

DESPITE THE VIGOUR of the Tuka movement, it did not influence adjoining regions, and the next reports of similar outbreaks
were to come from New Guinea, that vast island to the north of
Australia, on the west side of the huge Melanesian region.

It seems unlikely that there had been any direct contact between
eastern New Guinea and Fiji, though the possibility cannot be
precluded. The kind of contacts which might have been possible
means of spreading information were the visits of traders, whalers,
pearling-luggers, and also of native trade expeditions. None of
these are likely to have found their way into the historical record.
Many Whites would be more concerned to avoid having their
activities brought to the attention of authority than in reporting to
government officials. Native expeditions often covered extraordinary distances, and passed on news and information, not
directly from one end of the region to the other, but through a
series of intermediaries. The great trading expeditions of the
Massim islanders, with their extensions along the Southern coast
of New Guinea, are well known[1] and many similar trade routes
existed along the New Guinea coast, and between the mainland
and the islands off the coast.[2]

Whilst we cannot show any direct contact, then, between the
Tuka movements and the later New Guinea movements, we can-

[1] see Capt. F. R. Barton's description of the Hiri expeditions of the
Motu people in *Seligman*, 1910, and *Malinowski*, 1915, for the exten-
sions of this network in the Mailu area. The material on south-eastern
New Guinea trading expeditions is summarized in *Tueting*.

[2] see, for example, *Hogbin*, 1935.

49

not dismiss this possibility in many other cases. Europeans often underestimate the facility with which news and ideas, and even material objects, can be passed on even in societies lacking modern techniques of communication. Such transmission has been amply demonstrated, for example, in Mead's study of the Arapesh.[1] McCarthy has shown that even more startling distances can be covered over long periods of time, and that objects and ideas have been diffused from northern New Guinea as far as southern Australia via such trade routes.[2]

Through such indigenous means of transmission, natives have often been aware of developments in distant areas long before Whites have received word of them. Finally, labour migration is an important mechanism for spreading news, as natives from different parts are brought together on plantations, and then take new ideas home with them.

It would be ridiculous, of course, to look for external inspiration in every case. The important point is that, even if external inspiration is lacking, the existence of similar social situations, with similar social tensions, in entirely separated regions, might lead to similar results. Conversely, without a fertile soil, ideas imported from abroad would not take root. But ideas imported from outside often decide the particular form a movement of social protest takes.

Having discussed the channels available for the communication of ideas, we must now cast a glance at the state of Black-White relations at this period in order to see why millenarian notions, when diffused, had such great attraction for the natives. Some indication may be obtained from the area where the first cult broke out. Sir William MacGregor, the new Administrator of British New Guinea, was very concerned to ensure that 'the rapacious acts of the benighted heathen' gave place to 'law and good order under the munificent and wise guidance of a beloved Administrator'.[3] Sir William was determined to enforce recognition of the new authority of the Queen and of her representative. In one of the most politically developed societies of New Guinea, he enforced his authority in a typical manner. During a visit to the Trobriand Islands, he noted the Paramount Chief seated on his high platform. This custom ensured that nobody stood higher than the chief, and made it possible for his subjects to pass by him without their having to crawl on the ground. Sir

[1] *Mead*, 1938.   [2] *McCarthy*, pp. 173-95.   [3] *Thomson, J. P.*, p. 13.

William 'saw the chief sitting on high, in his seat of honour, walked straight up to him, seized him by the hair, and dragged him to the ground, and took his seat himself. "No one", said Sir William, "shall sit higher in New Guinea than I." '[1]

Sir William's activities on the eastern mainland of New Guinea are of particular interest in that they preceded the first outbreak in this area by only a few years.

Following the killing of the skipper of a trading vessel by natives of Chads Bay in 1888, MacGregor himself led an expedition to capture the offenders and bring them to trial. Among the results of this expedition was the arrest of one of the leading figures in the killing, an armed clash in which several natives were killed, the flight of the population of several villages into the bush at the advent of the Whites, the defiance of the inhabitants of Abioma village in Milne Bay, and the removal of several 'chiefs' from the latter village as hostages. Four of the natives were sentenced to death; five others were imprisoned for twelve months, one for eighteen months, and one was acquitted. As Thomson remarks, with unconscious irony: 'The proceedings throughout were closely watched with deep interest by a great number of chiefs and other natives, all of whom appeared to be much impressed by the solemnity of its progress.'[2]

The death penalties were carried out at various spots so as to impress natives over a wide area, and the hangings were watched by 'large assemblages', upon whose minds the 'impressive character of the proceedings had produced a salutary influence'. Whether the impact of European rule and the experience of trade with the Whites gave rise in fact to entirely 'salutary' responses was to be made clearer only five years later.

The Milne Bay Prophet Movement

In 1893, Mr R. J. Kennedy, Native Magistrate at Samarai, described in the Annual Report how a young native named Tokerua (correctly Tokeriu) of Gabagabuna village on the north side of Milne Bay[3] had become inspired by a spirit which resided in a traditionally sacred tree.

Seligman, however, states that 'it was not uncommon for living

[1] *Murray*, 1928, p. 331.   [2] *Thomson, J. P.*, p. 41.
[3] Further information about Tokeriu may be found in *Abel, C. W.*, pp. 104-28; Russell Abel's account is a condensation of this.

men and women to journey to Hiyoyoa [the other world—P.W.] and return to this world'.[1] According to his account, Tokeriu claimed to have visited Hiyoyoa itself. On his return, he prophesied the coming, in two or three months' time, of a great storm which would submerge the whole coast with a gigantic tidal wave. Existing villages, including Wagawaga and Gabagabuna, would be submerged by this wave which would cause the emergence of a new island in the middle of the bay.

Believers, however, were to be saved. The prophet enjoined various measures on his followers as the only way to ensure salvation. The White man's goods were banned: tin match-boxes, pocket-knives, and other such possessions were discarded, and the natives were to return to the use of stone implements. The people were also to wear long, narrow leaves in their armlets, as a sign of their 'entire repudiation of the White man'. They were to abandon their houses and retreat inland to seek refuge from the storm. Houses were burnt down and the people moved: the inhabitants of Gabagabuna village, for example, built a new village half a mile inland. It differed from the traditional type of village in that the houses were built in long rows with a long platform running alongside. In the centre was a larger house, the residence of Tokeriu.

Abel, the missionary, discovered the existence of the movement when, one Sunday, he found his morning service attended only by children. Everyone had gone to Tavara, the district where Tokeriu lived, he discovered, so with a colleague he immediately set out for Wagawaga, where there was a mission station with a native 'teacher', Biga. Only Biga and his wife and family greeted the party. Men, women and children had fled inland with their pigs and dogs.

Abel eventually found that the prophet had been told by a spirit that after the storm the south-east wind, the wind of the pleasant harvest season, would blow continually. Then the land would prosper, and yams and taro multiply in the gardens. Besides these traditional attractions, a sail would be sighted on the horizon, heralding the coming of a huge ship with the spirits of the dead on board, and the faithful would then be reunited with their dead kinsmen. Tokeriu would form a government, and have at his disposal a steamer much larger than the government steamer, the *Merrie England*. Since food would be so abundant, all pigs

[1] *Seligman*, 1910, pp. 655-6.

were to be killed and eaten, and food in the gardens consumed.

The people heeded his message. No work was done, and some 300-400 pigs were killed and eaten. This latter action indicates the powerful appeal of the prophet's message, for pigs were not only the major source of animal protein to these people, but also reservoirs of wealth, and invested with the greatest social value.

The people of Wagawaga, who had had experience of similar prophecies years before, asked the missionaries whether these prophecies were true. When Biga and the Whites exposed the stories as lies, they became enraged and prepared to wreak their vengeance on Tokeriu and on Gabagabuna. The mission party, with more peaceable aims, then went with them to Gabagabuna.

They found it practically deserted. Pushing inland, they came across the new village of Gabagabuna. The natives had received prior warning of their coming, for no women or children were to be seen, and the men sat in 'sullen silence' on the long platform, making no reply to the Whites' greetings. All inquiries were fruitless—Tokeriu had gone inland, the people said. Uninvited, the missionaries climbed on to the platform, but attempts to ingratiate themselves failed: 'I had in my wallet a long thin stick of trade tobacco, a delicacy very much prized by these people, and as I was sitting in the doorway of the chief's house I took it out, and threw it to some men who were sitting behind me in the dark. Almost before they had time to pick it up, it was hurled back and struck me on the ear.'[1]

Biga warned them that their lives were in danger every minute. Then, suddenly, Tokeriu arrived. 'He was not the grey-headed wizened man we had expected to see—the kind of old man who, in his dotage, might imagine he had held converse with a spirit in the night. Tokeriu was in the prime of life . . . he was a refined man, for a savage; and the marvel to us was that he could restrain his people, who were not in sympathy with him in the conciliatory course he was taking.'[2]

He was obviously trying to control his strong emotions, and listened in silence to the missionaries, but made no response.

Suddenly, he began to recite his prophecies. The people became more and more excited and hostile, and the visiting Wagawaga men, equally, were only held back with difficulty by the Whites.

Eventually, the Whites' party made for safety: they split up and

[1] *Abel, C. W.*, p. 118.   [2] *ibid.*, pp. 119-20.

found their way back to the coast in small groups, reaching their boats just before their pursuers could attack them.

The followers of Tokeriu eventually became disillusioned with him, when the slaughter of their valuable pigs turned out to have been in vain. The people now threatened to kill him; Government intervened, arrested him, and gave him two years' prison sentence in Samarai jail. Gabagabuna received a Christian teacher, and when Abel visited the village Tokeriu offered him a present of a large, new garden, full of crops.*

It will be noted that although Tokeriu made his peace with Abel, anti-Europeanism was marked in this movement. Later we will see that anti-European feeling was not necessarily present in the earlier stages of many movements though it quickly became added to most of them. The Tokeriu movement is, therefore, of particular interest since it is one of the earliest Melanesian manifestations in embryonic form of that consciousness of common cultural community, and of difference from other communities, that we call nationalism.

The Baigona Movement

There was a gap of some years before other movements were reported from New Guinea. Then, in 1912, came reports of the first of a new wave of prophetic cults in north-east Papua. This movement was led by a man named Maine. Maine claimed that he had been killed by a snake, Baigona, which lived on Mount Victory (Keroro). Baigona had taken him there, extracted his heart, and dried and smoked it in the fire. Then the snake gave Maine his heart back, taught him new doctrines and sent him to proselytize amongst his people.[1]

The new doctrine was mainly concerned with magico-medical curative techniques, although it possessed other overtones. Maine appointed other Baigona men as his agents all along the coast up to the Anglo-German border, and in the inland villages along the Kumusi River. He is said to have benefited materially from his teaching by the payments he received from initiating others into the cult-mysteries, but we must remember that there is a large

---

* A photograph of this extraordinary prophet, wearing leg-irons in Samarai jail, may be seen on p. 127 of C. W. Abel's book.

[1] For minor variants of this myth, see the Rev. Copland King, *Papua, Ann. Rpt.*, 1912-3, App. A.

amount of distortion in accounts written by people hostile to the movement. The charges of fraud and deliberate deception for individual profit constantly levelled at the leaders of these movements were sometimes undoubtedly valid, but very frequently they were not; often they involved a misunderstanding of native reciprocal exchange, ceremonial feasting, etc.

The native recruits—generally one or two from each village—now returned home to spread the gospel. These 'Baigona men' formed a kind of priesthood, but had more than merely religious influence: Maine passed on to them the messages he 'received' from Baigona.

Though they practised traditional cures, massaging evil substances out of the bodies of the sick, it was said to be the noncorporeal 'Baigona' which was massaged out rather than the traditional small material objects such as stones, splinters, etc. During these performances, young men sang songs around the patient or lines of drummers accompanied the doctor while other enthusiasts danced; indigenous herbal remedies, which were often quite efficacious, were also used.* Some of the Baigona men mixed their medical activities with sorcery; on this score, and on several others, they came into conflict with the Administration.

It is difficult to judge whether honesty or a desire to excuse failure was displayed by the Baigona man who, having failed to 'pull out' the Baigona by massage (the case being one of TB), returned the gift which the patient had made him, saying that the case was hopeless: it was a White man's disease, beyond his capabilities.

Baigona men had their followers do gardening work for them, while they themselves spent much time in personal adornment; they also marked their special status by observing certain taboos. Instead of drinking water, they drank coconut milk; sugar cane and cold coconut were also taboo.

One of the most important beliefs stemmed from the importance of the snake in cult doctrine. This was extended by other animals—sharks, crocodiles, monitor lizards, cuscus, etc.—all of which were

---

* At a Baigona performance in the Kokoda District in 1919, the Baigona man chewed herbs into a mixture which he plastered on to the body of the sick man, followed by plasters of kava, ginger, etc. It was said that the patient would see the spirit of the person bewitching him; the doctor then proceeded to the witch's hut, and found the magical substance which was shown to the patient and burnt (*Papua, Ann. Rpt.*, 1919-20, p. 63).

commonly believed to be reincarnations of the spirits of dead human beings. These beliefs of the Orokaiva tribes had been noted long ago.[1] Williams speaks of 'one general doctrine . . . common to all the Orokaiva . . . the doctrine of animal reincarnation'.[2] The animals in question were believed to haunt the bush, visit villages or appear in dreams, and were regarded as 'dangerous' and 'abominable' and had not to be offended.

Snakes are peculiarly suitable symbols for ancestral manifestations: they show a marked addiction for human residences, yet are dangerous if not handled carefully.[3] The spirits, significantly enough, were said to betray their presence 'by faint "sip sip" noises, like the chirping of geckos which haunt all native houses'.[4] But the symbolic significance of the snake goes even deeper than this, and will be discussed later.

One government officer received vivid testimony of the power of the new taboos. While out at sea, he ordered his native police to fire at a crocodile. That night the police dreamt that they had been visited by Baigona, who protested against this attack on a tabooed creature. All the guilty persons were thoroughly ill next morning as a punishment for their behaviour.

The leaders also claimed powers over the rain, and utilized to the full traditional possession-mechanisms, trances, fits, and speaking with tongues. The Administration advanced as a principal reason for the suppression of the Baigona movement its use of 'thoroughly obnoxious paroxysms of a peculiarly horrible nature'[5]

The content of the Baigona cult seems to have been particularly limited in its adherence to traditional modes of thought and action. But it was certainly influenced by the changed social position of the natives of the region.

The indigenous background of cult beliefs and practices should not obscure its novel features. Anti-White overtones were present even in this superficially 'non-political' cult. Indeed, according to one account, the cult was said to have begun when a European, Patrol Officer Hogan, died. A native named Aede took the credit for this magical 'killing'.[6]

An incident reported to one missionary throws light on native

---

[1] see *British New Guinea, Ann. Rpt.*, 1897-8, p. 47, and *Papua, Ann. Rpt.*, 1910-1, p. 139. [2] *Williams*, 1928, p. 25.
[3] cf. *Fortes*, 1945, p. 145. [4] *Williams, op. cit.*, p. 41.
[5] *Williams, ibid.*, p. 8. [6] *Papua, Ann. Rpt.*, 1912-13, p. 154.

attitudes to Whites as well as on the type of people who became leaders. Kaipa, an ex-policeman, was out walking with a mission-instructor friend of his named Harry. Kaipa was a Baigona adherent: when Harry sighted a snake and was about to kill it, he remonstrated with him in vain. Kaipa then asked the dead snake if it would take vengeance, and it moved its head, replying that it would in a few days' time. To propitiate it, Kaipa put the dead snake and some food and valuable necklaces in a canoe, and set it adrift, saying 'We did not kill you. It was the missionary. We are sorry, and are paying you with these necklaces. . . .'[1]

The hostile reception given to a government medical officer who tried to give the people of one village medicine to drink as a protection against ringworm was directly attributed to Baigona influence. Here, the natives put on a show of epileptiform fits to mask their resistance, claiming that 'God was speaking to them', and refusing the medicine; the women became 'possessed' in sympathy.[2]

These Black-White antagonisms must be understood in the light of the recent history of the area. The first large influx of Whites into this region took place in 1895, following the discovery of gold in the Yodda area. Government followed the prospector, and an Agent established himself on the Mambare River in 1895. He was attacked and killed by the natives after only two years. By 1908, there were two Resident Magistrates in the region—now known as the Northern Division—one at each of the main goldfields. But only the goldfields and the tracks up to the goldfields were fully under government control.

Most of the native labour was recruited from the Western Division. In those days, '. . . conditions on the Mambare goldfields were recognized to be the worst in the territory. Heavy loads had to be carried for long stages, there was no provision against epidemics, and the chilly mountain nights were death to natives accustomed to the temperature of the coast. The death-rate was 21% in 1903-4 . . . in 1906, it was still 17.7%. . . . All this time there was no medical officer permanently stationed in the Division.'[3] Natives deserted wholesale, often after their first day's work, abandoned their loads, and tried to get down to the coast. Local natives were offered rewards for apprehending these deserters.

One of the results of these conditions was that the local natives

---

[1] *Papua, Ann. Rpt.*, 1912-3, p. 154.   [2] *Williams*, 1923, p. 13.
[3] *Mair*, p. 123.

were unwilling to sign on as indentured labourers. Both in the
Purari-Vailala region and in the Buna area, it was noted that the
natives were willing to work locally, but not away from their own
localities.[1] In 1915, 119 out of 626 natives 'had their contracts
cancelled owing to complaints of ill-treatment'; others refused to
accept the pay of relatives who had died whilst working as indentured labourers, saying that 'the boys had been illegally recruited
and the Government could not make it square. . . . These experiences . . . made other natives hesitate to sign on at all.'[2] Yet
one Resident Magistrate, noting that natives feared that they would
'be taken to some far-away place and perhaps never reach their
homes again', could remark 'I do not know where they get this
idea from.' It was commonly recognized that there was 'a correlation between the high rate of desertions from the Mambare . . .
and the shocking conditions under which the men worked',[3] but
opposition from White miners forced Government to fix the
statutory minimum wage at 10/- per month instead of the proposed
£1.[4]

The local natives did not accept the invasion lightly, for early
reports describe them as showing a 'sullen silence, or yelling
defiance from the hilltops'. 'Whereas in other parts of the Possession
it has been found feasible to gradually bring tribe by tribe under
government influence, this . . . was rendered impossible by the
sudden rush of miners into the interior. . . . Strong tribes who had
never before come into contact with white people awoke to find
their territory overrun.' Fighting ensued, gardens were plundered,
and Black-White relations went from 'bad to worse'.[5] Violence by
local natives was followed by the public hanging of murderers at
Kumusi and Tamata in August and September 1903. Small wonder
that a Magistrate lamented that, what with the miners and the war-
like, populous tribes, this 'was the most difficult of the magisterial
Divisions to administer'.[6]

Under these conditions, the Baigona movement, though stem-
ming from indigenous magical beliefs, developed a new under-
current of political and proto-nationalist feeling.

Government certainly saw it as a danger. E. W. P. Chinnery,

[1] *Mair*, p. 129.   [2] *ibid.,* p. 125.
[3] *ibid.,* p. 130, and *British New Guinea, Ann. Rpt.*, 1902-3, p. 27.
[4] *Mair*, p. 133.   [5] *British New Guinea, Ann. Rpt.*, 1900-1.
[6] *British New Guinea, Ann. Rpt.*, 1905-6, p. 111.

then Acting Resident Magistrate, Mambare District, had fifteen Baigona men on the Gira River alone brought before court; he described them as 'most cunning rogues' with a 'craving for power'.[1] Such suppression seems to have been effective, and Williams claims that the cult was virtually 'stamped out' by 1914; but it persisted secretly in the interior and elsewhere, and where it was stamped out other cults emerged.[2]

On the whole, the cult appears to have been characterized by the use of simple, traditional-type magical techniques for the 'solution' of limited and minor personal problems. It was also passive, having no millenarian goal or expectations, and tended to lay the responsibility for the misfortunes of life at the door of the people themselves. This stress on the guilt of the people marks the cult off sharply from other Melanesian movements such as the Vailala Madness and, though the surface resemblance of possession-outbreaks masks this distinction, the element of penitence—perhaps coloured by Christian ideas—is further manifest in that the ancestors are said to have censured people for not having saved them from dying by becoming Baigona converts.

The Taro Cult

Although the Taro cult attracted most attention in its post-1919 phase, and might have been greatly stimulated by the unsettlement of World War I, it began even earlier.

No connection is known to exist between the Baigona and Taro cults; rather are they parallel developments arising from the same social situation. Certain features were shared by both the movements: shaking-fits, special taboos on the killing and eating of certain foods, etc. But the Taro adherents avoided eating plants as well as animals—red pandanus seed, sago, crocodile, different kinds of fish, frogs, eels, etc. In more important respects, too, it constituted a movement which differed from the Baigona, and had more lasting results.

The earliest account is by Chinnery[3] who described the Kava-keva (meaning 'giddy, mad') and the Kekesi cult of Manau village, both of which were later called generally the 'Taro cult'. These broke out in the area between the Gira River and Buna Bay. They

---

[1] *Papua, Ann. Rpt.*, 1914-5, p. 58.
[2] *Papua, Ann. Rpt.*, 1919-20, pp. 62-63.
[3] see *Chinnery and Haddon.*

elaborated indigenous beliefs concerning the intervention of spirits in human affairs and the need to placate them by offering food.

The leader of the Kava-keva was a native of a tribe on the lower Mambare River named Buninia (Williams' spelling; Chinnery: Boninia). Buninia had no particular reputation as a prophet or magician, but early in 1914 he toured other villages in his group and announced that he had been possessed by the spirit of the Taro.*

The details of the story of what happened to Buninia vary. He claimed that he was 'struck down' by the Spirit in his garden. A missionary reported that he had been visited by his father's spirit, which had been travelling in search of his son and had met some other spirits at Mitre Rock. Here they had had a 'ghostly picnic' of cuscus and taro, and had then found Buninia. Buninia gave an audience to Williams in 1924 in which he described this Revelation, and his followers re-enacted the scene in ballet form. Again, a woman named Kosivo, sister-in-law to Buninia, claimed to have been visited by the spirits of three men who, '*fleeing from the approach of the White men on the Mambare*' had been killed by hostile neighbours. Their spirits then found Kosivo, copulated with her, and gave her the spirit of the Taro, leaving her in a trance. Another variant traces the origin of the movement to a woman named Simberi.[1]

These variants suggest that the precise details of the Revelation, and the personality of the prophet, are not of major importance.

Buninia proclaimed that the existing methods of cultivation were dilatory, and should be abandoned. A special ritual was announced to be applied to gardening activities. Initially, there was little enthusiasm for this message and Buninia's instructions were ignored, in spite of his warning that the crops would be destroyed if his words were not heeded.

This lack of interest was replaced suddenly by a whole-hearted turning towards the prophet. In November 1914, a girl in a neighbouring village was 'struck down' by the spirit of the Taro; she became oblivious, and whilst in this condition began to sing the songs which Buninia had created as part of the cult ritual. Buninia

---

* Taro (*ba*) is the staple food of the Orokaiva. Although Williams remarks that 'there is no reason, as far as I know, why the yam should not flourish' (1928, p. 118), nevertheless elsewhere (p. 110) he acknowledges that the soil is 'often of poor quality on the plain' (i.e., in most of the area). Taro can grow in such areas, yams cannot; see *Conroy and Bridgland*, p. 76.

[1] *Chinnery and Haddon*; *Williams*, 1928, pp. 12, 15-17, my italics.

cured the girl, but she soon relapsed. In other villages more and more cases of the 'sickness' occurred, a state of affairs which induced the headman of the group to call a meeting. At this gathering those who had been 'struck' gave their messages and urged collective propitiation according to the ritual instituted by Buninia.

On November 25th Chinnery witnessed an extraordinary scene. Buninia was in charge of proceedings. The young men drummed, while the prophet sang his cult songs full of foreign words. Then one individual after another became possessed by a shaking-fit, jerking their heads, their bodies trembling, often with clenched fists and contorted faces. Whilst in this state, the possessed received messages about the planting of the taro and other instructions relevant to this central cult activity. Gardening was to be carried out with the greatest care and application, and various rules about the care of food were 'received'. During the performance several songs were sung, the first concerning the taro; then came other songs about sugar cane, banana and other foods which were important to the people. The shaking-fits were known as *jipari*, a term 'used of the sling as it is whirled before the stone is released; also of a branch swaying in the wind'.[1] Baigona convulsions were called *dutari*: to tremble, used of ague, shivering, etc., but it was the head-jerking which was peculiar to the Taro cult. Both natives and observers considered that these paroxysms were distinct from trances or madness or running amok.

Transmission was usually a collective phenomenon. Williams considered that individual possession was generally assumed, but collective genuine. Taro leaders, for example, willingly 'put on' realistic demonstrations of the fit for him. He observed one man staggering about in the grip of most violent possession, but always avoiding obstacles in his path. These individuals who were involuntarily possessed were probably psychologically predisposed to such reactions; other cases were stimulated, and men could induce or resist the fit. Continual possession left a man exhausted, and the fit was usually followed by a dream.

Besides being a mechanism by which instructions regarding the taro cultivation were transmitted, the very action of the *jipari* was held to exercise a beneficent influence upon the crop. In addition, like the Baigona men, and probably largely as a legacy from them, medicinal cures were effected by the Taro leaders. Sicknesses were

[1] *Williams*, 1928, p. 48.

of two kinds: natural, mild illnesses which normally disappeared by themselves, though Taro men treated them; and illnesses due to sorcery which were beyond the skill of the Taro doctors. The Taro doctors generally confined their treatment to cases of spirit-caused illnesses, following traditional techniques of 'sucking' out evil substances, massaging the evil substances out of the patient's body, and so on. The more highly favoured cases were those which took place to the accompaniment of drumming in true Baigona fashion. The doctor did not formally demand payment, but would nevertheless be given an appropriate present by the cured person.

Some Taro men professed to have power to control the rain, especially the power of averting it. When they failed, they attributed this to the maleficent actions of sorcerers. But the counteracting of drought, the principal danger in this region, was not attempted by the Taro men.

Besides this 'doctoring', Taro men also performed special magic designed to ensure a good taro crop. They chewed up small leaf-wrapped packets of medicines and betel, and sprayed this mixture from their mouths on to the growing crops. Since the Taro man was accompanied by a party of vigorous young drummers, this destroyed rather than multiplied the crop. Taro leaves were deliberately broken, presumably to imitate the withering away of the ripe taro, and medicines were placed in the holes made for the taro shoots. They were usually plants whose large leaves resembled those of the taro. Sometimes the magical herbs were planted so thickly that they smothered the growing taro!

Others believed that the wind brought waves of *jipari* trances, and that drumming for the south-east wind would cause the taro leaves to sway and stimulate the growth of the taro. Such practices as moving the head like swaying leaves, and drumming as if in 'gusts' of wind, were akin to similar ideas about the south-east harvest wind in the Milne Bay movement.

Taro leaders also called for quantitative improvements in production through the extension of existing cultivation and the clearing of larger gardens. The ancestors were then called to consume the taro, betel, cigarettes and other offerings displayed on platforms which were set up in the gardens while the living carried out the planting of the taro.[1] These structures, called *gaga*, were derived from the traditional *karau* offertory-platforms of the Orokaiva

[1] *Papua, Ann. Rpt.*, 1919-20, p. 62.

('sometimes with a miniature ladder from the ground which is meant to facilitate the spirit's access to the morsels of decaying food which have been left for it').[1] The offerings were intended to propitiate the spirits of the dead, for the ancestral cult preceded and persisted through the period of the beliefs in the spirits of the taro.

Large feasts, combined with singing[*] and drumming were the central Taro activity. These *kasamba* feasts resembled traditional inter-village feasts outwardly, but they differed from traditional feasts in that they were used as curative performances. There was also a symbolic change of name from *pona* to *kasamba*, and various practices were adopted to emphasize the distinctiveness of the new ritual: the taro was cut in a special way; special cooking-, serving- and eating-procedures were adopted; special houses (*ba oro*) with offertory-platforms were often erected for the use of Taro leaders and singers, remaining after the feast as a sort of Taro temple. Besides the Taro songs, new Taro drum-beats, Taro greetings, Taro cries and prayer-like phrases sprang into universal use. Even new words were introduced to replace pre-Taro Age terms. Many of these words were quite unintelligible, either as a result of confusion in the course of being constantly repeated, or because they originated in the dialect of one area and spread to other parts. But it was their wider not their narrower, semantic significance which was important. They symbolized the new life, as did the taking of new names, names of some kind of taro, by the converted.

The spirits had left Buninia (and other prophets) various special objects as well as the verbal ritual and songs: bags for carrying taro, forks for eating it, pots and dishes for cooking it, and so on. Taro medicines—leaves or weeds—had 'power' and curative properties which men hoped to acquire by rubbing them on to their bodies and on to the bags in which they carried taro. Similarly, men placed their digging-sticks and axes on the prophet's body to absorb his 'powers'.

The rapid spread of the movement over a wide area and the

---

[*] Dancing was important as part of the ritual only in certain sects. Vigorous singing, drumming and conch-shell blowing were prominent features in all, however. As the conch cannot be tuned, it is often out of tune with the singers. 'One can understand why a distracted missionary lit his Primus stove and placed it by his reading-lamp so that its roar might drown the discords of the *kasamba*' (*Williams*, 1928, p. 38).

[1] *Williams*, 1928, p. 26.

unity of its adherents did not develop of their own accord, no matter how predisposed the people were to some kind of radical change. The Taro men (*ba embo*), the priests and political organizers of the movement, were specially possessed by the taro spirit or the spirits of the dead. Although anyone might graduate to this status, a few outstanding men sprang to the fore, usually making use of the fits of involuntary possession to which other men succumbed. These Taro leaders organized the *kasamba*, officiated in ritual and ceremonial, practised *jipari* as a speciality, and observed certain taboos.

They used the Taro houses more than other men. Through their dreams new medicines, rituals, cries, words, and other features were introduced, thus strengthening their power. They increased their following not only by stimulating mass-possession, but also by initiating particular individuals into the mysteries.

These individuals, though they claimed to have received personal inspiration and knowledge through dreams, also admitted that they had received instruction from Taro men. The movement was taken from one village to another by relatives and other visitors, but it was also spread by deliberate proselytization. Men would organize *kasamba* in other villages, become seized with the *jipari*, and explain to the villagers that they would also get it, which they soon did, for they were anxious to receive the Taro. Even contact with Taro objects—medicines, lime-pots, etc.—could infect others with *jipari*. The recruits deferred to the men who initiated them as their superiors in the hierarchy, and salutes copied from the police were used. Initiates usually paid for their training, in keeping with native custom, and often had to undergo a period of trial and observe taboos; washing, for example, was forbidden. Some who found the taboos too irksome 'resigned' from their training. Even some varieties of taro itself were tabooed, nominally because they were 'dangerous'; the disciplinary aspect of the taboo is thus more important than the actual nature of the object tabooed. Special taboos were observed by leaders over and above these general restrictions. By these means, the Taro leader maintained control over converts.

Williams saw how the cult was deliberately spread when a party of visitors to Korisata village were given a demonstration of Taro performances by four different sects, each sect stressing the superiority of its particular doctrine.

The cult soon spread up the Mambare and Kumusi Rivers, and inland from Buna as far as Kokoda. To the north of the Orokaiva, it halted before reaching the Waria tribes who possessed a similar culture, but different languages. On the middle Gira, it did not exert much influence, possibly because of the influence of existing cults there and partly because of mission influence. But it spread southwards into the North-Eastern Division as far as Wanigela, amongst people of different language and culture.

Forecasts of the decline of the Taro Cult were frequently made, but were all proved premature. By December 1914, for example, the area in which Chinnery had seen Taro (*Kava-keva*) performances in November was no longer staging them. But isolated cases still occurred, and were particularly noted round the area of the headquarters of the Anglican mission station near the Mambare mouth. The whole coast was now infected through the proselytizing of the cult leaders.

The Doctrine of Amity

The Baigona cult in the same region had met with government suppression earlier not so much because it was explicitly anti-White, but because it represented a dangerous development—an independent and widespread native organization. But its suppression stimulated anti-White feeling, and the people had learnt how to organize through their experience of the Baigona movement.

It was noticed early on that the Taro Cult exhibited certain characteristics which set it off from ordinary religious movements. One of the messages which Buninia received from the spirit of the taro was to the effect that no weapons were to be carried in the gardens. This was symbolic of the stress upon friendliness, co-operation and the renunciation of violence between cult members. It was marked by the universal Taro custom of shaking hands—a custom which 'became a rage'. Williams tends to regard this as a matter of 'minor interest'[1] and suggests that it arose because of fear of sorcery by Taro men with whom it was politic to keep on good terms. But this misses the *political* significance of the custom. Nor was it a mere 'imitation' of Europeans: it was a symbol of the changed social relations between villages and tribes which had previously been discrete and isolated, often hostile, entities. Indigenous religious institutions had been tied to these limited units

[1] *Williams*, 1928, p. 46.

of society: the tribe, the village, and so on. But the 'Spirit of Taro' was a pan-tribal phenomenon; it was 'positively a new idea, and not an attempt to revive old customs'. Nor can we attribute this spirit merely to mission preaching on Christian brotherhood. Even whilst competing for members, the sects of the Taro movement all exhibited this same 'good fellowship' towards each other.[1]

The Taro cult thus went farther than the Baigona. It made use of the new opportunities for increased spatial mobility which European rule facilitated. But in making doctrines of unity, co-operation, comradeship, etc. central to the cult, it reflected not only the breaking down of old barriers between social groups, but also the new common interests which these groups had developed as subjects of the White man.

Williams himself noted this 'elementary tendency towards cohesion', though he did not develop this theme. But that acute observer A. C. Haddon had grasped the true nature of these movements much earlier. Unlike others, he never regarded them merely as fanatical and mystical cults, of interest as queer religious phenomena, but of little account otherwise. These, he said, *were* religious movements, but religious movements which strove to 'sanction social or political aspirations'. They were products of a situation of social unrest and of the 'weakening or disruption of the older social order'. He observed that some movements were related to 'purely native ideas', that others were 'obscure' in origin and content, but that many were responses to 'the encroachment of the White man' by 'communities that felt themselves oppressed' and which were awaiting the Messiah.

The Taro cult contained no millenarian expectation, and to this extent was more passive than the Milne Bay or Tuka movements. Yet, although more closely related to traditional religious movements and ideas, it contained new elements which call for its consideration together with the millenarian movements proper.

Indeed, although the central Taro doctrine relates to the propagation of magical rites to ensure good crops, the curing of the sick, and so on, its new features should be clearly distinguished. We have noted the wide spread of the movement and the sense of mutual interdependence between Taro adherents.

The movement also foreshadowed future organizational possibilities. Williams remarked on what he termed 'a sort of hierarchy,

[1] *Williams*, 1928, p. 19.

very ill-defined . . . but nevertheless containing the seeds of an interesting development'.[1] In this new Taro hierarchy, we see the beginnings of a political organization entirely separate from the traditional structure, headed by men who were not necessarily the leaders in the old society. The cult drew most of its ideological material from the old order of society and, even under the new régime, people were still vitally concerned about their crops, about the weather, about the maintenance of good health, about harmonious relations with the living and the dead, about the continuity of society as expressed in the ancestral cult. But new elements were equally marked, both in organization and in ideology.

It is significant that the movement firmly dissociated itself from the Christian missions. It therefore represents a conscious step towards the establishment of forms of organization, which, while not yet directly challenging European authority (whether government or mission), were independent both organizationally and ideologically. The Taro movement, though limited and passive as compared even with earlier movements elsewhere, still showed considerable evidence of anti-White feeling.

On the other hand, the leaders did not hesitate to use Christian elements for their own ends, as revealed in the 'disputation' between one of the Taro leaders and a Christian missionary. This leader, Dasiga Giama, requested a missionary to give him an outline of Christian doctrine. After he had heard it, he said: 'I knew all that before.' Later, on asking a missionary why the taro was not growing well and receiving an answer in horticultural terms, he replied roundly: 'No, they say it is because of God's anger'. The missionary then entered on a long theological wrangle with Dasiga who disputed vigorously and far from respectfully with him, and finally left with a parting-shot of 'unintelligible gibberish'. He then asked the missionary if he understood; on the latter's replying 'No', he was told 'God's praise'. The same missionary later met a minor leader, who was 'well groomed, with his hair neatly clipped, carried a walking-stick, and greeted the visitor with an English "Good morning". He wished to show him a letter from Jesus Christ and produced a stray missive which a neighbouring planter had sent to the master of the launch *Misima*, asking him to call for copra.'

He gave a long, and apparently sincere, account of how this

[1] *op. cit.*, p. 32.

letter had come to him after a vision of Jesus Christ, who had told him he was to be 'the New Guinea missionary'.[1]

There were other obviously Christian elements in the practices of this particular sect: special 'commandments', 'services' round a wooden pillar, speaking in meaningless 'tongues', 'reading' from the palm of the hand, and incantations such as *Jesu Kerisu Kaenaembo*: Jesus Christ the man for us.

The Sects of the Taro Movement

The Taro cult, despite its doctrine of friendliness, and rapid spread, was not a highly integrated movement with a unitary authority-structure. The reverse is the case, for the forces pulling local communities apart were very deep-rooted, and the forces drawing them together only developing. Local divisions were more significant than cultural ones, for the various Binandere dialects 'do very little to hinder the freest intercourse and conversation between members of the various tribes' and their culture 'is in all fundamental points remarkably uniform'. The Orokaiva are a 'strikingly homogeneous [people], not only in physique, but also in language and culture'.[2] But although they shared this common culture and common social position in relation to the Whites, most intensive social interaction took place within a limited range. There was little necessity for the people of different villages to act together regularly. But they had learnt methods of organization from the Baigona cult, and they knew the attitude of Whites towards such movements; suppression taught them lessons on security. The Resident Magistrate, who feared the revival of Baigona, and the Bishop, who saw little danger in the doctrine but who disapproved of the *jipari*, were carefully deceived.

The local divisions in the society affected the cult organization. There was a strongly fissiparous tendency, which found its channel of expression in the claims by numerous individuals to dream-inspiration, and who consequently elaborated and modified the existing doctrine in their own ways. As in all religions which allow individual communication with the supernatural without the mediation of church or priesthood, the possibilities of fission were strong in the Taro cult.

Thus several separate sects developed within the general Taro

---

[1] *op. cit.*, pp. 75-76.
[2] *op. cit.*, pp. 79-80.

movement, each with its separate customs, insignia, incantations, and so forth. These sects associated themselves with *varieties* of the taro plant, and with bananas, sugar cane, betel, coconuts and other plants. Nearly all these sects shared the belief in the central Taro doctrine, but one at least did not, though it practised *jipari*. In this sect, in Manau village on the coast, Christian elements were more heavily marked than in others, largely because Dasiga, the leader, was a mission convert of fanatical enthusiasm, and the people were more heavily under White influence through ex-policeman and indentured labourers, and through the teachings of missionaries. Here, people believed that the ancestors were coming with a fleet of steamers and canoes, unlike other areas where the cult held sway. The notion that the coming of the Whites spelt disaster for the native society was not new. One man, on seeing his first White man approaching in a ship, had told the people that death had now come amongst them; they should marry off all the young virgins without the traditional bridewealth payments, and kill off all their pigs.[1]

Though we know little of the social origins of most leaders, it is noteworthy that Dasiga was village constable of Manau, and Bia, the real politician who developed the movement on the basis of Dasiga's visions, had been a corporal in the Armed Constabulary. I have shown how the cult leaders were not necessarily leaders in the old authority-structure: they were often people who had had special experience of White rule.

These fissiparous tendencies were not new, for the Manau sect had first been reported in 1914 as the Kekesi, in contradistinction to the Kava-keva, i.e., the main Taro movement. The leader of the new sect was Bia, described by Chinnery as a 'notorious sorcerer and a most plausible rogue'. (Chinnery was hostile to these movements, but his opinion of Bia was endorsed by Williams.)

Bia proclaimed himself the agent of the spirit Kekesi. He claimed that whilst he was returning from Buna in November 1914 (i.e., after the beginning of the 'Kava-keva'), he received a visitation in a dream from a dead man who told him about Kekesi, who controlled the growth of food and whose residence was at Mitre Rock, not far from where Bia was sleeping. (Bia was clearly re-working earlier myths, since this is the third occurrence of Mitre Rock in origin-myths of the cults.) Kekesi was a friend of Jesu Kerisu, he

[1] *Monckton*, pp. 59-60.

said. If his laws were not followed, Kekesi would cause the food supply to fail. Later, the spirit of the dead man introduced Kekesi himself as the big chief of food and a strong spirit, 'all the same Jesu Kerisu and Government'.

Kekesi was seated, but kept bouncing up and down in an alarming fashion, gurgling the while. Boinumbai, the dead man, interpreted the gurgles as meaning that Kekesi was a chief who was to be obeyed, lest he ruin the crops. Food was to be cultivated with assiduity, and none wasted. The people were to obey the Government, but, at the same time, their own moral code was not to be neglected. He then instructed Bia in praise-songs to Kekesi, which were to be sung regularly, mostly in groups, but in varying positions, some while standing, other while kneeling and yet others while sitting.

The name Kesi which occurs in the songs is the name of Kekesi's steamer (though a whole *fleet* was to come). Disciplinary control was exerted over the people by various methods. When going to and from the gardens, the people had to 'fall in'. In the gardens, Bia's right-hand man, Yavevi, gave various Taro commands, e.g., 'A shun man!'—the words *shun, shen, sha* and *som* occur frequently in the polygot lyrics invented by Bia. Other English words occurring in the strange speech of Kekesi included 'missionary', 'Government', 'taro', 'Jesu Kerisu', etc., all learnt in Bia's days as a policeman; significantly enough, Bia was unable to repeat Kekesi's speech only two days later.

Bia's doctrine and organizing ability transformed villages under his influence. Even the physical appearance of the people changed. Old and young cut their hair like mission children, and senior men adopted the custom of carrying walking-sticks. Every day a service, called 'school', was held at Manau. In one 'service' Bia placed an empty box in the centre of the village ground, and Dasiga incanted with a stick in his hand, looking towards Heaven and turning round and round as he walked about. Bia then repeated the incantations, kneeling with his head on the box as if reading, with the villagers kneeling round him. After further incantations and speaking with tongues, with responses in Binandere (one incantation was 'Alleluiah salomi'), the people were told of their ignorance by Dasiga. They were all 'wicked' . . . 'say you are not village people, say you are the people of Jesus', he told them. Both he and Bia were illiterate, but Dasiga expressed his desire to go to school to learn reading and writing so that he might lead the people.[1]

The relations between Bia and Dasiga are interesting. Dasiga was the 'real visionary'; he is spoken of in some early reports as the initiator of the movement,[2] but, even if he was originally visited and not Bia, the latter soon took control. Bia, 'a man of strong personality and magnificent physique', exercised a control over the milder Dasiga which Chinnery considered to be hypnotic; Dasiga himself remarked that when he came near Bia he was liable to be seized by a 'fit'. Dasiga conducted much of the ritual and evangelization; and also carried out organizational work under Bia's guidance in the gardens. Whenever the ritual flagged, it would be revived by Bia's becoming 'possessed', or by the true possession of Dasiga or some other genuine enthusiast.

Bia's control over, and manipulation of, Dasiga can be paralleled time and again in these movements; the power exercised by the Taro leader Yaviripa over the 'visionary old duffer' Buninia is another example. Both Yaviripa and Bia, moreover, had been Baigona leaders.[3]

But the Manau movement, though more millenarian than other Taro sects, was still not particularly anti-European. Dasiga taught that crop failures were due to the actions of the spirits, and might only be avoided by faith in the Great Father, and his Prophet, Dasiga, who was to lead the people towards civilization; non-believers would be punished by fire.[4] Bia, too, stressed obedience to the Administration (at least to White observers), side by side with observance of indigenous moral codes. But jealousy of, or hostility towards, the Whites is implicit in the cult doctrine, as the equation of Kekesi with Government and Jesu Kerisu symbolizes. The cult had come a long way from simple garden magic or curative magic, though the precise degree of anti-White feeling is difficult to judge.

In November, despite Bia's professed loyalty, the movement was banned, but in December and January Bia visited the villages on the Gira River in secret. By late December, all the Gira people, and those on the coast as far as Tabara and the Eia River, had been converted to the Kekesi movement, and possessed the new songs.

---

[1] *Papua, Ann. Rpt.*, 1920-1, p. 46. [2] *Papua, Ann. Rpt.*, 1920-1.
[3] For photographs of these vital-looking men, see *Williams*, 1928, facing p. 72 and p. 200. [4] *Papua, Ann. Rpt.*, 1920-1.

Yavevi was active in spreading the movement southwards towards Buna. So strong was Bia's influence over this man that after Government had sent Yavevi to Buna under surveillance, away from Bia's influence, he nevertheless returned to Bia, who then sent him again to Buna, this time on an evangelizing mission. Such missions helped spread the cult down to Sanananda.

Of the other Taro sects, most were only minor variants of the normal Taro-Kava-keva movement. These were not independent cults, but minor divisions within the main movement. Such sects tended to follow village divisions, because the leaders commonly converted their own village; they were distinguished by name, by the symbolic use of the different varieties of the Taro (some twenty), and by other diacritical features, some physical, e.g.,facial decorations, and others behavioural: a distinctive 'whimper' affected by one sect, gazing heavenwards by another, various motor habits, jerks of the head, *jipari*, twitches, etc. There were special sect ways of eating taro with special objects, e.g. forks; the 'medicines' used by the different sects again differed. But these were merely minor variants. All shared a common body of belief and ritual: they believed in stimulating the growth of *all* taro, not merely their 'own' variety, though a few concentrated on magical promotion of their name-variety. The sects thus followed local lines of division, but were not separate cults.

One which was more clearly a separate movement was the Diroga cult, which flourished in the south, away from the main focus of the Taro cult round the Mambare. It is believed to have been initiated by Arai, a native of the Koena Lakes,[1] and concentrated largely on magical cures. Its members derived their power from visitations by the spirits of slain men, symbolized by spears, the main cult emblem. These *diroga* spirits manifested themselves as insects, fruit-bats or meteors and could be heard whistling as they passed overhead. Diroga men were also often suspected of sorcery.

Like the Taro cult, the Diroga cult had its sub-divisions, distinguished not according to varieties of taro, but according to different weapons. And though there were slight variations in Diroga (and Manau) doctrine, they shared a body of common doctrine with the Taro proper.

Another southern sect was the Rainbow cult, whose adherents were seized by *jipari* on the sight of a rainbow (following a dream

[1] *Papua, Ann. Rpt.*, 1919-20, p. 63.

72

of the founder). They also preached taro-fertility doctrines, though one man stressed that the rainbow influenced *hunting* rather than the cultivation of taro.

In the south-centre of the Division was also found the Hohora cult, 'Hohora' signifying both 'cock' and a variety of yam; its doctrines are inadequately known.

The mechanism of dream-inspiration was ideally suited to the expression of these local fissiparous tendencies. Men could become possessed by different spirits, which gave them special instructions and badges with which they started their own sect. The doctrines of the movement thus varied from area to area. Around the original focus on the Mambare, the main Taro doctrine held sway; at the mouth of the river, and in other coastal villages, the Manau Kekesi was dominant; and in the south and centre, the Diroga, Rainbow and Hohora movements. There was, moreover, a general tendency for the teaching to become modified in the direction of traditional belief the farther the movement spread from the Mambare. Thus we find that whereas Buninia stressed the taro spirits, which he termed *atiti*, to distinguish them from the traditional ancestral spirits (*binei, sovai, embaki, siango,* etc.), his followers changed this back into a belief in ancestral spirits which controlled the growth of the taro, for which, however, they (mis)used the new word *atiti*.

The Taro cult persisted longer than earlier outbreaks, partly because, being less radical and millenarian, it did not disappoint its followers with unfulfilled prophecies. In 1928 it was still strong. It is now difficult to relate the rise and fall of the movement closely to external changes, but it does not appear to have been greatly affected by specific events, rather expressing a general disturbance as a consequence of White control. Thus the introduction of 10/- tax in some sub-districts in 1920, did not immediately stimulate anti-Government feeling. But the shortage of taro in Kokoda District in 1924[1] as compared with earlier abundance, such as the crop of 1919,[2] did generate a new wave of Taro activity. In Manau, 'fear of Government' and the 'continuous teachings of the missionaries' subdued the enthusiasts.[3] Here the cult disappeared after a mission station was established and the village Christianized. By 1928, the Kekesi mythology had been virtually forgotten.

[1] *Papua, Ann. Rpt.,* 1924-5, p. 44.
[2] *Papua, Ann. Rpt.,* 1919-20, p. 62.
[3] *Papua, Ann. Rpt.,* 1920-1, p. 46.

The Taro cult, though focused upon traditional and still-vital interests, crop fertility, the curing of sickness and the cult of the ancestors, and although non-millenarian, exhibited many features which call for its consideration with millenarian movements proper. It exhibits, in elementary form, elements which were to become more marked in other movements, and provides an important example of the process of transition from indigenous cult to millenarian movement.

Although it resembles movements which must have occurred constantly in pre-White times, it possessed quite a new significance under the changed social conditions. It was not for nothing that the Administration frowned upon this cult, though because of its limited and passive character it was not suppressed as vigorously as the Baigona or Milne Bay movements. Since it looked forward to no violent change, and promised little, it could maintain its hold without achieving anything beyond personal psychological satisfaction. But all these movements were proscribed because they were not merely religious outbreaks, but had political potential as new kinds of independent pan-tribal organizations, now passive, but potentially menacing, and some, in varying degrees, already anti-White, anti-Government and anti-mission. Williams, after denying the *direct* influence of the Whites on the cult's development, goes on to remark how the 'unsettling and repressive' effects of government and mission policies had destroyed 'old belief' without providing a substitute, and blocked 'accustomed outlets'.[1] It is as a new *political* phenomenon that the Taro cult was of such importance. It was a cult which was trying to provide an answer not merely to ever-recurrent problems of life, but also to new ones.

[1] *Williams*, 1928, p. 80.

CHAPTER IV

The Vailala Madness

Ye are a stiff-necked people; I will come up into the midst of thee in a moment, and consume thee: therefore now put off thy ornaments from thee, that I may know what to do unto thee. . . .

Thou shalt not bow down to their gods, nor serve them, nor do after their words: but thou shalt utterly overthrow them, and quite break down their images.

Exodus 23:5-6, 24

THE BAIGONA AND TARO MOVEMENTS attracted considerable scientific interest, but did not receive as much attention as the now-famous movement which developed in the Gulf Division of Papua —the Vailala Madness.

This movement was first reported in 1919, some years after the commencement of the Baigona and Taro movements, when Administration officials were told that there was great excitement in the coastal villages of Nomu and Arihava. All the villages from Vailala as far eastwards as Keuru then became infected, and such was the excitement that Europeans became considerably alarmed. They called the outbreak the 'Vailala Kava-kava' (cf. Kava-keva) or 'Orokolo Kava-kava' (though, in fact, Orokolo was one of the few villages unaffected by the 'Madness').

Various other names were given to the movement: 'Gulf Kavakava'; 'Head-he-go-round'; its Motuan * equivalent *kwarana giroa* or *kwarana aika*; the Elema equivalent *haro heraripi* (*haro*: head; *heraripi*: whirling motion, e.g.,*bea heraripi*: whirlwind); *iki haveve*: 'Belly don't know', i.e., 'dizzy' or 'ecstatic'—the usual name given to the movement in the Gulf coastal villages themselves; and to the west, in the Purari Delta, *abo abo*: giddy, crazy.

The first witnesses of the excitement had reason for alarm. One observer entering one of the villages was confronted by the following sight: 'the natives . . . were taking a few quick steps in front of

* Motuan is the *lingua franca* of Papua, in its debased form 'Police Motu'. The Motu people live near Port Moresby.

them, and would then stand, jabber and gesticulate, at the same time swaying the head from side to side; also bending the body from side to side from the hips, the legs appearing to be held firm. Others would take the [*sic*] quick steps forward and stop, placing the hands on the hips, jabbering continuously, swaying the head from side to side, and moving the trunk of the body backwards and forwards, remaining in this position for approximately a minute. . . .'[1]

Even children were affected, but some individuals were more affected than others. At Nomu village, for example, one young man: 'stood on the *eravo* platform [*eravo*: men's house]; he was bending, swaying and tottering, hands on hips. He rolled his eyes continuously and uttered exclamations, which the onlookers said were unintelligible to them. When taken inside the *eravo*, he kept peering up into the roof. Subsequently he became quiet and went down among the people, where he seemed to be playing a leading part in the dancing which was going on.'[2]

Affected individuals felt strange sensations occurring in their stomachs. The common practice of literal ventriloquism stemmed from this belief, and the stomach was fanned to induce possession. One philosopher of the movement defined two stages of possession, initial ecstatic possession (*iki haveve*) and the later rise of inspiration (*iki pekakire*: 'belly he think'—*pekakire*: to climb), but most of those affected did not analyse their sensations to this degree.

There were three categories of people whom Williams termed 'Automaniacs': those who were swept away involuntarily, those who simulated possession, and those who could voluntarily induce it. It is this last category of person which provided the leadership of the movement, for it was well-organized despite its apparently wild and uncontrolled appearance.

But because they could consciously induce these symptoms, it should not be presumed that they were frauds. Some were, but many were very really possessed and believed in it, even if they could to some extent control its onset and cessation, and even if they consciously spread it. But many of the leaders used less stable individuals who were swept away by mass hysteria for their own social and political ends. We have already met this division of labour between the genuine prophet—often a psychotic—and the

---

[1] *Williams*, 1923, p. 10.   [2] *op. cit.*, p. 5.

more socially-conscious and not necessarily insincere organizer. Impostors were generally a small, if important, minority.

In some villages was to be found 'a pole of considerable length and weight, with a knob at one extremity which usually shows that the pole has been used in the manner of a battering-ram'.[1]

These poles were usually kept hidden from Europeans in the village cult temple, or on the veranda of the temples, a spot where people sat and became 'inspired'. The poles varied in size, one being up to 30 feet long and 6 inches in diameter, another 15 feet long with a snake-shaped head * and another, in Vailala West, even heavier.

The poles were carried on the shoulders of at least two men. They were said to move under their own power, and to take the bearers with them; the bearers had no control over the pole's movements.

The use of the pole was a development of traditional divinatory techniques. In cases of theft or similar offences, the pole would be brought out and hoisted on to the men's shoulders, with leading cult adherents in the two key positions at each end; the pole would then automatically go towards the house of the guilty party, who would thereupon confess.

The cult leaders at Arihava were quite agreeable to Williams' testing the pole by hiding some tobacco on the person of one of six men. The pole immediately found the tobacco at the first attempt. Williams then himself acted as a pole-bearer, but although they agreed to substituting Williams and three of his servants, the two 'end-men', delegated by the cult leader, remained at their posts, since without them, it was said, the pole would be passive, or—an alternative explanation—'too heavy'. In the next experiment, the pole was again immediately successful. In the third, two failures occurred before success, and in the fourth, three before success.

The operation of the pole was stage-managed with much panto-mime of 'automotive' action and staggering here and there after initially quietly walking it around. In one demonstration, the pole moved to the cult leader. He then addressed it, upon which it moved and stopped in front of Williams and then suddenly became more active. 'By this time, six men were shouldering it; the thing—

---

* see photo facing p. 34, *op. cit.* The origin of these previously un-known poles is obscure.

[1] *op. cit.*, p. 33.

which is virtually a tree-trunk—wheeled and whirled until the bearers were panting from their exertions. Biere (the cult leader) meanwhile shouted exhortations: "Come on, boy, come on, boy!"[1]

As Williams left the demonstration, the pole pursued him and barred his path, until, on advice, he told it to go to bed, which it did immediately.

The manipulation of the pole clearly fell upon the two end-bearers, who could be heard talking quietly to each other while in action. Nevertheless, it was sufficiently successful for belief in its efficacy to be buttressed, and if, in one case, it was realized that human manipulation worked the oracle, this did not impair belief in the ability of *others* to divine by supernatural techniques alone. Thus, divinatory failures by a particular pole would not under-mine belief, and even innocent people who were accused are said to have all accepted the verdict.

The leaders themselves were credited with special powers and accorded great respect, though many of them declared that any wisdom they possessed in their stomachs was not their own, but emanated from the ancestors. One man professed no wish to be 'cured' of his 'madness', which endowed him with the gift of heal-ing and the special power of exposing sorcerers. Modifications of indigenous curative and divinatory techniques were also employed, involving massage, the extraction of harmful objects from the body, etc., though the traditional chewing of bark and spitting on to the palms of the hand were abandoned.

Williams paid special attention to the psychological aspects of the movements, to the beliefs, the hysterical phenomena and the 'puritanism' rather than to the social, political and organizational aspects. This bias arose from his belief in the necessity and desirability of preserving as much as possible of tribal life. He unequivocally describes natives who had received some education as 'cultural hybrids' and 'Jesus Christ men'. They are, he says, 'denaturalized: they have ceased to be true natives'; 'horrible and wholly pathological', they 'literally make one's flesh creep'.[2] Else-where he writes that the movement may be evidence of a 'genuine innate weakness of the Papuan's character'. With such prejudices, Williams was prevented from making a sound sociological analysis of the movement. Moreover, he was bound to regard the movement in terms of 'social pathology', 'breakdown', etc., rather than as an

[1] *op. cit.*, p. 34.   [2] *op. cit.*, p. 60.

adjustment to a new social situation. Consequently, he over-weighted the importance of the hysterical aspects and the suppression merely of native ceremonies, and underestimated the political significance of the movement. Similar deficiencies are evident in his analysis of the Taro cult. In later years, he was to sugar the pill of the crude colonial phraseology cited above by expressing his views in terms of 'academic' functionalism, a doctrine which, in later years, however, he ultimately rejected.[1]

He consistently underestimated the effects of British and Australian rule on the Gulf peoples. Even before the arrival of Government, missionaries had made a considerable impact on this area. The Roman Catholics at Yule Island, who had been excluded from possession of a 'sphere of influence' under a 'gentleman's agreement' between the Methodists and Anglicans, had endeavour-ed to make up for a late start by vigorous evangelism. The London Missionary Society had established its first station at Port Moresby with which region the Gulf natives were in touch through trade expeditions: later the LMS extended its activities to the Gulf. The establishment of the administrative headquarters of the newly formed Gulf Division at Kerema in 1906 brought the people of this region under close government supervision; in 1913 Kikori became the new Delta Division headquarters. Easy access by sea to the coastal villages facilitated contact by mission and Government,* whilst the discovery of oil near the Vailala River in 1911 led to intensified European penetration. The Anglo-Persian Oil Company began boring in this region and employed many natives, some of whom were taken to Rabaul. Plantation owners also took men to the Rabaul area. It is noteworthy that the majority of the more active adherents of the Vailala Madness had been indentured labourers, and were 'proficient in Motuan, and even in English'.[2]

Though the Lakekamu goldfields was an area peripheral to the main strongholds of the subsequent Vailala Madness, the 1910 goldrush there must have had repercussions as word spread of the conditions under which labourers were working. Between January and June 1910, 225 of a total labour force of 1,100 died from dysen-tery and other causes.[3] 'The experience of some natives of the

---

* Magisterial Services staff increased from eighteen in 1911 to thirty in 1912 and forty-two in 1913 (*Mair*, p. 27).

[1] *Williams*, 1939; and 1940, pp. 406-10.

[2] *Williams*, 1923, p. 8.   [3] *Mair*, p. 124.

upper Fly whose first taste of labour conditions was on the Lake-kamu "had the effect of practically closing the district to recruit-ing."[1] The effects of recruiting in the Purari Delta were marked; in 1919 the area was said to be 'worked to its utmost capacity',i.e. over-recruited.

Back in 1912, an LMS missionary had found the natives of one village highly excited because they believed him to be one of their ancestors returned from the dead. This belief that White men are the returned ancestors was possibly indigenous; it was to receive a new twist in the doctrine that all natives would be White in the after-life. The disturbance of the indigenous social order by direct assault on established institutions * was accompanied by the dis-semination of new doctrines in the form of Christian teaching, as well as government codes and instructions which had to be carried out under threat of prosecution, e.g.,the cleaning of villages† and, in the Purari Delta, the building and maintenance of plank gang-ways across the mud-flats surrounding the villages. Character-istically, Williams regarded failure to maintain these as 'negligence . . . and . . . indifference to the most obvious improvements'.[2] Strong, the government anthropologist, more tolerantly recog-nized that 'it meant several days' work to the small neighbouring villages every two or three months . . . and that the natives were just as well off and happy walking through the mud; and that the only people who benefited by it were myself, who never used it more than once every six months, and perhaps an occasional trader, and that we might as well be carried'.[3]

It is significant that one of the few Purari villages affected by the Vailala Madness was Apiope, which had been under strong mission influence for many years before Government established control and 'had given up cannibalism as a result of the teachings of the Rev. Chalmers'.

The coincidence of the ending of the 1914-19 war with the out-break of the Vailala Madness may not be entirely accidental since 'Djaman' was the supposed language of the Vailala Madness leaders when speaking with tongues.

* The public burning of native religious esoterica was practised by some missionaries (see *Hogbin*, 1947, and *Lawrence*, 1954, for more recent examples).

† In the Delta Division, 116 convictions were recorded for 'refusal to clean village', and twelve for 'refusal to repair houses' in 1925-6.

[1] *Mair*, p. 125.   [2] *Williams*, 1923, p. 43.   [3] *ibid.*,p. xi.

We have noted the recruitment of the leadership from ex-labourers. Amongst them were organizers and propagandists like Kori, a village constable who had been in the Papuan Armed Constabulary for over twenty years. In 1905, he had been the 'right-hand man' of the only trader in the District, and had acted as guide and interpreter to important government officials during their visits to the largely uncontrolled Delta. Another cult leader had built himself a large, European-style bungalow and was interested in government schemes for establishing rice plantations.[1]

The originator of the 'Madness' is said to have been an old man named Evara. 'Brisk and intelligent', and 'obviously an outstanding personality',[2] he was much influenced by European activities as even his clothes bore witness. He was wearing a soiled coat of white duck when Williams saw him, with a 1919 Victory Medal suspended from his top button-hole on a red tape. His son, a government interpreter, related how his father had once been hunting and had fallen into a trance. The villagers searched for him for four days, but failed to find him, and he eventually found his own way home. He said that a sorcerer had 'ripped up his belly'.

Some time later, his father died. As Evara lay in a trance brought on by this shock, he was for the first time visited by the Madness. Then his younger brother died, and Evara was seized again. This time he told the villagers, who soon became greatly excited, and spread the news around, infecting others with the Madness.

For it was not merely the automaniac seizures that excited them. It was Evara's revelations. He prophesied the coming of a steamer, carrying the spirits of dead ancestors on board, who would bring with them the 'Cargo'. In the initial stages rifles were included amongst the expected goods, and 'vague ideas of Papua for the Papuans were current'.[3] Later teachings stated that the Cargo was to be allotted to villages by the signs of identity on the crates. The spirits had revealed that all the flour, rice, tobacco and other 'trade' belonged to the Papuans, not the Whites. The latter would be driven away, and the Cargo would pass into the hands of its rightful owners, the natives. To obtain these goods it was necessary to drive out the Whites. In view of the state of Black-White relations at the time, this is not surprising. Williams cites the case of a plantation manager who used a whip to silence the loud

---

[1] *Papua, Ann. Rpt.*, 1919-20, App. V., pp. 116-18.
[2] *Williams*, 1923, p. 28.   [3] *op. cit.*, p. 15.

lamentations of some 'boys' who were mourning a dead friend, and Strong sums up a common attitude of Whites as 'I want the nigger to work for me so that I can make my pile and leave the so-and-so country'.[1] Native views of White men were well summed up in the remark of one Papuan to an idle fellow: 'D'you think you're a White man, doing nothing?'[2]

At the same time, the ancestors were Whites, an idea which was often embarrassing to White men. One official, who was taken as the deceased father of a villager, was followed around, given presents of garden produce and betel, and, on requesting a small sample of sago for the purpose of making a chemical test, was offered as many whole trees as he liked!

The idea of the steamer and the Return were new elements; even an aeroplane was prophesied as the means of transport for the Cargo, though no aeroplanes had yet appeared in this part of Papua. The mystery was solved when Evara was found to possess a cheap English novel entitled *Love and the Aeroplane* with a crude cover-drawing of a man and woman precariously suspended by a rope from an aeroplane. But ideas of Heaven rather than aeroplanes were the probable source of rumours that 'papers' had fluttered down to Evara from the sky, and of the theme of inspiration from above in the form of a White ancestor or God striking the affected person on the head, and then communicating a message or delivering a gift. The significance of the theme of the White ancestors under these changed social conditions is implicit in Evara's remark that 'brown skins were no good . . . he wanted all the people to have white'.[3]

As the movement developed, many embellishments appeared. One man had a vision of Heaven, Ihova Kekere (Jehovah's Land), which was like the earth, only much better. In Heaven there was no forest, unlike Papua; houses were made of stone, not 'ground'. Food was very abundant, including the White man's limes, oranges, water-melons, sugar cane and bananas, whilst sheep and *arivara* (an animal like cow, pig and horse—probably water-buffaloes, seen in Rabaul) were also there. People wore long garments reaching from the top of their head to their feet, like those worn by the Yule Island missionaries, though variously coloured red, white and black. The chief man in Heaven was Ihova; under him were Noa, Atamu, Atamu's wife Eva, Mari (the daughter of

Atamu), Kori (a 'very large man'), and two children of Ihova, Areru and Maupa.

Many cult adherents called themselves 'Jesus Christ men'. Some had visions of God or Christ and received messages from them. Belief in the ascent of the dead to Heaven was a 'central doctrine', and the man who gave the foregoing account of Heaven also expounded a fair account of the Christian notion of the soul. Evara himself spoke of the 'Good Place', Hedi (Heaven), but many informants merely believed that people 'die finish'. Others confused Heaven with Yesu, and a 'faded but martial portrait of George V' was displayed as Ihova Yesu-nu-ovaki: Jehovah, the younger brother of Jesus. Another imaginative variation was Evara's analysis of a Lifebuoy soap advertisement depicting a field-hospital with a motor-ambulance and male and female figures in uniform. He pointed out one figure as being himself, and the others as his relatives, some deceased.

The most important addition to traditional notions was the idea of the Return and the Millennium. The immediate cause of the outbreak is believed to have been a sermon on the Resurrection preached by a White missionary. But most other elements in the ideology of the movement were traditional.

The fundamental doctrine concerned the spirits of the dead. The chief regular duty falling upon cult members was the obser-vance of mortuary feasts for dead ancestors, just as the traditionally important *Sevese* ceremony was initiated out of respect for the dead.[1]

But far from strengthening the *Sevese*, the new movement attacked ancient religious customs: all the masks and paraphernalia connected with the *Sevese* and *Harisu* religious rituals were burnt in piles before the eyes even of the women, and the rituals them-selves banned in nearly every village.

In their place came three elements of obvious European origin. Firstly, tables were set up, with benches around them, in a central position in the village. Seated at these tables in European style, relatives of dead men held feasts, dressed in their best, while women and children sat on the ground. The tables were ritually decorated daily with beer bottles full of bright croton flowers (and placed under the tables during the heat of the day); young coco-

[1] For an account of the *Sevese* see *Williams*, 1923, pp. 46-47, and 1940, passim, for the Orokolo version, the *Hevehe*.

nuts, husked ready for eating, were also provided, since otherwise the dead would be angry. Sickness was a sign that a feast was needed to appease ancestral wrath.

One report cites offerings of two bowls of rice, betel, and three bottles of flowers on a table which had a loin-cloth as table-cloth, and was guarded by a man lying nearby under a mosquito net. Confident in the arrival of the Cargo, villagers spent their time seated with their backs towards the tables, abandoned gardening and ceased their traditional trade. Two visiting vessels trading from Port Moresby were told to go away as the people were not making sago for exchange any more.[1] This behaviour provoked a violent response from one Acting Resident Magistrate: 'They sat quite motionless and never a word was spoken for the few minutes I stood looking at them. It was sufficient to raise anybody's ire to see them acting in such an idiotic manner; a number of strong, able-bodied natives, in mid-afternoon, dressed in clean, new toggery, sitting as silently as if they were stocks and stones, instead of being at work or doing something else like rational beings. They appeared to be fit subjects for a lunacy asylum.'[2]

Besides the tables, special cult temples were erected. These, the *ahea uvi* (literally, 'hot houses'), were called 'offices' in the east of the affected area; they resembled mission churches rather than European offices, since an atmosphere of quiet sanctity was preserved inside, untypical of indigenous ritual. They were square, neat, and well constructed,[3] and were usually in the centre of the village, but kept shut, entry being controlled by cult leaders, who used them more than other people. Inside were tables, benches and variants like a garishly painted sideboard.

In order to establish contact with the spirits of the dead, the leaders would sit on the verandas of the *ahea uvi* (as White men, for different reasons, sat on their verandas); one claimed to communicate with 'Goss' (God). In the east, the *ahea uvi* were less common, and information was eagerly sought about them. Some had special tables or parts of the building for different clans, and one temple contained decorated strips of bark-cloth, bearing distinctive clan designs.

The third major feature was the *parakke* flagpole (presumably a corruption of the English word). Years before, the LMS had in-

[1] *Papua, Ann. Rpt.*, 1919-20, App. V.   [2] *ibid.*
[3] A photo of one may be seen in *Williams*, 1923, facing p. 22.

84

troduced village flagpoles and flags for use on special occasions, especially on Sundays. Out of these, the cult made media of contact with the dead, though not everywhere. Some believed that the spirits could be contacted via the painted flagpole, and sickness cured by appeasing the ancestors. Others merely received messages through them, the leader standing at the foot, with the message coming down the pole into his stomach and out of his mouth in the form of meaningless songs, which were taken up by the people around him. Some poles possessed personal names, and a few seemed to be treated as actual personalities.

One trader claimed that they were imitations of the Persian Oil Company's wirelesses. He had seen a pumpkin hoisted to the top of one for transmission to the expected steamer, and considered that they existed for sending messages to the vessel. One pole had an 'aerial' with 'wires' of lawyer-cane and an 'operator cabin' at each end. The people looked forward to the steamer's arrival with glowing anticipation, despite disappointments; they would rush out in the middle of the night, shouting with excitement, and with torches blazing, **was** the cry of 'Sail ho!' raised.

Through their control of the *ahea uvi*, the table ritual, the feasting and the flagpoles, the intercourse with the dead for which they acted as mediums, as well as by stimulating waves of possession and dancing, the leaders had a strong grip on the movement. There was no overall control, but a few major leaders extended their influence by evangelization; they were respected by the people, and were themselves proud of their activities. Evara was proud of his reputation as the first man to have been possessed, even though he claimed that the 'Madness' no longer affected him.

Starting in Iori, the movement spread like wildfire, partly as a result of visits to the affected area by parties from outside, and partly through organized evangelism by such men as Kori, Village Constable of Nomu, and Harea of Haruape (Vailala West). Kori, styled by Williams 'the Paul of Papua', was 'a rather singular personality, more than usually cunning, but nevertheless a very faithful and energetic friend of the Government'.[1] Kori had originally gone to see the affected people with a friend, and before long both found themselves overcome. They returned home, and Kori organized 'parties of very militant enthusiasts' to the Maipuan villages and even to villages in the Delta. He swept all before him,

[1] *op. cit.*, p. 30.

making bonfires of the sacred objects, and brushing aside the trifling opposition. Villages which were converted were promised that they would be notified immediately on the arrival of the Cargo.

In some villages, the traditional authority-structure was quite undermined, though the extent to which this happened varied. In Vailala West, the cult leader, Biere, 'a very strong character', said to deserve 'to be a man of influence', had taken over *de facto* political power from the chief, an old man. Elsewhere small groups of leaders took over. The most interesting development was the emergence of the 'rudiments of an organization' among the coastal leaders, Harea of Haruape being the 'boss' in the eastern part. He not only spread the Word, but later carried out 'something like a tour of inspection'.[1] Here we see a similar political development to that which occurred amongst the Orokaiva, a feature described by Williams here as 'not unlike a mild and incipient shamanism' with an 'incipient priesthood'.

Indeed, the organization was probably even tighter in its earlier phases than Williams gives credit for.* Mr Murray, the Resident Magistrate in 1919, described how the 'bosses' made the people 'fall in' and salute them, and preached anti-White doctrines.

The disciplinary features of the movement were not limited merely to the organizational field. The movement formulated new ethical codes by which moral pressure was exerted on its adherents, and the powerful forces of subjective belief and individual conscience were made a buttress to the formal organization. Apart from positive injunctions to provide feasts for the ancestors, etc., members were enjoined to abandon stealing and adultery and to observe Sunday. Though many previous restrictions were abandoned—women and men participated equally in the feasts for the ancestors—social control was exerted by means of public accusation and confession, the guilty person paying a fine of a pig. Pigs were also given by cured persons in divinatory curings, the curing requiring not merely the traditional extraction of harmful objects, but also the confession of the sick person's sins. If he denied any, he was accused of lying.

Crimes were frequently exposed by a 'visiting preacher', i.e., a

---

* He visited the area some years after the vigorous beginning of the movement, after it had been strongly persecuted, and 'never witnessed any large collective demonstrations' (*ibid.*, p. 4).

[1] *op. cit.* p. 32.

86

cult leader. Thus Kori asked the women and children if they stole vegetables and fruit from the gardens. When they denied this, he confounded them by exclaiming 'You are all liars!'

Plainly, there are elements of Roman Catholic teaching in this stress on confession, but the significance of this insistence on a new morality and the abandonment of the old goes deeper than mere surface imitation of White teachings. Other doctrines insisted on the cleanliness of the villages, on clean eating, and on the faithful washing their hands. A 'primitive Puritanism' made people 'forswear their amusements, discard their ornaments, and settle down to a life of dull, prison-like regularity'.[1] Old ceremonies were accounted wicked, and villagers asserted that people should 'stop quiet along village'. 'Personal adornment was banned; feathers were snatched from the heads of vain unbelievers, and the forbidden lime-pot was dashed from their hands'.[2] Children no longer had their noses and ears perforated, as ear and nose ornaments were no longer used; hair was cropped short. This sharp break with the old morality, and the powerful emotions generated in the process, were emphasized by the public breaking of strict sexual taboos. Women became hysterical, threw off their garments, and fell on the ground. This was distorted by Whites as 'sexual abandon' when, in fact, the major emphasis of the movement was on strict sex-morality, the evils of adultery, and so on.

This renunciation of the old ways was accompanied by the adoption of European practices. The deep concern with European material goods, the root of the Cargo doctrine, is also apparent in the detailed description of the clothes worn by God when He visited one prophet. In another visitation, from an ancestor, his clothing was again detailed; coat, shirt, trousers, hat and 'foot'.[3] Mission policies also influenced cult practices. Missionaries had carried out 'considered suppression' of the ancient rituals. Like the missionaries, the cult leaders enjoined strict Sunday observance, and, in many villages, evening 'school', i.e., prayers led by cult leaders, followed by reading aloud from books, and a nine o'clock curfew. 'Reading' by wholly illiterate natives was common in this movement; they would hold Bibles in their hands, often trembling and twitching the while. One man walked into a White man's house smoking a cigarette, with the Gospel of Luke in his hand and a

[1] *op. cit.*, p. 40.   [2] *Williams*, 1934, p, 370.
[3] *Williams*, 1923, p. 27, and *Papua, Ann. Rpt.*, 1919-20, App. V.

pencil and paper, on which he made marks which he said were a
'letter'. On being ordered out, he went to the village trade-store,
where his behaviour terrified the white woman in charge. Taken
to the Resident Magistrate's office, he sang, slapped his chest, and
gave a performance like a Highland fling.

Other European elements included 'about turns', the stopping
and starting of dances by whistle-blasts, books carried under the
arm, and especially the use of pidgin English, mostly with a
plantation flavour. Williams cites a children's game (unconnected
with the cult) in which the children danced towards each other,
'shaping up' as if boxing, whilst singing *ai kikki bluddi as—Heh!
Heh! Heh!*' Phrases which occurred in the 'speaking with tongues'
were 'Me wantum kaikai (food)', 'He all right', 'Ihova', 'Heave
'em up', 'Come on, boy!' (the last from one leader to a divinatory
pole). This 'language' was said to be 'all-a-same Djaman', which
natives knew of both from visits to Rabaul, before 1914 German
territory, and through rumours of the War itself. 'German' was
favoured as an anti-Government tongue.

Changing native attitudes towards their own cultures were
typified by one village constable who urged the destruction of the
Sevese paraphernalia with the argument 'The White man doesn't
do such things: why should we?' Another, in the less elegant
language of the trader and planter: 'Throw 'em away, bloody New
Guinea somethings.' One person, a Christian adherent of the
movement, claimed to have been told in a dream that 'the first
men were bloody fools . . . no savvy anything'.

But if avid for the White man's goods and knowledge, the
natives saw the White man himself as the major obstacle between
them and their goal. Notions of 'Papua for the Papuans' in the early
phases, and the prophesied arrival of rifles with which to attain this,
aroused great excitement. Natives were 'disposed to be insolent'
and the cult 'bosses' urged natives not to sign on as labourers and
not to sell coconuts to traders; one 'shooting-boy' asked his master
if he could take his gun away to the village for a few days.[1]

Resistance to, and hostility towards, the Whites took odd forms.
Under the cloak of 'hysterical' possession, men behaved rudely to
the Whites, which they would not have dared to do openly. One
government official, who was attempting to introduce rice plantations, was received in a very hostile manner. The natives became

[1] *Papua, Ann. Rpt.*, 1919-20, p. 29.

collectively 'possessed', which he himself considered to be 'a protest against the rice-growing proposition' (p. 10); after two hours
of fruitless effort to bring things under control, he retired defeated.

The movement spread rapidly, both westwards and eastwards.
By 1923, it covered the area from the Purari Delta to the Biara
River. Inland, the Opau group north of Kerema, and many of the
villages up the Vailala, Tauri and Biaru Rivers were partly affected.
The oilfields were not immune from the infection, but many of the
natives were dissuaded from endeavouring to return home.

The Administration did not take this situation lightheartedly.
Large numbers of badly affected natives were brought into the
stations, where they were put to work and given plenty of food,[1]
since food was running low in some parts owing to the abandonment of gardening and to continuous feasting. The people had given
up sago-making, and were living on yam and taro only. Sixty-
eight affected men were brought in for eight days in November,
and quickly recovered. More radical was the arrest of several of the
cult leaders, two of whom were each fined 10/- for 'spreading
lying reports'. Some of them denied any responsibility for their
condition, saying 'I no savvy: God he savvy', and most of the
genuinely affected offered little resistance; if lined up, they 'fell
out' when ordered.

In the face of strong government and mission opposition the
movement became security-conscious. Officials entering the villages would be told that the movement had not affected that particular village, or had passed away. The purpose of the *ahea uvi*
flagpoles and tables was concealed, and native leaders said that the
dances were only festivities—'Xmas'. As the Resident Magistrate
was inspecting one village, he saw the flag on the flagpole of the
village on the opposite side of the river being hauled down!

The movement, then, expressed powerful native resentment at
their social and political position in the new order of things. It also
represented a considerable development of new political mechanisms in face of this new situation, and cannot profitably be discussed, as Williams tends to discuss it, in terms of 'hysteria' alone.
The hysterical elements are only too plain, and can be interpreted

---

[1] The Resident Magistrate's interpreter, who was affected by the Madness, lost nearly fourteen pounds in weight. 'Reasoning' had no effect on
him. The police were told that, if they became possessed, this would constitute a breach of discipline.

in terms of the frustrations arising from changed social conditions, the inability to find correct ways of dealing with these new problems due to lack of material techniques and knowledge, and the powerful emotions engendered by conscious mobilization to overthrow the old, deeply established ways and to adopt new ones.

For the sociologist, also, the interest lies in the attempt to reform the superstructure of society without effecting any really fundamental changes in the technology or agricultural economy of the society. Some have seen a contradiction between the belief in White ancestors and in an after-life in which all natives are to be White, and the anti-White sentiments held simultaneously. But there is only a contradiction if one is performing an exercise in limited and formal logic. The consistency underlying both these superficially contradictory notions is the desire to be like the Whites, a desire which, in native eyes, meant removing the Whites.

The Legacy of the Vailala Madness

From time to time different government officials reported a waning of the movement and predicted its end, only to be greeted by a new wave. The arrival of the first plane over the Gulf, for example, caused fresh outbreaks in some areas. But by 1923, the wild early phase had passed, and some villages which had destroyed their ceremonial equipment at the height of the enthusiasm now revived the ancient ceremonies. Certain spots, indeed, had never abandoned them. Other villages had cooled off, but old hotbeds still carried on with the movement. It was not until about 1931, after a period of some twelve years, that the movement may be finally said to have died out.[1]

But the effects of the Vailala Madness did not cease with the end of organized activity. The memory lived on in the minds of the villagers, and, as time passed, legends grew up. This phase sheds much light on the repeated reappearance of cult movements in the same area; in this area of Papua another such movement was to occur, in the Purari Delta, as late as the end of the 1939-45 war.

In 1934, people still firmly maintained the 'belief that those first years of the Vailala Madness constituted a brief age of miracles'.[2] The things which had been prophesied in 1919 were believed in 1934 to have actually taken place. It was recounted how, in that wonder time, 'the ground shook and the trees swayed . . . flowers

[1] *Williams*, 1934, p. 369. [2] *op. cit.*, p. 373.

90

sprang up in a day, and the air was filled with their fragrance. The spirits of the dead came and went by night—morning after morning the imprints of their European boots and even their bicycle tracks were found on the beaches . . . dogs used to rise from the ground and roam the village. They belonged to the . . . dead people.'[1]

Apart from these retrospective additions, the cult activities were remembered as true happenings, not frauds. The leaders *had* received messages via the flagpoles, and papers *had* appeared from invisible hands or from the sky. Informants 'remembered' hearing a warning hum in the poles, followed by a knock, and then the receipt of the message by the leader, who put his ear to the pole and transmitted the text to the people in 'Djaman'.

The steamer of the dead, moreover, actually *had* appeared. People had seen the vessel's wash, heard the noise of her engines, the rattle of the anchor-chain, and the splashing of her dinghy being lowered into the water and of the oars; similar noises were heard as it disappeared without ever having actually been seen. Others remembered obscurely seeing her large red funnel and three masts, and many saw her lights. The Victory Medal which Evara wore in the 1920's was given him by a ghostly passenger who threw it into his canoe as he paddled alongside! Clouds often obscured a proper view of the vessel, though the inhabitants of villages unaffected by the Madness had greater difficulty in seeing the vessel than the faithful.

One prophet, it was said, had 'died', and had lain for three days, guarded by other leaders who prevented friends and relatives from approaching. During this time rats actually gnawed his ears. On the third day, he rose again, and announced in 'German' in a loud voice that he had returned from the Land of the Dead, bringing back a new morality and the idea of the *ahea uvi*. He was carried around the village on a litter which he claimed to be the steamer of Lavara, a legendary ancestress who had returned to Papua.

These beliefs persisted in spite of a certain amount of disillusionment. When the steamer failed to arrive, some villages ate the food they had accumulated for the ancestors, as food was now short. Others were disabused of their faith by the exposure of rank impostures. By 1935 the tables and chairs of the Vailala Madness movement were being chopped up for use as firewood.[2]

[1] *loc. cit.*   [2] *PIM*, 20th December 1935.

But though failure and exposure eventually brought the Vailala Madness to an organizational end, they by no means undermined belief in it. In fact, as time passed, the era of the Madness became more wonderful in memory.

CHAPTER V

Spread and Development

*Behold the name of the Lord cometh from far, burning
with his anger, and the burden thereof is heavy; his lips are
full of indignation, and his tongue as a devouring fire. . . .*

*And the Lord shall cause his glorious voice to be heard,
and shall shew the lighting down of his arm, with the
indignation of his anger, and with the flame of a devouring
fire, with scattering, and tempest, and hail-stones.*

Isaiah 30:27, 30

THE TARO CULT AND THE VAILALA MADNESS are the best-
described of the early Melanesian cults. But they were only two of
the many movements which broke out between the wars. Few of
these are described in any detail; all that we know, in some cases,
is that a cult movement occurred. Our sources vary, therefore, in
quality and quantity, and many movements have taken place, in
all likelihood, without receiving any mention in the published
literature at all.

Generally, administrations only publish information on the most
striking and widespread of these movements, and there seems little
doubt that many movements have flourished secretly without even
coming to the attention of the authorities. But the records which
do exist show that an extraordinary number of cults did spring up
over the whole of Melanesia, and that they shared very many
features in common.

We cannot follow the different movements strictly chronologically, since this would obscure differences between movements
which, while occurring at the same point in time, represent different stages in the development of the millenarian cult. Such an
approach would also make it difficult to follow through a series of
cults in any one area. I propose, therefore, to preserve the general
historical time-scale, but to take area by area in a way that makes it
possible for us to look at both the sequence of events in each area
and the overall developmental pattern.

An early cult in the extreme south of the Melanesian area was the German Wislin* movement of 1913-14 on Saibai Island in the Torres Straits group—an island close to the Papuan mainland.

By 1913, Europeans—traders, government officials and missionaries—had long been established in the Torres Straits Islands, and at times considerable friction had arisen between the islanders and the Whites. The first missionary enterprise started in 1871, and commercial developments quickly followed. By 1901, 315 Torres Straits Islanders were working for the pearling companies[1] out of a population of less than 2,500. Thursday Island soon became a cosmopolitan centre for the pearling industry and, by 1916, 537 of the Islanders themselves had become lugger owners and pearlers.[2] They also experienced the vagaries of the new economy: in 1905, a year of low prices for pearl-shell, 200 islanders were suddenly thrown out of employment.[3] These developments had their repercussions on Saibai, even if the effects were not so severe as on Thursday Island.

The doctrines of the German Wislin were first put about in 1913, but it was not until early 1914 that it became an organized movement. It contained some novel features. The earlier Milne Bay movement, as we have seen, had included the notion of the coming of a vessel with the ancestors aboard. This would be the beginning of millennial conditions in which there would be bountiful crops, numerous pigs and so on. Except in so far as Tokeriu was to have a steamer, it was not envisaged that the ancestors would bring European goods for the people. In the German Wislin, however, we find for the first time outside Fiji the notion that was to become so important and widespread in decades to come—the notion of the Cargo.

The cult devotees did not anticipate millennial conditions in which yams and pigs would abound, but that the ancestors would bring with them money, flour, calico, tomahawks, knives and so on.

Leadership soon emerged in the shape of three men who were known as 'German Wislin', and who were called 'generals' or 'captains'. These generals and captains, it was distinctly stated, were *not* King George's Men. The leaders ordered all the men to

* or Wislun—presumably derived from 'Wesleyan'.
[1] *Peel*, p. 107.
[2] see Lieut. Mackenzie's chapter 'Pearl-shelling in the Torres Straits' in Bishop White's 30 *Years in Tropical Australia*.   [3] *Peel*, p. 110.

congregate on Good Friday, 1914, at the graveyard, between 8 and 9 p.m. The pressure brought to bear on every member of the community to attend was considerable: failure to be present would be visited by the wrath of God or of the *markai*, the spirits of the dead.

These and other threats of retribution are reminiscent of the lurid interpretations of Christian eschatology given by native mission teachers. One shepherd told his flock, who had been remiss in providing him with food: 'When you die you will go to the Big Fire. . . . And there will be nothing to eat. Nothing at all. You will come hungry, even as you have made me come hungry. You, too, will eat grass. And the grass will come dry in your stomachs. Then the fire will go down your mouths and set alight to that dry grass. And smoke and fire will come from your ears. Smoke and fire will come from your noses. Smoke and fire will come from your mouths. And it will burn for ever and ever, amen. I tell you you will all come damn' sorry you not been give plenty food to me. I have speak finish. Now, altogether stand up, open hymn-books and sing strong feller, and not forget what I been say.'[1]

In an oration delivered at the graveyard, it was prophesied that the ancestral spirits would appear that night; there was to be no more work done, as the spirits would provide. Each person masticated wild ginger, which he then spat on to his body, face and arms, rubbing it in.* After this, there followed prayers and songs. Frivolity was attacked and the errors of sceptics denounced. Non-believers would be brought to their senses, not merely by their being excluded from the money to be disbursed, but also by the loss of the money they now possessed.

The millennium was to commence in two weeks, it was said. When that period expired, the Day was promised for another three weeks' time, and when that period ended without the ancestors having arrived, the event was postponed once more. It was expected that a steamer, the *Silŭbloan*, would arrive with the spirits of the dead, and would tie up at a jetty which was to rise up out of the sea at the western tip of Saibai. One man claimed that

---

* Ginger played an important part in traditional magic. Among the nearby Kiwai people it was believed to enable men to see and handle the spirits of others (*Riley*, p. 294).

[1] *McLaren*, p. 135.

the steamer was coming from Canaan, but the *markai* were to embark at a place called 'German Town' in the far west.* The vessel was to call at Thursday Island, where the *markai* would overcome and kill the Whites, and then proceed to Saibai.[1]

Then would the Cargo be dispensed. Then, some said, the era of the equality of White and Black would begin, but since others prophesied that the Whites at Thursday Island were to be slaughtered, the theme of peaceful co-existence is a variable element in the prophecy. In native eyes, the basic point was the occurrence of a radical change in Black-White relations. Originally both had been equal; the White man had only established his control over key resources by theft; self-help, then, was a logical and parallel action on the part of the islanders.

Services were held on Friday and Sunday nights. The Christian God was prayed to for help, especially financial help, but the South Seas mission teacher was strongly opposed by the cult adherents. Considerable stress was laid on the finding of lucky objects, following indigenous beliefs, but now the objects were said to have come from the *markai*. The finding of such an object was notified to the 'German Wislin' leaders who consulted the *markai* in 'German Town' as to the genuineness of the find. In return for the usual verdict of genuineness, they received a fee for their intercession and advice.

The influence of the Christian missions, which exercised such strong control over the islands, is thus particularly striking in this movement, but the interpretation of Christianity by the enthusiasts was quite unorthodox. God was conceived of as working His will through the ancestors; we find numerous Christian elements transmuted in this ideology—the name 'Wislin' itself, prayers, services, God, Good Friday, and so on.

The name 'German' deserves some comment. Although Haddon says nothing on this score, it seems likely that news of the World War had percolated through to Saibai from Thursday Island; even before the actual conflict, the growing tension could easily have become known to the natives, especially in view of the likelihood of armed conflict between the British and German forces in New

---

* This geographical direction may derive from the traditional myth of the island of the dead, Kibu, which was said to lie to the west, but might equally refer to the general geographical direction of Germany.

[1] *Haddon*, 1935, pp. 46 ff., and *Chinnery and Haddon*, pp. 461 ff.

Guinea. In this atmosphere, the significance of 'German' as an anti-Government symbol becomes clear, and the emphasis on the leaders *not* being 'King George's Men' will be recalled.

In the German Wislin, then, we see a transition from magical practices designed to secure traditionally valued ends—an abundance of garden produce—to those aimed at bringing *new* kinds of produce, a transition from the coming of the ancestors in a ship into their coming with a ship-*load* of desired things.

In the Milne Bay movement, the steamer was both a symbol of power and a great material acquisition; in the German Wislin it became also the vessel of the Cargo. Such a common belief need not, of course, imply any contact between the two areas. Under conditions of frustrated wants and antagonism between Whites and Blacks, the notion of the withholding of these goods, rightfully the natives', by the Europeans is easily developed. We will find this theme of the arrival of the stolen Cargo increasingly stressed in other movements, and eventually the central theme of most of them.

Its significance is not hard to seek in social conditions where the natives were rapidly developing new wants for European goods which could only be obtained by working for Europeans, for there was, in general, little market for native produce. Working for the Europeans, however, generally meant leaving home. It usually meant risking death as a pearl-diver, and not everyone could satisfy their wants in this way. As far as the natives were concerned, the Whites received the goods by steamer from unknown parts; they did not manufacture them, and merely sent pieces of paper back. They did no apparent work themselves, yet refused to share their fortune, forcing the natives to work long and hard for a return of a small proportion of the goods they themselves obtained with such ease and in such profusion. Who made these goods, how and where, were mysteries—it could hardly be the idle White men. It was the natives who did all the manual work. If the goods were made in some unknown land, they must, then, be made by the spirits of the dead.

Whilst administrations often realized that these movements were the product of unsettling political and economic conditions, they frequently tried to strike at the shadow and not at the substance. Whether these movements were consciously and overtly anti-White or not, they were all treated with the utmost suspicion: thus the Kava-keva, the Kekesi, the Milne Bay and the Baigona movements were all proscribed. These bans, however, were often ineffective and, where the movements did decline, they generally did so for other reasons than fear of repression. Such attacks also often tended to convert relatively passive and harmless movements into something stronger.

As Marett remarked in characteristically pithy style: 'With the unfortunate precedent of Pontius Pilate, Governments should be chary of applying police methods to new movements in religion.'[1]

Under repression, the 'missionary zeal' Haddon had noted in early New Guinea movements was to develop into organizational and security measures of a much higher order in later movements. These cults, Haddon remarked, proved one thing, the falsity of 'the very prevalent notion of the permanence of all native institutions and of the supposed disinclination of primitive people to adopt new ideas or new cults'.[2]

The Rising Tide

The 1920's saw the rise of a number of millenarian cults all over New Guinea. In 1922, Timo, a native from the Huon Peninsula, prophesied that the world would come to an end and all the villages would be overwhelmed by falling mountains.[3]

In Dutch New Guinea, a movement emerged in the late twenties around Lake Sentani, where there had been initial resistance to European penetration until about 1925. Though the Sentani area had become largely Christian by that date, the coastal dwellers clung to their pagan religions. The missionaries caused the sacred spirit-statues to be thrown into the Lake, and, in some areas, spirit houses were burnt down by Government.*

In 1928, an independent native Christian movement developed, which was initially supported by the missionaries. At first it helped the missionaries in their work. Its leader, Pamai, declared that he was charged by God to convert his Papuan fellows, and his followers sent delegations to the mission to obtain teachers. The secret-society masks were exposed and smashed, or given to the missionaries, and the Creed and the Pater Noster were chanted all night long.

---

* Sixty of these statues were fished up in 1939; see Jacques Viot's *Déposition de Blanc* cited in *Rousseau*.

[1] *Williams*, 1928, p. xi.   [2] *Chinnery and Haddon*, p. 456.

[3] *NMB*, 30th May 1924, p. 24, quoted in *Höltker*, 1941, and *Lommel*.

Pamai then began to sell a healing liquid, and to take money in return for his teaching. He also started preaching against Government and mission, and told the people not to do any more public work for Government and to withhold their taxes. Government quickly arrested Pamai, and sentenced him to three years' forced labour.[1]

In 1929-30, there were reports of a myth of the 'Golden Age' amongst the Baining of New Britain; again there were rumours of the imminent resurrection of the dead. The mountains would collapse into the valleys to form a great plain covered with fertile gardens and fruit trees which would require no cultivation. Dead pigs and dogs would come back to life, but native sceptics and Europeans were to die in the earthquake.[2]

With the advent of the 'thirties, reports of Cargo movements came thick and fast. In 1930, there was the 'God the Father' movement at Suain on the north-east coast of New Guinea,[3] and in the Sepik region the first of a number of movements was reported.

The Sepik District

The coastal area of the Sepik District had been under European control for many years, and the Germans had established their first administrative station at Aitape in this District. Even so, administrative control only extended a very short distance inland from Aitape and Wewak even in the late 'thirties. But even if the effects of White contact were passed on to the inland villages only at second hand, they were by no means negligible. Reed remarks, for example, that the German way, when starting a new station, was to send 'armed police to the nearest native community to round up free natives for the work'.[4] Kidnapping from villages which refused to furnish labour-recruits was also common: 'of 138 recruits from the region near Berlinhafen [now Aitape] who were delivered to the Neu-Guinea Kompagnie at one time by the recruiter, Kernbach, 130 ran away after the first night to try to regain their own villages'.[5]

After the departure of the Germans, the new Australian admin-

[1] *Missionsblatt Barmen*, May, 1929, pp. 535 ff., quoted in *Eckert*, 1940.
[2] *Brenningmeyer*, p. 48; *Höltker*, 1941, p. 940; *Laufer*, p. 216.
[3] *Steyler Missionsbote*, Vol. LVIII, 1930-1, pp. 68-69, quoted in *Höltker*, 1941, and *Lommel*.   [4] *Reed*, p. 146.   [5] *op. cit.*, p. 147.

istration was generally welcomed as an improvement in the coastal and controlled areas, but in the marginal and semi-controlled areas Australian rule was often more resented than German. Writing of the Sepik, Reed remarks: 'The natives whose culture suffered less change from aboriginal conditions under German administration look back on those earlier times as the "good old days".'[1]

The reason for this resentment in the backward areas becomes clear when one takes into account the observation by Pfeil, German recruiter and official, concerning the 'widely-held native conviction ... that the foreigners were merely temporary visitors and that they would soon depart'.[2] It is difficult for us, with our knowledge of the deliberateness of colonization, to realize that the native notion that the Whites would not stay long was a reasonable one in view of their past experience. The shock of realization that the days of independence were gone for ever must have been traumatic for such peoples. And by the time this initial shock had been absorbed, the German government itself was overthrown by the Australians in 1914. This was only the first of several equally radical changes. After World War II one native ruefully remarked: 'We do not understand. We are just in the middle. First the Germans came—and the Australians pushed them out. Then the Japs pushed out the Australians. Later, the Americans and Australians got rid of the Japs. It is beyond us'.[3]

Therefore, when four prophets arose near Aitape, promising that all Europeans would leave the Territory within a few months, people took notice of them, especially since these men claimed that Government had no power over them, nor the police or village officials. The prophets claimed to be 'Kings'; they had been miraculously born and possessed supernatural powers. When the Europeans left, they said, all the property they left behind would accrue to the natives, and the crops would grow by themselves. Cooking-pots should be destroyed, as they would be replaced by new and better ones soon.[4]

The 'Black King' movement was also reported from Wewak,

[1] *op. cit.*, p. 154.   [2] *op. cit.*, p. 153.
[3] *Burridge*, 1954b, p. 937. To add to the confusion, New Guinea was a Mandated Territory, and became a Trust Territory after the war.
[4] *Steyler Missionsbote*, Vol. LX, 1932-3, pp. 107-8, quoted in *Höltker*, 1941, and *Lommel*; *PIM*, 20th December 1932, p. 46, and 20th November 1935, pp. 25-26; *TNG, Ann. Rpt.*, 1930-1, p. 96.

where the four 'kings' declared that the ancestors made all the cargo, but that the Whites illegally deprived the natives of the goods. After they began to prophesy that the government station would disappear into the sea, and to preach against payment of taxes, against the Government and against the mission, four of the leaders were gaoled, and three exiled to an island.[1]

In the following year, a startling development took place. The elders of Moagendo village took the missionary into their sacred spirit house, and offered him the finest of the sacred figures which were then dragged in procession on to the mission vessel, the *Stella Maris*. As the vessel proceeded along the river, village after village was found to be awaiting the arrival of the boat, with their sacred images ready for loading. Soon the boat was crowded with images. In one village, the elders received the news of the cult in the middle of an initiation ceremony which they rapidly brought to an end.[2]

The Madang and Morobe Districts

Spreading along the coast from the original focus in the Sepik District, the movement reached the neighbouring Madang District by 1935. It was anti-mission in content, and apocalyptic rumours of a strange Black King who lived in the interior and had a skin of iron and stone, and many hands, began to circulate.[3]

The adjoining Morobe District also had its share of cults in the 'thirties. In 1932-4, in the Markham Valley, a native began having visions of his dead father and of Jesus Christ. He prophesied that the ancestors would bring about the end of the world by causing an earthquake and floods: everybody, whether Christian or heathen, who wished to be saved should take refuge in the mountains immediately. Many people built temporary grass shelters, but before the movement advanced any further, Government arrested the leaders.[4]

This did not prevent the emergence of yet another movement in the Markham in the following year. This movement was led by

---

[1] *Steyler Missionsbote, loc. cit.*

[2] *Steyler Missionsbote*, October 1932, pp. 11 ff.

[3] Otto Bader, 'Im Dunkel des Heidentums', *Steyler Missionsbote*, 1935-6, Vol. LXIII, pp. 287-8, quoted in *Lommel*, p. 32 and *Höltker*, 1941.

[4] *NMB*, 15th August 1932, p. 63; 15th July 1933, p. 53; 15th April 1934, p. 27.

a man named Marafi, who announced that Satan had visited him and had taken him into the bowels of the earth, where he had seen the spirits of the dead who dwelt there.

Marafi had spoken to these dead people; they told him that they wished to return to the world of the living, but that Satan forbade them. Not until Marafi had converted the villagers to belief in Satan as the Supreme Being would the dead return to earth. The return of the dead would be heralded by an earthquake; the sky would turn black, and then heavy rain of flaming kerosene would burn houses, gardens, and all living things. In order to survive this cataclysm, the people should build houses large enough to contain entire communities. On the first shock of the earthquake they should immediately take refuge in these houses. Next morning, they would find the dead returned with cases of tinned meat, tobacco, loin-cloths, rice, lamps and rifles. The rifles would be more powerful than any the Government possessed. After the cataclysm, the people would have no need to garden.

Marafi was a capable organizer: he soon convinced some villages that he was in contact with Satan, and that he had been given miraculous powers by the Prince of Darkness. When he visited a village, he would be given presents—money, clothes, and so on—and, for his part, appointed deputies whom he instructed in cult songs and dances. These men were then to spread cult doctrines and rituals in other villages. Both Marafi and his deputies apparently deceived and cheated the villagers. When ultimately relieved of the presents he had received, he was found to have in his possession £2 9s. in cash, a blanket, two knives and an axe: these were restored to their owners. On the 'instructions' of Satan, moreover, he took women and young girls as his wives, or gave them to the young men.

He reassured waverers that, if Government tried to interfere, Satan would cause the earth to open and swallow them. As a further buttress to morale, he made the people assemble on dark nights near the cult houses, telling them that he would visit Satan. After solemnly warning them against spying on him, the penalty for which would be Satan's spearing the offender in the stomach with his long, spear-like finger, the prophet disappeared in the bush. Going round behind the house, he climbed the roof, and shouted down to the assembled multitude that he was flying overhead like a bird. Another time, he took a native into his house, where he introduced him to his dead father. Although the native could not see clearly because it was dark, he was convinced that he had spoken and shaken hands with his father.

Owing to the expectation of the imminent cataclysm, gardens were abandoned; deserters from employment hid in the villages, and the authority of Government and of native officials was undermined. But it was Marafi's removal of the women which proved his undoing. Natives now hid their wives and daughters in places of safety. District officers, proceeding to the area, released the young women, and sent them home. Although they showed signs of anxiety, they had not been molested.

Government courts punished the offenders in measure according to their offence. Many of Marafi's deputies publicly admitted that they had deceived the people, but on Marafi's instructions. Most of the villagers now realized that they had been deceived, and nearly all the communal houses were destroyed; others, however, remained faithful and did not destroy them.[1]

The most interesting aspect of this movement is its thoroughgoing ideological inversion of orthodox Christianity. As in many other movements, the cataclysm was to mark the millennium for the natives and the coming of disaster to the Whites, but few movements took the more rigorously logical step of adopting the White man's Devil as the natives' God. The movement thus did more than merely reproduce the Black-White situation in ideological form: it condemned the existing social order by creating a Heaven which represented the overthrow and inversion of the existing society in fantasy.

Marafi's movement still smouldered on in secret despite suppression and exposure, and another outburst occurred in 1936.[2] But the whole of the Morobe District was affected by similar cults by that time. Fresh outbreaks were reported from the Huon Peninsula in 1933, when a native named Upikno, a hermit who lived alone in the bush, began hearing 'voices' and working miracles.

He took the new name of Lazarus on God's instructions, and taught his disciples songs which he had learnt from his 'voices'. Upikno called for moral renewal: there was to be no more thieving,

[1] *TNG, Ann. Rpt.*, 1934-5, pp. 19-21; also *NMB*, 10th November 1934, pp. 83 ff.
[2] *NMB*, 10th February 1936, p. 13; 15th May 1936, pp. 35 ff.

no promiscuity and no sin. He claimed that the mission was working badly: frequently missionaries would desert their work and go away on leave. The missionaries were not needed and would be replaced in church and school by natives. All the White man's goods, including tools recently brought from Rabaul, should be destroyed.

A young boy of ten and a half now started hearing voices also, but his voices were rather less Christian in tone than those which Lazarus-Upikno had heard. If the people prayed hard, the boy said, the dead would return with food, houses, and riches for the faithful. The present bad houses and the bad skins would go. Their skins would be renewed, and life eternal would commence. God, who had made the Whites rich, would now help the Blacks.

These teachings led large numbers of people to destroy their goods. They assembled in mass gatherings for prayer, and the familiar shaking-fits occurred.[1]

Many similar movements were reported in these years from the Madang and Morobe Districts.[2] Some of these, such as the Letub, Kukuaik, and Eemasang movements reached their climaxes during and after the war, and are discussed below.[3] About others, such as the 'schwärmerei' in Kalangandoang village in the Rawlinson Range in 1933, the Sosom movement in the Goldberg mountains in 1936,[4] the Second Coming of Christ outbreak on the Rai Coast in 1936,[5] or the movement on the Töpfer River headed by a magician named Yerumot,[6] our information is very slight. A good account does exist, however, of the Mambu movement whose influence was to persist into the post-war era.[7]

The Mambu Movement

This movement sprang up in the Suaru-Ulingan-Banara area of Madang District. By 1937, native society had been profoundly disturbed. The Roman Catholic Mission at Bogia had begun setting up stations in the hinterland as long ago as 1915; migrant

---

[1] *NMB*, 10th November 1934, pp. 83 ff., and 25th July 1934, p. 55.

[2] *NMB*, 15th August 1932, p. 63; 15th July 1933, p. 54; 15th April 1934, pp. 26 ff.; October 1936, p. 13 and 20th August 1936, p. 13, quoted in *Eckert*, 1937.   [3] see Chapter X.   [4] *Eckert*, 1936, p. 473.

[5] Ignaz Schwab, 'Der Koch des Teufels', *Steyler Missionsbote*, Vol. LXV, 1937-8, p. 236, quoted in *Eckert*, 1937.

[6] *PIM*, August 1936, p. 68; *NMB*, 15th November 1936, p. 112, quoted in *Hölkter*, 1941.   [7] see below, Chapter X.

labour had made its inroads on the indigenous order,* and Government represented a third alien and disturbing influence. Many natives from inland villages were baptized Christians by the time of the Mambu movement.

Mambu, the prophet, was himself a baptized Roman Catholic. He had been a migrant labourer at Rabaul, and for some time after his return his behaviour was perfectly normal. Indeed, the Mission had contemplated using him as a Mission helper.

But one morning, at 5 a.m., when the missionary arrived for morning prayer, he found Mambu already at Church. He had even carried out the necessary preparations such as taking the coverings off the altar. These duties were normally performed by the sister sacristan, so the missionary rebuked him, asking him what right he had to touch these things. When Mass began at 6 a.m., Mambu disappeared. This strange behaviour was followed by another queer incident. Mambu now arrived at Bogia on the coast. The missionary there asked him about his odd behaviour; Mambu merely listened to his rebukes impassively. He was then sent off home, but as he was passing the church, the bell sounded for the evening Angelus. It was usual to stand and pray at this sound, but Mambu instead went down on his knees until the peal was over.

Shortly afterwards, one of the Sisters was sleeping in her room when she was awakened by a man who gripped her hand. This person was never caught, but natives at the station believed that it was Mambu's doing.

Following these first rumbles, the storm soon broke. News now reached the Mission of a new movement in the hinterland. Mambu was preaching a new syncretic doctrine compounded of both pagan and Christian elements, but anti-White, anti-mission and anti-Government in its general content. The Whites had discriminated against, and deceived, the natives, he was saying; therefore all obedience and submission to them must be renounced.

The ancestors lived inside a volcano on Manum Island, where they worked hard making goods for their descendants: loin-cloths, socks, metal axes, bush-knives, flashlights, mirrors, red dye, etc., even to plank-houses: but the scoundrelly Whites took the cargoes when they reached Rabaul.

* see picture of a 'finishtaim boy' (migrant labourer whose contract has been completed) with a coin in each hand, loin-cloth, etc., in *Höltker*, 1941, p. 206.

Now this was to stop. The ancestors themselves would bring the goods in a large ship. The coast behind Suaru would open to form a harbour, and the cargo would be discharged. Then there would be no more garden work, for amongst the cargo would be ample rice and bully beef for all.

Mambu told his followers that Government had no right to levy taxes. The villagers should refuse to pay these taxes; they should tell the tax officials that they had paid their taxes to the 'Black King'. They should refuse to work for Government, cleaning the roads or carrying; this the Whites should do themselves. The missionaries, equally, were exploiters. Roman Catholics should not go near the mission stations nor attend school; if they did, the coming of the cargo would be delayed. Non-adherents were boycotted. They would be excluded from the benefits of the millennium, and those who persisted in going to church would be burnt with the church buildings.

Mambu now instituted a series of rites for the faithful. Prayers for money were offered up at the ancestral graves, and temples were set up in the villages. But followers were baptized in the government rest-houses. The Chosen entered the rest-houses in pairs, a man and a woman together, symbolically taking over these places belonging to the White man's Government. The grass skirts of the women and the loin coverings of the men were then cut away, and their genitals washed or sprinkled with water. Only European loin-cloths and long female dresses introduced by the Europeans were worn; the old traditional clothing was said to be 'nogud', and was preventing the return of the ancestors.

Skirts were piled up high in one heap, and men's pubic coverings in another, and a grave dug by each pile. Then Mambu stood in each of the graves in turn, crucifix in hand, and made the sign of the Cross firstly over the crucifix and then over the two heaps of clothing. After he had jumped out, the two heaps were shovelled in and covered with earth. Thus was the past repudiated, and the native claim to European goods and European power dramatically symbolized.

The special status of Mambu was emphasized in several ways. He claimed special powers, such as invulnerability, and adopted the titles of 'King long ol kanaka',* or 'blackfela king' or 'black master'. When he left a place, he was given the ceremonial farewell

* *kanaka*: pidgin English word for native.

'Gudbai King'. And to stress his special position, he remained unmarried, 'like a mission-sister', as the natives said. It seems likely, from the unusual circumstance of Mambu's being unmarried at thirty years of age, from the genital-washing, and from Mambu's probable involvement in the incident of the nocturnal invasion of the Sister's room, that Mambu was not only gifted with unusual qualities of leadership, but was also sexually abnormal. To reinforce the spiritual allegiance of his followers, he provided them with food, miraculously sent by the ancestors: rice which had arrived by air, and fish which had come by river, though it was sea-fish. This was merely an earnest of joys to come. Better quality pigs would soon arrive, if the ancestors were not irritated by the failures of the living to carry out their religious obligations.

Mambu's message was mainly anti-Government at first, but soon became equally anti-mission. Initially, he met with a cool reception amongst his own people, so he betook himself to Tanggum country, where he achieved greater success and began to collect 'tax'. His activity was facilitated by the temporary absence of the missionary, and by a fire in the church at Bogia in January 1938, an event which Mambu may have used as a 'sign'. Tanggum had been a difficult country for missionaries in the early days, and now, once again, the old hostility reasserted itself. Next, Mambu moved to the Suaru-Banara hinterland, where the people were noted for their hostility towards Whites. In 1920 a recruiter had been killed there, and Höltker describes the country as 'ein undankbares, schweres Missionsfeld'. This area now became the base for Mambu's operations. The people built him a special house and a number of temples. He encouraged them to eat up all their food, and baptized many recruits. From here, the movement spread down to Ulingan. Only very remote villages remained unaffected, but even many of those which appeared superficially to be unaffected when visited by Europeans were noticed to be unnaturally quiet and full of natives wearing European dress.

Paradoxically enough, it was the migrant labourers, the people most affected by the disturbing effects of European rule, who were the weakest link in Mambu's plan of campaign. For although it was easy for the old people and the women to follow the call to abstain from contact with the White man and his goods, the migrant labourers had developed different wants, and had become dependent on their earnings to satisfy these wants and those of their relatives and dependants too. So it was the labourers themselves, by no means well-disposed towards the Whites, who refused to forgo present prospects of obtaining limited wealth for apocalyptic visions of ultimate luxury.

Of the Europeans, the storekeepers had rejoiced at the sudden spending-spree on European clothes. Others, however, were less pleased. The Mission became worried as the boycott became more and more effective. Government, at last realizing the seriousness of the situation, sent police to the area. In March 1938 Mambu was arrested, exiled, and given a sentence of six months' imprisonment at Madang.

His followers were unshaken; they claimed that he had only gone to spread the gospel elsewhere, and in May another wave of cult activity broke out. 1939 saw another revival in the Banara area and even an extension into the hinterland behind Rempi, where the earlier Kuduj movement had prepared the ground.[1] Though these new Mambu waves were suppressed by Government, the movement was far from exhausted, as we shall see when we examine its post-war manifestations.

Other Cults in Long-Contacted Regions

To round off our examination of pre-1939 cults in the Mandated Territory, we will mention one which occurred in an area long under administrative control, where the natives had had close contact with Whites over decades. This was the Namatanai sub-District of New Ireland. It was under complete control, was an area where White plantations were important, and had what, for New Guinea, were good roads and communications. The natives themselves were producing copra for sale and were described as 'perhaps . . . [the] most developed in the Territory'.

Here the cult movement took a somewhat different form. It was not particularly anti-European, a circumstance which may be related to the comparative prosperity of these small independent native producers in a period of slight recovery from the worst depths of the depression.

New processes of differentiation were evident in diverse fields of social life, and the work of both Roman Catholic and Protestant missions over many years had led to an even more direct attack

[1] Wilhelm van Baar, 'Ein ganz eigentümlich Vorgang', *Steyler Missionsbote*, Vol. LIX, 1931-2, pp. 127-8, quoted in *Höltker*, 1941.

upon, and questioning of, indigenous values and customs. More-over, in a situation where there were two Christian missions opera-ting, apparently preaching two different moralities, all morality was more closely questioned.*

Conflicts within the community thus did not follow the domi-nant Black-White lines of cleavage, but took the form of a clash between conservative elders and the younger people.† Only later did it take the form of a movement inspired by religious visions of a prophet.

The *casus belli* was an actual incident in a village, not a direct response to any specific external impulse. A young couple had en-deavoured to persuade Christian clergymen to marry them without their parents' consent, but the latter had refused since the couple concerned belonged to the same exogamous unit, and therefore, in native eyes, would be committing incest.

This refusal was clearly the last straw to the frustrated younger generation, whose protest took the form of a 'religious' outbreak. It was not headed by either of the young couple, but by a prophet who acted as spokesman for the younger people. At his meetings, he called for the abolition of the old exogamous restrictions and for the amendment of marriage custom. A spirit had told him in a dream that the new marriages, far from being a sin and leading to mystical penalties, would be blessed with numerous offspring.

The movement, however, soon got out of hand. One of the disciples of the prophet saw in his dreams a shipment of Cargo which was to be distributed amongst believers. It had already left Rome, and would be delivered in the village by the spirits of the dead. When the Cargo arrived, it was said, the young couple would be married, and would become famous as the originators of the new life. This message was vigorously propagated and widely accepted.

The sharpness of the internal struggle is revealed by the specific exclusion of the reactionary defenders of the old custom from the distribution of the Cargo. When 'subversive elements' of the move-ment developed, and people began to neglect their gardens, the

* The growth of conflicts within a native community through the existence of rival missions is best seen in the case of Rivo Island, near Madang, where the 300 natives, half Roman Catholics and half Lutherans, built a fence across the island to cut off social intercourse (*Gitlow*, p. 11).

† The changes and conflicts in modern village life have nowhere been more vividly depicted than in Hogbin's work (*Hogbin*, 1939 and 1951).

Administration finally took action, and, working through the 'saner elements', was successful in destroying the movement.[1]

Even though this movement had developed initially around internal social problems, and though the conflict was one between native and native, the quick widening of the movement from its original focus on marriage questions to Cargo doctrine and thence to 'subversion' indicates how convenient and attractive Cargo doctrine was as a medium for the expression of all kinds of discontents. It also shows how the expression of discontent over limited local issues could quickly lead to the expression of wider discontents. For, ultimately, these intra-village tensions were the product of the wider changes wrought by external forces, especially by the presence of the Europeans, their Government, their missions, and their plantations.

This movement shows particularly clearly that millenarism expresses not merely political and economic discontent, but also reactions to disturbances in many other social fields—changes in marriage customs, religion, legal mechanisms, in morality, in the relations between the sexes, and in the relations between young and old—even if these changes have been initiated by the coming of the Europeans. As we have seen for Namatanai, the missions have been extremely important agents of change in many of these fields, since they attacked ancient values and beliefs directly. This ideological assault did not unsettle native society in the same way as more material changes—labour migration, cash-crop farming,etc. —but it helped to undermine the social moves in a way which was to have devastating consequences. It brought every individual face to face with new and difficult moral choices. This is not to say that the missions were not more directly agents of material change. Some missions became quite important owners of plantation property, and employed large numbers of native labourers. It is this fact which explains the signs observed in New Guinea reading 'Most Sacred Heart of Jesus Ltd.' and 'Holy Ghost Ltd.' [2] These plantations generally provided funds for mission work inside New Guinea, but some of the Roman Catholic mission societies used profits from New Guinea plantations to subsidize mission work in other parts of the world.[3] Not unnaturally, when the question of abolishing the pre-war indentured labour system came under

---

[1] *TNG, Ann. Rpt.*, 1937-8, pp. 29-30.
[2] *Reed*, p. 237.   [3] *Hogbin*, 1951, p. 234.

review in 1945, those missions benefiting from this system opposed its abolition.[1]

*　　*　　*

Having examined the movements in the Mandated Territory, brief mention must be made of other cults in Papua in the late 'thirties. These included waves of pig-killing in the Northern and Northeastern Divisions, including the old Taro Cult area.[2] The Northeastern Division also produced the so-called 'Assisi' cult which continued right through the war and into the post-war period, its members defying excommunication by the Mission.

They expected Christ to arrive in a ship with the Cargo which would be stored in a cave in the hills. There would be no more work, and the brown men would turn white and rule their former masters, now brown of skin.

There followed great destruction of property, quaking-fits, speaking with tongues, and a revival of the ancestor cult. Mission services were imitated, and one prophet performed a 'Holy Communion' service, using coconut milk for wine and giving a parody of the prayer-book service.[3]

In the south, there was a wave of pig-killing in Kairuku in 1937[4] followed by two cult outbreaks in the Mekeo District in 1940 and 1941. In the first, which took place in a long-missionized village, a young girl of seventeen became possessed. This is one of the rare cases of female leadership in these movements. This remarkable girl, Filo, dreamt that God (or A'aia, who gave the Mekeo their laws and customs) had told her that the people were wicked. There should be no more gardening and pigs should be killed off. The people should set up altars and pray.

Her prophecies were ignored until the outbreak of an influenza epidemic which killed sixty people. Then her prophecies were remembered. Filo's parents collected money which was to be sent to Heaven to avert God's wrath, and Filo herself threatened the people that if they persisted in gardening or hunting they would be turned into weeds or transformed into pigs and cassowaries. Like-

[1] *Hogbin, op. cit.*, p. 199.

[2] *PIM*, January 1946, p. 52; *Papua, Ann. Rpt.*, 1937-8, p. 35.

[3] *Cranswick and Shevill*, Chapter 9, 'The Church and Strange New Cults', pp. 87-93; *Australian Board of Missions*, pp. 101-3.

[4] *Papua, Ann. Rpt.*, 1937-8, p. 35.

wise the wicked would die and unbelievers would be transformed into animals when the darkness came and the sky fell on the earth and the world turned upside down. She strongly emphasized the new morality and the abandonment of the old ways, and attacked stealing, lying, sorcery, etc. She herself defied ancient exogamous rules by marrying a close relative. Sorcery objects and native ornaments were to be thrown away. They would have no cause to worry about food, she said, as it would come from the ancestors in Heaven by aeroplane. God would also send lorry-loads of rifles and ammunition, with which the Europeans would be driven out. The Mission would be attacked first, for their religion was false, and then the police. Such retribution would only be just, for the Europeans were stealing goods sent by the spirits to the Mekeo.

The people then spent night and day dancing, singing round the altars, using both Roman Catholic prayers and their own. Women preached, and the congregation was overcome with mass hysteria.[1]

Leading the movement was a small group of Filo's relatives, including two uncles, one of whom called himself 'God' and another 'Jesus'. The movement used Filo's village as a headquarters. 2,000 people now concentrated there from other villages, and Filo deputed leaders for each community. Matters soon reached a climax:

'A day or so of this behaviour and the crisis arrived. A procession headed by Filo marched around the village and then halted in dead silence outside the mission compound. One man climbed the fence and rushed to the church door which he tried in vain to batter open. Inside the Sisters of the Mission had gathered all their schoolchildren. Father Coltré then came running up and was attacked by this native with a heavy sea-shell used as a receptacle for the holy water just outside the church door. A murderous blow was struck at the Father with its jagged edge. Fortunately, he managed to dodge and received only a glancing blow on the forehead, which caused him to bleed profusely. However, he wrestled with his assailant and threw him to the ground. The native was ejected by a Mission Brother and another priest. Several other natives then came in to belabour the Father with small sticks, but these were also dispersed and the affair came to an end. But the night was made hideous

[1] *Belshaw*, 1951, pp. 5-6.

for the inmates of the Mission who were given gruesome details from the Mission fence as to what their fate would soon be.

A Mission Brother escaped by bush paths and crossed to Yule Island by canoe. A magistrate and police arrived next morning'.[1]

This party hardly expected the enthusiastic welcome accorded them as presumed bringers of the Cargo. But this warm welcome did not deter the magistrate from making numerous arrests. Filo was detained on the station for a few months, and convicted of 'spreading lying reports tending to give trouble amongst the people'. Others received penalties of up to seven years.

The seriousness of the situation was shown by the recurrence of the movement in the following year. Filo resumed her activities, and the natives set up 'wirelesses' in the swamps and remote scrub. 'Miracles' bolstered the movement, in spite of hunger resulting from diminished horticulture and loss of pigs, from which the area suffered for several years afterwards. When Filo was arrested once more, other leaders took her place, and prophesied that she would make a triumphal return upon a white horse.* Indeed, a white horse was removed from the Mission, but the people failed to feed the animal so that it was weak and useless on Filo's return. But instead of the expected triumphal return, Filo came back under police escort, and was greeted by only a mild demonstration.

The movement persisted underground for a while, with people praying secretly in the bush for Cargo. The non-arrival of the Cargo, government and mission repression, and some coincidental deaths following the arrival of the police broke the movement organizationally, but in memory the people did *not* regard the cult as a fraud, and the Government was held responsible for preventing the fulfilment of the prophecy. The 'miraculous' happenings engineered by the leaders—the falling of objects from Heaven (tobacco, money, books, handkerchiefs, knives, permits for trucks, guns, etc.)—was firmly believed in, not merely at the time, but long afterwards when the movement had disappeared. Like the memories of the Vailala Madness, the miracles, in retrospect, had *actually happened*.[2]

* Perhaps inspired by Revelation 19:11.
[1] *Papua, Ann. Rpt.*, 1940-1, p. 21.
[2] *Belshaw, op.cit.*, p. 7; *PIM*, 5th March 1941, p. 18 and 15th November 1941, p. 50.

CHAPTER VI

The Continuity of the Cults: Buka

So that the fishes of the sea, and the fowls of the heaven,
and the beasts of the field, and all creeping things that creep
upon the earth, and all the men that are upon the face of the
earth, shall shake at my presence, and the mountains shall
be thrown down, and the steep places shall fall, and every
wall shall fall to the ground.   Ezekiel 38:20

────────

HAVING EXAMINED HOW MILLENARIAN CULTS appeared in various parts of Melanesia between the wars, we can now turn our attention to a more intensive analysis of a series of cult movements in one particular area. This will enable us to estimate the nature of the forces making for the persistence of the cults, and the direction of their development.

A notable area for the occurrence of Cargo cults before World War I was Buka, a small island at the northern end of the Solomons chain which had been long under European influence. Trading posts were established on the island in 1884, followed by mission stations and plantations, and many of the first native recruits to the German police force were drawn from Buka.[1] It is worth noting that Melanesian troops were used by the Germans in the suppression of the Maji-Maji rebellion in Tanganyika in 1905-6.[2]

One of the earliest millenarian movements on Buka occurred at Lontis,* on the north coast, but few details are known of its content. Its leaders, Novite and Muling, were arrested by the Germans, and taken to Morobe where Novite died. Muling was later allowed back. A French missionary claims that the movement was suppressed and its 'martyrs sacrifiés par le bourreau du gouvernement allemand',[3] but Döllinger, German 'Stationsleiter' at Lontis in 1913 denied this completely.[4]

---

* Stanner seems to have confused this with the German Wislin in his reference to 'the "German Wislin of Saibai" at Lontis, on Buka' (*Stanner*, p. 61).

[1] *Reed*, p. 141.   [2] *Sayers*, p. 75.
[3] *Montauban*, 1948, p. 135.   [4] in *Eckert*, 1937.

Under the Australians, the island remained a major source of labour for planters and Government.[1] No further outbreaks are recorded in the literature until November 1932, when a 'quasi-religious' movement was reported in and around the villages of Malasang and Gogohei. Its leader, Pako, was assisted by Muling, veteran of 1913, and Terasim, a Marist catechist. Muling claimed kinship with the sun and moon. When he prophesied that a tidal wave would come and sweep away many villages, five hundred alarmed villagers took refuge overnight on a hilltop. He also prophesied the arrival of a Cargo ship with iron, axes, food, tobacco, motor-cars, and, significantly, firearms. Work now ceased in the gardens.[2]

One of the prophets is said to have gone to Heaven, where Saint Peter told him that the people were to go to church regularly, to abandon their old dances and rituals, and to levy tolls and demand higher wages from the Whites.[3] Owing to this ban on work, Malasang, the centre of the pot-making industry, ceased production.

Most accounts depict Pako as the main leader. Pako was no mere village native. He had travelled abroad and seen the ways of the Europeans, and on his return had built himself a European-style house. After a time, he began to have dreams*; he called for the renunciation of both paganism and Christianity, but advocated the placation of the ancestors at the village burial-grounds, which were decorated with garlands, the crosses painted red, and pigs sacrificed to the ancestors.

This break with the past was emphasized by the abolition of in-law taboos: the secrets of the men's initiation ceremonies were revealed to the women, magic was renounced and individual property in money abolished. This last practice did not imply merely a revulsion against things European; it emphasized rather the solidarity and primitive communism of the movement.

Pako also preached that natives were to become the equal of Whites, and that storehouses should be built for the reception of the Cargo.[4] Wharves and docks were actually built at Malasang. Pako soon had 5,000 followers and united the whole of Buka for

---

* cf. the dream (unconnected with the cult) about the government yacht, a deceased daughter, a black-skinned captain, etc., in *Blackwood*, p. 575.

[1] see *TNG, Ann. Rpt.*, 1921-2, p. 23.

[2] *TNG, Ann. Rpts.*, 1933-4, p. 22, and 1935-6, p. 21.

[3] *Eckert*, 1940, p. 32.   [4] *O'Reilly and Sédès*, pp. 191 ff.

the first time.[1] The movement even had its own red or black flags, with the letter P and a white cross. Vehicles and aeroplanes were shortly expected from Australia, via Germany, and thence to Buka, and one White man passing through Buka Passage was attacked.[2]

About this time the natives had to be forcibly prevented from boarding a trading vessel. The boat and her Cargo were theirs, they said, and the White crew were their ancestors.[3]

Pako, Muling and Terasim were soon arrested and exiled to Madang, where Pako died: Muling and Terasim were later allowed back to Buka.[4]

Things remained quiet for only a year or two. Then Sanop, ex-*tultul* and leader of the movement in Gogohei village, fell into frequent trances, and prophesied the coming of the Cargo ship. When it arrived, they would become the rulers of Buka, and Gogohei the leading village. Like Pako, Sanop did not have pacifist notions, or extend his egalitarianism to the Europeans: if the Government interfered, the police were to be shot. But whereas Pako had influenced all Buka, Sanop only controlled Gogohei.

Stores for the Cargo were built on the beach, but no major revival occurred until Sanop announced that the Cargo would not arrive while there was plenty of pig and taro to eat. One of the leaders prophesied a 'coming darkness', and precipitated a rush to trade-stores for miles around to purchase lamps and kerosene. As there was to be an earthquake which would dash the pile-dwellings to the ground, many people hurriedly built dwellings on the ground. Good Friday came, but no Cargo. Sanop mollified the villagers, but after a week of abstaining from work, things went back to normal. Sanop was finally arrested and given six months' gaol.[5]

The emphasis upon the abandonment of social distinctions, the sharing of property and the abandonment of worldly wealth was strongly marked in this movement, reflecting a high degree of social differentiation intensified by new social and economic developments. Besides the giving up of personal cash property, prophets stressed that the Cargo ship would bring tinned food for those

---

[1] TNG, *Ann. Rpt.*, 1933-4, p. 22.   [2] M(aurice) L(enormand), p. 83.
[3] *Leenhardt*, p. 63.
[4] see *Montauban*, 1934: *Eckert*, 1937; *PIM*, 20th December 1932, p. 46.
[5] *Die Katholische Mission*, Nov. 1934, pp. 309 ff., quoted in *Lommel*.

who lacked it, and that those owning large gardens or many pigs should give their food away in feasts if they wished to qualify for a share in the Cargo.

This emphasis upon democratic solidarity, symbolized in ascetic acts of renunciation and dedication to a new ethic is typical of all movements of this type. They have been vividly commented upon in medieval and Reformation movements by Engels:

'asceticism . . . is to be found in all medieval uprisings that were tinged with religion, and also in modern times at the beginning of every proletarian movement. This austerity of behaviour, this insistence on relinquishing all enjoyment of life . . . is a necessary transitional stage without which the lowest strata of society could never start a movement. In order to develop revolutionary energy, in order to become conscious of their own hostile position towards all other elements of society . . . they must begin with stripping themselves of everything that could reconcile them to the existing system of society. They must renounce all pleasures which would make their subdued position in the least tolerable. All the prophets of rebellion started with appeals against sin, because, in fact, only a violent exertion, a sudden renunciation of all habitual forms of existence could bring into unified motion a disunited, widely scattered generation of peasant grown up in blind submission'.[1]

These elements we have already noted in Melanesian movements —the sobriety and piety, the stress upon new rigorous moral observances, and restrictions of many kinds. But it is the 'violent exertion' which is the feature of greatest significance, and this takes other forms than asceticism. Thus, in Buka, the wealthier villagers were urged to share their wealth, but those who benefited in fact increased their intake of the good things of life. Their feasting, indeed, was the obverse of the renunciation of their wealthier fellows.

In Melanesia, the break with the past and the stress upon solidarity were often emphasized not only by the adoption of a severe ethic, but also, in accordance with traditional custom, by the holding of communal feasts, the obverse of asceticism. The people rejoiced in the prospect of the Coming, for it was to be a Coming

[1] *Engels*, pp. 74-76.

which they would enjoy, and for which they need not exert themselves; they had only to observe the prescribed cult ritual.

The arrest of Sanop did not cure him of his millenarian proclivities. Though other villages lost faith, Gogohei cleaved to him, and in 1935 signs of the revival of the burial-ground worship were noted by missionaries. The new movement spread into Bougainville where many of the northern groups had marked cultural affinities with the people of Buka.[1]

The people did not believe that Pako had died. They considered that he had been hanged by the Government and had given up his life to ensure the arrival of the Cargo. He had then risen from the dead and returned to his old house at Malasang. Sanop now moved to this place from Gogohei and held meetings at which Pako's spirit appeared to invited gatherings of men from all over Buka, telling them to organize and prepare for the Cargo ship. From a secret room in Pako's house a hidden man, probably Pako's brother, simulated the spirit. Sanop used to appear occasionally amongst the crowd outside the house in order to avoid the charge of ventriloquism, and listened to 'Pako' with the rest. In other 'miracles', Pako made rice and meat. Once more, an earthquake was to signal the arrival of the ancestors; then the people were to assemble at the cemeteries. Crowds now rushed to be baptized, and those who were already Protestants tried to change to Roman Catholicism.[2]

To propitiate the spirits and ensure a share in the Cargo, the villagers helped clean the cemeteries and erected flower-bedecked crosses and flagpoles on which flags were hoisted. At one village, a stone traditionally credited with magical power was moved from its site in the bush to a clearing and pulled across the newly-swept paths of the graveyard. Its power was said to be much increased. On Pororan Island, a mast was decorated with the old traditional plaited girdles of wild banana bark. On Bougainville, dogs and pigs were killed, in-law avoidances were abolished; women were now allowed to eat with the men and were allowed to see the initiation masks.

The movement became openly anti-European when an expedition to kill the Europeans at Rabaul was discussed. Then the Whites on Buka were suggested, missionaries amongst them. Sanop promised the arrival of motor-cars, planes and rifles, and

[1] *Blackwood*, pp. xii-xiii, 16-17.   [2] *O'Reilly*, 1937, passim.

each village started drilling with dummy carved rifles and sticks. The Germans were also said to be bringing the Cargo by some. 'Into the sea with the Whites!' was the order of the day, and victory was confidently expected. The Europeans were accused of hiding part of Christian doctrine and ritual: they concealed the fact that it was the ancestors of the natives who made the goods the Europeans received. Proof was available in the inability of Europeans to repair mechanical contrivances when they broke down; they had to be sent away for the ancestral spirits to repair.

On Bougainville, the movement appears to have been less radical. Flagpoles were erected for communication with heaven, but the teachings resembled those of orthodox Christianity. The people were to obey the missionaries and to go to church regularly; they were to give up pagan customs, such as polygyny, though the prophets were permitted by God to have more than one wife. On the material side, higher wages were demanded, and it was said that the provision of tools for government work should be the Government's responsibility.[1]

Beginning in April 1935, the movement assumed great proportions by September, the people expecting the imminent arrival of the Cargo and the establishment of native rule. Some of the Roman Catholic catechists and their followers expounded the message in the churches. Two Roman Catholic teachers and three *tultuls* were in the leadership, and even three of the Paramount Chiefs failed to report the movement to Government, because they were waiting to see what would happen.

An earth-tremor at Buka started the desertion of plantation labourers who proceeded immediately to assembly points. The Government now acted. On Bougainville, about 100 people were arrested.[2] On Buka, Government burned down Pako's house, arrested the leaders, but failed to seize Sanop who eluded them for two weeks before he was captured. When he was eventually taken, faith in him had deteriorated to such an extent that he had to be protected from an angry crowd.[3] And on Bougainville a famine resulting from the destruction of property sobered down the enthusiasts. There was now a return to the initiation cult, and

[1] *Montauban*, 1934, quoted in *Eckert*, 1940, p. 32.
[2] *Lommel*, p. 35.
[3] *TNG, Ann. Rpt.*, 1935-6; *O'Reilly and Sédès, loc. cit.*; *PIM*, 20th November 1935, pp. 10, 25-26.

those who had revealed the secrets of the masks were strongly attacked.

In spite of this disillusionment, many still expected the Germans, whose arrival, they said, had been frustrated by the Australians. Revived activity was noted in early 1939, possibly stimulated by a severe earthquake in southern Bougainville, but this outbreak was also suppressed.[1]

The final crisis came with the arrival of the Japanese. Now at last the millennium was clearly at hand. On the departure of the Administration, government stores were looted by the excited natives. Plainly, the strange Japanese were the expected bringers of the Cargo, not the Germans, and they were greeted with wild joy. Many believed that the Japanese, like the British, would soon leave also. It was decided to get rid of government-appointed native officials and to elect new governments of young men unafraid of Administrations. The Japanese suggested appointing a supreme chief for all Buka, but, owing to clan and other sectional rivalries, no agreement was reached on a candidate, and the scheme lapsed.[2]

By December 1942 each village had its own military organization with wooden guns or spears, and organized bodies of soldiers, messengers and police. Chiefs were provided with guards of honour, and were greeted with special ceremonial, including the Japanese bow. The natives found the Japanese ancestor cult particularly congenial.

The Japanese organized work-teams under strict military supervision to cultivate huge gardens for their own and the natives' food supply. The people were enormously impressed. 'Now', they said, 'we have the secret of riches which the Whites withheld from us.' This feverish activity was taken as a sign of the imminence of the Coming, and many visionaries prophesied the arrival of a 'King'.

This honeymoon was destined to end in tragedy, however, for conflict soon broke out between the natives and the Japanese. The details are somewhat obscure, but the real cause of the dispute was resentment at forced labour, at the false promises of the desperate Japanese and their growing thefts from household and garden, all of which, combined with Allied machine-gunning and bombing, reduced the people to misery and starvation. Alarmed

[1] *TNG, Ann. Rpt.*, 1939-40, p. 27.   [2] *Montauban*, 1948, pp. 136-7.

by the existence of a strong armed native movement of resentful islanders, the Japanese now sent two planes to arrest the leaders. After having been tortured, three of them were executed and the rest committed to prison. But some natives still persuaded themselves that the Japanese were hostile only to these leaders.[1]

With the arrival of the Americans there was great relief. A government officer told the people that a new life would begin after the war. The aim of the Government was to raise living standards to those of the Europeans. Wages would rise, hours of work would be reduced, and war damage compensation would be paid. Village Councils would be set up, and boys trained to take part in the Government with the Whites. The people would be allowed to build their villages wherever they liked. He then asked for suggestions from the islanders themselves.

At this, there was such great debate and so many meetings that the Government had to request calm. Eventually it emerged that the chief question was that of wages. No other problems were mentioned. Ex-soldiers argued that wages of as high as £1 per day should be demanded, but ultimately a claim of 4/6 per day was lodged. Wages were eventually fixed at 15/- per week plus food and tobacco. The Chinese traders were quite pleased, since this meant more trade in the stores, but White planters were not so pleased. The natives themselves were highly dissatisfied, and for long refused to offer for work. Finally, they began to drift back to work reluctantly, and even then a 'go-slow' policy was adopted by government labourers.

Only at Ieta was a Council formed—by a chief, without consulting the people at all. At the first meeting, fines of £1 for adultery and fornication were introduced—as Montauban cynically remarks, 'donnant ainsi champ libre aux plus fortunés'. The District Officer rebuked the people for their lack of initiative in the use of the Council.

War damage claims, prepared two years beforehand, were eventually paid. This delay had led to great distrust of Government's intentions, but in the end the people received amounts varying from £100 to £200, part of which was to remain in bank accounts. The schools were now strongly patronized, since these were the places where one could learn about the acquisition and counting of money. Older youths, however, became restless at merely learning

[1] see *O'Reilly*, 1947.

about money, and wanted to acquire some, and they began to drift to the plantations.

The persistence of these movements on Buka shows that mere failure of a prophecy is no assurance that a cult will lose its hold on the people. Indeed, failures can be interpreted in such a manner that they contribute to the strengthening of the basic concepts involved. A particular failure could be admitted without undermining the belief that other movements and other rituals might hold the key to the Cargo. Moreover, failures could always be attributed to the malice of the Europeans who were preventing the ancestors from coming. And although failures were real enough and directly observable, the reasons for the failures could not be so easily shown. Since there *was* no existent reality to which they referred, they could not be verified or disproved. The non-arrival of the spirits did not prove that they did not exist, and to the natives the non-existence of unobserved phenomena could only be asserted, not proved. And one could always point to happenings which could be attributed to ancestral intervention.

For throughout this period the fires of Cargo faith were fed by the inexhaustible fuel of social dissatisfaction. To people desperate for some explanation of the irrational and unjust world in which they lived, desperate for a solution to their problems and for a faith to steer by, attempts to prove deception by their leaders and attempts to tell them about the production processes of modern industry and to suppress the movements by force were futile. Stanner has remarked that 'to proscribe them would be like trying to tie water with string'.[1] Yet the tying has been constantly attempted.

[1] *Stanner*, p. 72.

CHAPTER VII

The Coming of the Japanese

Blow ye the trumpet in Zion, and sound an alarm in my holy mountain; let all the inhabitants of the land tremble: for the day of the LORD *cometh, for it is nigh at hand;*

A day of darkness and of gloominess, a day of clouds and of thick darkness

The sun and the moon shall be darkened, and the stars shall withdraw their shining

The LORD *also shall roar out of Zion, and utter his voice from Jerusalem, and the heavens and the earth shall shake: but the* LORD *will be the hope of his people, and the strength of the children of Israel . . .*

And it shall come to pass in that day, that the mountains shall drop down new wine, and the hills shall flow with milk.   Joel 2:1-2; 3:15-18

━━━━━

THE SWEEPING ADVANCE OF THE JAPANESE across the Pacific caught the various colonial Powers unprepared. New Guinea proved no exception; Rabaul was captured on 4th January 1942, New Britain and New Ireland occupied, and the coastal regions of the Mandated Territory mainland taken. The Japanese advance carried them into Papua and threatened Port Moresby; civil government came to an end in Papua with exodus of higher officials to Australia in mid-February. In areas such as Bougainville, New Britain and New Ireland—under Japanese occupation for over three years—the illusion that the Japanese were the expected deliverers was speedily dispelled, especially towards the end of the war when 'the Japanese, beleaguered and hungry, drove the natives from their villages and gardens, forcing them to live like nomads in hills and caves, and almost completely destroyed all crops, even devouring the taro stems and leaves'.[1]

In some areas, opportunity was taken for the wiping out of old scores. The handing over to the Japanese of a group of missionaries by natives of the Waria Valley was attributed to grievances going back to the early gold-prospecting days.[2] Höltker claims that

---

[1] *Stanner*, pp. 88-89.   [2] *Mair*, p. 200.

where Europeans were murdered or handed over to the Japanese, heathens were usually the culprits.[1] Some spots seem to have been at least generally sympathetic to the invaders, but, apart from the long-occupied regions, generalizations about Japanese-native relations are not easily made.

Rumours of the imminent Japanese arrival stimulated a wave of cults in many different areas, In the Gona-Buna area, old stronghold of the Taro Cult, an outbreak just before the Japanese landing was said to have had a 'prejudicial effect'.[2]

The Japanese sometimes attempted to manipulate Cargo movements for their own ends, and promised a rosy future under their aegis. On Karkar Island, a Japanese Officer told the natives that the Japanese had tried to come before, but had only just succeeded. Japanese, he said, worked; Europeans did not. Natives worked hard for the Whites, but received a poor return. Unlike the Whites, the Japanese did not eat apart from the natives. If they worked with the Japanese against the Europeans, they would receive motor-cars, horses, pinnaces, houses and planes. This speech was followed by a lavish distribution of loot.[3]

But this honeymoon was soon over in most areas. Over a quarter of the population were killed or died of sickness during the war in the Kokopo area alone. Health and social services were non-existent under the Japanese, but the invaders, on the other hand, did not place such heavy demands upon the local population for labour as did the Allied Forces.

After the physical devastation of people and livestock, huts and gardens, the large-scale dragooning of native labour was the most shattering effect of the War upon the lives of the native people. Compulsory carrying had never been popular. In Papua people had complained 'We are not horses or mules . . . let the Government get other beasts of burden.' But in order to supply the needs of the military for carriers, and to extend production of rubber and copra, a great drive for labour took place in the areas subject to Allied control. At its height the labour drive secured 28,000 men— more than double the pre-war labour force—from Papua, and 21,000 men from the diminished area of New Guinea under control, plus 5,000-6,000 volunteers.[4] Even the two- to three-year indenture period eventually established by mid-1943 was renew-

---

[1] *Höltker*, 1946, cited in *Lommel*, p. 38.   [2] *PIM*, January 1946, p. 52.
[3] *PIM*, November 1946.   [4] *Mair*, p. 190.

able by the military administration without the labourer's consent. And some of the methods used to get labour were not to be easily forgotten: 'hostages were held, and even men returned home not allowed to land until the required number of replacements presented themselves. As late as 1944 an experienced District Officer ordered signed-off labourers who refused to re-engage to be flogged—a means of persuasion which proved effective. Sometimes native police were sent on recruiting expeditions.'[1]

By drafting 5,000 labourers to the rubber plantations of Papua, production valued at around £3-4M was achieved for the period 1941-5. But many villages had been deprived of nearly 30% of their able-bodied males, and, in some cases, 40% and over. The increased burdens thrown upon the remaining men, women and children were often further added to by demands upon them for various services by the Military Administration, by local units, etc. And 61,000 natives were evacuated; in the extreme, the houses of people refusing to move were burnt down. Legal controls counted for little in such a period: the Lakekamu district, over-recruited in 1943, was subjected to an intensive recruiting-drive in 1945, contracts being for twelve months, with two-year contracts for natives who tried to avoid it.[2] The legal protection of the labourer was often minimal under these conditions; officials were instructed in 1943 that inspections disclosing complaints against natives were to be dealt with immediately; proceedings against employers were not to be instituted without higher authority.

Under these arduous conditions, in spite of vastly improved medical services, the health of the natives was undermined. Sick wastage among native carriers on the famous Kokoda Trail was 30% at its worst, and malaria and dysentery were introduced into the Highlands, previously free from these diseases.

Native experience of the hardships and horrors of the war had often been met with promises of the improvements to be expected on the expulsion of the Japanese. Yet expectations about the post-war world must have been given an ominous twist by the re-appearance of pre-war price discrimination in those areas subject to Allied control even before the war ended. The ratio of net profit to turnover in the case of merchandise sold to natives was two to three times higher than that for European trade.[3]

The natives, however, though they distrusted the New Guinea

[1] *op. cit.*, p. 188.　　　[2] *op. cit.*, p. 191.　　　[3] *Stanner*, p. 84.

'old hands', had a different attitude towards the Australian and American troops they met. Since German missionaries before the war had always referred to the representatives of the Administration as 'English' (in contradistinction to themselves), the natives also regarded the Australian officials and employers as 'English'. The troops they met in the war, however, called themselves 'Australians'. These 'Australians' were remarkable for their friendly egalitarian attitudes to the natives, the 'English' for their maintenance of colour discrimination, master-servant attitudes and contempt of the natives. ANGAU,* the administrative unit of the military, was classified as 'English'.[1]

The Mansren Myth

The most striking instance of the Japanese impact upon an area where millenarian cults had been occurring for many decades was reported from Dutch New Guinea. In the far west of the island, round the shores of Geelvink Bay and in the islands round the Bay—Numfoor, Biak, Japen, the Radja-Ampats, etc.—millenarian manifestations had been reported for a very long time. To understand later developments more fully, we must first look at these older manifestations.

It was in this area that the earliest instance of a millenarian prophecy in Melanesia occurred, as early as 1867, when a native declared himself to be a *konor*,† a herald or forerunner of a redeemer who would bring salvation and usher in the millennium.[2]

The myth round which this prophet built his doctrine has been recorded in considerable detail by several writers; we are fortunate in possessing, in addition, more than a dozen accounts, mainly by Dutch officials, of the various movements connected with the myth. These cover a period of some sixty-five years.

The myth of Mansren tells how, long ago, there lived on the islet of Miok Wundi an old man whose skin was wrinkled with age, and whose body was covered with sores, from which circumstance he was nicknamed Manamakeri, 'he who itches'.‡ Manamakeri

---

* Australian New Guinea Administrative Unit.

† The word *konor* is said to have been used by the Roon people of Geelvink Bay as a term for a shaman or magician (*van Hasselt, P. J. F.*, p. 93).

‡ Variants: Mandamakeri, Mansarmakeri, Mandarmiaki, Manarmaker, etc., from the root *maker*: to itch (*van Hasselt, P. J. F.*, p. 92).

[1] *Read*, 1947, passim.   [2] *Kamma*, p. 148.

greatly relished the wine which he obtained by tapping the flowers of a large *marĕs tree* (*Calophyllum inophyllum L.*). So greatly did he love this drink that he climbed the tree day after day to change the bamboo containers, in spite of his great age. But he began to notice that a thief was removing some of the liquid.

In order to trap the thief, he lay awake one night at the foot of the tree, and waited for him. But on climbing the tree later, he found that the thief had eluded him, for the tubes had been emptied, and he had heard nothing.

Next night, he waited again, but at the top of the tree. Before long the thief appeared, and Manamakeri grabbed him. It was none other than the Morning Star, Kuméseri!

The Star was ashamed and terrified. He besought Manamakeri to let him go, as dawn was approaching, and he feared the burning power of the sun. 'If you let me go', he said, 'I will compensate you for the thefts.' Manamakeri agreed, but waited to see what he offered before releasing him.

Firstly, the Star offered him a wand which would produce an abundance of fish. But Manamakeri said that he was not interested in the wand, for he got plenty of fish from his kinsmen, and he refused to release Kuméseri.

Then the Star, in desperation, showed the old man a tree whose leaves, if hung up near the house, would make Manamakeri famous and rich, and a great maker of praus. But Manamakeri refused this offer contemptuously, saying that he was too old to savour such pleasures (though he was lying, and only wished to get more out of Kuméseri).

By this time, it was growing very light, and the Star now offered even more attractive enticements. He now gave the old man some fruit from a *marĕs* tree and told him that if he threw this fruit at the breasts of a maiden she would become pregnant, and women would be attracted to him.

Manamakeri took the fruit contemptuously, but still did not release the Star.

Kuméseri now gave him a piece of wood. 'Whatever you draw with this staff', he said, 'will become real when you stamp your foot.' Then the old man released the Morning Star, though with ill grace, and made his own way home.

On his way, he met a beautiful maiden named Insoraki who was bathing in the sea. The old man threw the fruit at her, but missed.

However, the fruit flew by its own power so as to hit the girl between the breasts. Astonished, she threw the fruit away, but it kept returning by itself to her breasts.[1] She then left the water in terror, and Manamakeri went home, grinning.

Insoraki now became pregnant, much to her surprise and her relatives' anger. Their furious questions as to who was the father could only be answered by professions of ignorance, but she was naturally disbelieved.[2] And when Insoraki gave birth, her child was no ordinary mortal, for the boy spoke immediately after birth.

Her parents and kin were determined to find out who the father was. The child would recognize its father, they said, so they arranged a dance around the mother and child. Firstly, the young men danced, but there was no response from the child. Then the middle-aged men danced, with no result. Then the older men were tried, unlikely as that was. Manamakeri kept clear of the scene, frightened of the people's wrath. But eventually the child was brought even to him. To the people's horror and fury, the boy immediately claimed him as his father. At this time, the child was only two or three weeks old.

The furious islanders now decided to abandon the old man and his wife and child. The crime would infuriate the ancestral spirits, they said, and they would all perish if the trio were not expelled. The people thereupon destroyed their houses and gardens, and embarked in their canoes, some to Biak, others to the north, and others elsewhere. They also destroyed anything that might be used as a vessel by the outcasts.

Insoraki now upbraided Manamakeri, and the hungry child began to pester his mother for food. 'Go and ask your father for the flakes of his skin for food!' she shouted. 'I too am hungry.'

The child then went to his father, and the old man replied 'Go and look in the house; there is plenty of food there.' And indeed, there *was* food in abundance there, created by the magic staff.

Manamakeri began to feel that he did not suit his young wife. He therefore made a fire and stood in the flames. Then his old skin fell off, and changed into valuable brass gongs and armlets. Stepping out of the fire, he looked at himself in the water in a large shell. He was dissatisfied with his light colour, so he stepped back into the fire, until finally he was satisfied with his appearance. Then he

[1] *Tijdeman*, p. 254.   [2] *Encyclopaedisch Bureau*, p. 123.

donned the armshells, put decorative feathers on his head, and proceeded home.[1]

Insoraki was surprised to see a handsome youth and ran off, the youth pursuing her, while she shouted that she was a married woman and warned him that her husband was due home soon. Manamakeri succeeded in quietening her, and when he produced the brass gongs she began to believe him. But it was the miracle-child who finally convinced her by immediately recognizing his young father.

The trio now became rather lonely, so Manamakeri, taking the magic staff, drew a prau in the sand. He stamped his foot, and it sprang into reality, equipped with many rowers. Then they left the island, and made for the open sea and Biak.

During this wondrous voyage, Mansren * (the name by which the old man now became known), created various islands, because the little boy wanted to play on the land. Many social groups, too, claim their origin from this time: some claim direct descent from Mansren's family. The Numfoor people say that their four chiefly houses were originally created by Mansren to provide company for Insoraki. Mansren further gave the people their laws and customs, and instituted the men's houses.

On this miraculous journey, the prau moved *under* the water.[2] The details of the route vary considerably and it is clear that these variations are not without meaning. It is generally held that Mansren visited the islands between the Padaido group and Numfoor, Waigeo in the west, and the Mamberamo River in the east. The child is supposed to have died at Numfoor.

The route of the final departure also varies from one account to another. This final departure is held to have been caused by the doubts of the people. Mansren had always taken care of them, provided for them, and cured their sicknesses, but once, when he promised to save a sick child, and told the mother not to worry even if the child died, the mother became furious with him. Mansren, in his turn, became angry at this sign of little faith. He then left in a small canoe and was never seen again.

* or Manseren, meaning 'the Lord', from the root -*sren*: lord, ruler, etc., and the masculine prefix *man*-. This title is used with various accompaniments, e.g. Mansren Manggundi: the Lord Himself; Mansren Manamakeri; Mansren Koreri: from the *koreri* or millennium; Mansren Kakado, etc., etc.

[1] *van Hasselt, P. J. F.*, p. 94.   [2] *Encyclopaedisch Bureau*, p. 125.

It is clear that this myth follows the pattern of many traditional origin- and creation-myths. It validates existing social groups—chiefly houses, tribes, villages,etc.—as well as the physical environment. And the people point to the 'remains' of this wondrous Creation Period which give the existing social order mythological backing: Mansren's cooking-pot, now a stone; the ashes of the fire, Mansren's shell-mirror, a stone which was Mansren's gun, a big rock which was his anchor; at Miok Wundi, a very old *marĕs* tree, the one, it was said, from which he had extracted the wine, a big black stone which was his sharpening-stone, etc. Also on Miok Wundi was the site of his house.

Plainly, the variations in the details of the route of Mansren's final journey, the places and groups he created, and similar variations are not merely accidental variants, but reflect the different social origin and interests of the various informants who gave the different accounts. It is thus **probable** that there is, in fact, no one 'correct' version of the myth, but this aspect cannot be very precisely studied from the existing literature. Other indigenous origin-myths were later added in.

A complete text of an epic poem derived from the legend gives the words of Manamakeri, and recounts the people's hopes of his return.* For it was said that Mansren would return, and when he did, the Golden Age would begin. At the place where he now lived,† Mansren would plant a coconut which would grow into a huge tree reaching to heaven. Then it would overbalance and fall slowly down until it touched Miok Wundi. The *konor*, the miracle-child, would run across the trunk to Miok Wundi.

Then the delights of the Golden Age would commence: the old would become young, the sick well and the wounded unblemished of body. The dead would return; there would be plenty of women, food, weapons and ornaments. Youth, beauty, wealth and harmony were to be the order of the day in the *koreri*.‡ There would be no more work and no 'Company' (i.e.,the Dutch Administration), no forced labour and no taxation.

---

* dramatic enactments of the Mansren myth also occurred; see photo of a man acting the role of Mansren in *Held*, p. 203.

† in some early versions, Soep Kalinga, i.e. Indonesia; later, Singapore or Holland (*Hartweg*, pp. 46-58).

‡ etymologically derived from the root *-rer*: to slough the skin, e.g.,of snakes, or even of lobsters, according to most authorities.

Prophets of the Lord

The Mansren myth was noted as early as 1857. German Protestant missionaries had arrived in the area in 1855, followed by the Utrecht Missionary Society in 1862. Various reports in the journals of these societies, plus information obtained from a schooner captain, brought the Mansren myth to the notice of a few western European specialists.[1] But when the myth became associated with social movements, more attention was aroused.

In 1867, a native who gave out that he was a *konor*, a herald of Mansren, told the people to abandon their gardens and to begin dancing a 'murder song'. The enemies of the people were listed. But the information about this *konor* is slight; we know more about a later prophet who emerged in 1883.

This man, the Korano Baibo of Mokmer, a powerful village on the south coast of Biak, was the first *konor* to achieve a reputation outside his home area. When a comet appeared over Miok Wundi, he suggested that this was a sign of the wondrous return of a *konor* —none other than himself. The Korano was an astute but insincere man who had made a special journey to the Radja-Empat Islands and to Tidore, receiving from the Rajah of Tidore his title of Korano and some gifts. This gave him only limited authority among the people, especially since he merely used his new-found authority to claim women and 'presents' for himself and his family. But when he claimed to be a *konor*, people were attracted to Miok Wundi from all round Geelvink Bay. Only interested in personal gain, the Korano did not develop the revolutionary possibilities of the millenarian doctrine, but merely preached mild fertility doctrines, urging the people to multiply and to cultivate assiduously. He therefore encountered no opposition either from the Rajah of Tidore who claimed suzerainty over this region, and whose vassal in the Radja-Empats exacted annual tribute from the Papuans, or from the few Europeans.

By 1894, the Korano's star was on the wane, though the people feared to demand their presents back. He attempted to buttress his power by marrying his daughter to a Chinese, Lan Sen, a court interpreter for the Administration, who, like his wife's father, used his position to oppress the natives. But Lan Sen was finally exposed, and the Korano lost most of his power.[2]

[1] *Goudswaard*, pp. 84-94.　　　　[2] *Encyclopaedisch Bureau*, p. 74.

There then arose a succession of prophets, some of whom claimed to be merely heralds of the Lord Himself, others to be Mansren in person. Most of them were deported. One visited a mission station and suggested that the missionary should worship Mansren and pay the prophet. Another said that Mansren could fish Dutch dollars and blue cotton cloth up from the sea, could change little pieces of cigar into guns and the leaves of trees into fish. He could make old men young, turn grey hair black, and replace old teeth by new. The Wandamen prophet who appeared sometime later quickly lost his glory. He had instituted special songs, and assured the faithful that only they would secure the bliss shortly to come.

In 1886, a missionary reported the rise of another *konor*, again on Miok Wundi, in the Utrecht Missionary Society journal for that year (p. 66). This was the first prophecy of the coming of a ship full of goods, and the message found a wider audience than that of earlier prophets. A schooner captain who visited Miok Wundi at this time found the island full of people from different tribes: Roon, Waropen, Wandamen, etc. Such visits were kept secret from the missionaries.

A marked deterioration in Papuan-White relations appears to have set in around this time, though the Biak people had been feared by Europeans for a long time. The murder of the skipper of the *Corredo*, a small Dutch steamship, was due to the agitation of a *konor* who had believed himself superior to the Whites.[1] J. L. van Hasselt himself had had a narrow escape during riots a couple of years earlier, and blamed the hostility of the people partly on this *konor*, who ordered the people to sing all the time. The natives, lined up in troops, used to parade in front of their 'lord' singing such words as: 'We want to come to you, but we cannot; the strange Dutch birds are closing the door.'

When the boat of a Dutch official got stranded up the Mamberamo river, this was attributed to the power of the *konor*. Later the factories at Korido were attacked by a fleet of a hundred praus led by three men, one of whom was a *konor*. Twenty-two people are said to have been killed, but the *konor* himself escaped, and later even became a government headman, though with no special influence.[2]

In 1901, a District Officer received a mysterious gift of two

[1] according to J. L. van Hasselt in the Utrecht Missionary Society journal of 1887.   [2] see *Horst*.

marĕs leaves, on which little mannikins were drawn. This came from a man who had just arrived on Numfoor, though *neither by prau nor ship*. He had ordered the natives to take this 'letter' to his 'son', the District Officer. The officer would be sure to understand it.

The islanders spoke of the miracles performed by the *konor*. He had pulled an ironwood tree out of the ground; he had revived the dead; and he had said: 'When my son reads this message, he will come.' The officer consequently stayed put, only to see the prophet himself arrive in a beflagged prau to visit his 'son'. He told the official that he had come from heaven, and that he had decided not to call in at Mansinam Island as this would have caused it to sink into the sea! But the Dutchman, unimpressed, clapped him in irons; after his release the prophet had little further influence.

There were no further prophets until 1909-10, when an expedition of exploration up the Mamberamo started a new wave of excitement. An ethnologist on another expedition found himself taken for Mansren, for his medical cures soon gave rise to the rumour that he could revive the dead, make gold out of sand, etc.[1]

Some Papuans believed that the Whites were looking for slaves or gold, but the more sophisticated said that they were really searching for Mansren, who had disappeared on the upper reaches of the river. A native named Mangginomi started this rumour, which led to a general Papuan expedition to the Mamberamo from all the villages on the coast and on the various islands. The Papuans soon found that the Dutch expedition had retired, defeated by beri-beri. Hostile natives had predicted that their vessels would turn to stone, and, although this particular disaster did not occur, the expedition had indeed met with no success. And no one claimed to have seen Mansren except Mangginomi.

On his return Mangginomi based himself on Numfoor, and announced that he was a *konor*. He proclaimed the imminent coming of Mansren who had sent him.

If vast quantities of food were prepared for Mansren's reception, as well as women and many pieces of cloth, Mansren would appear at a special house built for the 'King of Papua', a building which was remarkably decorated with carved symbolic figures.

Mangginomi's influence grew rapidly, so that Government soon became alarmed. Attempts by officials to reach the island failed

[1] *Moszkowski*, p. 327.

owing to high seas supposedly sent by Mansren. Feeling now ran high, and riots broke out. It was said that a house had miraculously split in two, that the Rajahs of Tidore, Djailolo, Ternate and even the Rajah of Holland had all appeared—to announce the coming of the greatest of them all, the Rajah of Papua, Mansren.

Protestant teachers who attempted to undermine Mangginomi's influence were threatened with physical and mystical punishments, and their followers sneered at.[1] Excitement grew when Mangginomi declared that Mansren would not come whilst there were strangers in the land. He also urged passive resistance to labour for the Government and to payment of taxes. Mangginomi was thereupon arrested in May 1911, and sentenced to five years' hard labour. He appeared to be sincere and steadfast in his beliefs. Whilst he was in prison, the villagers sent praus carrying presents to relieve his sufferings, and when he returned from gaol in May 1916, his influence was still great on Numfoor.

When these events were drawn to the attention of regional specialists in Europe (via Moszkowski, and Orelli's *Allgemeine Religionsgeschichte* of 1913), it was suggested that this Redeemer myth would prove a valuable advantage to missionaries working in this region.

Similar myths have since been noted elsewhere in western New Guinea. In the Wissel Lakes region, the Migani have a myth concerning their culture-heroine Situgumina, who had gone away to Holland taking with her the power, cowries and other riches which then accrued to the Dutch.[2] Such myths seem to be modifications of existing myths adapted to the new situation created by the coming of the Europeans. How far some of them reflect Hindu or Islamic influences via Indonesia is impossible to judge, but millenarian ideas and millenarian movements were not unknown in that part of the world.* We have seen, too, that there was considerable intercourse between this part of New Guinea and eastern Indonesia. Many of the elements added to the myth, however, are clearly

---

* notably the expectations of the return of Jayabhaya, the twelfth-century Javanese king, the periodic rise of Muslim mahdis, *ratu adil*, and other prophets and messiahs in Java. Java witnessed the Samin movement as late as the 1920's. Borneo had its *njuli* movement, the Minehassa region of the Celebes its *mejapi*, and the Bataks of Sumatra the *parhu damdam* (*van der Kroef*, passim).

[1] *Tijdeman*, p. 255.

[2] *Rhys*, pp. 183-4, 187, 189; cf. *Quinlivan*, passim.

of European origin. The notions of original sin and of ultimate salvation in the Mansren myth were no doubt added under Christian influence.

By the time of the Mangginomi outbreak, this whole region had long been under White influence. The Utrecht Missionary Society had established itself at Mansinam around 1860, and at Manokwari in 1878. By 1908, there was a mission station at Nusbundi. The Dutch Administration established itself in the area in 1898, and in 1913 the first administrative officer was appointed to Bosnik island. It was after 1908 that the Mansren myth began to assume Christian elements and became more revolutionary in tone. Its interpreters now forecast the inversion of the present social order: Papuans would become Whites, and the present Whites would have to clear gardens while their former subjects ate rice.

The Mansren myth was thus, in its earliest phases, harmless enough. Indeed, the earliest clashes with the Dutch were not couched in terms of the Mansren ideology at all: the uprising of 1906 in Makuker and Arwan, for example, was occasioned by the imposition of forced labour for road-building. Even the risings of 1921 and 1926 under Aweho and Aduweri were not connected with the Mansren belief.

But although political resistance was thus not limited solely to millenarian forms, the latter remained very common, especially as the open secular expression of anti-Administration feeling was dangerous. Moreover Christianity, which supplied so much of the new content infused into the Mansren myth, became very widespread during this period. Between 1905 and 1940, 30,000 natives were nominally converted to Christianity on Biak and Supiori alone. They built their own churches and often the missionaries let them carry on with the work, only giving occasional advice. It may well be that we have here an instance of a phenomenon amply documented from other areas, i.e., a trial period in which the people experimented with Christianity as a means of obtaining material rewards.

Following the secular incidents of 1921 and 1926, two minor prophets sprang up, though with little success.[1] But a movement in 1928, headed by one Wasjari, was more effective. He prophesied the coming of Mansren in ten days' time and urged the people to stop working. In order to save the faithful in the terrible darkness

[1] *ten Haaft*, 1948a, p. 113.

to come, when the world would sink, he drew a large canoe in the sand. Once more, the Government intervened and arrested the prophet, who was sentenced to eight months' imprisonment.

This led to yet another outbreak. Representatives had been sent to Wasjari from people living in the Gulf of Manjalabit. The Gulf people now adopted the movement and, despite the suppression of Wasjari, a new prophet arose in their midst, a man named Tanda. Tanda began to have visions of Mansren and revelations that Mansren would come to earth at Tanda's village, arriving in a ship two miles long. Huge crowds now collected and people prostrated themselves before Tanda, who slept in his house, covered with a white cloth. But after eight nights' vigil Mansren failed to appear.[1] About this time, Wasjari was freed, and thousands flocked to see him at the house built specially for the reception of Mansren. He was now rearrested and gaoled once more, for four months.

Two more pre-war prophets must be briefly noted because they made important additions to Mansren ideology. In 1934, a *konor* predicted not merely the coming of a four-funnelled steamer with Mansren on board but an event which was to become a very important element in the Cargo ideology of northern Dutch New Guinea movements: the miraculous coming of a factory. This *konor* made considerable profit out of the large crowds who visited him from tribes living as far as 150 miles' journey away.

In 1936, a prophet claimed to have seen Mansren accompanied by the Queen of Heaven. He not only demanded that the teacher, missionary and district officer should all be killed, but, before he died in 1938, is said to have predicted that Mansren would cause a war between the Japanese and the Dutch.

The Fight for Deliverance

We have seen how nearly every year during the decade leading up to World War II saw the rise of a *konor*. The constant suppression of independent native organizations built up to a situation which was bound to end in violence. Little by little the Mansren myth strengthened its hold upon the imagination of the natives: not only was the order of society to be inverted, but even the order of Nature itself. Yams, potatoes and other tubers would grow on trees like fruit, while coconuts and other fruit would grow like tubers. Sea-creatures would become land-creatures, and vice versa. In-

[1] *Kamma*, pp. 151-2.

deed, 'not only the whole world, but the whole cosmos [was] involved'.[1] All temporal boundaries were to be destroyed and a new heaven and earth would replace the old.

This ideological inversion of the cosmos was given the seal of religious authority by identifying the natives and their villages with figures and places mentioned in the Bible. Villages were renamed Galilee, Jericho and similar names, and one leader, who called himself 'Mozes', retired for divine inspiration to a mountain which was renamed 'Mount Karmel'.

By these actions, the enthusiasts symbolically resumed their long-denied rights: the special connection of the Papuans with Christianity and the Bible, which the Europeans had for so long usurped, was reasserted. The Whites had hidden the fact that Jesus Christ was a Papuan by tearing out the first page of the Bible. But the cult leaders exercised special Biblical powers: they could raise the dead, speak with tongues, etc. Psalms and hymns consistent with the message of Mansren were sung, and Biblical texts were selected which favoured the cult doctrine.

The Bible, with its multiple component strands of religious thought, allows such selection to be easily made. These Papuans are typical of all millenarists who select not those passages favouring acceptance of their earthly lot but the apocalyptic passages prophesying the imminence of the millennium, and the message of hope contained in the Resurrection. They select not those passages enjoining resignation in the face of hardships and miseries on this earth but those which imply 'muscular Christianity', the righting of wrongs by the faithful themselves. They do not believe in the perpetuation of a universe in which there is for ever to be a miserable life on earth and an ultimate heaven after death. Their millennium is not a vague, remote dream. They seek to make heaven on earth, in the here and now. And they draw strength from the many close parallels between the simple life of Old Testament society and their own; plainly, it cannot be their idle and luxury-loving rulers who are the true heirs of the Bible. It is the native people themselves who must be the Chosen, for they are simple peasants and herdsmen, people whose customs—initiation, polygyny, etc.—are often similar to those depicted in the Old Testament. Like the Jews, also, they have laboured under oppression and wait to enter the Promised Land. To such people,

[1] *de Bruijn*, p. 6.

the Old Testament and the apocalyptic writings of the New generally have the greatest appeal.

Of the many Mansren movements which developed on the basis
of this appeal, the first to spark into large-scale violence were those
which led into and developed out of World War II.

In 1939, an old leper woman named Angganita, a baptized
Christian living on a small islet off one of the Schouten Islands,
had recovered miraculously on several occasions when she had
seemed to be on the point of death. Five times she was expected to
die, and five times she recovered. She seemed to possess the secret
of eternal life, and first her family, and later others from near and
far came to see this miracle-woman. She now began to have visions
and saw lights and heard voices.[1]

Her activity was first reported by native teachers to the Administration. An official then came and interrogated the village
headmen who were clearly trying to conceal something. As the
people seemed hostile, and the islet was well populated, the official
had to send for help. Angganita was then taken to Serui, but was
allowed to go in a canoe, paddled by her own clansmen. When she
arrived, it was found that the relevant papers had not been sent
with her; no investigation could be held, as the only witnesses were
Angganita's own people. Public sympathy for Angganita was great
in Serui, and collections were made for her, so the Administration
was obliged to release her, after extracting a promise from her and
her clansmen that they would desist from subversive activities.
These promises might have been kept had public interest not been
so powerful a pressure, for shoals of canoes now came to visit
Angganita. She told these people how she had outmanoeuvred
Government, and began to preach resistance to the Dutch. She
recounted the stories of other *konors*, and foretold the comings of
ships with many masts, bearing the ancestors aboard and loads of
Cargo. There were rumours of miracles in which houses 'grew'.
Angganita now renamed the islet Judea, and another, Gadara; her
village became Bethlehem, and a small river, Jordan. She instituted rites of initiation into the movement, went into trances, and
spoke with tongues, as one native significantly remarked 'like the
early Christians'.[2]

The Government now struck. Angganita was arrested and
gaoled. But the movement could not be held back. All Biak was in

[1] *ten Haaft*, 1948b, pp. 163-4.   [2] *Teutscher*, p. 414.

uproar: riots broke out in which one native official was killed and another wounded.

The movement now began to snowball. It was said that Mansren had gone to the Netherlands after leaving New Guinea, but was returning to Biak via Germany or Japan. Native songs told how Holland had been defeated and occupied because Mansren had left Holland—where he had gone before the war to buy Cargo— and set out for his homeland. They sang of the Coming of Mansren, when the Deluge would take place and a vast Heaven ship would come floating on the waters. To prepare for this event, large numbers of praus and rafts were built. Moreover, the leaders proclaimed, manna would not fall from heaven unless the people did their share by dancing and singing a special dance, full of power-creating magic. Hundreds of men and women danced day and night in ecstasy, praying to the ancestors and expecting an earthquake, the sign of Mansren's arrival, hourly.[1] The songs became martial, exciting the people; they told of incidents in the life of Mansren—Tuan Allah—and of his power. And the people poured forth presents to the *konors*: sago, bird-of-paradise feathers, and so on.

Strangers were excluded from these ceremonies, and it was preached that there was no longer any need to pay taxes. Gardens were harvested and pigs slaughtered; if this were not done, the *koreri* would never come, manna would not fall, and the people would be condemned to a life of toil in the gardens. The movement had become at this stage 'far less a religion than a self-conscious Papuan cultural nationalism'.[2] In their songs, the natives sang of their native land, and of their culture-heroes, prophesying the extension of their rule over areas where those heroes had once held sway.

The weapon of Christianity was turned against the Europeans who brought it. The natives, among 'the most educated and civilized of Papuan peoples',[3] even attracted Ambonese Christians to their secret meetings in the jungle. They utilized such themes as the Virgin Birth, declaring that Mansren had been born in this miraculous fashion. The theme of inversion was symbolized politically by the adoption of the Dutch tricolour in reverse as the flag of the Papuan kingdom. This was only justice, since, like the hidden part of the Bible, this flag was really theirs, but had been taken from them.

[1] *Lekahema*, pp. 98-99.   [2] *de Bruijn*, p. 10.   [3] *Pos*, p. 561.

By 1942, just before the arrival of the Japanese, the movement was becoming more and more violent and revolutionary. Real leadership passed from Angganita to Stephanus Simiopiaref, a Biak man serving a gaol sentence for murder, who was released by the Japanese when they swept into the area. Many government coolies and missionary trainees were also returned home.

These men were thus predisposed to help the Japanese and to listen to their propaganda, which told them that all Papuans were going to be free and promised them a share in the Japanese Co-Prosperity Sphere in East Asia. There had been no military resistance. This sweeping victory by an Asian army over the now-interned Whites; the vast numbers of the Japanese and their plentiful equipment, especially their trucks; their feverish activity in building roads, airdromes and defence works—all these made the deepest impression upon the Papuans.

When Stephanus returned to Biak, he found a large meeting in progress; he now stepped forward with prophecies of a Papuan empire from Gebe to Hollandia. Secret army units were now formed—supposedly to the cabalistic number of 8,888 men—and houses were built in a new village ready for the millennium.

Stephanus Dawan, an important leader who had killed the policeman earlier, prophesied that a warplane factory would appear. The Administration had kept 'modern things' from the natives, and deceived them with 'rubbish and lies'. Now goods in abundance were to be theirs, including the most modern equipment.

Visions were now seen on all sides, and one leader gathered thousands of the faithful together in a large stockade to await the Coming. Stephanus Dawan claimed that he had been taken to heaven with his wife Theodora, and that Jesus himself was Theodora's child. Stephanus assumed the title 'Ara Supiori' (?Allah; Supiori: an island); other leaders took such titles as 'Administration', 'Mansren Allah', 'Guru' (teacher), 'Mansren Jesus', 'Radja Masi' (Prince of Baptism),etc. Theodora had the title 'Wilhelmina' and Angganita became 'Radja America', or according to other accounts, 'Maria'.

Stephanus Simiopiaref was 'Radja Damai' (Prince of Peace), a title also used by other leaders such as Jan Simiopiaref, his brother, and Korinus Boseren. This reflects the uncentralized nature of the movement and the lack of coordination—even, at times, the hostility—between the various groups. Each village had its own 'radja' with his staff, and each group their own flag. Strongly organized in military fashion, they were nevertheless independent units, though with some recognition of Stephanus Simiopiaref's special position; but even leaders could not control their followers always. Leadership was vested in the equivalents of generals, high-ranking officers, lieutenants and privates, the last being known as 'apprentices'. Even 'doctors' were appointed, together with 'ministers' and 'radio telegraphists' for the 'radio stations'. Frequently, home-made uniforms were worn, with turbans appropriate to the rank; leaders wore cloth badges of rank. The troops were armed with wooden 'rifles' and bush-knives which were to be transformed at the Coming into real weapons. Special agents made note of non-cooperators and arrested hostile elements, but confidence was more positively reinforced by propaganda about the magical efficacy of a holy-water drink of invulnerability. This would effectively protect the user if certain taboos were observed. Bullets striking the user's body would turn to water.*

The ideology was spread and strengthened by the appointment of special 'apostles'. One of the reasons for native backwardness, they said, had been their ignorance of other languages; they would be taught Dutch, English and Chinese by special teachers in the millennium.

The movement developed rapidly under Japanese rule. Though the latter were greeted as liberators at first, these illusions soon died, and hopes of asking the Emperor of Japan to recognize the official flag of the 'Papuan Kingdom' were speedily dispelled. A few leaders still assisted the Japanese, but the others were soon in violent conflict with them.

Preparations were made for resistance, with some effort at organizing a commissariat. The destruction of the gardens was stopped, and at one time Korido supplied Biak with sago. But famine eventually appeared as the rapacious Japanese collected food-levies. Their rule was specially severe because this area contained their administrative headquarters, where they employed hundreds of natives in building work. The rule of the Dutch was now seen to have been replaced by something worse. Before long, the doctrine of freedom from all foreign control was in the air.

---

* Similar beliefs have been found in many uprisings, for example in the Maji-Maji Rebellion of 1905-6 in Tanganyika and in many well-known Islamic uprisings (*maji*: water in Kiswahili).

Dutch missionaries had been attacked and killed, churches and schools burned down. Now, the death of many Japanese, but of none of the natives, during Allied air-raids was a sign that the Papuans were the Chosen People, and that the turn of the Japanese had come.

Stephanus Simiopiaref's group had already captured Sowek on 6th July 1942, taking prisoner Chinese traders and an Ambonese teacher whom he imprisoned and tortured. Next day, an attack on Korido was narrowly averted, though prisoners were taken. The Japanese now decided to strike, and were probably assisted by Ambonese informers. On the 13th July, a captured Dutch vessel was sent to bombard Rani, and as the Mansren followers sailed out to the attack in their canoes, convinced of their invulnerability and waving their wooden rifles, they were met with a withering hail of fire from machine-guns. There were many casualties, Stephanus amongst them, though some say he was beheaded later, together with Angganita.

Even this slaughter did not mean the end of the general movement. Those villages which refused to join in were attacked; Japanese patrols were captured and killed. Papuan security precautions were very effective, and diversionary action was sometimes taken by delivering up innocent villagers to the Japanese as Mansren adherents; these unfortunates were tortured and beheaded. In revenge for the killing of Japanese, one prophet named Nimrod was shot on Serui football ground.

The fight was now carried on by groups scattered all over the islands and the coast, each for itself in a confused rash of fighting. Some who had cooperated with the Japanese, like Stephanus Dawan, now began to talk of cooperation with the approaching Americans. The Japanese therefore arrested him and beheaded him to discourage further defections.

Jan Simiopiaref's group set up its headquarters near Mokmer airstrip, which became an assembly point for the people, who ignored the Japanese when they arrived. After issuing threats that the airstrip must be cleared, the Japanese returned a month later and, finding the people massed on the strip, machine-gunned the crowd. Some five hundred were killed in this slaughter in which Biak policemen, collaborating with the Japanese, proved themselves particularly vicious.

On Biak, the band under Korinus Boseren was now the principal group still fighting. Korinus had been imprisoned in 1932, but had succeeded in escaping to Biak. The District Officer, aware of this, wrote to the authorities, but received no answer, Korinus was therefore able to stay on Biak, and even ultimately became a village headman. He was a model of cooperation. He was catechized and christened, went to church regularly, cooperated with the Administration, and collected and paid in the taxes promptly. But fate caught up with him when he was sent for by the District Commissioner on a false pretext, and gaoled until the Japanese released him.

Korinus' group was very aggressive. He cooperated with Jan Simiopiaref in a raid in which Chinese shops were looted and a mission teacher killed. A White official had been killed earlier. The people of north Biak now concentrated in his 'town' at Wopes. A Japanese representative now visited Wopes, accompanied by some Biak collaborators from one of Stephanus Dawan's groups, and an Ambonese interpreter. The Japanese officer made a threatening gesture with his sword while speaking. Korinus, taking no risks, leapt forward and struck the officer down with a bush-knife. The interpreter was also wounded in the mêlée, and later died.

In revenge, the Japanese despatched a punitive expedition. The inhabitants of one village were mostly wiped out and many tortured. Korinus himself died an ignominious death, stabbed by a member of his own family, who was tired of resisting the Japanese.[1]

There were also smaller groups in west Biak, on Numfoor, and one on Japen Island under the command of a teacher. This latter, however, terrorized teachers and even raided Serui itself. But despite the raid, and the propaganda among the people, the authorities were able to stop the further spread of the movement.

In general, the Japanese succeeded in crushing these bands one by one before they became too dangerous. Fearful that their airstrips would be endangered, they ruthlessly deported whole villages, beheaded and tortured many people, and laid heavy burdens of forced labour upon men, women and children. But if the Japanese had turned out to be false liberators, there were others at hand. Rumours of a new Saviour were stimulated by the sight of stranded lifeboats, and by garbled stories of submarines belonging to the approaching Allies.

It was with immense relief and joy that the people welcomed the

[1] *ten Haaft*, 1948b, pp. 3-4.

American attack on Biak in 1944. The 5,000 Japanese soldiers were speedily disarmed and then began the operations which probably made more impact upon the islanders than the actual military victory itself—the unloading of the war material. Just as prophesied, ships and landing-craft of all kinds poured out their cargo upon the beaches. The air was thick with rumour: more and more huge *konor*-ships were coming. Biak, which had never been a great sago-producing area, was short of food. The natives were given food by the Americans and were even handed weapons to help in hunting down the Japanese stragglers. One Dutch guilder was offered for a Japanese head; later only two ears had to be produced.

Plainly, these were the true deliverers, though there was sometimes a little friction with them: islanders objected when enthusiastic American souvenir-hunters snapped up nearly all their everyday equipment, even when they were paid well. But the removal of the population from Miok Wundi in order to make room for a U.S. Navy Base was taken as a particularly happy augury, in spite of the hardships entailed for the islet's population. The goods and stores here and elsewhere were plainly foretastes of future riches. As they paddled their canoes, the people sang, 'When the Americans go, all will be ours.'

The restarting of schools in 1944 aroused little interest since people felt it hardly worth while going to school when the millennium was at hand. In addition, anti-mission feeling still ran high, and there were even a few who expected the return of the Japanese.[1]

But the millennium did not come, and the American cargo did not accrue to the people. Bit by bit, the hard facts were borne in upon the Papuans, and the belief in the imminence of the *koreri* waned. Symbolically, the now huge coconut tree of Manamakeri at Miok Wundi was bulldozed out of the ground by the U.S. Navy.

Elsewhere in Dutch New Guinea, resistance to foreign rule, both Dutch and Japanese, was less highly organized, except for movements in the Hollandia area. Here a man named Simson carried on the tradition of the earlier Lake Sentani prophets. He prophesied that a Papuan Messiah, now in the Netherlands, was about to appear, and all strangers would be wiped out. The Japanese countered this threat by killing Simson on Sentani airstrip.

Hollandia was later the base for 400,000 American troops. The Papuan population was astounded by the equipment of the Ameri-

[1] *ten Haaft*, 1948a, p. 77.

cans, who were served by 200 cinemas, but, as with the Mansren movement, there was no further millenarian outbreak in the area until after the Allied troops had departed.

The effect of this invasion was visible in one post-war outbreak in the Nimboran area when people built special Cargo houses in the cemeteries and, imitating the troops, constructed 'hospitals' staffed by 'doctors' and 'nurses'. There was special stress on the expectation of a factory rising from the earth, an event which the Dutch officials were invited to witness.[1]

We have now seen how the most advanced of the cults were developing away from magical techniques towards secular political action. But amongst more advanced sections of the population, orthodox secular political movements were beginning to emerge side by side with the more bizarre millenarian cults. In such areas as Biak, where the people were far removed from tribalism, there was a growth of secular political movements, some of them stimulated by, and in contact with, the revolutionary movement in Indonesia.[2] These movements appear to have been suppressed at a later date.

Many of the features of the Dutch New Guinea movements are thus strikingly similar to those found in the territories to the east. How far this may be attributed to direct contact it is difficult to say, though the war did much to bring the natives of the various parts of Melanesia into closer contact with each other. But even if notions of the Deluge, a Heaven-ship, etc. are found elsewhere, the Dutch New Guinea movements have certain ideological elements of their own, particularly the notion of the miraculous appearance of a factory. The course of development of the Mansren movement, however, is a particularly striking instance of a process we have already noted. It began with the use of an indigenous myth as a passive and non-violent millenarian reaction to Administration and mission control. It ended by the creation of well-organized and disciplined bodies which used armed force in the effort to drive the foreigners from Papua.

[1] *van Baal*, 1952, p. 494; and 1953, passim.
[2] see *UN*, Irian Committee, 15th August 1950, for remarks on the emergence in Dutch New Guinea (Irian) of the Komite Indonesia Merdeka (KIM), the Freedom Party of Indonesia Irian (*PIDRIS*), etc.

CHAPTER VIII

The Movements in the New Hebrides

> *But the fearful, and the unbelieving, and the abominable,*
> *and murderers, and whoremongers, and sorcerers, and ido-*
> *laters, and all liars, shall have their part in the lake which*
> *burneth with fire and brimstone : which is the second death.*
> Revelation 21:8

THE ISLANDS OF THE NEW HEBRIDES GROUP suffered greatly during the last century from 'blackbirding' of labour recruiters who took thousands of natives from the islands, often by force or deceit, and shipped them to the plantations of Queensland or Fiji, from which many of them failed to return. Disease and mortality rates on the estates were high; at the very worst they reached as much as 750 per 1,000.[1] And there was little interest in seeing that the labourers got back to their own islands after their term was over.

A disastrous decline in population took place in the Solomon Islands and in the New Hebrides. The population of Aneityum, in the New Hebrides, for example, declined from some 5,000 in 1839 to 199 in 1943; that of Tanna from between 15,000-20,000 in 1872 to 6,000 in 1926; that of Aniwa from 192 in 1894 to 140 in 1910.[2]

These inroads on native society soon attracted the attention of scientists. The views of Rivers, who attributed the bulk of the decline to 'interference with social customs, notably head-hunting, this promoting lassitude, lack of interest in life, and therefore decreased will to have children'[3] were for long widely accepted.

Belshaw, however, sums up his authoritative survey of the question by observing that 'violence and the introduction of new diseases would appear to be the prime causes of depopulation'. It is therefore to the blackbirders, who introduced firearms and diseases, that the decline in population must be attributed.

---

[1] *Belshaw*, 1954, pp. 39-40.
[2] *op. cit.*, pp. 188-90, and *New Hebrides, Col. Ann. Rpt.*, 1921-2, p. 4.
[3] *Belshaw, op. cit.*, p. 92.

And of labour recruiting after the establishment of the Anglo-French Condominium over this group of islands, Belshaw remarks: 'Since the Condominium the graver abuses have been checked, but still, in 1946, numerous accusations were being made of traffic in liquor, of the use of women as decoys, and of debt to force labour to work beyond its contracted period. Inspection by most administrative officers of the Condominium was an empty formality.'[1]

Even after the suppression of the worst excesses of the black-birding era, European diseases and the sale of alcohol and arms all continued to devastate the population. Deacon remarked of Male-kula in the 1920's: 'Whole districts have vanished, while in the areas remaining the population consists largely of men back temporarily between periods of work in the big plantations. . . . The result is that the pattern and flow of native life is broken; the body politic is a desiccated corpse.'[2]

But if the islands were valued as a source of labour, they did not become important centres of plantation development themselves. Only four or five settlers lived on Ambrym, for instance, before World War II. The Condominium Government had slender financial resources and small staff. It is therefore universally spoken of as an example of ineffectiveness which has become almost a byword, symbolized in the popular name of 'Pandemonium'. Education and medical services were described recently as 'not worth mentioning'.[3]

In this vacuum of civil government the power of the missions was greatly enhanced. The first Protestant missionaries arrived in 1848; it was not until 1906 that the Condominium Government was established. The missions reigned supreme, with their own courts and their own laws.[4] Their interference in the lives of the natives early attracted official notice and criticism. Comments on the suppression of native institutions were severe, and the 'would-be civilizers' were said to have 'no consideration of the effects, positive or negative, good or ill, of such instruction on the native mind or character'. Those things in which the natives took pleasure, it was said, were suppressed.[5]

[1] op. cit., p. 36.   [2] Deacon, p. 22.
[3] Belshaw, 1950a, p. 92; see also the figures on p. 14.
[4] Barrow, p. 379.
[5] New Hebrides, Ann. Rpt., 1923, p. 5.

Espiritu Santo: *The Naked Cult*

On the island of Espiritu Santo, the impact of the Europeans had disastrous effects. By the turn of the century the island was in a state of anarchy: feuds, infanticide and epidemics were rife. Outbreaks of violence were common, and several Europeans were killed. Most of these killings were straightforward murders, as in the case of the Greig family murders in 1908, but the murder of a British planter named Clapcott in 1923 at Tasmalum in the south of the island was somewhat different.

The Clapcott murder, it transpired, contained millenarian elements, though the idiom was pagan and not Christian. 'Clapcott had been for some years on rather bad terms with most of his native neighbours, who accused him of interference with their women. He had been subjected to assaults and some destruction of his coconut trees.'[1]

The killing was sanctioned by an ancient myth which told how, when a noted native murderer was finally done to death himself, all his victims came to life.[2] The murder had been carried out on the orders of a native named Runovoro or Rongofuro[3] who had been educated at the Presbyterian central school and who was now organizing a movement aiming at the extermination of all Europeans. Clapcott had been the first to go; Runovoro promised that if the other Europeans were killed, the dead would arise, and the ancestors would return from a far land where the Whites had sent them. He soon gained a wide following in central Santo, and charged a fee for admission into the movement, ranging from 5/- to £1. His agents covered the whole island in their organizing campaign.

Runovoro prophesied that the ancestors would arrive after a Deluge in a great white ship loaded with Cargo. This would only be distributed to paid-up members. His followers built a large store for the Cargo; once they nearly seized a recruiting schooner, for 'every passing sail aroused great excitement and fire-signals from the anxious watchers posted on the beach'. Plantation workers were convinced by Runovoro's ability to write meaningless marks, and the prophet was credited with having raised from the dead not

---

[1] *Guiart*, 1951c, p. 86; other accounts describe Clapcott as an inoffensive man.

[2] *Williams*, 1928, p. 100.   [3] see the account in *Guiart*, 1956b.

only human beings, including one of his followers who 'died' in the excitement of a dance, but also a dead cow.

The awakening of the dead was constantly postponed, but this only strengthened the more radical wing of the movement. The demand 'Santo for the Santoese' was put forward, and the death of the Whites called for, since they were preventing the resurrection of the dead.

'The culmination was a tragedy which occurred on the 24th of July last year [1923]. Ronovoro was holding a great "sing sing" at the conclusion of which the resurrections were to take place. Probably it was decided then that the Europeans were to die. A half-caste visited this "sing sing" and was recognized by Rono-voro as his deceased son. The resurrection bodies were to be white-skinned. The half-caste did not appreciate his adoption and took the first opportunity for flight. In the middle of the "sing sing", Ronovoro's wife died and when all attempts to raise her to life failed, he declared that Clapcott was the cause and must be killed before she would come to life. Five men were sent to shoot this planter, who was an inoffensive man, deaf and in a very lonely place. He was shot, his body mutilated, and parts of it eaten.'[1]

In retaliation for the murder, HMS *Sydney* shelled the bush.[2] Eighteen men were arrested and seventeen tried, one having died in the meantime. Of these, six were sentenced to death (three of the sentences being commuted), and six others to varying terms for stealing the dead man's goods: five were acquitted. Ronovoro himself firmly believed in his own invulnerability, as he had already returned from the dead once, and faced execution quite fearlessly.

Little further was heard of the movement, though it was known to be persisting among the inland tribes, until an outbreak in 1937 was suppressed, and the leader arrested; he later died in prison. Once more, the Cargo myth and the theme of the White man's interference were put about; now, however, the Cargo was to be landed where Clapcott had been killed.[3]

Friction between White and Black was still strong. In the early part of the war, when a volcano erupted on Lopevi, the population

[1] The Rev. Raff in *Williams*, 1928, pp. 100-101.
[2] *Harrisson*, pp. 380-1.
[3] *Guiart*, 1951a, p. 128; see also *Simpson*, pp. 114-9.

was evacuated to Paama, and settled there. But the evacuees refused to accept government assistance in the shape of food. Earlier, there had been refusals to accept Coronation medals from the High Commissioner, since this was feared to be the prelude to the introduction of poll-tax. One chief of Paama was found guilty of spreading 'false rumours' and imprisoned for creating trouble, but even worse rumours circulated after his release.[1] And native attempts to play off the British against the French were standard tactics by this time.

The full impact of the war was not so devastating in the New Hebrides as in those parts of the Solomons, the Bismarck Archipelago and New Guinea directly affected by the fighting. But the large-scale activities of British and American forces in the New Hebrides, and rumours of events in the north, had powerful repercussions.

With the end of the war, missionaries on Santo began to be alarmed by the recrudescence of Cargo notions. At first only two small villages were affected, but the movement—now called variously the Naked Cult, Malamala or Runovoro School—spread to a large number of villages by 1948, and was openly anti-White. Over a third of the population of some districts in the southern half of the island was affected.[2] The originators of the cult, in central-west Santo, had difficulty in controlling the eastern area.[3]

The leader of the movement, Tsek, advocated the destruction of native-owned European goods as well as the products of indigenous crafts, the killing of all stock, and refusal to work for Europeans. Existing huts were to be burnt down and replaced by communal houses, two in each village, one as sleeping-place for the men and one for the women. It was forbidden for families to cohabit at night, and this domestic communism was reinforced by the construction of a large kitchen for each house, where cooking was allowed only in the mornings.

Special steps were taken to emphasize the abandonment of the past: many important taboos were scrapped, clan exogamy and bridewealth abolished. Although the movement embraced many different language groups, a new 'language' was now adopted. It

[1] *PIM*, 15th March 1940, p. 45.
[2] Belshaw notes that 'the inland villages of Aoba and Espiritu Santo are not visited' by administrative officers (1950a, p. 12).
[3] *Miller*, pp. 330 ff.

was said that it was America who would bring everything the people wanted, and that there would be no death.[1] Thus the destruction of property was not merely asceticism; it was an affirmation of faith in a future of plenty. The replacement of the ancestors by the Americans is common in these post-war movements, and reflects the effect made upon native consciousness by the plentiful equipment of the U.S. forces.*

Although the practice specially insisted upon was the ban upon clothing and ornament, and although dances were also proscribed and cleanliness and purity stressed, this was not in the name of any primitive puritanism. It was rather an emphasis upon purity of heart and freedom of self-expression to such a degree that the sexual act was to take place in public, since there was no shame in it; even irregular liaisons should be open affairs. Husbands should show no jealousy, for this would disturb the state of harmony which the cult was trying to establish. Bridewealth was also abolished and exogamy converted into endogamy within the lineage.[2]

Tsek was little concerned with the Whites. His main aim was the removal of all quarrelling and friction, which were the causes of illness. To further its aim, cult members were formed into separate villages, containing, on the average, between twenty and forty people. One large village contained three sections, two being made up of cult members, and the third of traditionalists. Cult solidarity was also emphasized *across* village boundaries, for much intervisiting went on, but only between cult villages. Status differences were weakened in the stressing of unity, and wealth differences obliterated by the killing-off of pigs. This rigid morality proved too much for some of the weaker vessels who at first joined, but later reneged; others resented the destruction of their property, and became opponents of the cult.

A road several miles in length was built to the sea at Tasmalum, the scene of Clapcott's death, for the use of the Americans; at the end of it, a 'dock' was built to receive the Cargo.

The Administration now began to take heed of the missionaries' warnings, and launched an attack on the cult. The 'dock' was

* Natives in some parts of New Guinea believed that 'Australia had no troops and only aeroplanes; others . . . that only American land troops were fighting; yet others . . . drew conclusions from the Australian preponderance in all arms' (*Stanner*, p. 88).

[1] *Miller, op. cit.*, and *Poirier*, passim.   [2] *Guiart*, 1956b, p. 196.

burned down, but despite this attack, the movement persisted, though driven underground. New elements were added: a 'special house for a modernistic ritual including preaching and community singing', poles and creepers representing a 'wireless belong boy', shaking-fits, prophesying, and so on.[1] Later, a European was asked to leave the area where the ship was expected to land.

The spread of this movement on Santo showed that an indigenous organization could unite a large number of separate social groups over a wide area. This was even more apparent in the movement which developed on another island, Tanna.

Tanna: John Frum

Tanna, a large, fertile and well-watered island in the southern New Hebrides which had suffered in the past from the activities of the blackbirders, was beginning to show signs of population increase once more by the 'forties, though there were still less than half the number of people there had been a century before. Blackbirding depredations left their effects in a 'legacy of bitterness which is not yet dead',[2] as well as in reduced population.

The people came under administrative control in 1912, and since 1916 had had the same Agent, a Briton named James Nicol.* Just as on Santo, Government was weak, and the missions strong. Economically, the island was ill-developed; most revenue came from the sale of native copra or from the wages of migrant labourers. In the years just before World War II only four traders lived on Tanna, one being Mr Nicol's assistant.

There were three mission stations: the Presbyterian, the most powerful, on the west coast; the Seventh Day Adventist, also on the west coast; and the Roman Catholic in eastern Tanna. The White staff of the missions was small; from time to time it included female missionaries and nurses.[3]

A critic of the missions writes:

---

* Nicol's attitude to natives is shown by his action when Sir Harry Luke asked him who a certain native woman was: 'He went up to her, slowly pulled up her head by her top-knot so that he could have a good look at her face, opened her mouth and inspected her teeth like a vet judging the age of a horse, and said "Oh that's Rosie"' (*Luke*, p. 149).

Nicol originally went out as engineer of the Government yacht. Sir Harry describes him as a 'rough and ready old Aberdonian'.

[1] *Guiart*, 1951a, p. 128.   [2] *Barrow*, p. 379.

[3] *O'Reilly*, 1950, pp. 69 ff.

'The Presbyterian Mission . . . first to arrive . . . acquired a preponderant position, which it has jealously guarded. . . . Later, English district agents were appointed, but often they could hardly be other than the secular arm of the Mission.

With the praiseworthy intention of preventing the alienation of native lands, the Mission had been given custody of the greater part of the coast; but, as proprietor in the eyes of the law, it profited by expelling those whom it considered undesirable.

Convinced of the intellectual inferiority of the native, the Presbyterians neglected educational work.'[1]

The dissatisfaction of the natives with mission teaching predisposed them to radical change. One native told a District Agent that he had been so disappointed with prayers and hymns all the time, and the 'little practical gain' of missionary activities, that he had joined another Church. Here also he found 'pray, pray, pray and sing, sing, sing, all the time'.[2] Except for one missionary, no European could communicate with the natives in anything but pidgin and none had the confidence of the natives or lived with them.[3] Under these conditions, movements of protest on Tanna naturally took on an anti-Mission flavour, and drew their recruits from existing Christian congregations, above all Presbyterian.

Millenarian tendencies had been noted just before the turn of the century, when there had been rumours that Jesus would descend and lead the Christians to Heaven while Tanna and the pagans were consumed by fire.[4] But the first important signs of native unrest did not become apparent until much later. In early 1940, there were signs of disturbance, exacerbated no doubt by a fall in copra prices. Meetings were held from which Whites were excluded, as were women. These meetings were to receive the message of one John Frum (spelt sometimes Jonfrum),* described as a 'mysterious little man with bleached hair, high-pitched voice and clad in a coat with shining buttons'. He used 'ingenious

---

* Rentoul derives the name John Frum partly from 'Broom' (Frum—the broom with which the Whites would be swept from Tanna) and considers that the 'John' reflects the breakaway from the John the Baptist Mission and the formation of an independent native church (*Rentoul, loc. cit.*).

[1] *Guiart*, 1952a, p. 172.   [2] *Rentoul*, p. 31; cf. *Poirier*, passim.
[3] *O'Reilly*, 1950, passim.   [4] *Guiart*, 1957.

stage-management . . . appearing at night, in the faint light of a fire, before men under the influence of kava'.[1] John Frum issued pacific moral injunctions against idleness, encouraged communal gardening and cooperation, and advocated dancing and kava-drinking. He had no anti-White message at first and prophesied on traditional lines.

The prophet was regarded as the representative or earthly manifestation of Karaperamun, god of the island's highest mountain, Mount Tukosmeru. Karaperamun now appeared as John Frum, who was to be hidden from the Whites and from women.

John Frum prophesied the occurrence of a cataclysm in which Tanna would become flat, the volcanic mountains would fall and fill the river-beds to form fertile plains, and Tanna would be joined to the neighbouring islands of Eromanga and Aneityum to form a new island. Then John Frum would reveal himself, bringing in a reign of bliss, the natives would get back their youth, and there would be no sickness; there would be no need to care for gardens, trees or pigs. The Whites would go; John Frum would set up schools to replace mission schools, and would pay chiefs and teachers.*

Only one difficulty prevented the immediate attainment of this happy state—the presence of the Whites, who had to be expelled first. The use of European money was also to cease. A corollary was the restoration of many ancient customs prohibited by the missionaries: kava-drinking above all, and also dancing, polygyny, etc. Immigrants from other islands were to be sent home.

This was not simply a programme of 'regression'. Only some of the ancient customs were to be revived, and they were customs banned by the missions. And the future envisaged was not the restoration of primitive tribalism and hand agriculture, but a new life with 'all the material riches of the Europeans' accruing to the natives.[2] John Frum would provide all the money needed.

Natives now started a veritable orgy of spending in European stores in order to get rid of the Europeans' money, which was to be replaced by John Frum's with a coconut stamped on it. Some even hurled their long-hoarded savings into the sea, believing that 'when there would be no money left on the island the White

---

* Chiefs were not paid, and teachers were supported by the faithful and by small allowances from the missions.

[1] *Guiart*, 1952b, p. 166.   [2] *O'Reilly, loc. cit.*

traders would have to depart, as no possible outlet would be found for their activity'.[1] Lavish feasts were also held to use up food. There was thus no puritan or medieval European 'asceticism' in these general joyful expectations of plenty. Rather, solidarity between rich and poor alike was expressed in this orgy of consumption, since existing wealth was meaningless in the light of the prodigious riches to come. Friday, the day on which the millennium was expected, became a holy day, whilst on Saturdays dances and kava-drinking took place. 'A certain licence accompanied the festivals', Guiart remarks. We may be sure that this represents some socially recognized breaking of existing conventions.

The movement was organized through messengers known as 'ropes of John Frum'. The enthusiasts broke away from existing Christian villages which the missions had set up under Christian chiefs, and broke up into small family units living in 'primitive shelters', or else joined pagan groups in the interior. This development, though formally the opposite of Santoese domestic communism, symbolizes the same basic social fact: a break with the mission-controlled villages and the old pattern of group life.

The first John Frum wave in April 1940 occasioned little alarm, but the revival of the movement in May 1941 created considerable perturbation. Large amounts of money were suddenly brought in by natives. Even gold sovereigns, which had not been seen since 1912 when they were paid to the chiefs who accepted the authority of the Government, appeared; this perhaps symbolized renunciation of the agreement. Some natives came in with over £100 in cash; cows and pigs were killed, kava drunk, and there was allnight dancing at the Green Point villages on the west coast where the movement had its centre. The Presbyterian missions, on Sunday the eleventh of May, found their services unattended. One of the most influential chiefs had given the order to abandon the mission and their schools. Dominican services were equally neglected.

After a lapse of a week, Nicol visited Green Point, only to find it empty except for a few women and children. He summoned twenty police reinforcements from Vila and, with the aid of one of the chiefs, arrested the John Frum leaders. A menacing crowd followed him shouting 'Hold firm for John Frum!'

In the trial, it transpired that John Frum was a native named

[1] *Guiart*, 1951b, *loc. cit.*

Manehivi in his mid-thirties.* He was illiterate (though he pretended to read), and refused to say where he had obtained his gold-buttoned coat. Manehivi was sentenced to three years' internment, and five years' exile from Tanna; nine others received a year's imprisonment. Nicol had Manehivi tied to a tree and exposed as an impostor for a day, and made five chiefs sign a statement asserting that they renounced John Frum, and fined them £100.[1]

The movement still flourished in spite of repression. December 1941 was the significant date of the next major outbreak. News of Pearl Harbour had percolated through even to the natives of Tanna, though the defeat was credited to the Germans, who were going to win. Because of growing anti-British feeling, Nicol had twenty men arrested and sent to Vila, and recommended the establishment of a permanent police force.

Meanwhile the John Frum leaders in Vila were active. Manehivi was not the real John Frum, people said; the latter was still at large. Missionaries intercepted messages written from Vila by a second John Frum, a Tanna police-boy, Joe Nalpin, and addressed to a west coast chief and two other men. They contained a new theme: John Frum was King of America,† or would send his son to America to seek the King, or his son was coming from America, or his sons were to seek John Frum in America.‡ Mount Tukosmeru would be 'covered by invisible planes belonging to John Frum'. Nalpin actually helped to direct the new phase from gaol, where he was serving a nine months' sentence.

In January, Australian Catalina flyingboats on patrol were the probable origin of the rumour that three sons of John Frum—Isac, Jacob and Lastuan (Last-One?)—had landed by plane on the

---

* see photo 75m in *Luke*. Guiart states that Manehivi was handed over to justice to protect the real culprit. Further information on native-mission relations is given in *Guiart*, 1956a.

† *Guiart*, 1951c, p. 87. Mr G. S. Parsonson informs me in a private communication that the theme of the Coming of the Americans, and also of the Coming of the Japanese (both of these nationalities being well known to the natives of the New Hebrides), was in fact quite an old theme and was not just a product of the war. Indeed, none were more surprised than the Tannese when the Americans and Japanese actually did appear on the scene. This helped to swing the people towards John Frumism, about which they had previously been sceptical. A full account of these early manifestations is being prepared by Mr Parsonson.

‡ Rusefel (Roosevelt), King of America, was also frequently referred to.

[1] *O'Reilly, loc. cit.*

other side of the island from Green Point. 'Junketings' were going on night and day, as it was believed that John Frum's advent was imminent. The appearance of the first Americans and of numerous planes added fuel to the flames.

The three sons of John Frum 'were half-castes, had black hair, and were dressed in long robes and jackets. They showed themselves near a banyan tree, and gave their orders to Gladys, a girl of twelve, who translated the words which the other young boys and girls heard without understanding. A sack of magic stones had to be laid at the foot of the banyan tree to ensure the Coming of the divine children. . . . Isac was the mouthpiece of his brothers. . . . He was to be king of the south-east part of Tanna. The other two were also to be kings.'[1]

The movement thus had two separate foci, apparently following the lines of traditional east-west rivalry. Young girls and boys were dedicated to the new gods and lived together in a common dwelling. They bathed together ritually by day and danced by night, and went on pilgrimages to Green Point, the place of origin of the movement. This area, evidently, had at least ritual superiority.

The Administration became greatly alarmed when natives began to guard villages and escort strangers, and when one man asked a Chinese merchant's son the price of his father's store, because he expected the Chinese to leave with the Europeans.

Nicol found that young girls were 'waiting' on the leaders, and that another run on the stores was in progress. One store had done £300 worth of business in January, following on a very slack period. He then arrested Isac (Siaka) and others, and sent them to Vila for a years' detention; one sentence was imposed for 'incest' and others for 'adultery'.

As the Americans moved in to meet the Japanese threat, the news of their arrival swept the islands. A man was arrested for saying that Mount Tukosmeru was 'full of soldiers'; it would open on the Day, and the soldiers would fight for John Frum. But the most astounding piece of information was the news that many of these U.S. troops were *black!* It was prophesied that large numbers of black Americans were coming to rule over the natives. Their dollars would become the new money; they would release the prisoners, and pay wages.

Consequently, the Americans met with a splendid response

[1] *Guiart*, 1952b, p. 168.

when they set out to hire native labour. The movement now revived on Tanna, and kava-drinking and dancing were the order of the day, especially on the east coast; the missions were still boycotted. More arrests were made, and the prisoners sent to Vila, where many were allowed to work for the U.S. Air Force.

At the beginning of 1943, Nicol left Tanna for a period. His replacement, Mr Rentoul, noted the atmosphere of tension as soon as he arrived. He attributed this partly to anti-mission feeling and partly to price fluctuations and to the absence of consumer goods in the stores.[1] John Frum adherents now adopted a new approach. John Frum himself asked for permission to attend services while in custody, and in June 100 native notables asked to visit the Residency to 'make it up with Government.'[2]

In October, Nicol returned. His arrival precipitated a new John Frum demonstration which was broken up by the police. Natives armed with guns and clubs resisted arrest and reinforcements were summoned. A new leader in the north of the island, Neloaig (Nelawihang), proclaimed himself John Frum, King of America and of Tanna. He organized an armed force which conscripted labour for the construction of an aerodrome which the Americans had told him to build for American Liberator planes bringing goods from John Frum's father. Those who refused to work would be bombed by planes. This pressed labour was resisted by a few natives who were wounded. The District Agent, under the pretence of demanding a ship to evacuate him from the island, radioed for help. He arrested Neloaig when the latter visited him at his office.

The arrest of Neloaig produced demands for his release. The supporters of John Frum, undaunted, went on feverishly building the airstrip, and a band of Neloaig's followers even attempted to liberate their leader from gaol. The police reinforcements, with two U.S. officers, were quickly despatched to the John Frum airstrip. There they found 200 men at work, surrounded by others with guns. After the latter were disarmed, an American officer spoke to the natives, trying to persuade them of their folly. This was backed up by a demonstration of the power of a tommy-gun turned on a John Frum poster pinned to a nearby tree. Many fled in panic; the police then burned down a John Frum hut and took forty-six prisoners. Neloaig received two years, ten others one year,

[1] *Guiart*, 1957.   [2] *O'Reilly, loc. cit.*

and the rest three months. Later Neloaig escaped from gaol and hid in the bush on Efate for three years before he gave himself up. In April 1948 he was committed to a lunatic asylum. His wife was detained at Vila, but the people of north Tanna still paid homage to her.

Though illiterate, Neloaig had pretended to read and had started his own schools. When the missionaries at Lenakel tried to restart classes in 1943, only fifty children out of a total population of 2,500 attended. Dances and kava-drinking still flourished, and villages were allowed to fall into untidiness. John Frumism still flourished. Pagans, too, provided recruits: pagan leaders had long attempted to play off Government against mission, Neloaig's father among them.

There were two more arrests in 1945. In 1946 a revival started, and contact was established with the prisoners at Vila and on Malekula. The growing tension came to a head in April 1947 when, in reaction to high prices, natives raided a store, mounted the counters, and tore the price-tickets off the goods. This, they announced, was on orders from John Frum, who objected to the colours of the tickets, and who asserted their rights to these things: 'John Frum like black now white.'

Iokaeye (Yokae), the new John Frum, claimed to have received and transmitted orders from Isac, John Frum's son, who spoke like a man, at a special place in the bush on Thursday evenings before sunset. Isac abhorred the colours red (blood), blue (sickness), and yellow (death), and women were forbidden to dye their skirts with these colours; only black and white were allowed.

Iokaeye and fourteen others were now arrested; Iokaeye and two other men received five years, the rest two years plus five years' exile, but all fourteen had been involved in the outbreak of October 1943, and had clearly been little overawed by their previous failure. Two villages were declared out of bounds to other villagers.

Towards the end of 1947, four coconuts arrived from exiled John Frum adherents with instructions that the nuts be planted on the sites of four of their houses which had been demolished on European orders. There is doubt as to whether these coconuts were a mere gift or some esoteric sign of rebellion, but the coconuts were dug up. Continuous suppression seems to have weakened the movement by this time. At their own suggestion, 133 people signed an undertaking not to have anything to do with John Frum and to help the Government.[1] But the explosive potentialities remained great.

From 1948 to 1952, however, complete calm reigned on Tanna. The economic disorders of the war gave way to an era of high copra prices, which rose from £25 per ton in 1947 to £78 in 1952. Then, in 1952, the price fell again to around £30. These fluctuations were regarded as the deliberate work of local European traders.[2]

New signs of unrest appeared in various parts of the island: the daily wearing of leaves normally only worn on ritual occasions; the boycott of European stores; visions of the dead and of 'Jake Navy', a figure derived from a popular brand of cigarettes, and so on. John Frumism was clearly still alive. A whole series of rumours began to circulate: some people had seen the indigenous god Mwayamwaya; others had seen the mythical mannikins who were believed to live in ravines; some saw Isac and Lastuan once more; and the recently-arrived British Delegate was said to be an avatar of Noah, who was now equated with John Frum. There was little sign of any immediate decline in the movement's appeal.[3]

Yet, despite these undercurrents, Government reported that the natives were 'in general very happy . . . and had . . . few desires for exterior expression'.[4]

Malekula: Cargo Cooperatives

One of the newer developments on Tanna was the setting up of cooperatives in order to dispense with the services of the distrusted European traders. This tendency was very much more marked on Malekula, an island to which the John Frum movement spread, partly through the exile of cult leaders there, and also through direct evangelization, which often followed traditional lines of communication. The Tanna leaders thus had some influence on the peoples of Ambrym and Malekula, Epi and Paama. On Malekula, for example, secret night-time meetings and dances were held only three miles from the mission.

But events on Malekula took a less directly political turn, though many people were influenced by John Frum and Naked Cult agents. Independent native organizations on Malekula did not concentrate on an expected supernatural coming of the Cargo; they set out to

---

[1] *Barrow*, p. 382.   [2] *Guiart*, 1957.   [3] *op. cit.*
[4] extract from the *New Hebrides Ann. Rpt.* for 1948, noted in *Simpson*, 1955, p. 149.

advance native economic interests by the cooperative efforts of the producers themselves.

In 1939, three natives, chief Paul Tamlumlum, Kaku, and Ragh Ragh (Charley), formed a company to produce and market copra. The profits were to be placed in a community bank and used for the benefit of the community: at first, for the free distribution of goods, and later for the building of schools, hospitals, etc.[1]

A great deal of coconut planting was done, and a deputation was sent to Vila to make arrangements for sale. A British planter was eventually asked to take over the marketing and to administer the bank, under the control of a British official. When this arrangement came to an end, the bank was handed back to native control. The first trouble came in 1941 when Paul Tamlumlum was sent to prison because chiefs had been illegally putting pressure on people to carry out collective clearing and planting.

The arrival of the Americans meant the exodus of many men to Santo where they were employed in unloading operations. The wealth and generosity of the Americans amazed the natives. Even today native families still possess crockery and furniture left to them by the Americans. Pro-American feeling was strongest in the cooperative area, where the American flag was hoisted. But there was much more behind the pro-American sentiments. Ragh Ragh announced that an American, Capt. W. Otto, had described the riches which would be given to the natives after the war. Ragh Ragh, Paul Tamlumlum and a Pentecost islander named Bule John were then arrested and imprisoned.

After the suppression of this first wave of American-inspired enthusiasm, the movement took some time to regain its impetus. By 1945, the cooperative movement had been revived, but now with a very different purpose: land was to be cleared, not for agriculture, but to make roads for the expected lorries, and to mark out an aerodrome for Capt. Otto's planes. Roads were also made on Pentecost; Bule John was now rearrested.

Paul Tamlumlum and chief Etienne now resumed more orthodox cooperative activities, and in mid-1949 persuaded the son of their old White representative on Santo to assist them. Under his guidance, the 'Malekula Native Company' was formed. Though there were a number of 'councillors' as local representatives, the White agent on Santo in fact dominated the movement. He sent a

[1] *Guiart*, 1952b, pp. 429 ff.

boat round to pick up copra, and also to collect labourers, who were not to work for any other European except him. Profit went into the Company's bank, but before long there was trouble with the Administration over the books.

In northern Malekula, complaints were made. Here there was a division of interest between the rich indigenous landowners and refugees from uncontrolled Big Nambas country existing on small borrowed plots. The larger landowners had a correspondingly larger share in the cooperative and the immigrants were under their economic domination. And though payments were made to cooperative members for the copra marketed, they only received about a third of what they were entitled to.

The use of former members of the New Hebrides Defence Corps to impose a quasi-military discipline over the workers soon aroused alarm. Medals stamped with individual numbers and 'Malnatco', originally issued as a means of identification in sales, gradually became badges of rank. Little by little, Cargo elements began to re-emerge; there was talk of the arrival of arms and ammunition and a black flag. Ragh Ragh, who was in touch with the John Frum leaders, was thereupon expelled from the Company by moderate elements who wished to develop the cooperative as a purely economic venture and to avoid the government suppression which the continued presence of Ragh Ragh in the leadership would invite.

The movement now gained rapidly in strength on Malekula, on Pentecost and on Ambrym. Despite mission disapproval, there were large group-enlistments cutting across religious affiliations. The Company now began training truck-drivers and building roads, and diverted a considerable amount of labour from the plantations. The channelling of the movement into harmless courses led the Administration to abandon attempts to suppress it, and it forged ahead.

Religion on Ambrym

The importance of the missions in the New Hebrides has been noted for Tanna and Espiritu Santo, where the cults were particularly anti-mission. A more detailed examination of the effects of mission influence on native society can be made for another island, Ambrym, where Christian proselytization produced complex social differentiation, even though social change there had been much less radical than on other islands.

In 1952, contact with Europeans was limited, especially with government officials. There were sporadic visits from traders buying copra, and one or two Roman Catholic missionaries and sisters. There was only one planter, and little migrant labour as compared with other islands. But shortage of labour had resulted in improved conditions for workers, and employer-employee relations were relatively harmonious. Migrant labour held less of the terrors of the past, and tended to attract youths eager to see the world. Many signed on for a different area each time. This produced a 'great intermingling of the natives of the archipelago which in a few years should make a more uniform development of the archipelago possible—and all the more so as the last refractory tribes accept, and even seek to sign on, in their eagerness to make up their leeway'.[1]

Besides sporadic visiting traders buying copra and selling trade goods, White traders have established stores run by native clerks. Unlike other islands, native entrepreneurs have not yet set up their own stores, but the growth of commerce has resulted in a new social differentiation, undermining the traditional hierarchy of wealth and rank of the Mage society. And traditional kinship rights and duties are flouted: one native catechist, for example, 'entertained relatives . . . at his home (a hut belonging to the mission) and when they were leaving, he presented them with a bill of expenses for his hospitality'.[2] Another individual profited from the devaluation of the pound by buying dollars from bush natives. The devaluation was attributed to the illness of the King represented on the money.

Today, the major social divisions among the 1,500 natives are between the various Christian groups and the heathens. The former do not oppose the heathens as a single bloc, for they are divided into various denominations; mainly Presbyterian, a large Roman Catholic group, and some Seventh Day Adventists.

We have seen how elsewhere the recruitment of converts into Christian villages under Christian 'chiefs', who were often 'teachers' and not from traditional ruling families, disrupted native communities. On Ambrym, this was not done to the same extent. This fact, together with the persistence of a strong, consciously independent, heathen community, had meant a lesser degree of disturbance than on Santo and Tanna, and is reflected in the relative freedom of Ambrym from millenarian cults.

[1] *Guiart*, 1952a, pp. 256 ff.   [2] *op. cit.*, p. 259.

But the considerable powers vested in the Presbyterian teachers have inevitably weakened the authority of the chiefs. The teachers, untrained in religious matters, but trusted by missionaries to spread the gospel, hold a key intercalary position between the Whites and the islanders. Some teachers have used the authority of the missionary for their own ends. They also exert considerable influence over the White mission staff who rely on them for information on matters affecting the natives, since only two missionaries speak native tongues. For the native who is illiterate (as with nearly all the Presbyterians), or cut off from personal Bible study because the Bible has not been translated into their tongue, the teachers have access to unique knowledge and authority.

The Roman Catholic catechists form a similar élite. Village life was further disrupted when the Catholics centralized their flock round the mission church, and then later dispersed them. The Seventh Day Adventists restrict the authority of their teachers to the religious sphere and have no 'chiefs'. Yet this mission's policies have also profoundly altered native life. The discipline enforced by their teachers is stricter than that of other denominations; acceptance of this discipline is facilitated by the attraction of technical training in joinery, carpentry and elementary iron-working given by this mission. Others have joined because of dissatisfaction with existing missions. The Adventist teachers are also trained to see farther than their own locality: they are taken away for training to other islands as part of a deliberate policy of welding the small Adventist groups into a solid body on an archipelago-wide basis.

New systems of authority, prestige and status, residence and association, have thus developed. They are replacing, and competing with, the old and with each other. The Roman Catholics, for example, forbid marriages between Catholic and 'unconverted' natives. And all denominations seek to recruit the 'heathen'.

The missions have little influence in the interior of the country, except the Presbyterians to some extent. Here the central institution is the Mage society, with its hierarchy of age-grades, entry to which is gained by the payment of pigs: £A300-400 in pigs is the estimated cost of entry to a medium grade.* The men of the highest grade, the *Mal*, provide the secular and religious leadership of the community.

* cf. the Mangki society of Malekula, *Deacon*, Chaps. X-XIV.

Two men held this highest rank, one of them an ex-Queensland labourer, the other a native assessor and a conscious defender of heathen independence. The assessors, appointed to assist European officials, included another heathen, two Roman Catholics and two Presbyterians. Thus the religious divisions of the island were recognized in the governmental structure, and the internecine struggles for power were carried into the sphere of the assessorship.

There seems little doubt that both assessors and teachers used their power illegitimately not only for forced conversion, but also for quite secular ends, though Guiart's critical analysis has been challenged by a former Presbyterian missionary.[1]

Native leaders have seen that the strengthening of their religious power also meant the strengthening of their political power, and the aim of 'achieving equality with the Whites' has never been far below the surface.* The heathens have suffered serious blows in their attempt to maintain their independence. The pigs which form their principal source of animal food and of wealth, and which are vital to their social institutions, have been the object of attack by mission and Government.

Pig-rearing is 'seen as the *sine qua non* of heathenism'. It is attacked in the name of hygiene and the protection of gardens, but other evils have resulted from the abandonment of swine-culture by Christians, such as dietary deficiencies, increased in the case of the Seventh Day Adventists by religious taboos on the eating of such foods as shellfish and fish without scales (and on less beneficial things such as alcohol, tobacco, tea and coffee). Although Christian villages are no cleaner than the heathen ones, the campaign against swine-culture was vigorously carried on until 1952. Using mission and government authority, some native Christian leaders had an excuse for a field-day against the heathens' pigs, which they slaughtered, often when the pigs were not in fact damaging gardens. The heathens passively resisted government orders to pen their pigs.

---

* *Guiart*, 1952a, p. 262. Cf. Deacon's remarks on the character of those Malekulan natives who took to Christianity with enthusiasm: 'the Christian converts . . . form a small band, corresponding . . . to the (idealistic) social revolutionaries of the Bakunin type in Europe; they are out for the destruction and reconstruction of native society' (*op. cit.*, p. 20).

This perspicacious analogy goes far to explain why the Christians were so readily attracted to millenarism.

[1] *Paton*, passim.

These attacks on the heathen community are only one side of the picture, however, for the heathens attempt to utilize divisions in the Christian ranks for their own ends, and set Catholic against Presbyterian, and even Englishman against Frenchman. They thus offer protection to natives who have offended Christian rules, e.g., women fleeing from their husbands. For such action, however, one heathen assessor was nearly imprisoned; he fled, and his brother was taken as hostage for six months. His fear and suspicion of Government and mission were intensified until a rapprochement was effected. This suspicion is evident in the heathen resentment of educational and medical services which they consider to be the thin end of the religious wedge. And one heathen leader accused the Presbyterian Mission of wanting to annex the island for Britain when Mr Paton distributed some Condominium flags.[1]

In spite of these ideological and political divisions, the people are still bound together by economic and other activities: 'the ways diverge, but there is a certain compensating economic interdependence between the Christian and the heathen regions; the latter are customers in the stores of the Christians; while for their part they supply the Christians with bamboos and creepers for house-building, with native remedies and even with foodstuffs at the time of the gathering of the harvests. The Christians can put sailing canoes on the stocks on behalf of the inland groups of heathen.'[2]

But the opposition between the factions was such that when the John Frum movement spread to Ambrym, it did not succeed in unifying the whole population, but was canalized by existing divisions. It was principally among the Presbyterians that the movement had its success, though these, of course, did form the largest group on the island.

Once more the exiling of John Frum leaders led to the spread of the movement to other islands where these leaders were deported. Exiled leaders at Port Sandwich thus used traditional channels of inter-island communication, as well as Ambrym islanders evacuated to Malekula following an earthquake, to start the movement up on Ambrym.

The growth of the movement at Uro village, on military lines, showed how much had been learnt from the war. Village entrances were guarded by a militia commanded by 'captains' and 'lieuten-

[1] *Guiart*, 1952a, pp. 262 and 267.   [2] *op. cit.*, p. 260.

ants'. This force exercised daily and changed trousers (i.e., uniform) on handing over duties. On entering Uro, one had to give one's name, and the reasons for one's visit or transit, all of which were entered in a register. The newly widened and cleaned roads were flanked with notices saying 'Halt!', 'Stop!', 'Mouia!', 'Compulsory Stop!',etc.

The people were ready to abandon the missionaries; they could run their own religion and schools, they declared. Government would not touch them, for they would take refuge in the mouth of the volcano. As on Tanna, Temar, the ancestor-god of the volcano, was worked into the ideology: 'young boys played at putting leaves in crabholes and at telephoning to Temar . . . speaking into tinned food tins. . . . An old woman . . . was said to have seen a light in a craggy portion of lava and had heard what seemed to be the sound of a bell. In the evening, the village went in procession to the music of the guitar and dancing, to the lava flow. They heard the sound of the bell and waited. As nothing happened they began to kill the cats, at the direction of the old woman. The dogs were tied up in the village during the evening, and, of course, began howling.'[1]

Store debts were paid off, and money thrown into the sea, for it was soon to be replaced by new. A white steamer (the colour of *Le Polynésien*, the Messageries Maritimes vessel) would bring vast stores to John Frum followers from America. Watch was kept through the night, but the cry of 'Sail ho' was not made. When *Le Polynésien* did arrive at Craig Cove, the chief of Uro went to ask the priest if the Cargo was really consigned to him.

The John Frum movement now spread to other villages; mission regulations were ignored, and men discussed holding women in common. Paama, a fully Presbyterian island, also received the cult, again along traditional channels, and pig-killing and money disbursement broke out.

On Ambrym, the Presbyterian teachers appeared to have succeeded in stamping out the cult, but it would be rash to say that it was dead. Guiart remarks that the collapse of heathen resistance might well provide 'fresh impetus to John Frumism; and this is the more probable since distrust of the Whites is general'.[2] The dynamism of the John Frum cult might be the stimulus to the building up of a unified, independent and probably anti-European move-

[1] *op. cit.*, pp. 170-1.　　　　[2] *op. cit.*, p. 267.

ment which some native leaders have attempted to establish by manipulation of the various Christian denominations. These existing channels, however, might well prove more satisfactory, since, on Ambrym, anti-mission feeling does not seem to have been as strong as elsewhere, and considerable liberty of action was afforded to native leaders by the missionaries. Indeed, in 1948, the native Presbyterian Church of the New Hebrides achieved its independence.*

But the field is evidently open for intensive recruitment to movements promising amelioration of present conditions. Fluctuations in copra prices, news of technological innovations at Vila, and other economic matters were matters of concern to the natives of Ambrym. Equally, there was deep fear that the New Hebrides might share the fate of the islands to the north during the last war. Knowledge of the war in Viet Nam stimulated this fear, and the anthropologist Guiart was suspected of being occupied in preparing for the next war.

On Ambrym, native aspirations towards self-expression have taken the form of religious factions. But the basic pattern is not unlike that of other islands, even if there are local peculiarities. As in other islands of the New Hebrides, where there are channels easily open to independent native enterprise (e.g., the cooperatives on Malekula) *within* the framework of the existing social order, millenarism has failed to strike deep roots, even though no large opportunities for political advancement are available. But demands for the latter will come. The frustration of such demands could lead to the development of orthodox political movements, but it could equally lead to a revival of the cults. The wider possibility of the linking up of such movements on an archipelago-wide basis has been shown to be quite feasible.

Nevertheless, existing sectional divisions have as yet hindered the development of such a unified, proto-nationalist movement, except to some extent on Tanna. Whether the reported interest of educated half-castes will affect this process remains to be seen.

The process of economic differentiation in native society can best be seen from the Malekulan cooperative movement. Here the veer-

* The missions, for example have not attempted a frontal attack upon traditional marriage customs, including polygyny and child betrothal, because these are still supported by all natives, but attempts are made to 'render them less brutal'.

ing of the Company between the poles of orthodox economic enterprise and millenarian Cargo activity may be seen not as a shift of the whole membership from one side to the other, but as the epiphenomenal expression of internal differences within the movement. We have seen the differentiation of society into men with large land-holdings on the one hand, and poor dependent immigrants with small borrowed plots on the other, and the newer growth of wage earners and entrepreneurs among the natives. This precipitated a struggle for power in the post-war period which culminated in the success of the new native entrepreneurs, their explusion of the radical millenarist Ragh Ragh, and the consequent direction of the movement by the economically dominant moderates along the lines of increased production and the further growth of their economic strength. Their programme appealed also to the poorer natives, since it met with some initial success in a favourable world economic climate.

It was therefore able to counter much of the appeal of Cargo propaganda by showing that real economic advancement, whilst not on the prodigious scale envisaged by Cargo leaders, was actually possible under existing conditions by orthodox secular means. Such policies may have lacked the dynamic, root-and-branch appeal of millenarist solutions, but they did represent a fresh approach to the question of native economic and political advancement which was likely to be a more effective threat to White rule, and more beneficial to native interests in the long run, than millenarian activity.

CHAPTER IX

From Millennium to Politics

For thus saith the Lord of hosts; Yet once, it is a little while, and I will shake the heavens, and the earth, and the sea, and the dry land;

And I will shake all nations, and the desire of all nations shall come: and I will fill this house with glory, saith the Lord of hosts.

The silver is mine, and the gold is mine, saith the Lord of hosts.

The glory of this latter house shall be greater than of the former. Haggai 2:6-9

Marching Rule

FOR A BRIEF MOMENT at the height of World War II the eyes of the world were turned to the Solomon Islands, where a grim struggle was being fought out. The name of Guadalcanal will be for ever prominent in histories of the war. Once the Japanese armies had been thrown back, however, the Solomons became once more a rather unimportant backwater.

But if the Solomons had become once more merely remote 'South Sea islands' to the outside world, they looked very different when viewed from inside. Changes had occurred 'with such concentration and with such devastating effect that their results can justifiably be described as revolutionary'.[1]

Malaita, the island on which nearly half the population of the British Solomons is concentrated, had suffered severely from the depredations of blackbirders in the past. Most of the Western Pacific natives taken to Queensland had been Solomon Islanders, mainly from Malaita, and large-scale depopulation had ensued. This drop in population continued even after the establishment of the British Administration: from a high estimate of 150,000 people in 1929, the population fell to only 90,000 in 1939.[2]

Before the war, copra production (principally by Levers Pacific Plantations) had been the main type of European enterprise, and

[1] *Belshaw*, 1950a, p. 72.   [2] *Belshaw*, 1954, p. 188.

between 1936 and 1941 over 20,000 tons of copra were produced per year. Labour was drawn mainly from the more heavily populated areas such as Malaita. The Administration was not very vigorous: its activities were limited by lack of revenue, and out of a total expenditure of some £50,000 in 1935-6, nearly £30,000 was spent on European emoluments. While 30% of the total revenue came from native taxation, medical expenditure, for example, amounted to only 2/- per head before the war.[1]

The last remaining areas were brought under control by the 'thirties. This extension of government control had not always taken place without conflict. One of the final acts of violent resistance was the killing of a District Officer and a cadet during a police patrol on Malaita in 1927. But no sooner did these clashes cease than labour disturbances began to occur. In 1935, unrest was reported on Malaita, where Europeans were threatened and defied; on Gizo, a plantation manager was assaulted.[2] Dockers demanded higher wages, and violent resentment was expressed against those recruiters who took on cooks and other labour, paid them six months' wages, and took them away for good. The influence of foreign socialist seamen was suspected in this agitation.

Economic and political agitation was growing, but the organs of Government were weak. Before the war, Government on Malaita was represented by a District Officer at Auki and some police, with whose aid he collected the head tax levied on males between 16 and 60. At the head of each administrative division of the island were headmen chosen by Government, who received £12 per year and had police under their control.[3]

The potentialities of the situation were shown by the development of the 'Chair and Rule' movement, partly stimulated by a European missionary who encouraged the natives of Santa Ysabel, Gela and Savo to agitate for a seat on the nominated Advisory Council. He had emphasized the need for a chairman and proper procedure; from this developed the symbols of a flag, a wooden chair and wooden rule which gave the movement its name. When the movement put forward demands for increased wages, and established contact with natives on San Cristoval, they were punished and the missionary asked to leave. Even in 1954, however, his memory was still revered. This Chair and Rule movement

---

[1] *Belshaw*, 1948, pp. 95-98.
[2] *PIM*, November 1935, p. 5 and p. 56.   [3] *O'Reilly*, 1948, p. 149.

did much to stimulate Government to introduce Native Courts and Councils.[1]

With the coming of the war, the plantations were abandoned, 'leaving native employees to find their way home as best they could. Many natives were left stranded throughout the war'.[2] Unlike other areas, however, the Resident Commissioner and the Bishop of Melanesia stayed on. Very savage fighting ensued, and many islands suffered both from the actual fighting and from the depredations of the armies, though Malaita was spared this devastation. But the depredations of Allied troops were as nothing compared to the wholesale looting of the Japanese. It is worth noting that Hogbin rejects charges of Japanese atrocities in the form of rape and mutilation as 'not . . . substantiated' or 'unproven'.[3] But it would seem that had it not been for Japanese brutality and robbery the native population might have received them with sympathy; as Belshaw notes, 'the original instructions of the British officers that [natives] should move from their coastal villages into bush hideouts were at first ignored'.[4]

The subsequent impact of the vast Allied invasion force on the Islanders can be judged from the comments of one native: 'These I saw on 1st January 1944, and I was surprise to see them: (i) plenty of people, (ii) the ships on the sea, (iii) the aeroplanes, (iv) the motor cars and jeeps, (v) the ship it goes in sea and land, (vi) all sorts of launches, (vii) all sorts of different languages, (viii) all sorts of men, white and brown and black. Every tribes are in here (1) Americans, (2) Solomon Islander—there are plenty in here, (3) New Zealanders, (4) Australians, (5) Hawaiians, (6) Fijians, (7) Englanders.'[5]

The Solomon Islanders were greatly struck by the size of this sudden invasion, by the diversity of nationalities involved, and especially by the numerous black and brown American negroes, Fijians, and others, who wore the same clothes, ate the same food and used the same equipment as the White soldiers. They were equally astounded at the abundant supplies and equipment which the troops treated so casually and handed out so liberally. In the Russell Islands, by 1947, 'the villagers [had] acquired their own telephones and electric lighting system, and rebuilt their houses

[1] *Belshaw*, 1950b.   [2] *Belshaw*, 1950a, p. 66.
[3] *Hogbin*, 1951, p. 8.   [4] *Belshaw*, 1950a, p. 69.
[5] *op. cit.*, p. 143.

entirely of timber . . . every one of the 6,000 people in Gela . . . had acquired a stretcher bed and mosquito net'.[1]

3,000 men, mainly Malaitans, were recruited into a nominally Volunteer Labour Corps, under American control and receiving American food supplies, but with ex-planter officers. They received £1 per month pay. Free labourers, however, received wages up of to £14 per month; and for those non-Labour Corps natives who flocked to work for the Americans the value of their wages was over-shadowed by the value of their side-earnings. Other natives carried on a profitable trade in curios and fruit. The British administration was highly unpopular when it used police in an attempt to stop the drift of labour into these channels.

At the end of the war, the copra industry was shattered. £2M worth of fixed investments had been destroyed, and the military installations were no substitute. Copra production was very low, since only some 1.5% of the pre-war acreage was under coconuts. This meant that there was no outlet for those areas which had become dependent on wage labour even before the war, and where wants had increased enormously in the meantime.

Towards the end of 1945, dissatisfaction was apparent. Natives were refusing to work for less than £12 per month. 'The people are not strong in government order as in the day passed. They say they didn't like the British now . . . not like America men they give us everything for nothing', said one native.[2] This pent-up feeling finally broke out in a new political movement called Marching or Masinga Rule.* Some of the members of this movement were no doubt spiritual descendants of the Chair and Rule movement; others were stimulated by American troops (some of whom were said to be Communists) who pointed out to the natives their disabilities, urged them to organize politically, and roused in them the hope of radical improvements after the war.

It would be futile to search for the origin of Marching Rule

---

* The persistent perversion of this name into 'Marxian Rule' is, of course, merely a case of political hysteria. Other versions are Masinga Lo, Maasina Rule, Martin Lo, Masinga Law, Marssinga Rule, Mercy Rule, Masian Rule, etc., etc. (*PIM*, June 1950, p. 37; August 1947, p. 66, etc.). The name is actually derived from *masinga*, a word meaning 'brother' or 'brotherhood' (or 'young shoot of the taro') in the Ariari tongue, according to Allan, the best authority. Cf. *maasi*: fraternal, brotherly (*O'Reilly*, 1948, p. 150).

[1] *op. cit.*, p. 69.   [2] *op. cit.*, p. 144.

merely in such special external stimuli; primarily it was the result of internal responses to the violent upheaval of the war. No one leader emerged at the head of the movement; rather a number of energetic leaders emerged on different islands, and established contacts with each other. Most of them were drawn from the ranks of hereditary political, religious and military leaders or from amongst mission teachers. One of the chief leaders was Nori, a man of about forty, who had worked for European enterprises for most of his life. Though illiterate and pidgin-speaking, he was plainly no mere millenarian leader filled with religious enthusiasm but ignorant of White society. One settler, however, states that in 1947 Nori was baptized at his own request and claimed to have been inspired by the sight of an American general on Guadalcanal smoking a golden pipe. When he asked the general how he could become rich, he told him to start Marching Rule.[1] It is possible that this version can be attributed to some of Nori's followers, for though the leaders were generally straightforward politicians, the rank-and-file often held millenarian ideas.

Another important leader was the Solomon Islands war hero, Vouza. Vouza had had a remarkable career. He had retired from the Constabulary on a pension in 1941,[2] but fought during the war as a scout. He had been captured by the Japanese, tied to a tree, slashed with a sword and severely bayoneted and left for dead.[3] Vouza later received the George Medal and the American Silver Star for his heroism, and became a headman.

Before long, he began to try to set up political control over the whole of Guadalcanal, but Government frowned on this activity, and sent him and other headmen to Suva for a course in local government.[4]

Timothy George, the third major leader, had been born in Queensland, where his father had been taken as a worker. He is described by one missionary as an 'opportuniste intelligent', had been educated in Australia, and wrote well and spoke fluent English, unlike other leaders. At one stage, he collected £1,900 with which to organize the direct sale of copra to the U.S.A. He was under the influence of Protestant missionaries, however, and

---

[1] *PIM*, June 1950, pp. 37-38.
[2] see *MacQuarrie*, passim, for his early career.
[3] *Central Office of Information*, p. 28.
[4] *Belshaw*, 1950a, p. 127.

later, when Nori and others were arrested, he stood aside from the movement.[1]

Marching Rule thus grew up in several separate areas and with several leaders; it was complicated by a web of intrigue, rumour and internal rivalries and dissensions.

The Administration found many of the aims of the movement 'admirable': the cultivation of larger gardens, the concentration of villages, cooperation with Government and mission, and so on. Other features they found less palatable: rumours of the coming of American ships and of the imminent entry into Paradise, and demands for American rule and the replacement of government chiefs by true indigenous authorities. The revival of certain ancient customs and the nationalist attitudes of what had become a highly organized and disciplined mass movement were equally less admirable.[2]

The movement soon spread and coalesced with other movements in adjoining areas. By 1944 it had become well rooted in the Koio and Ariari Districts of Malaita; later it spread to the hill villages of southern Malaita, and by 1945 was strong on Ulawa and San Cristoval as well as Malaita and Guadalcanal.

In north Malaita, the people expelled their missionary in 1947 saying: 'You have taught us all that was in the Bible. You have taught us to read. Now let us manage our religion ourselves.' Again, people now demanded payment for small services which they had always performed free for missionaries in the past. On being accused of ingratitude by a missionary who had spent his whole life educating them and curing the sick, natives replied: 'But it's your work, isn't it?'[3]

By 1947, the movement had spread northwards to Ysabel and Gela (Florida), and later reached the Western Solomons and the Santa Cruz group, and even some of the Polynesian outliers.

On Malaita, Marching Rule had become a highly organized movement headed by Nori and Timothy George; the latter was said to have commenced signing his decrees 'Timothy George Rex'.[4] Allan has described how they divided Malaita into nine districts, roughly corresponding to the existing administrative Districts. Each district elected a 'head chief', but these met only rarely, and were assisted by 'full chiefs' in charge of sub-districts.

[1] *O'Reilly*, 1948, p. 151.
[3] *O'Reilly*, 1948, p. 151.
[2] *BSIP, Ann. Rpt.*, 1948, p. 26.
[4] *PIM*, October 1946, p. 7.

The people were then concentrated in 'towns' which were governed by 'leader chiefs', and in large towns, each clan had its 'line chief'. The new 'towns' were built on the coast, partly, possibly, because this was the practice of the U.S. Army, but also because of greater ease of communication and transport, and because good farming land was only to be found there.[1] The 'towns' were laid out, like U.S. camps, with roads, and had special meeting-houses and other buildings.

At all levels there were clerks who despatched instructions, drew up lists of members, etc. The 'towns' were picketed night and day by young men called 'duties' armed with truncheons; they controlled entry and exit and also provided escorts for 'leader chiefs' and guards of honour for visiting 'head chiefs' .When off duty, these security forces were drilled by 'strife chiefs', roughly equivalent to a kind of NCO. They also enforced the laws and rounded people up for work in the new communal gardens, marching the women to and from the gardens, where their work was supervised by 'farmer chiefs'.

Local customary law was codified by the clerks, and put into practice in the courts set up under 'custom chiefs', who thus relieved 'head chiefs' of judicial burdens. Fines and gaol sentences were employed to punish breaches of the law: failure to pay taxes, failure to go to meetings, and so on. And, in spite of strong enthusiasm for independent native organization and self-expression, blind anti-European prejudice was not evident. Indeed, help and cooperation from Europeans were expected in order to implement plans for improved educational and social services, and it was proposed that the administration of communal farms should be directed by European farmers. The sources of revenue envisaged included not merely taxation and fines, but also rents from the leasing of land to Europeans, and the Marching Rule legal code still envisaged the committing of serious cases to the District Officer. White technical officers were also wanted, and salaries could be offered to them, since the leaders of the movement had considerable money stored away. On the other hand, 'equal pay for equal work' was the slogan of many of the ex-Labour Corps men, who strongly demanded that natives should manage and even own the plantations, since it was their work which built them.

The institution of certain administrative changes in 1944 did

[1] *Belshaw*, 1954, pp. 96-97.

much to shape the development of Marching Rule policy. There had been some pre-war experiments with Native Councils and Courts, but the new plans were more ambitious, and envisaged the ultimate establishment of a Grand Council for the whole Protectorate. The Councils, however, were 'purely advisory and legislative. People with this kind of power want above all to act constructively; and yet there appeared to be nothing for them to do but talk.'[1]

The Councils and Courts remained very much under close Administrative control: in the elections for district headmen, for example, the elected candidates had to be approved by Administration. These bodies, consequently, set up after considerable delays and possessing very limited powers, did little to solve urgent problems. Some of the Councils pressed on with such matters as 'paying school-teachers, dressers, and clerks, or buying boats, pigs, and similar equipment'.[2] And if these moves were later found to be impracticable or were forbidden by the Administration, the blame was laid on the Europeans; 'the money was kept for the purpose, it was rumoured, of driving the European from the islands!'

Marching Rule now took over many of the functions denied to the New Native Courts and Councils: the codification of native customary law, for example, had been initiated by the Administration, as a result of prewar protests at the ignoring of native custom, but never carried to completion. The movement commanded widespread mass support in contrast to the boycotted Native Courts and Councils. Contributions poured in, and the chiefs, who were wealthy in dollars, backed precept with practice when they paid their followers the £12 per month minimum wage which was being demanded from Europeans instead of the ruling 10/-.

Non-adherents were said to have been deprived of land and expelled into the bush or otherwise discriminated against, but such measures were rarely necessary. The movement embraced both Christian and heathen, and, although largely underground until 1946, came out into the open in the middle of that year with huge demonstrations of thousands, especially at the administrative station at Auki on Malaita.

Administration repression generally only led to stronger re-

[1] *Belshaw*, 1950a, p. 120.   [2] *op. cit.*, p. 122.

sistance.* Some chiefs, however, began to dissociate themselves from the mass demonstrations and preached cooperation with Government, but this did not save them from arrest in the following year.

Side by side with these orthodox political developments, millenarian elements were present, though they became less and less important as time went on. Many natives regarded the British as a people who refused to disgorge their property, and the Americans as the saviours of the people who were coming once more in their LST's and Liberty Ships.† The people built storehouses to receive the goods, which were expected to be distributed by the Americans free. One missionary saw a line of forty-three storehouses 'sited and completed with military precision—a very neat, workmanlike job—and all empty'.[1]

It was not these millenarian aspects that worried Government, however, but the existence of what had become a militant political party, expressing an embryonic nationalism and uniting scores of formerly separate and minute social groups. Though existing social institutions, such as clubhouses and churches, were utilized to spread the movement, these were not the units of organization, for new social units were created, even in the economic sphere.

Marching Rule had by now become the *de facto* government of large parts of the Protectorate, and adopted its own flag with a central panel bearing a bow and arrow device and the letters NUC (Native Union Council) and five horizontal yellow stripes on a blue background on either side. The people refused to offer for labour, and only a few joined the police, even when the wages offered—35/- per month, with £2 10s. per month for a second term—were high. Nor would they pay any taxes.

At the same time, people believed that Government would recognize and assist Marching Rule. These notions were speedily dispelled by the arrest of the nine leading chiefs and of many others on Malaita and Ysabel in September 1947. At the same time, HMAS *Warramunga*, HMS *Contest* and other naval vessels 'showed the flag' in the area; the submarine HMS *Amphion* was

* Forty arrests are cited in *PIM*, October 1946, p. 7.

† Belshaw notes that expansionist notions about the extension of U.S. authority over the Solomons and elsewhere were openly expressed at all levels of the U.S. Forces in wartime and may have influenced natives (*op. cit.*, pp. 130-2 and 70).

[1] *PIM*, November 1947, p. 9.

also at Santa Ana island in the south, and the aircraft carrier HMS *Theseus* and the destroyer HMS *Cockade* passed through on the way back to Hong Kong from Australia.[1] The arrested men were charged with 'terrorism and robbery', illegal drilling and other offences, and were committed for trial at Honiara, the capital. After a trial of twenty-nine of the leaders, lasting twenty-five days, nine were sentenced to six years' hard labour, four to periods varying from one to five years' hard labour, and six found 'not guilty'. The defendants claimed that the 'care of children, and similar objects' had been their aims, and that Marching Rule 'duties' had only acted as 'fire brigades and as nursemaids and kindergarten attendants'.[2]

The trial was followed by a government offensive: in November, an order to remove village fortifications was issued. Raids were made on villages in the Koio area where 'ambitious palisades . . . with lookout towers' were destroyed, together with a Marching Rule gaol and barracks for the 'duties'. Numerous arrests were also made, but the leaders and many supporters were forewarned and escaped.[3]

These measures soon drove the movement underground on Malaita and San Cristoval, the strongest Marching Rule areas; it seemed broken on Florida, Ysabel and Guadalcanal. To supplement these negative measures, Government opened a school to train students for posts in government Courts and Councils. In March 1949 Marching Rule was still continuing: one area of Malaita was 'openly defiant' and elsewhere there was 'passive resistance'. But the movement had lost ground in the western Solomons, where Native Councils had been established and where copra production had revived. By this time, Councils had been established on Choiseul, Ysabel, the New Georgia group and the Gela group, though progress was slow on Guadalcanal and San Cristoval.[4]

In the areas of highest resistance, such as Malaita, it was said that stories of the Cargo type were being used to boost morale. Bishop Caulton reported that horses' hooves were drawn in the sand and fires lit in the bush at night by leaders who announced that these were signs of the imminent arrival of the Americans.[5]

---

[1] *PIM*, October 1947, p. 71.
[2] *PIM*, March 1948, pp. 29-30.
[3] *PIM*, December 1948, p. 44.
[4] *PIM*, March 1949, p. 32.
[5] *PIM*, August 1950, pp. 45, 47.

1949, 2,000 political prisoners were still held,[1] and even as
March 1950 some 500 prisoners were still detained at
a. Marching Rule was said to be 'as strong today . . . as at
ne'. The people were 'staunchly faithful' to the movement[2]
an... ere awaiting reforms.

This claim, however, ignored the fact that by November 1949
Government had succeeded in breaking down the last of the stock-
ades, and had induced half of the population to accept both the
reimposition of a poll tax after a gap of eight years, and the taking
of a census which had previously been resisted.[3] Census-taking
began in December 1949, but Marching Rule leaders urged resistance to it. In April 1950, the census had to be abandoned again
because of non-cooperation from the islanders.

In some areas also, the tax was refused; mass demonstrations
took place, and rumours of violence filled the air. In February
1950 a District Officer's patrol was attacked and a constable
seriously wounded; he later died of his injuries.[4] By mid-1950,
stalemate had been reached. But on the King's Birthday, 1950, the
nine chiefs were released on condition of cooperation with Government. Native resistance became weaker. Some labour was now
offering for work,[5] and most of Malaita was now administered,
though still hostile and providing no labour.

In 1950, the revision of the constitution was announced. An
Advisory Council consisting of five Solomon Islanders, five other
non-officials, and four officials was to be set up. By late 1950, six
local Native Councils were in existence in the Western Group,
with assets of £9,550, and a Native Administration school and a
cooperative had been started.

In 1951, the Marching Rule leaders changed their tactics by
encouraging constitutional resistance through a new movement
called 'Federal Council'. This aimed at the setting up of an administration[6] in Malaita independent of the Protectorate Administration.
Marching Rule continued to boycott the Administration, and its
leaders were therefore arrested, convicted and imprisoned.

In 1952, Government offered Malaita an Island Council. Pro-
tracted negotiations now began: in July, forty Malaita delegates

[1] *PIM*, July 1949, p. 43.   [2] *PIM*, March 1950, pp. 30-31.
[3] *Col. Off. Rpt.*, *BSIP*, 1949-50, p. 5.
[4] *Col. Off. Rpt.*, *BSIP*, 1949-50, p. 39.
[5] *PIM*, August 1950, p. 41.   [6] *Col. Off. Rpt.*, *BSIP*, 1951-2, p. 48.

were elected to the proposed Council, but thirty-one of them, in the end, refused to attend owing to a boycott ordered by Federal Council.

Nevertheless, the breaking of the movement in some areas, and the weaning away of support and of leaders in others, resulted in a diminution of Marching Rule-Federal Council power. But non-official Whites still insisted in 1954,'The Government Only Hopes it is—But "Marching Rule" Nationalism is not Dead in BSIP'.[1]

Malaita was still the key, both in terms of labour supply and of political importance. And wartime devastation had not been overcome to any significant degree. From the end of the war up to 24th October 1947 only 963 tons of copra had been produced, and 534 tons exported. In 1948, 4,450 tons, as compared with the pre-war 21,000 tons per month, were produced. Even by late 1950, production had only doubled over the figure at the end of the war. Much of the increase, however, now came from small native producers rather than from large foreign-owned plantations. The most vocal criticism of Government came from settler organs which favoured the ending of British control and the integration of the Solomons and the New Hebrides with the Australian territories. Except for the copra industry, there had been no new investment since the war, the critics said, and the Protectorate was financially dependent on grants from the UK and on royalties from sale of scrap iron and war-disposals materials.[2]

The breeding grounds for the Marching Rule agitation were plainly the economic dislocation of the war, and the increased desire for self-rule which the war also created. With the revival of the economy, support for Marching Rule became less whole-hearted. Prices of copra rose from £18 per ton to £70/12/6 per ton by 1948; wages of natives trebled. New experiments with cocoa production were also launched. And people had grounds for objections to Marching Rule extremism. Numbers of people had died, for example, through being obliged to work long hours exposed to the heat of the sun in the communal gardens. In this situation, Government acted shrewdly and abandoned its earlier policy of simple repression.

In September 1952, the political breach was finally healed by the new High Commissioner who went to Malaita in person and met the various factions, including the non-cooperators. He pro-

[1] headlines, *PIM*, March 1954, p. 59.   [2] *PIM*, March 1950, p. 59.

posed a Malaita Council with a President chosen by the delegates, and, if the Council so desired, a number of Solomon Islanders on the Advisory Council—if they would recognize the authority of Government, cooperate with District Officers, and obey the laws.

The Federal Council leaders finally accepted these proposals, and later the inaugural meeting of the Malaita Council was announced for the following January. Salana Ga'a became President, and Vouza was one of the four islanders elected to the Advisory Council.

*   *   *

The Marching Rule party, at least in its later stages, marks the end of an epoch in Melanesian political development (excluding the more advanced territories of Fiji and New Caledonia). Initially, it contained within it the millenarian heritage of past movements of protest, but it soon developed into a proto-nationalist political party of a new kind. It is possible that further discontent might bring about a recrudescence of millenarian notions, or lead to violence, if the immediate results of constitutional political activity, especially of participation in the running of Councils and Courts, do not lead to any significant results. And economic instability is another unknown factor. The recovery of 1948 no doubt weakened the revolutionary wing of Marching Rule, but it might become powerful once more if wages and copra prices slumped again.

It would be a mistake to pay too much attention to the millenarian aspects of this movement to the exclusion of the more important political, social and economic demands which are the ordinary stuff of world politics. The demands for minimum wages, for improved educational and social services, for independence and self-rule, for national self-expression, etc., are the important features of Marching Rule, not the lingering myths of the Cargo. And there is little doubt that in general the leaders were not affected by Cargo beliefs, even if some may have utilized them; their aims were much more mundane and attainable.

We have here, in fact, a modern nationalist body with overwhelming popular support; we leave the realm of the Coming of the Cargo and we enter the world of nationalist politics. Marching Rule, then, was not a cult, but a political party. We will see the final consummation of this transition to completely orthodox politics in another important post-war movement, which shows an even clearer abandonment of the millenarian dream—the Paliau movement.

The Paliau Movement

Manus (correctly, Great Admiralty Island), the largest island of the Admiralty Group, to the north of the New Guinea mainland, had been one of the earliest parts of New Guinea to be brought under German control. This island region was inhabited by socially distinct land-dwelling and seafaring groups, each of which produced specialized commodities—fish, pots, garden products, etc., which were exchanged through a complex system of trade.

The Manus sea dwellers lived on pile-houses in lagoons near Great Admiralty Island or off the lee shores of smaller islands. The land dwellers on the main island—the Usiai—and those on the smaller islands—the Matankor—spoke many different tongues and had markedly different customs. The Manus were culturally more homogeneous, but, though they spoke mutually intelligible dialects, they possessed no overall political unity. The special power of the Manus derived from their monopoly of the all-important trade which took place between the South coast and the smaller islands either in the form of barter or of sale for shell and dogs' teeth money.[1]

Indigenous differences of wealth between one community and another, and wealth and status differences within each community, were marked. The Manus, for example, were much richer than the Usiai, and had adapted themselves rapidly to the new conditions. Rank differences cut across clan divisions in the indigenous order, but the new wealth did not necessarily accrue to those of high traditional rank. Many of low rank found new opportunities for self-advancement in the European order. But some of high rank became even richer, and some of low rank remained poor. And all developed many new wants which they could not satisfy. Society was riven with tensions.

Buying and selling, the mounting of trade expeditions, economic competition in many different forms, were the keynote of Manus life, and are well known from Mead's *Growing up in New Guinea*. Young men were completely dependent upon wealthy seniors who financed their costly marriages, and thus gained domination over these helpless young men and involved them in pro-

[1] *Mead*, 1942, passim.

tracted economic exchanges. By becoming ruthless traders themselves they could eventually put an end to their dependence. The European economy now offered another means of escape, though it ensnared the islander in new relations whose full significance only later became apparent to him. As one administrative official remarked: 'Never have I met a people so individualistic . . . every man is jealous of his property rights and privileges however great or small. [Differences of] . . . wealth and poverty . . . are seldom so apparent as in Manus. It is for this reason that one meets so many Manus men who leave their homes to work for non-natives and who never wish to return. They are the poor and poverty means no standing in the community and no wife.'[1]

Manus men early became the mainstay of the police force. But the same official stressed their hostile attitude to Europeans, their sensitivity to White affronts, and their independent self-confidence.

By the 'thirties, labour recruiters, Catholic, Protestant and other missions, and the representatives of Government had become well-established figures in the Admiralties. And before long, there were signs of reaction to these changes. The Rabaul Strike of 1929, for example, was largely organized by Manus police-'boys'; these same police were to provide the future leadership for many an independent native organization. In the 'thirties, too, there was a marked swing towards the Roman Catholic missions, such as we have seen elsewhere. This was partly because the Catholics taught Pidgin English,* the key to a wider world, rather than local tongues; partly because they made less insistence on collections from the faithful than the Protestants; and partly because private confession appealed to a people who had previously had to expose their sins in public. The 'thirties also saw the first hints of millenarian developments to come: prophecies were spread about that the Devil would send a week of darkness on earth, when the Blacks would become white, and vice versa.[2]

Reformers of one kind and another now came to the fore. Some were concerned with long-standing problems: one man, for example, suggested a device for avoiding quarrels arising from the ghost cult.[3] Others had their eyes on the future: in 1939, an ex-policeman attacked the traditional marriage system and advocated

---

* now called Neo-Melanesian.

[1] *TNG, Ann. Rpt.*, 1937-8, p. 31.   [2] *Eckert*, 1940, p. 33.
[3] *Mead*, 1956, p. 96.

a modern way of life, including 'working for money, buying European goods, and dressing like Europeans'.[1] Another policeman, Paliau, set up a fund to pay the fines of those who failed to pay their taxes.

But these developments had not gone far when the Japanese invasion transformed the situation. The Japanese occupation was uneventful, but their ruthlessness and duplicity were bitterly resented by the natives. On the other hand, official Allied propaganda was unimaginative in the extreme, amounting to little more than the simple formula: 'The Japanese are bad. Kill them . . . We are coming back'.[2] The unsettled islanders, however, were looking for a more satisfying and comprehensive programme than this. Two of the central issues they were concerned with were economic reform, including the overthrow of the authority of the elders, and racial equality.

When the Japanese were expelled by the U.S. forces, Manus became the site of a truly enormous base for the mounting of the campaign in the west. For a while, the possibility of Japanese counterattacks inhibited labour recruitment,[3] but the immensity of the U.S. forces flocking into Manus soon dispelled these ideas. No less than one million American troops passed through this base during the war; the effects on native life were prodigious. At times, too, the number of Negro troops exceeded that of Whites. And native labourers received U.S. Army food; they witnessed the abundant American mechanical equipment doing the heavy work; they were deeply impressed by the pains taken and the services available to cope with health problems. This medical system, too, was part of a different system of thought from indigenous or mission medicine, which so often connected illness with sin and moral lapses. And the islanders were touched by the generosity of the American soldier. For the first time they saw a European society—albeit an extraordinary military one—functioning as an entity, instead of being presented with scraps of European material and mental culture. Their reactions were correspondingly comprehensive and fundamental.

They formed the general conclusion that the Americans placed the highest value on the preservation of human life and on the removal of arduous physical toil, and saw that all this was made

---

[1] *op. cit.*, p. 215. [2] *op. cit.*, p. 216.
[3] *Stanner*, p. 90.

possible by their 'having plenty of things'.* On top of this, the Americans treated them as brothers and as human beings. Unlike the Australians, they were 'casteless and classless' in their attitudes; 'Australian' became a deprecatory term applied to people who took things from others by battening on their relatives or by fleecing people in gambling. For the islanders, the American era was 'the time without taboos'.

The effects of this extraordinary invasion showed themselves soon after the end of the war. In 1946, Paliau, the man who had earlier set up the fund to pay the fines of tax defaulters, now appeared at the head of a new movement of popular discontent. A former sergeant in the New Guinea police, he was also an orator possessed of great dynamism, organizing ability, and literacy in Melanesian pidgin. He had been in Rabaul during the war, and had been given authority over all village officials in the Rabaul area by the Japanese. The Allied authorities did not charge him after the expulsion of the Japanese, since, as a native, he was considered to have 'owed no allegiance to the King or the Australian Commonwealth',[1] and since many Australian officials had told the natives to obey the Japanese.

Paliau soon had some third of the 13,000 natives of the Manus District under his influence, and between 1946 and 1950 established control over most of southern Manus. He recruited many followers from the ranks of those expelled from the Roman Catholic mission, from which large numbers of people now defected. He also gained support from immigrants who needed land which they could not obtain from the land-owners, and from the younger men who wanted the abolition of bridewealth. Many of these youths, too, because of the war, had not become involved in what Mead calls the 'economic treadmill' of the traditional economy, and were looking for other more modern and constructive channels for their energies.

Paliau's stronghold was the village of Mouk, a populous trading community on a small island, and the 'most remarkable aspect of the movement [was] . . . the achievement of Paliau in getting the

* This account of native reactions inevitably leans heavily on Margaret Mead's analysis (*Mead*, 1956, Chapters 7 and 8); a full study of the Paliau movement is being undertaken by her co-worker, Mr Theodore Schwartz.

[1] *UN*, 1951, p. 6.

traditionally hostile seafaring and land-dwelling Manus native population groups to work together'.[1]

He not only organized his followers politically, but even built up an independent church whose services and daily prayer resembled those of the Roman Catholic church, and whose ideology was based on the utopian aspects of Christianity. The Garden of Eden would exist once more if only sin were abolished. The sins most attacked were quarrelling, stealing and similar anti-social behaviour. It would be erroneous to overweight the mystical aspect of Paliau's doctrine, however, in spite of stories of visions, dreams, inspirations, etc., as Government itself pointed out. Paliau's feet were well on the ground. He preached a break with the past, the abandonment of burial feasts, of the use of dogs' teeth currency, bridewealth and polygyny.

The converse of this was a heavy emphasis on social improvement: on peacefulness and good-neighbourliness, on elementary hygiene and sanitary improvement, on the wearing of clothes, and on better housing and schools (in which these doctrines were to be taught). He called for economic cooperation, communal organization and the concentration of population in a way which would wipe out the distinctions between the former separate communities. This programme was partly expressed in quasi-Biblical terms, but Paliau used his new organization for very secular ends: the organization of communal food supplies, the building up of financial reserves, the cleaning of villages, the planting of crops, and so on.

He was bitterly attacked by White opponents, who accused him of establishing a totalitarian régime, including 'customs'—passes to permit the movement of people—marching, drilling, curfews, etc. Most of these accusations were malicious misinterpretations of the facts. Paliau also gave sanctuary to women fleeing from their husbands as part of his campaign to raise the status of women: he attacked the old marriage system in an attempt to make marriage easier for young men. Mead tells us that in Australia Paliau was 'played up as the harem-keeping mogul of a "Cargo cult"'.[2]

Paliau's programme swept him to success. With the aid of lieutenants called 'besmen' (?boss men, ?face men) he gained control over Baluan and the surrounding islands in 1946, organized a boycott of the Administration, and is said to have urged the ex-

[1] *TNG, Ann. Rpt.*, 1950-1, p. 27.   [2] *Mead*, 1956, p. 208.

pulsion of the Europeans and Asians. In 1947, he was arrested, and his movement accused of 'terrorism', the desecration of churches and the burning of administrative records. With other natives, he was taken to Port Moresby for an 'orientation' course. Here he was told of government plans for social development, and the working of Government was explained to him.

Some of the allegations levelled at Paliau were derived from the activities of a Cargo cult called 'The Noise', which had sprung up concurrently with the Paliau movement. This arose on Rambutjon island, under a prophet named Wapi. Village census-books and the hats of government-appointed officials were now burned; people became seized with twitchings and saw visions; property was hurled into the sea, especially traditional objects and even the skulls of the dead so important in the ancestor cult; people claimed to have *seen* the Cargo ships unloading. Planes were coming; the ancestors were returning; and docks were built for the Cargo vessels. People rejected the mission, and spent their time waiting in their homes for the Cargo, or praying in church. The Secret of the Cargo, so long hidden by the Whites, was now revealed in the form of the 'Long Story of God'.

Eventually, the failure of the Cargo to materialize produced a violent revulsion, and Wapi was killed by his disappointed brothers. Government force helped to finish the cult off.* In Peri, where Mead worked, for example, and where a dock had been built for the Cargo vessels, all the leaders were arrested.

Paliau himself was involved in the mystical upsurge for a short period, but soon broke with these excesses, and his movement soon attracted support away from the cult. Things remained quiet for a month or so and Government set up a special sub-station in the area. Batea Tapo, who stepped into the breach as acting leader, stoutly affirmed that the government officers had no real power, and that Paliau was the true legal authority.

Paliau returned on 29th July 1947. He now attacked Cargo fantasies, and vigorously set about organizing communal agriculture in which once-hostile communities cooperated. Important reorganizations took place. Manus villages moved on to the land; Usiai villages moved down to the coast. The movement now embraced members of no less than thirty-three former villages.

* There were later flickers on Johnston Island, which proved abortive. The Usiai of Bunai were also affected.

Paliau and his followers also established village councils which Administration officials attempted to guide.

By the end of 1949, one sixth of Manus was under Paliau's control. Recognizing the power of Paliau's position, and that simple repression was ineffective,* hostile Administration officials devised what Mead calls a 'Machiavellian' scheme. This was to establish a Council which would give Paliau authority over Baluan and adjoining islands, which contained a smaller proportion of the Manus who formed Paliau's strongest following, even though Baluan was actually his original home. This division meant that only a half of his followers could be included in the new Council area and would leave his Manus followers on the main island isolated, and thus weaken both halves of the divided movement. The plan was largely successful: Paliau was made *luluai* of Baluan in May 1949, but establishment of a Council was deferred. He thus possessed very limited official powers over about half the area actually under his control. His followers on the main island, though split off from him, still adhered to the movement, led by his lieutenant, Samol. And, despite his limited powers, Paliau accomplished much in a short time. There was no shortage of food; indeed, food was sold to the District Officer and traded with the mainland villages for sago and building materials. Housing showed a 'marked improvement'; every married man had a 'spacious and suitably constructed house', and 'ample accommodation' was available for single men. There was no anti-Administration propaganda.[1]

The following month, Administration attitudes stiffened. Life was said to be 'completely regimented', with military drill, fines, prostitution, the banning of money and its replacement by barter-exchange, clandestine councils, bans on government and mission schools, on government and mission medical services, on government courts, and on any other contact with Whites. But the preaching of the brotherhood of man had awakened a 'new consciousness in the minds of the people', and was favourably reported to the United Nations.[2]

Had the Paliau movement, then, changed from being creative and progressive in November to being sinister and subversive in

---

* Paliau was once arrested for 'adultery'—'the principal legal recourse against unpopular local leaders, rather like income-tax accusations in the United States' (*Mead*, 1956, p. 192).

[1] *TNG, Ann. Rpt.*, 1950-1, p. 28.   [2] *UN*, 1951, p. 6.

December? It would seem, rather, that the character of the movement had not changed, fundamentally, but the way in which it was being reported had. We have frequently been obliged to use inverted commas and such phrases as 'it is alleged . . .', 'it is said . . .', etc., not because of any desire to 'write down' unpleasant truths about these movements, but because nearly all our material comes from sources hostile to the movements. Frequently, internal evidence reveals contradictions, but often one can only infer from comparative knowledge that certain interpretations are distortions, either through lack of understanding, or deliberate. Such distortions, of course, provide valuable insights into the attitudes of those who make the reports. The shifts in tone in regard to the Paliau movement thus constitute a classic, but by no means unique, case. For the Solomons, for example, the introduction by natives of social changes, long advocated on paper by the administration, which then denounced this 'racing ahead' as 'subversive', have elicited the following bitter comment from one writer: 'unless the Solomons can experience an economic revival of a democratic kind, and the fruits of sound political and legal innovations, bitterness will continually hamper the efforts of administration, however well-meaning. If such a happy state could be achieved the other Melanesian colonies would have much to learn from the interesting experiments in progress. As it is, they may well profit from the errors which need not be repeated.'[1]

The projection of these errors on to the natives in the form of charges of 'subversion', etc., should not mislead us into acceptance of such analyses at face value. It was not to be long before official bodies were vying in paying compliments to the movement and in ridiculing past alarums and excursions.

There was undoubtedly some degeneration in relations with Government, however. This was not due to a wave of subversion, but to the delay in setting up a proper Council on Baluan. The frustration of people in this situation has been graphically described by Mead for the people of Peri village, who were similarly awaiting their own Council when she was there. In order to keep interest alive frequent meetings were held, and even the smallest issues were discussed at length. But enthusiasm for a powerless body diminished, and men took to gambling as an alternative focus of interest.

[1] *Belshaw*, 1950a, pp. 128-9.

Dissatisfaction with this state of affairs culminated in a campaign in early 1950. This was not a revolutionary campaign, but called for the establishment of Village Councils. At meetings of hundreds on Baluan Island, it was declared that 1951 was to be the year for the establishment of the Councils. Rumours of the usurpation of magisterial powers by some native leaders were unsupported by any evidence, it was reported.[1] But in April Paliau was arrested. On arrest, he had £1,000 worth of funds. He was charged with spreading false reports that he had legal powers which he did not in fact possess, and received six months' hard labour.

The arrest was a bombshell to the people. Deputations flocked to the District Commissioner in protest. They were told that Government would set up Village Councils 'soon', when an official was available to organize them. At meetings of native officials with the United Nations Trusteeship Council Visiting Mission on 22nd May 1950, 'impertinent' questions were asked. One man demanded to know what country was governing the people of Manus? On the same day, a native speaker, 'obviously an ardent and intelligent supporter of Paliau', complained of Paliau's arrest and was strongly supported. 'Paliau brought us light', the speakers said, 'He is in gaol. What shall we do?' 'The atmosphere was such that the Mission felt that a statement was necessary'.[2] One of the members then told the people that the Government of Australia was their legal Government.

The Mission took leave to doubt government claims that the movement had lost ground since Paliau's arrest. They considered that Paliau had known that he might be arrested, and welcomed the publicity this gave him. He again left a well-briefed acting leader. 3,000 natives were now said to be 'deeply involved'; of the 6,000 Roman Catholics, at least 1,500 had severed all relations with the clergy.

An officer was now quickly appointed, and established a Council at Baluan. The people eventually elected both Paliau and non-Paliau members. Other Councils were later to be set up in nearby areas under Paliau's influence.

During his imprisonment, and for a few months afterwards, Paliau was in Port Moresby, where Administration officials, including an anthropologist, talked to him. He attended local Village Council meetings, saw an educational centre and local cooperatives,

[1] *TNG Ann. Rpt.*, 1950-1, p. 28.   [2] *UN*, 1951, p. 6.

and accompanied an Infant and Maternal Welfare party on a visit to some villages. He also visited Kerema District with the Cooperative officer and saw copra being produced with government assistance, and attended book-keeping classes run by the Cooperative section. He said he had learnt a lot, which he would put into practice on his return, and denied any subversive intent; others were responsible, not he.[1]

Paliau was released in October. On his return, he cooperated with Government, as did his followers. By 1951, he was being described as a 'popular figure [who] has carried out his duties enthusiastically and intelligently'.[2]

Baluan Native Village Council, with Paliau as Chairman, covered only a small area as compared with his earlier sphere of influence, though in 1952-3 its area was extended. Large funds collected before the official Council was established were handed over to the new body. The Council raised £2,328 in taxes in 1951-2, and spent this on education, health, agriculture, water supplies, etc. In July 1951, a cooperative for the marketing of copra was set up, and a trade-store established; two native medical assistants were accommodated, and cocoa plantations started. The 1953 UN Mission reported that there had been 'undue apprehension'. The Mission found 'one of the most orderly, progressive and prosperous communities that it had encountered anywhere in the Territory'. The Paliau movement had been 'absorbed', and 'its adherents were the people who pressed for the establishment of a Council which now, composed of these as well as many people not associated with the movement, has shown excellent results.'[3]

* * *

Thus the Paliau movement was an advanced movement of the Marching Rule type. It was not millenarian, though millenarian ideas were in the air concurrently. And if Paliau had organized an independent church in the early phases, it was not in any expectation of the millennium. He expected the attainment of Paradise through the elimination of sin, much as the missions did, but his Paradise, like theirs, was in the remote after-life, not an imminent heaven-on-earth. The morality he preached was a morality which would consolidate the unity of the people for the achievement of

[1] *TNG, Ann. Rpt.*, 1950-1, p. 29.
[2] *TNG, Ann.Rpt.*, 1951-2, p. 33. [3] *UN*, 1953, p. 10.

practical aims. How little this was a mystical phenomenon, and how much a political one, is evident from the ease with which the church organization was relegated to the background.

In important respects, Paliau's movement, despite its strong proto-nationalist content, was not as revolutionary as the simple Cargo cult. But the Cargo cults were suffused with fantasy and preached illusory programmes which could not be implemented. Paliau secured more practical gains than any radical Cargo movement, for, if his objectives were limited, they were real and attainable.

The more radical aims, however—the expulsion of the Whites, independence,etc.—were not achieved and, to this extent, the movement disappointed the radical wing. This policy of gradually canalizing the movements into safer channels, rather than meeting them with head-on resistance, became more and more widespread. It was greatly facilitated by the gradual recovery of the island territories from the destruction of the war and by the normalization of the economy.

Such policies were used, for example, in the case of the organization headed by Tommy Kabu in the Purari Delta of Papua. This movement was primarily an economic enterprise rather than a political one. Kabu, the only Papuan to serve with the Royal Australian Navy, had started a cooperative, and quickly collected thousands of pounds.[1] As with Paliau, many of Kabu's followers misinterpreted his Christian propaganda for millenarism[2]: with great enthusiasm they destroyed piles of ceremonial objects and set up a para-military organization. But when the organization ran into financial difficulties, Government eventually established control over it, and split it into smaller units.*

Despite the abandonment of his earlier aims, Paliau was much more successful than Kabu, then, in forcing concessions out of Government and gaining political office whilst retaining his position in the new movement he had set up. And it would be wrong to think that the larger aims of the movement have been abandoned for good and all.

Outside Marching Rule, the Paliau movement is at present the only example of a large-scale, successful independent native political

* An independent native movement among the Nagovissi of Bougainville was similarly brought under government control (*Mair*, p. 202).

[1] *Mair*, p. 202.   [2] *South Pacific Commission, Allen*, passim.

organization in Melanesia (excluding Fiji and New Caledonia) which has been recognized by authority. The course that it takes, therefore, will be of great interest and significance for the region as a whole.

CHAPTER X

A Period of Transition

'SONG THAT IS SUNG IN REMEMBERANCE OF
HOMES LEFT BEHIND'

We have left our homes and beaches
To labour for the war in different places,
In far flung places. In these hard times
We wander aimlessly faraway from home.

Places that were never seen before
We now have seen by toil and sweat
Who has caused this dredded parting???
To be out on scatterd places

In our little homes before the war
Partings from dear ones was unknown
We have worked in different places.
To return is something dim.

We now wonder by our camp fires
Of our homes, our dear ones, and our wives
Longing, hoping, Praying deeply,
To return to home once more.

(From H. Ian Hogbin's
Transformation Scene, pp. 13-14)

THE WAR DID NOT AFFECT all areas of New Guinea equally. Where it did touch it destroyed utterly: 'North of the Huon Peninsula New Guinea was unrecognizable . . . there were not more than half a dozen buildings intact in the main European centres such as Wewak, Madang, Lae, Finschhafen, Samarai, Salamaua, Rabaul or Kavieng. Shops, stores, docks and wharves were little more than wreckage . . . even by 1949 no substantial reconstruction had been made except on the plantations and goldfields.'[1]

15,000 native lives had been lost, 20,000 buildings destroyed and 100,000 pigs killed. On top of this, on 'Black Monday', the two territories were plunged into chaos by the abrupt announcement to the huge body of native labourers that they could go home.

[1] *Stanner*, pp. 86-87.

They proceeded to do so. In August 1945 there were 34,000 men; in February the following year only some 4,100. The production of Papuan rubber declined from wartime figures of 5,000 tons per annum to 2,600 tons in 1953, because of the absence of large supplies of unskilled labour. This demand for unskilled labour was as much the main feature of the post-war economy as it had been of the pre-war. The achievement of about three-quarters of the pre-war volume of copra exports in the Trust Territory by mid-1950 was made possible by a gradual re-expansion of the labour force from 1946 onwards at the rate of about 10,000 a year, reaching a total of 48,185 in mid-1950.

In 1948, 35% of this force was employed on plantations, 18% in mining, 31% (a great increase because of reconstruction) by Government, 10% in shipping, commerce,etc., and 6% in domestic service.[1] Whereas the volume of casual labour was six times higher than that of June 1941, the amount of indentured labour decreased by two-thirds.[2] As before the war, however, certain areas supplied the bulk of the unskilled migrant labour for plantations and urban areas. The Sepik supplied most: 12,259 Sepik men worked outside the District at 30th June 1952 as compared with 1,755 within the District. But a new source of labour had now become significant: in 1952 the Central Highlands District produced 3,602 workers within the District, and sent 5,882 to other parts of New Guinea and 2,546 even to Papua in 1952.[3]

Native production was greatly increased, some 20% of the Papuan copra exported coming from this source in 1952.[4] In New Guinea, native copra production reached 3,208 tons in 1950. Quantities of other crops were also marketed by natives. Other fields of activity were entered by native entrepreneurs: in 1953 there were three times as many trucks in native hands in New Guinea as pre-war; already by 1951, 110 drivers' licences had been issued to natives in Kavieng alone.[5] Among this stratum, Cargo notions were giving way to orthodox political and economic movements. A new class of petty traders was coming into existence and was destined to play an important role in future events.

In addition, a new, but small, class of casual non-indentured labourers was springing up in a few centres. Amongst these, and even amongst indentured workers, strike action, which had been

[1] *Stanner*, p. 139. [2] *ibid.,* p. 137. [3] *UN*, 1953.
[4] *UN*, 1954. [5] *UN*, 1951, p. 12.

extremely rare before the war, became common after 1945, usually on a small-scale, local basis over minor issues. At Lae in 1945, a large demonstration and a wave of wage demands followed the rumour that the soldiers of the Pacific Islands Regiment had achieved pay rises by methods akin to striking; at Rabaul, native medical orderlies left work *en masse*; and at Wewak in May 1946, 250 men ceased work in sympathy with the native police.[1]

During 1947-8, there were nine industrial disputes, involving from three to three hundred natives at a time, a total of 448 natives altogether: this is typical of the post-war level of strikes. The workers struck on a variety of matters: hours of work, overtime, clothing, rations and other issues, rates of pay, abuses by employers, and so on. The shortest strike lasted an hour, the longest five days. The different rates of development in different areas are reflected in the range of wage demands at different times in various areas: 10/- per day at Rabaul, £12 per month at Lorengau, £2 per month at Maprik, 5/- per day at Skotolan (Bougainville). With good markets, coastal natives could often satisfy their wants by producing cash crops. The less favoured areas were still almost solely exporters of men.

The advanced regions had thus passed from the Cargo cult to the strike, the Native Council, the Rural Progress Society and the cooperative.* Under the stimulus of the Paliau movement, Government brought into existence other Native Councils: two in New Britain and three in the Rabaul area by 1953, as well as Paliau's Baluan Council. After Papua and New Guinea were joined together in an administrative union in 1949,† two native members were appointed.

* Petitions to UNO were also made, especially by educated, richer and more politically conscious natives in the Bismarck Archipelago, cf. petition from Paramount Chief Tongania of New Britain complaining of commercial companies, missions,etc.,and from a native technician, Chairman of the New Ireland Native Club, concerning price discrimination by Chinese copra-buyers,etc. (*UN*, 1951, p. 26).

† An action which some members of UNO declared to be contrary to the principles of Trusteeship. Criticism was voiced on other topics: 99% of the schools in New Guinea were still in mission hands; only eight natives were receiving higher education,etc. India complained that after thirty-five years nobody had yet successfully completed secondary education; the USSR that despite record profits, there was no company tax on foreign companies, etc., etc. (*UN*, Press Releases, T. R. 1045, 24th June 1955 and T. R. 1046, 27th June 1955).

[1] *Mair*, pp. 216-7.

Cooperatives were developing rapidly in certain areas, with a Cooperative school at Sohano. The Buka-North Bougainville area, once ridden with Cargo cults of which there were now only the faintest flickers,[1] significantly became an area of rapid cooperative development; fourteen societies flourished on Bougainville by 1952 with a turnover of £3,000, and twenty-one on New Ireland with a turnover of £10,891. Likewise, in the area of the former Taro cult, cooperative activity was considerable, despite the opposition of private commercial interests. Native concern to develop their own trading enterprises was probably stimulated by fear of the re-emergence of the pre-war situation, for the handing-over of store-trade to private interests by the wartime Production Control Board resulted in immediate price increases of from $11\frac{2}{3}\%$ to $46\frac{2}{3}\%$.[2]

All these developments indicated a large-scale turning away from millenarism in the more advanced areas. But while Cargo movements were disappearing in these areas, the wheel had come full circle in those areas just recently brought under administrative control. Here Cargo ideas were just beginning to spread, particularly to the Highlands of New Guinea.

The Central Highlands

First discovered some twenty years ago, the Highlands of New Guinea are still in the process of being opened up, a process which is portrayed in the world press as the discovery of one 'Shangri La' after another. The opening up of these populous, mountain-girt valleys has been speeded up in the post-war period, partly because of the Trust Territory status of New Guinea, and partly because of the need to solve the ever-present problem of procuring new supplies of labour. For long recruiting in the Highlands was not allowed, and entry by Whites rigidly controlled. During the war, 'Army orders were issued more than once forbidding the recruiting of highland natives for work in malarious regions'.[3] In fact, recruiting went on: as a consequence many of these natives died at the coast, and malaria and other diseases were introduced into the Highlands. Later, recruiting was officially allowed, and by 1949-50 nearly 4,000 Highlands natives were in outside employment.

Long before the Europeans themselves actually penetrated these areas, the inhabitants received information about them via in-

[1] *TNG, Ann. Rpt.*, 1948-9, p. 58.   [2] *Stanner*, p. 84.   [3] *Mair*, p. 197.

digenous channels of communication such as the Markham Valley. Under the stimulus of the European invasion, Cargo ideas began to take root. As early as 1940, two natives from the Sepik had brought news of the 'Black King' movement,[1] and sparked off a Highlands outbreak near Mt. Hagen, the leader of the movement being gaoled. But even in uncontrolled areas, there were fantastic rumours of houses made of glass, of the coming defeat of the Europeans by the natives, and so on. An ANGAU patrol into the largely uncontrolled region between Wabag and the Dutch border in 1946 found that the people were killing off their pigs in antici-pation of the imminent descent of 'Great Pigs' from the sky follow-ing three days of darkness. Supplies of food, water and firewood were stored up to see the inhabitants through the Big Night, and large Cargo houses were built. Wonderful visions were reported by men who had talked with possums, or visited lake-bottoms covered with valuable gold-lip pearl-shell. And one man had even seen the tail of a Great Pig—which turned out to be a cow's tail![2]

Even where the Europeans had not yet established their rule, or where they had temporarily withdrawn in wartime, there was always the sight of a sporadic aircraft, a crashed plane or a White man fleeing south before the Japanese to remind people of the existence of the Whites and to keep Cargo ideas alive.

In the eastern Highlands, ANGAU officers reported the exis-tence of Cargo activity in areas near the Markham Valley as early as 1943. They found there large 'wireless houses' in which bamboo cylinders were placed with 'wires' running from these cylinders to a bamboo 'insulator' in the roof and thence to a rope 'aerial' outside stretched between two poles. The patrol suspected the presence of Japanese; they lay hidden till next morning, when they witnessed the villagers assemble outside the house to practise drill with canes instead of rifles. Two natives whom they seized explained that the cult had been started by Markham natives who had told them of the imminent Coming of Jesus. The wireless would give them advance notice of the Coming. Then rifles woud be issued, and the ready-trained natives would expel the Whites. Several 'wireless houses' were found and destroyed.

In the centre of the houses were poles with rungs to which Jesus was to come, or up which the natives would climb to Jesus; the natives were also equipped with cane 'flashlights' with which to

[1] see above, Chapter V.   [2] *Simpson*, 1954, pp. 254-7; *Blood*, passim.

see Him. The officer who dealt with this movement informed the natives that 'Jesus would notify his coming to the "Governor" in the first instance . . . but it would be many years before such a thing happened; and if it ever did happen the news of his coming would emanate from the "Governor" himself and only from him'.[1]

The repression of this cult seems only to have aggravated it, and to have provoked anti-White feeling. In the next outbreak, two years later, the people now believed that the Whites had been intercepting the Cargo coming from the ancestors. The affronted ancestors would now bring the goods direct and in person, out of a large mountain in the south; a 'wireless' pointing to the mountain would receive the news, and a house was prepared for the ancestors. Graves were cleaned up, and native weapons and other goods destroyed; only enough food and goods for the interregnum period was preserved, the rest destroyed. Believers were anointed with coconut oil from the Markham at the foot of the poles. When the millennium arrived, black skins would be shed for white, and the White man's goods would go to the natives.

Deliberately breaking the rules excluding women from the men's huts, all natives, male and female, lined up daily outside the huts, and then entered one by one saluting the leader as they entered. Inside they waited reverently while he communicated by 'wireless' with the returning ancestors, and then sang songs. Planes engaged in aerial combat were said to be fighting battles between the ancestors and the Whites.[2]

These movements soon spread further into the Highlands, thriving on the disturbance and alarm created by the war: military concentrations at government posts, the bombing of mission and administrative stations, land-fighting near Kainantu, plane crashes and so on. The notion of the shedding of black skins for white and the use of dummy rifles were carried from the coast right into the Highlands.

Nevertheless, there was a period between the time of the first contacts with the Whites up to the importation of Cargo notions from outside during which the ground was prepared for these ideas. During this period the people independently developed some of the central notions of the Cargo movement.

When the first planes had been sighted in the 'thirties, there had

[1] ANGAU report quoted in *Berndt*, 1952-3, p. 230.
[2] Patrol Report cited in *Berndt, op. cit.*, pp. 230-2.

been great alarm. The noise itself created consternation, but the actual sight of the huge 'Bird' drove the people to hide their faces, to protect themselves magically, and to seek explanations. J. L. Taylor, one of the pioneers of Highlands exploration, describes the effect of air-drops on the inhabitants: 'Each time the machine . . . tore down the clearing . . . rice, flour, axes and goods of all descriptions came hurtling to the ground. . . . The local people sat in awe and wonderment, their eyes wide open at the sight. To them the aeroplane was a messenger from the heavens bringing food to spirits who had become stranded.

'Some old men actually told us by signs that they were ready to depart with us to our world above. . . .'[1]

Small wonder that the myths of the Cargo developed! And when people visited Kainantu and saw the White men actually emerge from the Bird's belly, they believed them to be reincarnations of the spirits of the dead. Once this initial fear had been overcome, they welcomed the Whites because of the material riches they brought.

These initial feelings of awe are reflected in the rumours that the Whites had sent snakes which would enter the vulvae of pregnant women and kill them.[2] (This rumour probably arose because Europeans had had sexual relations with native women at Kainantu and elsewhere.) Various measures were taken to counteract these snakes: people assembled in large houses for mutual protection and stayed there until their stores of food and firewood were exhausted. There were other rumours of a maleficent spirit; and a rumour that all black pigs would die and rot led to a slaughter of these animals.

A new phase was entered with the story that the ancestral dead had returned to Kainantu and were to make their friends and relatives wealthy. Now the initial reactions of mystification and awe, which had led people to adopt negative magical precautions, were succeeded by positive expectations. Perturbation was temporarily relieved through the promise of future certainties and through providing an outlet in action to a people desperately searching for a solution. In Berndt's words, the people were 'ready to be credulous given the opportunity'.[3] Consequently, Cargo beliefs spread like wildfire, especially since European goods were

[1] TNG, *Ann. Rpt.*, 1938-9, p. 144.   [2] *Berndt*, 1952-3, p. 53.
[3] *op. cit.*, p. 64.

already filtering into the area, even before the actual arrival of the Whites. And news that goods could be obtained through wage labour also reached the uncontrolled areas.

At this stage, the idea grew that the spirits (Europeans) were withholding the goods, since these were so slow in arriving. Moreover, during the war, the missions withdrew and the work of the Administration was considerably restricted. In some 'controlled' areas inter-village fighting again broke out. The consequent diminution of the flow of European goods exacerbated anti-European feeling. At the end of the war, the Cargo doctrine reached the area. By 1947, when administration was resumed, a large number of villages had been affected by a 'Ghost Wind' which had blown across the land, affecting all it reached with shaking and shivering like the *jipari* of the Taro cult.

People lived in daily anticipation of the arrival of the Cargo, but they were not merely passively waiting for its arrival: they took action themselves. Experiments were carried out to test the validity of the doctrine. They took various forms. Commonest was the placing of objects inside a specially-built hut: 'they collect oven stones, cut lengths of wood and pick leaves; the house . . . is regarded as a store, while the stones, leaves and wood represent commodities—paper and rifles and knives.'[1]

Salt and letters were also represented; ancient stone mortars, commonly found in the Highlands, were also used as symbols of the Cargo. Pigs were killed and the meat placed on platforms in front of the houses for the spirits to consume; the blood was used to anoint the objects and the house, following the pattern of traditional blood-sprinkling rituals. The surrounding area was cleared and swept in European style. Other experiments involved digging out and transplanting trees, digging for the expected goods, and so on. Instructions about these procedures were given in dreams to visionaries by ancestral dead or by Europeans or, in one case, by a pig.

There were familiar bans on gardening, exhortations to kill off pigs, taboos on the use of water, etc., as well as certain local ritual peculiarities. Conventional behaviour was abandoned: men and women resided together in the large houses, fighting was abandoned, and so on.

And constant failure did not diminish faith. Failures were ex-

[1] *op. cit.*, p. 57.

plained in terms of human deficiencies or the use of inefficacious formulae, or attributed to interference or trickery by other people, but the spirits themselves were not blamed, nor was belief in the truth of the Cargo myth weakened. Missionized natives who sought to expose this belief as nonsense were not regarded as public benefactors. There was 'sullen resistance' to their scepticism; people listened to them, 'sullenly staring at the ground' and said that the objects had failed to turn into Cargo because of them. 'We were on the verge of receiving rifles, axes and so on, and you spoilt it all', they said.[1] Failure was thus couched in terms of the belief. Morale was further boosted in the face of failure by concrete 'evidence' of success: cartridges from wrecked planes, newspaper,* calico and other trade goods were often shown as magical first fruits of the harvest to come. Most experiments, too, were on a small scale and were very localized; failure in one area did not necessarily undermine faith somewhere else.

Conscious deception was common, though other experimenters were as honestly surprised as their followers, and some repaid their supporters for losses entailed in the experiments. The fakers would make their noses bleed, and then claim that the spirits had done this. Others heated bamboos to make them explode to simulate rifle-shots. Yet another buried a knife and an axe in a swamp until they turned black in order to make them look unusual 'spirit' products.[2]

Such deception often brought retribution to those who deceived their fellows. But frequently it followed the lines of traditional cleavages between hostile villages: Cargo trickery now became a new weapon to use against one's enemies.

Where no obvious cause of failure could be found, failures were often blamed on the Europeans, whom the natives had been encouraged to hate by the Japanese in wartime. One man even armed a group of his followers with wooden rifles, but they were disarmed and ridiculed by mission natives. Nevertheless, the stress on obtaining rifles to drive out the Europeans increased.

Since it was becoming dangerous, the movement was now faced

* Because of wartime shortages, newspaper was used to make cigarettes in parts of the Highlands. A missionary could obtain five pounds of European potatoes, or pay for half a day's labour with a half-sheet of the *New York Times* (*Gitlow*, pp. 80-81).

[1] *Berndt*, 1952-3, p. 60.
[2] *Berndt*, 1954, pp. 215, 217, 219.

with repression. A series of arrests and imprisonments drove it underground and the leaders were dealt with by both formal and informal courts.[1] These very actions convinced the people of the truth of the Cargo myths, and thus partly reinforced their belief in them. But finally, because of powerful pressure both from White missionaries and officials, from Government-appointed native officials and from mission catechists, and because of eventual disillusionment, the movement gradually waned.

Thus the earliest native reactions had been merely reactions of awe and curiosity, and of concern to find an explanation of the doings of the Whites. To this end, they performed various magical actions in self-protection which had cathartic subjective effects. This stage was followed by the use of the new Cargo magic to try to secure the material goods which had begun to penetrate the area. There is no doubt that 'the desire to obtain material goods was . . . basic'.[2]

In the eastern Highlands, there was no building of airstrips with decorated borders to receive the Cargo planes, as elsewhere in the Highlands.[3] Planes replaced the steamers of the coastal Cargo cults because this region was only accessible by air. But the growth of air transport affected cults outside the Highlands too, and Cargo warehouses were even built to resemble aeroplanes.[4]

The intense desire for European goods was common to the whole people. They were willing to work and trade for the goods, but had little opportunity to acquire them in this way. The intensity of this common desire is reflected in the collective possession of the Ghost Wind. But despite these common aspirations, the movement did not have the mass character of, say, the Vailala Madness. Amongst a people who only yesterday were involved in local hostilities, intensely divided and fearful of their neighbours, the spread of the cult and of the experiments was localized and limited: people would ask kin in nearby villages to bring them enlightenment by selling them the shivering. But even if it never covered a vast area at any one time, the cult halted hostilities over quite considerable areas, and by cutting across sex, locality and other barriers, brought whole areas into a new kind of rudimentary community and consciousness of their common cultural identity. The

---

[1] *op. cit.*, 1954, p. 267.   [2] *Berndt*, 1952-3, p. 62.   [3] *Mair*, p. 66.
[4] see *PIM*, May 1950, p. 85, for a photograph of one of these Cargo houses.

leaders, though frequently people of authority in the traditional order, were not necessarily drawn from this category: some derived their power from new sources, such as their connection with the European order, and some were women. If Cargo magic did not lead to the achievement of the material and objective satisfactions explicitly aimed at, then, the activity itself led to a temporary psychical and subjective satisfaction. It damped down frustrations through the constant regeneration of hope, even if this hope gradually diminished.

*   *   *

While Cargo notions were only just taking root in the Highlands, they were flourishing with renewed vigour in those intermediate areas where change had not been as profound as in the towns and some coastal rural areas. Vast areas had still only the most superficial direct contacts with Whites, apart from that entailed in labour migration, and had gained little of positive value from this contact. One observer caustically summed up the major imports of the Goilala district of Papua, for example, as 'police, gonorrhoea and Christianity', an observation which could be applied to many areas of Melanesia.*

Cargo cults became a major problem to the Administration in areas such as these. Soon they were the subject of a special Report called for by the Trusteeship Council of the United Nations Organization.[1] Whereas in 1942 it had been possible for Reed to write a history of the Mandated Territory which did not even mention millenarian movements, in the post-war era they were widely recognized as a major administrative problem. News of them percolated through to the Australian public: the Sydney *Sun* printed an article entitled 'Cargo Cult Natives Await their Great White Ship' on 21st June 1950.

'Explanations' of the Cargo phenomenon now became very popular. Most observers regarded the movements as preponderantly religious phenomena, and stressed the savage irrationality of the Melanesian.[2] White settlers saw in them a dangerous step towards native self-determination and towards the subversion of the

---

* though these remarks by McAuley were challenged later by A. M. Bottrill (*South Pacific*, Vol. 7, No. 11, pp. 901-3).

[1] *TNG, Ann. Rpt.*, 1950-1, pp. 24-26.

[2] e.g. Nevermann's essay 'Die Südsee und der Kontinent Australien' in *Westermann*, pp. 261-2.

whole superior position of the Whites. One of their spokesmen, Mr N. M. Bird, posed the 'sixty-four dollar' question of the segregationist 'Would you let a native marry your daughter or sister?'[1]

The Europeans were thoroughly divided on the Cargo issue. Many settlers still blamed the missionaries for these troubles. The missionaries, in turn, hit back and blamed the settlers' treatment of the natives and their master-servant attitudes. One missionary claimed that the natives of his area had been let down by the Whites, who had promised them protection when the Japanese invasion was threatening. And, he claimed, although missionaries had allowed natives to call them by their personal names, this practice had been forbidden by minor officials of the Administration. One native who had done this had been punished by a warrant officer. Settler representatives did not remain silent in the face of these charges.[2]

Whilst this debate raged, the cults were spreading. From the Ninigo Islands of the Manus District to the Loyalty Islands of New Caledonia,[3] Cargo cults abounded. They were not without their amusing moments. The Loyalty Islands movement, due to the activity of Communists, had a peculiar flavour: it was the Communist Party of France which was to send a ship with the Cargo. At Talasea in New Britain, a cult leader named Batari 'scored a strong point on one occasion when a crate marked "battery" was unloaded from a ship—but not delivered to him.'[4]

In Papua, movements broke out on the Lakekamu and in the Goilala District,[5] and later among the Gogodara people[6]; the pre-war Assisi cult still continued in the North-Eastern Division.[7]

Among the Baining of New Britain, the old millenarian ideas of pre-war times smouldered and finally flared up in 1955 when a violent crowd of Cargo enthusiasts attacked a patrol which fired back and killed two natives.[8]

---

[1] *PIM*, 19th July 1946, p. 45.

[2] *PIM*, 18th June 1946, pp. 44-45; see note by the Editor.

[3] *Guiart*, 1951a, p. 129.

[4] *Mair*, p. 66.   [5] *PIM*, 19th November 1945, pp. 69-70.

[6] *Elkin*, p. 39.

[7] *Cranswick and Shevill*, p. 93; *Australian Board of Missions*, pp. 101-103—see Chapter V.

[8] *PIM*, July 1955, p. 67; August 1955, p. 8; September 1955, p. 163.

The major areas of Cargo activity in the Mandated Territory during the post-war era, however, were the Sepik, Madang and Morobe Districts. The backward Sepik region, now exporting more labour even than pre-war, had had its share of the pre-war movements. When the Japanese left, the District was in a most disturbed state.[1]

In places, the Japanese had been welcomed as heralds of the millennium, and Japanese propaganda that they would return once more had some effect on the people. On the Keram River, a Cargo movement broke out in 1944, reviving the old myths of the coming of a native king and the return of the ancestors.[2] Natives on an island near Wewak built an aerodrome to receive the Cargo.[3] On Buka, too, there was a slight recrudescence of Cargo activity which was stimulated by the Japanese promise that they would return in sixteen years' time; Japanese shrines in the bush were said to be venerated by the natives.

The Cults of the Madang and Morobe Districts

The most important, and best described, of the post-war movements come from the Madang and Morobe Districts. Some of the pre-war outbreaks which we have already examined had persisted right through into the post-war period. These movements have been analysed in developmental terms by the professional anthropologists Lawrence and Burridge and by the missionaries Hanneman and Inselmann. Their analyses, therefore, enable us to review processes of development common to many other Cargo movements, and form a fitting conclusion to our presentation of the evidence. I will therefore follow these movements through from the known beginning.

Coastal natives had been terrified when they saw the first Whites, whom they took to be gods (*tibud*) or returned spirits. One native, on seeing his first European vessel, declared that 'Tibud Anut' was passing by, smoking a large cigar.[4] Indigenous myths were thus modified to incorporate strange happenings. The Russian

---

[1] see *Stanner*, pp. 89-90.

[2] Ignaz Schwab in *PIM*, 18th September 1944, p. 16.

[3] *TNG, Ann. Rpt.*, 1948-9, p. 58; *PIM*, March 1948.

[4] *Hanneman*, p. 941. Anut was the chief creator-deity of some of the Rai Coast people. Nevermann records that the Marind-Anim, on first sighting a European vessel, concluded that the spirits of the dead had come from Surabaya to collect coconuts.

explorer, Mikloukho-Maclay, who lived on the Rai (or Maclay) Coast in 1871-2,* long before Government or mission became established there, records how the figure-head of a European vessel washed up on the islands in pre-European days was said to have come from the distant country in the south-east where Anut lived.[1]

Mikloukho-Maclay's relations with the natives had been amicable, but relations between later Europeans and the inhabitants were less friendly. Traders and recruiters deceived and cheated the people; one famous recruiter used to arrive in a village wearing an outfit resembling that of the Ku Klux Klan: he then performed 'magic' with rubber snakes, and astonished the villagers by 'drinking' bucketfuls of salt water (which in fact disappeared into a waterproof bag concealed under the robe). By this sort of trick, natives were impressed and finally persuaded to sign labour contracts for two and three years.

In 1884, the German Government established its control over northern New Guinea, and twice they planted their headquarters in the Madang region, once at Madang itself and another time at Bogadjim. Government was followed by the Lutheran Mission in 1886. Before long, Romilly could remark: '. . . it is almost certain that the natives were not so hostile to the whiteman as they have now become . . . the civilizing process . . . received at the hands of the whiteman since that time has made terrible savages of them.'[2]

The missions had great difficulty in the early days in making any headway at all. Natives would neither send their children to day-schools nor to boarding-schools, and in desperation some missionaries even paid children to attend. Finally, the material attractions offered by the missions won the day: metal tools were the greatest attraction of Christianity to the stone-using natives.

For a long time, the Europeans were not regarded as all-powerful, but as rather pathetic, ignorant people who could be easily cheated or stolen from. Their ignorance of sorcery was lamentable. 'These are not men, they are merely gods' said the natives, judging the Whites to be beings whose lives were inferior to those of living men. Again, they spoke the indigenous tongues very badly; why should

---

* and later in 1876-7 and 1883.

[1] *Mikloukho-Maclay*, Vol. III, p. 149. Earlier, he had thought that Anut was the name of a group (Vol. I, p. 247). The natives even then knew of the existence of metal tools, large houses and clothes in the Land of Anut.

[2] *Romilly*, p. 65.

one bother trying to make out their uncouth speech? And if one did associate with them, was it not likely to provoke the wrath of the ancestral spirits? Surely the country of the White man must be a very bad place, or why would they leave it? Or were these, perhaps, refugees who had fled their country to escape some punishment? Others mocked the prayers and hymns of the missionaries. In face of such opposition and disinterest, the missions were unable to make converts: it took one mission thirteen years before they could persuade one person to become baptized. The natives soon became 'tired of hearing about Jesus so often', and before long began to take active steps to resist the growing pressure from the Europeans. Their increasing hostility was reflected in the new twist given to ancient myths. It was now said that the Cargo was made by the ancestors, and not by Europeans.

On the small islands off Madang plans were laid to kill the Germans, but the plot went awry, and the rebellion was put down by force in 1904. From 1904 to 1912 there was a period of passive resistance, followed by another rebellion which was suppressed in 1912. This time the whole population was exiled from the Madang area until 1914. The Australians then returned the exiles to their homes.

The natives now appear to have held a series of meetings, and to have come to the conclusion that they could gain nothing by further armed resistance, but might gain much by cooperation. Having taken this decision, they decided to follow through its logical implications to the hilt. They flocked to the mission stations in droves, and suddenly became cooperative and enthusiastic Christians. Between 1920 and 1935 mission control was established over most of the southern half of the District, mainly by Lutherans. It is clear that the natives saw 'conversion' as a means of fulfilling their material wants; they believed that by becoming Christians the 'secret' of the Cargo would be passed on to them.

They persevered with Christianity for a long time. By 1929, however, they were becoming impatient. 1930 saw a Cargo movement on Karkar, and finally, in 1933, a petition was addressed to the missionary Rolland Hanselmann asking why the Cargo was being withheld.[1]

From this time onwards, a full-blooded Cargo movement, op-

---

[1] *Hanneman*, p. 946.

posed to orthodox Christianity, sprang into life. The vast difference between the lives of the natives and the lives of the Whites was
aptly symbolized by myths which stressed that the Whites had
flowers and the natives *taro*. Flowers now became Cargo symbols
everywhere, and the red flowers were said to represent the blood
of Jesus coming out of the earth.

The air was thick with rumours of an imminent improvement
in native fortunes. The missionaries, who did no work, were to be
excluded from these benefits. A new myth was now spread about
concerning an Administration official at Aitape, up the coast, who
had found a tribe with the 'as* bilong cargo', the secret of the
origin of the Cargo.

The strength of this belief in the Secret of the Cargo has been
graphically illustrated, with a novelist's touch, by Burridge:

'One evening, when I was strolling home, a man . . . followed
. . . . me. From time to time he would murmur, "Hm . . . Ha!
Hmmm . . . Yes!" in perfect imitation of what is, perhaps, our
own stereotype of a punctilious civil servant. Occasionally he
would say "Hmm . . . Okeydoke!"

I stopped for a smoke and offered him some tobacco.

"Thank you, brother", he said.

We remarked on the weather and then he told me he was a
man who knew (understood). *"Mi save"*, he said, *"mi save"*.
"What is it that you understand?" I asked him.

Straightway he commenced to draw a map in the sand. (See
diagram). The dot in the middle, he explained, was where
"Bigpela bolong ol kat up".[1] About him was snow in the upper
layers, night and day (represented by concentric circles). There
was water. "He" said the word and lands came up.

My informant drew the four cardinal points from the circles
and labelled them—wrongly. He identified Rabaul, Moresby,
Manam, Aitape, Manus, Tokyo, North America, South America, England and Germany. All these places were in the Green
Sea around the cardinals. A triangle was then drawn offset from
the cardinal labelled West. From England one had to cross the
White Sea and then the Blue Sea in order to get there.

---

* derived from 'arse' (*as*), the pidgin English meaning of which has
been extended from the original 'buttocks' or 'underside' to 'place of
origin', and thence to 'underlying cause'; see *Murphy*, p. 24.
[1] where God or the Creator appeared or manifested himself.

"And what is the name of *this* place?" I asked, pointing to the triangle he had drawn.

"You know . . ." he replied with a crafty look.

"But I don't", I said.

"Oh yes, you do!" he insisted.

In such a way the informant continued to maintain that I knew what this place was like, what grew there, whether it was hilly or flat, and what sort of people lived there. He maintained too that he also knew all this—so that, as we both knew there was no point in himself telling me what I already knew. At length, after long argument, it was admitted to me that no one in the world had seen this place or knew its name'.*

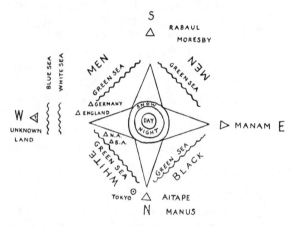

We have already seen how, before the War, a large number of mellinarian outbreaks had occurred in the coastal zone where Burridge made these observations, and we have traced the rise of different movements and their interconnections from the Sepik District and the Madang and Morobe Districts of the Mandated Territory to the north coast of Papua.† We have deferred for consideration until now the Letub movement which first sprang up in Madang District in 1939-40. Letub was a traditional cult

* 'In Tangu I was told of a mysterious place, far away and beyond the seas, where everything could be learned and the good things of this world obtained. This place was identified as Sewende (Seventh Day?)'[1]

† e.g. the Black King movement, the Assisi cult, the Mambu and Pamai movements; see Chapter V.

[1] *Burridge*, 1954b, pp. 936-7.

practised at a large mossy rock in a stream, with which was associated a special dance.[1] Another traditional element woven into
this cult-movement was the creation-myth of the two brothers,
Kilibob and Manup, who had given the various peoples their
material culture and customs and had even created the islands at
the beginning of time, but who had subsequently quarrelled and
finally disappeared.*

This myth was now merged with the Biblical myth of the dis-
inheritance of Ham and his black descendants, so that Kilibob-
Shem-Japheth became the ancestor of the Whites and had the
Cargo, whereas the descendants of Ham-Manup did not.[2] In other
versions, the natives had been offered the choice of the Cargo or
of traditional material culture, and had chosen wrongly.

Invocations were made to the ancestors at the village cemeteries,
asking for Cargo. In some parts, the bones of the dead were dug
up and placed on altars. Planting ceased, and pigs were killed off.[3]
Followers were encouraged to learn English, so that they could
learn the secrets in the Bible, but they abandoned the Mission.
The missionaries had only given them the shell; they wanted the
kernel, they said. In 1940, one *luluai* tried to set himself up as
King of the whole Madang area. The cult dances, which had to be
purchased, spread like wildfire, and prophets with powers of
healing sprang up, some of them women.[4]

One man declared that he was the apostle Paul, and that he
could communicate direct with God by wireless. In a cave behind
Alexishafen, it was said, the ancestors could be heard building
Cargo ships. Another man was jailed for saying that a King was
coming, and several native officials were imprisoned for not
checking the movement. They declared that they had only waited
to see if it was true or not.

Villagers who heard of the cult went to converted villages expecting to find the Cargo already there, and when a prominent

---

* see *Bodrogi*, 1953, for variants of this myth. The first White men in
the area were believed to be Kilibob and his friends returning. Kilibob
was light-skinned (Melanesian physical type?) whereas his brother, Manup,
was dark-skinned. Similar myths have been recorded elsewhere in
Melanesia; see *Guiart*, 1957, for a Tanna version.

[1] *Hanneman*, p. 948; *Inselmann*, p. 102.

[2] *Lawrence*, 1954, pp. 13, 17.

[3] *PIM*, 18th June 1944.

[4] *TNG, Ann. Rpt.*, 1939-40, pp. 27-28.

Letub man died, people watched his grave for months, waiting for a message.[1]

Other spontaneous native movements had developed side by side with the Cargo cult. Some of them received the blessing of missions which saw in them signs of the reception of the Word into native hearts. Like the Poreporena church in Papua,[2] a semi-independent and 'puritan' movement, native Christian movements sprang up in the Madang District also.

The first of these was the Eemasang movement, which had begun as early as 1927 as an orthodox native Christian movement,[3] but under the influence of Cargo thought had become more and more imbued with non-Christian ideas and practices. The dividing line between all these movements became less and less definite.

Just before the war, for example, the Eemasang leaders in several villages ordered the people to assemble in their Sunday clothes for some undefined purpose connected with Cargo beliefs.[4] Eemasang 'English study-groups' now became Cargo breeding grounds where the people were taught that the missions were God's agencies for the dispensing of Cargo on earth.

Missionaries in the Morobe District reported the building of Cargo houses which were guarded by youths by day and night. These houses were ritually consecrated by pouring the blood of sacrificed pigs near the doors and on the doors themselves; the meat was eaten by the villagers and by the cult leaders. Pigs' blood was also poured near pools, in the cemeteries and at other spots.

But all this activity failed to bring the Cargo. The community decided to make a new effort, this time devoted to the improvement of church buildings. Old, rickety churches were pulled down and replaced by new buildings; others were repaired. The earth around the churches was cleaned, and even dwelling-houses and latrines which were not in good condition were condemned. The whole community 'fell in' for church service, and prayed for the Cargo for whole days and nights.

This experiment also failed. Plainly, there must be some defect, if not in the ritual, then in the people. The root of the trouble was sin. Sin must be rooted out by public confessions and public punishment. But after the confessions had been made and the

---

[1] *Inselmann*, 1944, pp. 102-36, and 1948, pp. 41-49.   [2] *Hurst*, p. 114.
[3] *Flierl, L.*, passim, and *Freytag*, p. 50.   [4] *Hanneman*, p. 953.

sinners punished, still the Cargo failed to arrive. The villagers now went into their gardens, stripped them bare and ate all the food, killed their pigs and hens, and implored the ancestors and the spirits of dead missionaries who were buried nearby to help them.

Next they imposed taboos on certain foods, on sexual cohabitation, and so on, with very severe penalties for any infringements.

Finally, the desperate cult leaders were driven to direct fraud. Samples of Cargo which had already 'arrived' were now produced, including a cross stolen from the mission cemetery and other stolen European goods—a deception which was soon exposed.[1]

Like the Eemasang, the Kukuaik movement on Karkar Island began as an orthodox independent Christian body and later turned towards Cargo cultism. In 1940, a sermon by a missionary on the theme of Christ's resurrection precipitated mass seizures, falling on the ground, foaming at the mouth, speaking with tongues and numerous visions.[2] There were rumours of the approaching overthrow of both the social and natural orders: Karkar Island was to turn upside down.[3]

Christ was coming and there would be a great Darkness. There was a rush on the stores to buy lamps. When the Cargo arrived, a native kingdom would be set up.

Plantation workers began to flock home to await the great day. Government immediately arrested the leaders of the movement, and tried them at Madang. But the prophecy of the Coming came true: it was the exact day of the first Japanese bombing of Madang. In December 1942, the Japanese occupied Madang, and in January they were on Karkar. The Whites fled; their plantations were looted, and the remaining labourers returned home. The Japanese were friendly towards the natives, who welcomed them warmly.[4] Under the stimulus of Japanese propaganda, Cargo ideas flourished vigorously, and during 1941-3 many visionaries arose.

The natives soon became disillusioned with the rule of the Japanese, and began to long for liberation. Visionaries now prophesied the arrival of the Allied armies which they had seen in dreams.

When liberation finally came, however, in 1944, it soon became apparent that the Cargo dream was not to be fulfilled. Attitudes towards the Whites now changed, Cargo leaders began to tell the

[1] *Hanneman*, pp. 954-5.   [2] *Hanneman*, pp. 948-9.
[3] *Mair*, p. 66.   [4] *Höltker*, 1946.

people that the Whites were stealing their goods, including mechanical equipment. They should now drive them out. Shortly, their black skins would be shed and replaced by white. This message aroused great fervour, and a rash of religious meetings ensued, with mass hymn-singing.[1]

When the U.S. Army began to exhume the bodies of its dead, this was taken as a sign of imminent change, and fitted the cemetery-worship well. It was said that the bones were being removed before the natives could get them, and thus obtain the secret of riches. Christ had died once more, leaders proclaimed, and His bones were being gathered at the U.S. cemetery at Finschhafen en route for the U.S.A.!

Large imitation U.S. camps were now set up all round Madang on deserted Army camp-sites, filled with devotees white-hot with enthusiasm, even though residence in these camps entailed journeying several miles for food and firewood. At daybreak, the people 'fell in' with their 'commanders', 'paymasters', 'sergeants', 'RT operators', 'guards' and even their women and children.[2] The influence of this cult eventually spread even into the Highlands.

But the 'soldiers' were armed not merely with dummy rifles; they also had stolen grenades and other equipment. In the end, an armed revolt broke out in 1944 in the Bagasin area, but was soon put down.[3]

Its leader was a man named Kaum, a former police-boy at Rabaul who had prophesied the return of the Japanese and the expulsion of the Europeans. He was arrested and gaoled for nine months; on his release, he revived the movement and was again arrested, and gaoled for six months. In 1949, he was gaoled once more.

Neither the failure of the rebellion nor his sojourns in gaol dampened Kaum's fanatic enthusiasm. He next took employment in Madang, where he instituted another movement in the Labour Compound. He claimed to have been killed whilst in gaol, and to have gone to Heaven where God had named him Konsel (Council?). He had seen the dead ancestors there making Cargo, and had been given special ritual and a special symbol (probably a gun-shell) by one of the indigenous deities. In deference to his special status, other workers cooked Kaum's food for him.

---

[1] *PIM*, 19th November 1945, pp. 69-70, by N. M. Bird.
[2] *PIM*, July 1947, p. 9.   [3] ANGAU report cited in *Berndt*, 1952-3.

His rituals included various Europeanisms: prayer round a table, flowers in bottles, plates of food and tobacco, and so on. Kaum slept by the table at night, establishing dream-contact with Paradise, as a result of which he prophesied the coming of a tidal wave which would destroy the Whites. He also sent agents to nearby tribes to institute the new ritual.

As a result of the activity of men like Kaum, the whole of the region was thrown into a state of ferment. Among the Garia people, for instance, Lawrence found that no less than ten cult movements had taken place, only one of which had sprung up spontaneously in Garialand itself.

But even Kaum was a minor figure compared to the man whose name is specially associated with the Madang cults—the famous Yali.

Yali, the man who became the outstanding Cargo leader on the Rai Coast, had had a remarkable career. He had been a Sergeant-Major during the war, had served with distinction, and on his discharge, had returned home with enormous prestige. His influence over the Rai Coast people became so strong that when Japanese soldiers were discovered hiding in the bush, it was to Yali that the matter was reported and not to the Administration. At this stage, a missionary described Yali as 'sincere, energetic, and . . . a beneficial influence on the natives'.[1]

Government, appreciating the hold Yali had over the people, now succeeded in persuading him to cooperate with them in a rehabilitation scheme, and for a while all went well. Then, in 1946, the old Letub Cargo movement broke out with renewed vigour.

The Letub enthusiasts began to utilize Yali's name to advance their own cause. During the war, Yali had visited Australia where he had seen munitions and other factories. According to the Cargo leaders, however he had been killed during the war, had visited the King in Australia and God in Heaven, and had received God's promise that the Cargo would soon arrive. He had then returned to earth as a spirit.

The Cargo leaders now appointed lieutenants to carry this message over a wide area, and did so in the name of Yali. Believers were concentrated into large villages, and mass baptisms took place at the hands of native Lutheran evangelists.

Yali himself publicly attacked Cargo ideas at first,[2] and when

[1] *PIM*, April 1947, p. 69.   [2] *PIM*, April 1947, p. 69.

Letub leaders visited him he listened to their requests that he become their leader with reservation, though he did not spurn them. But after a visit to Bogia, in 1946, he became thoroughly disillusioned with Christianity, with the missions and with Cargo cults based on Christian notions.

On his return, he attacked the missions, saying that they were resisting the abolition of the indentured labour system which Government was set on. Yali walked from the Rai Coast to the Sepik spreading this message, one writer declared, and as a result, the people no longer feared the missionaries. He had been greeted like a Black King. Yali had told the people to get their wages from the missions, and so powerful was his influence that one European's labourers refused to follow their master on the next stage of their journey until Yali had given them permission.[1] Cult leaders, however, spread the story that Yali had been to Bogia to arrange for the delivery of the Cargo,[2] which would include war material for use against the Whites.

In 1947, Yali was summoned to Port Moresby, the capital of Papua-New Guinea, for talks with Administration officials, who were becoming most alarmed about his activities. While he was there, he was told that the Europeans did not believe in the Cargo. A native then showed him a book on evolution; this, he said, was what the Europeans really believed in. Yali was deeply shaken; the Europeans, then, really believed in descent from animals, the old totemic religion of his own people. He felt cheated, and now became violently anti-mission and turned once more towards the religion of his ancestors.[3]

On his return, he made speeches urging the people to concentrate on conventional development projects such as cooperatives, cash-crop farming, etc. He was greeted with wild enthusiasm by the people who held huge 'sing sings' for him, decorating the roads, and building platforms for the holding of great feasts.[4]

In 1948, the Letub men contacted Yali once more, and this time he welcomed their advances. Because Yali was now strongly anti-Christian, and because they wanted him badly as a figure-head, the Letub leaders now dropped the Christian elements from their doctrine and substituted the myths of Kilibob and other indigenous deities. The movement now became violently anti-

[1] *PIM*, April 1947, pp. 49-50. [2] *Lawrence*, 1954, p. 5.
[3] *Lawrence*, 1955, pp. 6-13. [4] *PIM*, May 1950, pp. 3-5.

mission under Yali's influence. It spread very rapidly up the Ramu and Sepik valleys as far as Wewak, and round Bogia there was practically a state of rebellion.[1]

Though he could read and write, Yali now had his own clerk to cope with his correspondence. Labourers returning home from work were greeted by their rejoicing comrades who were led by Yali lieutenants or 'kings'. Soon 'haus-Yali' buildings which resembled the traditional spirit-houses in design replaced the mission churches as social and religious centres in the villages. One missionary described how his clerk, a Yali leader, lived in a fine house with a lawn and a large star outlined in shrubs. When accompanying his master on his tours, this clerk used the opportunity to carry out his own independent activity: writing down village populations, making speeches, and so on.[2]

As the cult snowballed, missionaries were threatened with violence, non-believers were gaoled, and illegal taxes were levied. The cult was fast becoming a dangerous threat on a mass scale, and violence was increasing. Consequently, in 1950, Government arrested Yali, who was charged with incitement to rape, and extortion of money. He was eventually sentenced to six and a half years' imprisonment.

Thereafter the movement lost momentum. By 1953, it was dead on the Rai Coast, although the belief still lingered in people's minds. On Coronation night, 1953, there was an outbreak in Madang, but, as Yali was in gaol, he had nothing to do with this directly. In 1955, he was finally released.[3]

The Yali movement, then, represents the last link in a long chain of events reaching back to the days of Mikloukho-Maclay. We have seen how the arrival of the first Europeans was explained in terms of traditional religious beliefs. The Europeans were taken as spirits of the dead, or as manifestations of gods who brought with them material gifts for their descendants.

In the early days, when mission and Government were comparatively weak and could provide but few material attractions with which to wean the natives away from their customary pattern of life, this explanation of the Whites' presence was adequate. But as the activities of missionaries, traders, recruiters, and officials

---

[1] *PIM*, 17th September 1947, p. 58.
[2] *PIM*, September 1950, pp. 45, 47.
[3] Information kindly supplied by Dr Peter Lawrence.

began to impinge more directly upon native society, there developed a corresponding reaction, on the part of the natives, of increased resistance and hostility.

Soon the natives became involved in the European economy, because of the attractions of the Europeans' goods, despite their dislike of the new, inferior social role allotted to them. They then developed the myth of the Cargo created by the ancestors to account for the European possession of these goods from whose ownership they were excluded. After the failure of direct armed rebellion, there followed a period in which there was a turning towards mystical methods of gaining their ends. The people turned to Christianity in the hope that they would thereby require the Secret of the Cargo. Then came disillusion with mission Christianity, the creation of Cargo movements based on Christian myths, and, eventually, the revival of the notion that it was not the Christian God who made the Cargo, but the ancestors of the natives themselves. This time, however, the belief was shared over much larger social areas than in the early days, and not confined to particular peoples.

Yali's personal role greatly affected later developments. In 1945, he had been moving in the direction of orthodox political activity, not millenarism. But whereas the Paliau and Marching Rule movements had developed away from millenarism, Yali was sucked into the vortex of the cults when he felt himself cheated by the Whites.

Though this history has its own particular peculiarities, it helps us to establish a developmental paradigm for the cults. In order to understand the general significance of the cults, however, we must turn to an examination of their content and function from a comparative standpoint.

Conclusions

IN RECENT YEARS there has been a growth of interest in the history of enthusiasm, to use the term resurrected by Ronald Knox, amongst workers in various fields: historians, anthropologists, political scientists and others. And Fränger's suggestion that the painting of Hieronymus Bosch was conditioned by his connection with the millenarian sect of the Brethren of the Free Spirit has stimulated lively debate amongst art historians.

The kind of movement we have described for Melanesia is by no means peculiar to that part of the world. There is, in fact, an enormous literature on millenarian movements in most parts of the globe, even in some of the earliest records of civilization. The history of apocalyptic religions and of messianism is of special interest to people whose culture has included a central belief in One whom they believed to be *the* Messiah, who died for mankind and with whom they hoped to be reunited in Paradise.

This Messiah, however, has not been the only messiah. We have already seen how the millenarian vision of the Melanesian movement was often the vision of the return of some culture-hero, or of the Devil, or even of a 'multiple' messiah such as the spirits of the dead.

Similar cults have occurred to a greater or lesser extent in the other major regions of Oceania—Polynesia* and Micronesia.† Africa, North and South America, China, Burma, Indonesia and Siberia have also had their share of cults, and the history of Europe provides numerous examples.

A great deal of material on the African movements has been skilfully collected together by Katesa Schlosser in her book *Propheten in Afrika*. The movements she describes are not exclusively millenarian, however, for she includes diverse related forms of politico-religious organization. Amongst these are prophetic cults, witch-finding movements, separatist sects and so on.

* notably the Hau Hau movement in New Zealand among the Maori.
† e.g. the southern Gilberts movement of the 1930's.

Some, like Mwana Leza amongst the Ila of Northern Rhodesia, drew their inspiration mainly from Christian sources; others, like many of the North and West African movements, drew on Islamic beliefs; and yet others, like the Mumbo cult among the Kenya Luo used indigenous religious beliefs as the basis of a cult ideology. Schlosser classifies the cults on the basis of the provenance of the religious ideas which form the predominant ideological content of cult doctrine, i.e., pagan, Christian or Muslim. This seems to me at best only a preliminary classification; more importantly, the movements need to be analysed in terms of social process and not merely fitted into pigeon-holes. This African material, therefore, still awaits an adequate sociological analysis. But if the comparative social scientist has neglected this field, at least two of South Africa's finest novels—Sarah Gertrude Millin's *The Coming of the Lord* and Jack Cope's *The Fair House*—have been inspired by movements of this kind.

For North America, and to a lesser extent, Central and South America, there is an abundance of literature on prophetic and millenarian cults. Just as the message of the Delaware Prophet of 1762 was used by Pontiac to weld the Indians together against the Whites, so the great Tecumtha used the mystic visions of his brother in his effort to unify the tribes in defence of their independence. Their failure to achieve this allowed the Whites to complete their occupation of eastern America with comparative ease. So rapid was the subsequent sweep to the west that the tribes there had little possibility of establishing any form of combined resistance. Though prophets arose amongst the Kickapoo in the 1820's and amongst the Winnebago in the 1830's, for example, they only had local influence.

This piecemeal defeat of the tribes was followed by a last great move towards unification amongst the recently conquered western tribes. The two great waves of the Ghost Dance in 1870 and 1890 promised the return of the dead if people would only abandon sin and adopt the cult. In most tribes, the cult was interpreted in passive terms. To the Sioux, however, who had suffered a series of radical shocks, including the loss of their lands, and the loss of the buffaloes which had been wiped out in a fantastic slaughter, and who had been cheated of their treaty rights, the coming of the Dance helped to set off a train of events which culminated in the bloody massacre at Wounded Knee, when 300 out of 370 Sioux were mown down by machine-guns. From henceforth the Indians turned to quietist independent Christian sects or to pacific cults like peyotism.

Turning to China, we find abundant records of millenarian thought, particularly among secret societies following unorthodox schools of Mahayana Buddhism. They emphasized the idea of the redemption of mankind and the coming of a future Buddha who would usher in a reign of bliss, or encouraged the hope of attaining the Western Paradise of O-mi-t'o fu (Amitabha). Such societies, at times, became linked with movements of discontent, particularly among the peasantry, and were therefore visited with repression. Chinese history is studded with accounts of risings led by Buddhist sectaries, in many of which an actual messiah was believed to have appeared.

Orthodox Buddhism had little attraction for those who looked for an activist solution to man's problems, though it offered a solution in terms of resignation and escape. For orthodox belief stressed that it would only be given to the few to become saints and enter into Nirvana, the state of absence of desire and striving. Unlike the Judaeo-Christian and Islamic faiths, which promised salvation to those who led the good life on this earth, Buddhism offered no such hope to the many. Such a doctrine might be congenial to the rulers of a stationary agrarian society and to their resigned subjects, but it could not appeal to a rebellious peasantry. It was therefore not this fatalistic doctrine which commanded the allegiance of those who developed the millenarian side of Buddhist theology. Rather was it the notion of Paradise and of the return of the Messiah that they stressed.

But by far the most striking Chinese millenarian movement was the Taiping Revolution of *c.* 1850-1865, in which Taiping armies swept from Kwangsi Province almost to Peking and threatened the very foundations of the Empire. The movement was initiated by a visionary, Hung Siu-ch'üan, who had been influenced by Christianity, and who formulated a new creed based on the Ten Commandments. His call to cleanse the world of demons and unbelievers by use of the sword found a ready response among the millions of peasants labouring under an oppressive bureaucratic machine and ruled by the foreign Manchus, and among Chinese of all levels of society who felt humiliated by the defeats newly inflicted on China by the European Powers.

In India, on the other hand, that other major cyclical world religion, Hinduism, appears to have been remarkably free from millenarist sects. It would seem that the cyclical beliefs of Hinduism were very rarely interpreted in any millenarian sense. This does not mean that mobility and protest were unknown. Mobility within the apparently rigid caste system did take place, though more by whole groups than by individuals, but revolts against caste as a system only made a new caste of the rebels, since the basic structure of society remained unchanged. The only important Indian millenarian cults which I have found in my researches occurred as a direct result of the coming of the Christian missions, among the Mundas and Oraons of Chota Nagpur. One awaits with interest the explanation of this absence of millenarism from Hindu India, which can only be attempted by an Indologist. It will entail, no doubt, detailed consideration of alternative channels for the expression of social protest and of popular aspirations, particularly among the peasantry, as well as the analysis of the history of theology and political theory in India. As yet, the peasant does not seem to have stepped on to the stage of Indian historiography.

Islamic history contains many important millenarian movements and millenarian ideas. The Shi'a belief in the second coming of the 'hidden Imam', the Mahdi, who will restore the true religion, conquer the world for Islam, and usher in the millennium, and the belief in the second coming of 'Isa'(Christ) both provided ideological ammunition for uprisings, factions, sects and prophetic movements at many points in history. One of the most famous prophetic movements, though not specifically millenarian, was the Mahdiya of the Sudan.

For Europe there is an enormous literature of millenarism, particularly for the Middle Ages. Professor Norman Cohn's *The Pursuit of the Millennium* is the outstanding contribution to our knowledge of this field. He has shown how, while there were heretical groups at all levels of society, it was amongst the lowest strata, particularly amongst the uprooted and disorientated peasants who had been turned into unskilled urban workers or into beggars and unemployed, that millenarian fantasies took strongest root. Right through the Pseudo-Sibylline Prophecies, the belief in the 'Emperor of the Last Days', the Peoples' Crusades, the Flagellant movement, up to the more familiar English Peasant Rising of 1381, to the Taborites of Bohemia, Thomas Münzer and the Reign of the

Saints in Münster, there runs a thread of radical millenarian tradition transmitted from generation to generation and constantly reviving in one form and another. After the Reformation, however, with the defeat of the activist left wing, millenarism became more and more passive, no longer supported by the most forward-looking elements of society, but becoming more and more associated with the most backward elements.

A Religion of the Lower Orders

Certain obvious conclusions emerge from this brief comparative survey. Firstly, the activist millenarian movements—those which anticipate the coming of the millennium in the near future and which set about preparing for this event—have found support at all levels of society at one time and another. But it is amongst people who feel themselves to be oppressed and who are longing for deliverance that they have been particularly welcomed: especially by the populations of colonial countries, by discontented peasants and by the jetsam of the towns and cities of feudal civilizations.

Expecting, and hoping for, the millennium, people have destroyed their cattle, their crops, their means of livelihood. Southern Bantu died in their thousands in the nineteenth century through killing off their cattle and destroying their crops in response to a prophet's appeal; in this century, Eskimos in Greenland became so convinced of the imminence of the millennium that they stopped hunting and ate into their stores of food.

And in order to hasten their entry into the Promised Land, people have actually killed one another or committed suicide. In Crete, in the fifth century A.D., a band of Jews drowned themselves in their millenarian enthusiasm; in Baffin Land, in this century, Eskimos sacrificed two men to hasten the day; and a group of four hundred Guiana Indians massacred one another in order to be reborn in white skins.

Millenarian beliefs have recurred again and again throughout history, despite failures, disappointments, and repression, precisely because they make such a strong appeal to the oppressed, the disinherited and the wretched. They therefore form an integral part of that stream of thought which refused to accept the rule of a superordinate class, or of a foreign power, or some combination of both, as in Taiping China. This anti-authoritarian attitude is expressed not only in the form of direct political resistance, but also through the rejection of the ideology of the ruling authority. The lower orders reject the dominant values, beliefs, philosophy, religion, etc., of those they are struggling against, as well as their material economic and political domination. It is therefore natural that millenarian doctrines often become openly revolutionary and lead to violent conflict between rulers and ruled. Because of this revolutionary potential, millenarian movements are usually treated with the utmost suspicion by Church and State and have often been proscribed and persecuted.

The history of Europe, to take one region alone, provides us with a constant succession of schismatic movements, of which the more extreme frequently had a millenarian flavour, particularly in the Middle Ages. These sects, frequently underground movements, helped to pave the way for the Reformation and represented a tradition of resistance to the established authority of Church and State. The persecution visited upon them, especially by the Inquisition, was an equally continuing feature of medieval history.

Christianity itself, of course, as recent interpretations of the Dead Sea scrolls emphasize, originally derived its *élan* from the millenarist traditions of the Essenes and similar sectaries at the beginning of the Christian era. These people looked for the establishment of an actual earthly Kingdom of the Lord which would free the Jews from Roman oppression. Later this doctrine commended itself as a message of hope to the downtrodden of the Roman Empire. By the time Constantine made it the official religion of the Empire, however, the millenarian beliefs had been pushed into the background. Paul, for example, was initially influenced by apocalyptic ideas, and expected the Parousia* of the Lord in his lifetime, but later preached that the millennium was a symbolic ideal and not a political possibility on this earth. The Kingdom of the Lord now became an extremely remote event, not an immediate likelihood, and the faithful were urged to seek entry into Paradise in the after-life through leading virtuous lives in the here-and-now—and virtue included due respect for the Establishment.

From the time of Augustine, millenarism was specifically condemned by the Church Fathers as a heresy: Montanists in Asia Minor, Joachimites in Calabria, Flagellants, Beghards, Taborites —all were condemned and persecuted. The Kingdom of God on

* the Second Coming or Return of Jesus Christ.

earth, orthodox dogma had it, *had been* established by Christ's first Coming, and was being perpetuated in the Church and its members. The gradual perfection and growth of the Church would lead to the New Jerusalem.

These two streams in Christian thought—the orthodox and the millenarian—have thus persisted for hundreds of years in varying forms. During the Middle Ages, when the Church played such a dominant role in social life, heretical-millenarian movements were the form in which much of the most advanced critical thought was expressed. Marx once described the agrarian history of the Roman Empire as its 'secret history'; the secret history of the Middle Ages is the history of millenarian and allied sects, a history which is only now being written.

The Integratory Role of the Cults

The cults thus serve as an expression of reaction against what is felt as oppression by another class or nationality. But there are other important political characteristics shared by groups prone to millenarism, whatever their cultural differences.

The cults generally occur among people divided into small, separate, narrow and isolated social units: the village, the clan, the tribe, the people of a valley, etc. They occur, firstly, among people living in the so-called 'stateless' societies, societies which have no overall unity, which lack centralized political institutions, and which may lack specialized political institutions altogether. They have thus no suitable machinery through which they can act politically as a unified force when the occasion arises, except on a temporary, localized or *ad hoc* basis. They often have no chiefs, no courts of law other than the council of elders or of prominent or wealthy men, no police, no army and no administrative officials. In Melanesia, for example, centralized or even federal organs are often absent. Indeed, villages and clans speaking the same languages or dialects of one language and sharing a common culture get in a state of intermittent hostility with their neighbours, the very people with whom they trade and intermarry.

Such highly segmented societies are incapable of offering resistance to the incoming Europeans. When the need arises for large-scale joint action by members of these separate groups, now faced with the same common problems, they cannot act politically and militarily at all. Thus in Melanesia the discrete units were absorbed or defeated piecemeal by the colonial Powers in the nineteenth century.

The main effect of the millenarian cult is to overcome these divisions and to weld previously hostile and separate groups together into a new unity. The social necessity which produces this drive towards integration is the subjection of all the separate units to a common authority—the Europeans. Since the people have developed new common political interests where previously they had none, so they must create new political forms of organization to give expression to this new-found unity. It is precisely this integratory function which is served by the millenarian cult. It is therefore especially common in colonial countries in the early phases of the establishment of colonial régimes, particularly where the societies involved are without State machinery.

The second major type of society in which millenarian cults develop is the agrarian, and especially feudal, State. Such societies, of course, have indeed an elaborate formal hierarchical organization unlike stateless peoples, but the cults arise among the lower orders —peasants and urban plebeians—in opposition to the official régimes. These groups, like stateless Melanesians, lack any overall political organization. Their position has been well put in a famous passage by Marx:

'The small-holding peasants form a vast mass, the members of which live in similar conditions but without entering into manifold relations with each other. Their mode of production isolates them from one another instead of bringing them into mutual intercourse. The isolation is increased by bad means of communication and by the poverty of the peasants. Their field of production, the small-holding, admits of no division of labour in its cultivation, no application of science, and therefore, no wealth of social relationships. Each individual peasant family is almost self-sufficient; it itself directly produces the major part of its consumption and thus acquires its means of life more through exchange with nature than in intercourse with society. A small-holding, a peasant and his family; alongside them another small-holding, another peasant and another family. A few score of these make up a village, and a few score of villages make up a Department. In this way, the great mass of the French nation is formed by simple additions of homologous magnitudes, much as potatoes in a sack form a sack of potatoes. In so far as millions of families live under economic conditions of existence that separate their mode of life, their interests and their culture from those of the other classes, and put them in hostile opposition to the latter, they form a class. In so far as there is merely a local interconnection among these small-holding peasants, and the identity of their interests begets no community, no national bond and no political organization among them, they do not form a class. They are consequently incapable of enforcing their class interest in their own name, whether through a parliament or through a convention. They cannot represent themselves, they must be represented, their representative must at the same time appear as their master, as an authority over them, as an unlimited governmental power that protects them against the other classes and sends them rain and sunshine from above. The political influence of the small-holding peasants, therefore, finds its final expression in the executive power subordinating society itself.'[1]

This explanation of the 'cult of the individual' in nineteenth-century France sheds a good deal of light on peasant society in other times and climes. Like people in stateless societies, peasants are divided into tight-knit discrete groups. They are associated in a hierarchical framework, but lack their own common political institutions. Due to the material conditions of their lives, they lack any organization which could give practical expression to their common interests, and they do not see their common interests except in times of social crisis.

When confronted with the necessity of taking concerted action, they are obliged to throw up a centralized political structure *a novo* just as much as any primitive society.

In the particular circumstances of nineteenth-century France, the peasants were thus likely, Marx suggested, to produce a Bonapartist cult, but as we have seen, under other social conditions they look for deliverance not to secular individuals but to supernatural powers. Secular Caesarism flourishes in advanced agrarian society, but, under conditions of much greater cultural backwardness, peasants may equally look up to prophets who

[1] From 'The Eighteenth Brumaire of Louis Bonaparte', *Marx-Engels*, pp. 302-3.

promise a mystical solution to their problems and fulfilment of their hopes. The millenarian cult is thus typical of early phases of peasant political organization.

There is a third type of social situation in which activist millenarian ideas are likely to flourish. This is when a society with differentiated political institutions is fighting for its existence by quite secular military-political means, but is meeting with defeat after defeat. One may cite the case of the rise of the prophet Nongqause at a time when the Xhosa people were beginning to realize that they were losing the long-drawn-out Kaffir Wars.

Again, when the political structure of a society is smashed by war or other means, or fails to answer the needs of a people who wish to carry on the struggle, then a prophetic, often millenarian, leadership is likely to emerge. Significantly, the Hau Hau movement among the Maori arose after the military defeat of the Maori Wars, when many tribes and many tribal leaders had ceased fighting and when others felt that resistance was hopeless. Renewal of the battle called for superhuman and special measures in one last desperate attempt, and took the form of a religious appeal to join the divinely-inspired forces of liberation. There is more than a mere resemblance of names between the Hau Hau and the Mau Mau, for both arose when other political organizations had been broken, and both used extraordinary methods to revive the spirit of resistance and to weld the people together.

The millenarian movement thus brings together, for the first time, social units which have not only been separate from each other—though possessing some cultural links—but often even hostile, for the combination of hostility and cooperation between the very same groups is common. Other related types of religious organization have achieved this result, however, without being specifically millenarian. Professor Evans-Pritchard has shown how in Cyrenaica an Islamic Order, the Sanusiya, succeeded in unifying the small, discrete Bedouin tribes, which feuded amongst themselves, into a solid resistance movement opposed to the Italians.

But the stimulus which drives a people to unite need not necessarily be something external to the society, such as conquest by foreigners. There are many instances of millenarian cults whose cutting edge has been directed not towards foreigners or conquerors but towards members of other classes within the same society. Internal, and not merely external, antagonisms can equally produce millenarism.

For Melanesia, we have seen a general trend in the development of the cults away from apocalyptic mysticism towards secular political organization, a trend from religious cult to political party and cooperative. This development is by no means unusual. But when secular political organization has replaced millenarism, the cults which persist into the era of secular politics almost invariably lose their drive. The revolutionary energy is drained from them; they become passive. The Day of the millennium is pushed farther back into the remote future; the Kingdom of the Lord is to come, not on this earth, but in the next world; and the faithful are to gain entrance to it not by fighting for it in the here-and-now with their strong right arms but by leading quiet, virtuous lives. This transition to passivism is particularly marked in two situations: where the cult has been defeated, and where political aspirations are no longer masked in religious forms, but are expressed directly through political parties.

There are two outstanding examples of this transition to passivism in European history. The Taborites, the communist millenarists of Bohemia during the Hussite Wars, defeated five crusading armies thrown against them. In 1434, they were finally crushed, though the independence of the town of Tabor was recognized. In 1451, the town itself was attacked and the Taborite Government overthrown. The community was dispersed, and hunted down. Later it began to reform as the Bohemian Brethren. But the effects of the defeat showed themselves in the new stress upon peaceful, anarchistic communism and in the replacement of communist social ideals by the profession of charity and by a practical concentration upon industry and frugality.

Similarly, following the defeat of the revolutionary Anabaptists who ruled Münster from 1532 to 1535, this movement also took a much more pacific turn. By 1626, it had even won toleration in the Netherlands, and most notably survives even today in the completely pacific form of the Mennonite community in the United States. Similar trends can be noted in many countries: in South Africa, the millenarian cults which were such important factors in mobilizing whole Bantu groups against White incursions disappeared as modern secular political organization arose. Today, the predominant form of native independent religious organization is the separatist sect, which promises personal salvation in the after-life, where the colour bar is often expected to be reversed.

Where millenarism survives in countries with popular secular political organizations, it is generally escapist and quietist. It rarely looks forward to the millennium as an immediate possibility. Even the Jehovah's Witnesses movement, which still looks to an imminent millennium, is a pacifist body.

Such movements often blame the world's evils not on the rulers of society on a dominant Church or on a foreign government, but on the people themselves as worldly sinners. Their sins are the root of evil; salvation can only come by the recognition of guilt and by self-purification, not by war against the ungodly Establishment.

Movements of this kind are at another pole altogether from activist millenarism. One well-known case is that of the witch-finding movements of Central Africa, where the blame for social discord was not laid on the Whites, but upon the maleficent activities of witches. During the campaign to expose the witches, large quantities of magical equipment were cast out; much of this proved to be equipment used in curative, protective or other positive magical rites, and not in evil magic, but so strong was the belief that witchcraft was on the increase, and that the wickedness of the people themselves was responsible for the increasing discord in Central African society, that *all* magical materials were cast out whatever their purpose.[1] Later witch-finding movements in East-Central Africa showed a trend towards passivism. In the earlier movements there had even been millenarian elements and anti-White overtones, but, as trade unionism and the African National Congress took over the representation of African political and economic interests more and more, the cults came to concentrate upon personal guilt and upon 'divine inspiration, the sharing of sins by confession and "back-to-God" moral rearmament'.[2]

The failure of cults of this kind often leads to a desperate experimentation with all manner of movements which offer some gleam of hope. Frequently one finds that people turn back to Christianity once the cults built upon traditional religion have failed them. The Christianity they turn to, however, is anything but orthodox.

Cora Du Bois, writing of the failure of the Ghost Dance among

[1] *Richards*, passim; cf. *Guiart* (1956c) for a Melanesian parallel, in New Caledonia (pp. 36-37). [2] *Marwick*, p. 112.

the North American Indians, notes how, after the defeats of the Modoc War of 1872-3, the Indians turned to passivist Christian revivalistic cults often derived from, and linked to, fundamentalist White Christian groups: 'The growing influence of Christian ideology . . . mirrors the accumulating despair of the Indians and their realization that there was no room for them in the new social order. Christian beliefs, which were the outgrowth of a not dissimilar cultural situation, offered a ready-made escape into supernaturalism from realities which had become intolerable because they offered nothing but defeat.'[1]

Today, outside such backward regions as Melanesia, where they have a dynamic character, millenarian cults represent an escapist, passive trend and are principally confined to backward communities within the wider society: the White backwoodsmen and the Negroes of the southern States of the USA or the frustrated urban Negro population which has thrown up figures like Father Divine.*

The proliferation of Negro religious cults is *not* a product of any 'inherent religiosity' of the Negro, as Herskovits and others have postulated. It derives from 'the comparatively meagre participation of Negroes in other institutional forms of American culture'.[2] But this self-expression through the medium of religion is gradually giving way to secular forms of expression and organization.

Writing of American White sects, Clark has remarked how they

'originate mainly among the religiously neglected poor, who find the conventional religion of their day unsuited to their social and psychological needs. Finding themselves ill at ease in the presence of an effete and prosperous *bourgeoisie*, their emotional natures unsatisfied by a middle-class complacency, their economic problems disregarded by those who have no such problems to meet, and their naive faith and simple interpretations smiled upon by their more cultured fellows, the poor and ignorant revolt, and draw apart into groups which are more congenial.'[3]

The passivity of these sects is very marked. Clark finds it a 'strange fact' that

* There have been times when independent revivalism has also carried on the democratic 'log cabin' tradition of independence among peripheral communities.

[1] *Du Bois*, p. 150.   [2] *Fauset*, p. 107.   [3] *Clark*, pp. 16-17.

'these sects of the poor make little or no attempt to ameliorate the condition of their adherents. None have any program of social reform, except insistence on temperance and opposition to the liquor traffic. Not one takes an active hand in the labor struggle; most of them, indeed, look upon such matters as political questions to be wholly avoided. Some sects do not even allow their members to vote or hold public office. However they may work and practise as individuals, as Christians they seem to have settled down into a state of resignation, and they expect God to reward them in the world during the millennium of heaven after death. . . . The small sects are nearly always conservative. They insist on the commonplace and the ancient in theology, practice, and manner of life.'[1]

If we examine the statistics published by the Jehovah's Witnesses movement, we find a further significant fact. While the United States is the chief centre of the movement, and while countries like Western Germany, Britain and Canada contain important bodies of Witnesses, the colonial connection of the movement is very important. Four of the ten countries with the largest membership are in south-central Africa—Northern and Southern Rhodesia, Nyasaland and the Union of South Africa—and two other 'underdeveloped' territories, Nigeria and the Philippines, are also among the first ten:

United States	.	.	.	.	24,417,154
West Germany	.	.	.	.	6,466,407
Northern Rhodesia	.	.	.		3,867,515
British Isles	.	.	.	.	3,779,503
Nigeria	.	.	.	.	3,737,390
Nyasaland	.	.	.	.	3,038,594
Southern Rhodesia	.	.	.		3,022,422
Canada	.	.	.	.	3,010,938
Philippines	.	.	.	.	3,001,852
South Africa	.	.	.	.	2,964,391

Table. Hours of activity by members of Jehovah's Witnesses for various countries (source: Watch Tower, 1st January 1955, pp. 27-29, '1954 Service Report of Jehovah's Witnesses World-Wide').

In addition, we find Bantu languages like Lozi, Shona, Sotho,

[1] Clark, pp. 219, 223.

234

Bemba, Nyanja and Zulu side by side with English and German among the chief languages in which the Society's journals are published.

The reason for this striking success in south-central Africa lies in the appeal of the doctrine of the not-distant Coming of the Lord to Africans. The movement is not anti-White as popularly believed, but it is pacifist and has therefore come into conflict with Government. It has been banned in the Belgian Congo (where the alternative native outlet of Kibanguism became an enormous force) and has been 'controlled' in Northern Rhodesia, especially during World War II. The simple democratic canons, rituals and procedures of the movement are also a powerful attraction, and Africans are particularly attracted by the belief that in the USA, as opposed to Britain or Belgium, Negroes are members of the Society and of *society*, side by side with the Whites; there they live in amity, and the success and wealth of the movement are shared by Black and White alike.

The appeal of this doctrine to those who feel a sense of national or racial grievance is obvious, and it explains the enormous political importance in the early stages of colonial independence movements of what Chesneaux has called 'Christian colonial heresy'. The narrower causes of the emergence of this or that particular form of expression of these underlying discontents will emerge from further analysis of the history of evangelism in Central Africa. The reasons for the development of precisely this or that form of movement and belief—Cargo cult, prophetic movement, separatist sect, etc.—must be sought in specific historical analysis of the kind we have attempted for Melanesia. This colonial connection of fundamentalist, revivalist, millenarian and similar sects in the metropolitan countries is thus often very marked, especially the connection between colonial cults and Negro parent-sects in the United States.

Plainly, though, there is no sharp dividing line between the millenarian cult and other related movements. We cannot neatly separate off the millenarian from the ordinary prophetic movement, or from the independent native separatist sect. In addition, the future millennium is often envisaged in terms of a past Golden Age which may represent a folk-memory of an actual earlier epoch in the society's history, however idealized. Or the messiah may be some historical figure expected to return once more—a secular folk-hero usually invested with a religious aura. Stenka Razin, Marko of Serbia, King Olaf of Norway, Charlemagne, Barbarossa, Alexander, Nero, Cromwell, Napoleon, King Arthur, Bruce, Owen Glendower, Drake and countless other heroes have been expected to return one day. Both millenarism and the folk-memories of stateless societies are often merged in more advanced movements with secular utopias and with visions of a classless society in the future. In isolating the limited field of millenarism for the purposes of analysis, then, we do not imply any rigid separation in reality. But some delimitation must be made, otherwise a very large part of world history could be subsumed under the rubric of religious heresies, enthusiastic creeds and utopias.

To illustrate the overlapping, we have seen how the millenarian movement serves to unify people on the basis of the expectation of deliverance in the near future. Some expect that deliverance will be effected by supernatural intervention, others by human action. Yet there have been many religious movements led by prophets—the Mahdi in the Sudan; Joan of Arc; Makana, Nongqause and Umlanjeni in South Africa—which were not specifically millenarian, but which had a similar political function. Again, separatist sects *without* prophets have filled this integratory role, e.g., Cilembwe's church in the Nyasaland Rising of 1915, the Sanusiya in Cyrenaica, and, to some extent, the 'Ethiopians' in the Bambata Rebellion among the Zulu in 1906. And sometimes secular political leaders consciously manipulate millenarian doctrines for their own political ends, as Pontiac used the visions of the Delaware prophet. Or, like Joan of Arc, the prophet may have a purely secular aim—the expulsion of the English.

There are thus many variations of form; the basic division, however, is not between millenarian and non-millenarian movements, but between activist and passivist movements. Whether the activist content is expressed in the form of separatist sect, prophetic cult, or millenarian movement, or in some combination of all three, these are similar responses to similar social situations. And all ultimately result either in the emergence of secular political organization or turn into cults of passive resignation.

The political functions of these activist movements are thus clear enough. But, one may ask, why do the movements take a religious form? There are innumerable cases of secular political and military resistance to invaders by colonial peoples, and by peasants to their rulers.

The answer lies in the divisions within this type of society. In a society split into numerous component units, jealous of each other but seeking to unite on a new basis, a political leader must avoid identification with any particular section of that society. He must avoid being seen as the representative of the interests of any one group, particularly, of course, his own. He must therefore show that he seeks to establish his movement on the basis of a higher loyalty. By projecting his message on to the supernatural plane, he clearly demonstrates that his authority comes from a higher sphere, and that it transcends the narrow province of local gods and spirits associated with particular clans, tribes or villages. He is thus able to build upon existing social foundations, to use the small units of village and clan as elements in his organizational scheme whilst at the same time transcending the cramping limitations of these units by incorporating them in a wider framework.

By this projection on to the supernatural plane he thus avoids sectional discord. This is always backed up by specific injunctions to love one another, by calls to forget the narrow loyalties of the past, to abandon those things that divide them and to practise a new moral code of brotherly love.

This 'externalization' of the source of the prophet's authority thus meets the demands of highly segmented societies. The same mechanisms may be seen at work in Evans-Pritchard's account of the organization of the Sanusiya religious Order among the Cyrenaica Bedouin. The founder of the Order, he emphasizes, took great pains to ensure that it did not become identified with the partisan interests of any one Bedouin tribe or other group, and the close followers of the founder were themselves mainly foreigners. Again, the headquarters of the Order were deliberately sited in the remote desert oasis of Jaghbub, among other reasons to avoid association with any one tribe through use of a particular tribal territory.

Höltker has suggested, indeed, that the prophet always goes without honour in his own country, but is accepted abroad—as in the case of Mambu—because he is not identified with sectional interests. In fact, the majority of the Melanesian prophets succeed in spreading their message among their own people. Their 'neutrality' is assured because they derive their authority from extra-human sources altogether.

This projection of common values on to the supernatural plane, against a background of lesser private conflicts, is a phenomenon of wider relevance than the study of millenarian cults alone can show. It has been strikingly analysed in a recent study of a village among the Mwinilinga Lunda of Northern Rhodesia by Dr V. W. Turner who shows how, while common values are accepted by groups and individuals, their private interests nevertheless clash. They then try to manipulate these ethical ideals in their own interests, each appealing to the same moral code. The values themselves are unquestioned: they are removed from the realm of dispute by being expressed in religious terms. When social life threatens to become seriously disrupted, however, cathartic religious ceremonies are performed which reaffirm the ethical values of the society and which make possible the restoration of harmony between the disputing parties. This subjective removal of hostility, of course, does not remove the real causes of the conflict, and tensions therefore build up once more. There is therefore a cyclical process of dispute growing towards conflict, reaffirmation of religious values, and the fresh development of conflicts. The religious rituals represent a recognition that there must be a basic quantum of agreement and that quarrels must be contained if social life is to continue within the existing framework. More serious tensions cannot be resolved in this way, and may cause one of the parties to move away or may result in open rupture, such as violence.

There are other corollaries to the low level of political organization which we find in societies of the types which we have shown to be predisposed to millenarism. These are not so much structural resemblances as cultural, for these societies also lack advanced technological and scientific knowledge. The people are ignorant of the findings of advanced natural science on the aetiology of diseases, on variations in soil fertility, on the changes of the seasons, the movements of the planets, etc. They have little power either to predict the onset of natural disasters or to control or counteract them. Such ignorance in its turn is primarily determined by the low level of their technological equipment. These deficiencies in scientific knowledge and practice, especially knowledge of European society and above all of European factory production, provide ample room for the elaboration of fantastic 'explanations' in animistic or other supernaturalist terms, and for the use of magic to try to solve practical problems. The primitive peasant is thus predisposed to the acceptance of supernaturalist interpretations of reality: the soil is ready tilled for the millenarian leader. As pragmatic social experience increases and as education spreads, the ground becomes less fertile for millenarism.

Lawrence has shown, too, how Melanesian religion is essentially concerned with material rewards. He points out that native theologians do not so much sit down and consciously construct a body of syncretic religious dogma which they compound from Christian teaching and indigenous religion like some logical exercise. Their very assumptions, indeed, and their interpretations of the White order and of Christian thought, are cast in indigenous moulds of thought. They do not, that is, merely reflect upon Christianity, interpreting it as European Christians do, and then proceed to select congenial items. Selection of this kind is indeed made, but the very Christian ideology from which the conscious selection is made is not that taught by the missionary; it is Christianity as they understand it.

Lawrence shows that for the Garia their understanding is conditioned by their traditional belief in a pantheon of tutelary deities who created the artifacts, ceremonies, etc., which men possess, and who revealed to man the technical and the magical means by which these things were made. Empirical technical knowledge and magical knowledge are equally important. The really esoteric magical knowledge, however, is only given to a few men who know the secret names of the tutelary deities. Knowledge of these names gives one power over crops, animals, and so on.

Again, propitiation of the ancestral spirits ensures that they help living men, who give services (dances, rituals, offerings, etc.) in their honour and in their turn receive protection from misfortune and positive benefits. As Lawrence remarks: 'Garia religion is preoccupied almost exclusively with material welfare. It is concerned with the acquisition by human beings of material benefits in this world rather than of spiritual blessings in the next . . . as in all Papuan and Melanesian societies, relationships are expressed and understood most easily in terms of the giving or exchange of material goods and advantages.'[1]

These beliefs profoundly affect the Melanesians' understanding

[1] *Lawrence*, 1954, pp. 10-11.

of Christianity. The natives believe that acceptance of Christianity would bring with it the material riches of the Whites, rather in the spirit of the Samoan chief who remarked:'Now I conclude that the God who has given to His White worshippers these valuable things must be wiser than our gods . . . the God who gave them should be our God.'[1]

In accordance with traditional notions it is thus believed that the Whites possess some esoteric *secret* which enables them to obtain the Cargo. Unlike traditional goods, which could not be obtained by magical means alone, but only by a combination of magic and hard work,[2] the Europeans' goods were plainly obtained by magic alone: 'It is no exaggeration to say that the natives cannot appreciate that Europeans engage in any physical labour at all, and that consequently they imagine that the "work" by which they obtain their supplies of cargo is secret ritual. Therefore ritual is inevitably stressed to the exclusion of physical labour.'[3]

These conclusions about the importance of the pre-European ideology in moulding native reaction to European contact are borne out by Burridge's work. The Tangu, whom he studied, spoke of Cargo ritual as 'work'. The word *'uap*, used of work in the gardens, was used to describe Cargo rituals, which represent 'an effort directed towards producing the means of life'.[4] There is thus a similar belief in the efficacy of ritual alone in attracting Cargo, ritual which among the Tangu was a fusion of Roman Catholic rites and indigenous fertility magic.

Besides this general predisposition to misinterpret European activity, there are other special reasons why a supernaturalist interpretation of the European order is made. As in most colonial regions, organized mission activity is a powerful force in Melanesia. Religious proselytization takes place on a vast scale, and the powers possessed by the missions are very extensive, particularly in the fields of education and health. The power in the hands of missions, consequently, can be compared with that in the hands of the Church in the Middle Ages. Education is almost entirely a mission province. Native understanding of White society, therefore, is coloured by an education which lays special stress on the religious elements in our own culture. The mission has also considerable material resources and powers in its hands, and often constitutes a

---

[1] *Keesing*, p. 230.   [2] *Malinowski*, 1935, passim.
[3] *Lawrence*, *op. cit.*, p. 15.   [4] *Burridge*, 1954a, p. 247.

small theocratic state within a state. The missionaries themselves are in close contact with the people and often wield more real secular authority than the government officials who only visit the area sporadically.

Mission education is also one-sided in its limited range of subjects taught, and provides a basis for the Cargo myth of the 'secret' part of Christian knowledge hidden by the Whites. The natives are aware that there are other fields of knowledge—natural science, history, geography, political science, economics, etc.—which only a handful of natives are ever taught. And they know that there are partial translations of the Bible in circulation, and that new parts are constantly being translated. But do the Whites, in fact, ever translate *all* the Bible? When political and social aspirations are blocked by lack of suitable channels, or by deliberate policies—colour bars, repression of indigenous organizations, etc.—energies are diverted into the only available channels, those of organized religion. The lack of outlets for the activities of energetic, capable and ambitious leaders helps to explain the extraordinarily fissiparous nature of native independent separatist sects.

As well as being given to splits, the sects are also fond of ranks, titles, offices, badges,etc., as we have seen in the case of the Fijian 'cricket' clubs, the Mansren movement, the Marching Rule movement, and several others. The psychological satisfactions which these honours provide for frustrated individual leaders will be obvious enough, but there are deeper social reasons for the constant splitting and the 'plethora of offices'.[1]

The prosperity and worldly success that many sects achieve through enjoining upon their followers a 'Protestant ethic' of industrious devotion to one's calling in life itself often introduces new distinctions of rank and status, a tendency to abandon the old puritan codes in favour of more comfortable beliefs and practices. Fundamentalists then react against this by calling for a return to the old simplicity of faith and the former rude democracy in organization. Thus new splits are born from the clash between the prosperous and the doctrinal modifiers on the one hand, and the lowly and the fundamentalists on the other. The process of fission, too, is facilitated by the fundamentalist reliance upon direct inspiration; this allows anyone to claim divine inspiration. Fissiparity, therefore, is an outstanding feature of movements of this kind.

[1] *Banton*; see his discussion of this point at pp. 365-6.

In the Union of South Africa, for example, Sundkler lists 878 sects alone and refers to 123 'newer' sects. These sects arise by secession, often from the English and American (especially American Negro) fundamentalist or nonconformist parent churches, and their importance is strengthened in a situation where people tend towards escapism because of the past failure of direct resistance.

Both the integratory political function of the millenarian cult and the absence of a rich body of scientific knowledge are features of societies with limited and primitive technological equipment and a restricted division of labour. These tendencies are reinforced by the organized activity of missions in colonial territories, as they were once by the influence of the Church in the Middle Ages.

We have already shown how the instability and unpredictability of the European economy and of the European political order produced confusion in native minds. There were the fluctuations and declining returns of an economy of boom and slump, the changes and varieties of governmental apparatus: German, Australian, Japanese, British, Dutch, French, Condominium, Mandate and Trust Territory; and the destruction and chaos of World Wars. Given this background, and given the conditioning beliefs derived from indigenous religion, the millenarian cult may thus be seen not as an irrational flight from reality or a regression from the present into the past but as a quite logical interpretation and criticism of a European-controlled order that itself is full of contradictions which seem inexplicable in rational terms to the natives.

Writers like F. E. Williams, for example, have attempted to explain the cults in terms of abnormal psychology.[1] Interpretations like those of Linton, which stress the 'nativistic' character of the movements also seem to me wide of the mark.[2] This widely-used term 'nativism' itself lays stress on the regressive, backwards-looking aspects of the movements.

More recently, however, students of these movements have begun to see them in much more positive and dynamic terms. Firth has remarked that the 'movements are part of a process of imperfect social and economic adjustment to the conditions arising directly or indirectly from contact with the West. They are not mere passive responses, the blind stirrings of a people who feel

[1] *Williams*, 1928, passim; cf. also *Seligman*, 1929.
[2] see Appendix.

that they are being pushed around. Absurd as they may seem when considered as rational solutions, they are creative attempts of the people to reform their own institutions, to meet *new* demands or withstand *new* pressures. In the broadest sense their aims are to secure a fuller life.'[1]

Firth thus stresses that the cults are attempts to solve new problems posed by the colonial structure of society, and are not mere regression into the past. And a recent American student of these phenomena has termed them 'revitalization movements'.[2]

The Idea of the Millennium

We have already outlined the most favourable pre-conditions in which the emergence of millenarian cults is likely. The basic condition is a situation of dissatisfaction with existing social relations and of yearnings for a happier life. Since these conditions have been constantly renewed throughout history, millenarism has been a trend of thought which has therefore constantly revived, and which has died down only to be resuscitated once more. It is no accident that the millenarian idea, when introduced into suitable social situations in societies where the idea itself was previously absent, has flourished like the bay tree.

Without these pre-conditions, millenarism does not flourish in its activist form. Mooney has shown how the Navaho, very rich in flocks and silver, were one of the few Indian tribes who remained unaffected by the Ghost Dance of 1890, because they felt no need for a messiah. Obviously, where people actually suffer some material loss—such as the loss of their land due to the coming of the Europeans—resentment will be high, and this provides a basis for millenarism. But a people may remain quite untouched materially, and yet become violently dissatisfied, because of new *wants* which they have acquired. Interpretations of these cults in terms of deprivation, therefore,[3] must take into account not only actual material loss. The people of the east-central Highlands of New Guinea, for example, had lost nothing in material terms, but, actuated by a desire for the goods of the White man, who had not yet even entered their country, they developed a Cargo cult.

Firth has shown how a 'climate' of Cargo ideas may exist, without producing any actual Cargo organization. On Tikopia,

[1] *Firth*, 1953, p. 815.   [2] *Wallace.*
[3] e.g. *Barber. Nash.*

there were ideas of the bringing of the Cargo in the name of a deceased Tikopia; rumours of an approaching hurricane also caused people to uproot their crops; yet these elements did not fuse into a Cargo cult.[1] I myself found a similar situation among an Australian aboriginal tribe: the belief that the Whites could summon unlimited quantities of goods from the cities of Australia and Europe; the rumour that a new Bible had arrived foretelling the imminent end of the world, the destruction of the Whites and the salvation of the Blacks; and creation-myths of the Kilibob[2] type, 'explaining' why the Whites were rich and technologically advanced and the aborigines poor and backward.[3] Yet again these elements did not combine to form a coherent Cargo doctrine, let alone a cult organization. Plainly, the tensions which aroused these ideas were not yet sufficiently intense to bring them into coherent Cargo form. In such a situation, however, flashpoint might easily be reached if suitable leadership appeared or if friction became intolerably great.

Without the situation, activist millenarian ideas are unlikely to arise, or if they do arise will be confined to a clique. There are many examples of eminently suitable mythical material in indigenous mythologies which was never used as the basis of millenarian movements until the coming of the White man. Thus the North American Indians had cycle-myths of the renewal of the world and the return of the culture-hero.* In Melanesia, the myth of Anut on the Rai Coast, the belief in the return of the culture-hero among the Baining, and similar beliefs about Mansren in western New Guinea, all show that the mythical material was there to be used. Many of these myths may have contained some folk-memory of visits by foreigners,† but there are clearly many which are not the product of external influence—and even those which are serve a quite separate function as the basis of cults than they do as historical records. They are both at the same time.

But it was not until the coming of the Whites that such myths

---

* see Spier's analysis of the prophet-dance, an important cult tradition which later formed the core of the Ghost Dance religion (*Spier*, 1927 and 1935).

† cf. Bogesi's evidence that a record of Mendana's visit to the Solomon Islands (156) has been preserved in indigenous oral tradition (*Bogesi*, p. 354).

[1] *Firth*, 1955, passim.   [2] see below, Chapter X.
[3] cf. *Warner*, pp. 536-7.

were transformed into expectations of proximate deliverance and turned into burning programmes of action by organized cults. Plainly, there is nothing 'inherently' revolutionary or 'inherently' escapist or passivist in any of these beliefs; what determines whether an idea will be socially selected, what determines the way in which it will be interpreted, is the specific social interest it serves. Thus, in Reformation times, the belief in the millennium was revolutionary in one situation, but later became a sort of 'protestant ethic' of asceticism and industry in others.

But the situation does not *inevitably* or automatically produce millenarian ideas. Protest can take numerous forms, as we have seen. But since the idea is a peculiarly suitable one, when it is introduced into a situation where people are ready for it, it is seized upon. Among the Mundas and Oraons of Chota Nagpur in India, for example, there had been anti-landlord rebellions since the second half of the eighteenth century, especially in 1820 and 1832. Christian missions arrived around the mid-century, and people flocked to join them, in order to gather 'new strength to offer fresh resistance to the aggressiveness of their alien landlords'.[1] Finally, in 1881, they developed an independent millenarian movement, 'The Children of Mael', and in 1895-6 the Birsaite movement, which ended in violent clashes with police and Government.* This is a classic illustration of the injection of Christian apocalyptic ideas into a region seething with discontent, and the selection of the elements most congenial to the people to form a new cult. The Taiping Revolution in China, of course, is another such case.

The greatest single agency for the world-wide spreading of millenarism has been the Christian mission.† On the other hand, some missionaries themselves (e.g., Höltker, Inselmann and others) have blamed only the fundamentalist sects, such as the Seventh Day Adventists, for the spread of millenarian ideas.

These fundamentalist sects have undoubtedly been a powerful influence in spreading millenarian ideas, but those who have been looking for such ideas have often found them even in less apocalyp-

---

* Mr R. P. Katriar of Ranchi informs me that Birsa is venerated as a saint by the people today.

† though Christianity, like Islam, draws much of its millenarian inspiration from ancient Judaism.

[1] *Roy*, 1912, p. 266.

tic versions of Christianity. People select these aspects of Christianity, whatever the mission teaches them. To quote the words of a Jesuit who was strongly opposed to making the Bible directly available to Chinese peasants because of the conclusions they drew from reading it: 'from any point of the exegetical compass, a Chinaman can find his way up to the great rice problem'.[1]

To ascribe the spread of millenarism, then, merely to the activity of fundamentalist sects is incorrect. We have seen how understanding of Christian doctrine is affected by existing religious concepts, and how selection is not necessarily even a conscious process. Indeed, one missionary in Fiji has remarked that the setting up of the Kelevi separatist church was merely a formal organizational and ideological recognition of the quite unorthodox syncretic doctrines which are believed in by Fijians who actually remain in the Methodist church. The 'Methodists' are no less unorthodox than the separatists in their actual beliefs.

In addition to this unconscious reinterpretation of Christian thought which Lawrence has described, there is conscious selection by the theologians and politicians of the cults. But no matter how ready they are to seize upon suitable ideas, people do not always automatically produce specifically millenarian notions. The millenarian idea, then, is often introduced from the outside and injected into the movement. It then acts as a catalyst among people whose wants are rapidly developing, but who feel frustrated, deprived and helpless. The tensions generated by the contradiction between the people's acceptance of what Merton calls 'cultural goals' and the lack of 'institutionalized means' through which to attain these goals result in a peculiarly explosive and emotionally-charged situation. The goals Merton discusses are those of American society, especially the achievement of monetary success. The goals of the Melanesian are different. They are conditioned by his notion of a *right* to the possession of the Cargo, which the Whites are perversely denying him. This right is not the same thing as the socialist's conception of rights in a product which is socially produced but privately appropriated. The Melanesian conception is conditioned by cultural and social values which include the idea of much wider rights in the property of others than we conceive of in our society. To exaggerate somewhat, deliberately, one might say that the product is privately produced

---

[1] *Wolferston*, p. 102.

but socially appropriated. In a kinbound society, without marked formalized differentiation, where most social relations are face-to-face, private property is subject to many more over-claims by kin and relatives than in our society. The cultural goals of the Melanesian, therefore, are conditioned not solely by the desirability of the goods which the White men made known to him, but also by his traditional attitudes towards property. The incompatibility between his wants and the means of satisfying them is thus aggravated by the notion of a *right* to these goods. It becomes a particularly powerful source of resentment and frustration, charged with emotion. To get these goods, men are tied to a mode of life they hate. Once new wants have been created, they shackle the native more effectively to the European order than any legal or political compulsion, and render the latter much less necessary.

The hysterical and paranoid phenomena—mass - possession, trances, fantasies, twitching, and so on—which we have found in so many movements are thus no mere accidental features. They are the product, firstly, of the lack of means to satisfy enormously inflated wants. Feelings of deprivation and frustration are heightened by the apparent irrationality of White society, whose incomprehensible economic and political changes the natives vainly strive to understand and manipulate in their own interest. Though there is no real solution in the Cargo cult—for the Cargo will never come—the ardent wishes and hopes poured into the movement bolster it up and revive it time after time despite failure. And large-scale activities, some of them quite practical, are carried out under the stimulus of these fantastic yearnings. There is not merely destruction and avoidance of rational economic activity. We have seen also the cultivation of large gardens and the building of stores, sheds, jetties and landing-grounds for the reception of goods which will never come. But the latter activities are just as rational to the people who carry them out as increased production in the gardens. As Firth has pointed out, the work itself is an emotional outlet: 'They seek their solution in an imaginary projection. But they bolster it up by elaborate work. In one sense then, the work is not ineffective. It is in itself part of the satisfaction sought. It is part of the symbolic validation given to the idea that the things wanted are morally justifiable. Part of the message of the airstrip or the cargo wharf to the observer is "What we want is right." It is part of an affirmation of native claims, native community solidarity, native values, in the face of what is conceived to be an impassive, unsympathetic, or hostile outside world.'[1]

The cults thus express social and moral solidarity and independence in a highly charged emotional situation resulting from the overthrow or questioning of ancient ethical values. This confusion of values is heightened by the direct assault of missions on ancient belief, by rivalry between missions which profess to be servants of the same God, and by the discrepancy between White men's behaviour and the Gospel of the missionaries.

Those things which formerly brought a man high social status, such as being a polygamist, are now the objects of attack by missionaries and their followers. Men of low status are thrust into key political offices by Government, while aristocrats are ignored. The most sacred beliefs and rites are dubbed pagan superstition. Young men defy their fathers; they know more of the new life, and as labourers have greater access to the cash and knowledge which now count for so much.

The moral and emotional tensions which build up under these circumstances have been graphically described in Burridge's account of a visit to Manam Island. The fact that Burridge treated the islanders sympathetically and on terms of equality produced this reaction: 'When prayers were over I was asked if I would shake hands with the assembled villagers. As I was about to depart in any case I said I would be glad to do so. So I passed down the line of people shaking hands with each one in turn. The ritual commenced in silence. About halfway a tension had been built up which could be sustained no longer. One and all broke into tears and sobbing.'[2]

We can now understand why millenarian cults are so highly emotional, and why emotion manifests itself in motor phenomena such as twitching, convulsions, and similar habits familiar to psychologists who have studied individuals subject to similar strains in different cultural situations. As social tensions build up to a situation like the one Burridge describes, action of any kind is a relief. At one level, this relief is gained through the performance of large-scale social tasks such as gardening or building Cargo houses. All of this helps to compensate for the long-standing failure to control the outside world, which is now to be controlled in man's own interest. And personal catharsis is gained from the actions of

---

[1] *Firth*, 1951, p. 113.   [2] *Burridge*, 1954b, p. 936.

motor behaviour which spread throughout the community as if by contagion. One of the most graphic accounts in literature of the psychological atmosphere of these movements occurs in Manzoni's great novel *The Betrothed* where he describes the hysterical-paranoid witch-hunt during the Milan plague, when the mythical 'anointers' were held to have been responsible for the outbreak. Here is a description of another outbreak of enthusiasm in Reformation Germany:

'[Women] tore their breasts, stretching their arms out so as to form a cross, whilst others lay upon their backs, foaming at the mouth, staring up at the sky with a look of anxious expectation. Then they would spring up raving, grinding their teeth and clapping their hands, invoking blessings and curses from Heaven at the same time . . . some saw a great fire with blue and black flames descend from Heaven and cover the city; hysterical laughter and crying were heard on all hands. Ever and anon a group of men and women would be seen rushing through the streets shouting "Repent and be baptized! Slay the unbaptized heathen!" Suddenly the rays of the sun struck a newly-gilded weathercock . . . dazzling the eyes of those who looked that way. The assembled women fell on their faces and, with folded hands, cried "Oh! Father, Father, most excellent King of Zion, spare thy people!"'[1]

This emotionality is heightened by the cults' insistence on deliberately breaking with the customs, traditions, habits and values of the past. One missionary, writing about the Naked Cult of Espiritu Santo, remarked that 'the function of the cult seems to be to break all existing ties, of whatever description, and unite people on the exclusive basis of the cult'.[2] The Naked Cult therefore 'cut across all family ties and totem ties'. We have seen the political implications of this overriding of old divisions, but the break with ancient custom does more than this. It welds the devotees together in a new fraternity of people who have deliberately flouted the most sacred rules of the old society. They are bound together by their sense of guilt and by the feeling of having cut themselves off irrevocably from the old life. There are present very deeply ambivalent feelings for the rules which are being flouted are values which

---

[1] *Bax*, pp. 135-6. [2] *Miller*, p. 334.

the people themselves have been brought up to cherish, or which are cherished by many people in the community. Consequently much of the ritual often bears signs of feelings of guilt. In the end it is the fount of the marked hysteria and emotionality which we have so often found. This most radical rejection of the past generates the most powerful emotional energy. In order to flout the old values, men have to summon up extra untapped sources of energy and resolution; when they have done the act which creates this energy, they are bound together in mutual guilt and mutual support in opposition to all those who still accept the old beliefs.

The ritual breaking of taboos is thus a most powerful mechanism of political integration and generates intense emotional energy. We are all familiar with the use of the oath and of deliberate contraventions of taboos in the Mau Mau movement (though one must dismiss much of the evidence, and question the validity of a lot more). The energy liberated by breaking taboos which are considered particularly powerful—sexual, religious and others—is strong enough to bind people together under the greatest difficulties and hardships. It has been noted that some of the leaders of cults are on record as having committed some act which isolated them from their society; in Melanesia, both Filo and Tsek, for example, married in defiance of exogamic rules.

Some can see nothing in these acts except brutal perversion. The same accusation has been hurled at men throughout history who have used the same mechanism of a radical smashing of taboos in pursuit of a higher ideal. Fränger's study of the 'Millennium' of Hieronymus Bosch, however, has shown that a very positive ethic permeates a painting previously regarded as a sordid venture in eroticism and diabolism. In showing this positive content in Bosch's work, Fränger has shed much light on cult symbolism generally.

If we examine the many cases of 'sexual excess', 'erotic communism', 'morbid asceticism' and all the other labels pinned to ritual obscenity and sacrilege, it becomes clear that we are not dealing with unbridled lust or with ascetic perversion. We are dealing with the deliberate enactment of the overthrow of the cramping bonds of the past, not in order to throw overboard all morality, but in order to create a new brotherhood with a completely new morality. The role of ritual obscenity as providing an occasion for the statement and reinforcement of moral norms is well known from many societies,[1] but here it has a revolutionary content, the statement of a new morality. Sexual communism and sexual asceticism, both so common in millenarian movements, are thus two sides of the same coin—the rejection of outworn creeds.

It is for this reason that we find such heavy emphasis laid in all the cults upon a new morality. The social order is to be transformed by radical political and economic changes. But the new order must also have a new morality: it cannot continue with the outworn indigenous ethics or the code of its former rulers any more than it can continue with the old tribal structure or with the colonial régime. All prophets, therefore, stress moral renewal: the love of one's cult-brethren; new forms of sexual relationship; abandonment of stealing, lying, cheating, theft; devotion to the interests of the community and not merely of the self. Such doctrines are the spiritual concomitants of the new life if the political and economic changes are to be infused with any humanist content.

The symbolism of the movements amply bears this out. I cannot hope to emulate the subtlety of Fränger's study of Bosch's symbolism, but I can indicate certain outstanding themes. The 'cultural goals' which the cult devotees strive towards are clearly symbolized in European objects like money, 'Cargo' itself, the 'offices' of the Vailala Madness, or the use of flowers or European-introduced crops like rice. The 'institutionalized means' people use in their fantastic efforts to reach these goals are also often derived from the European order: flagpoles, wirelesses, poles and ladders with which to get into touch with God and the ancestors; flashlights to see Him with; and books, paper and the Bible as both symbols and means of acquiring the Secret of the Cargo.

Other less transparent themes are those of *renunciation* and *rejection*, symbolized in the destruction of animal and other material wealth, the abandonment of gardens, the throwing away of money, and, on the spiritual level, the deliberate burning of sacred paraphernalia and the exposure of secret sacred objects to women and children. This is associated with deliberate *defiance* of the authority against whom the movement is reacting, symbolized in the use of the forbidden kava by the John Frum devotees. The extreme expression of this defiance and the most positive rejection of the present way of life is the *inversion* of the existing social order.

[1] *Evans-Pritchard*, 1929, passim.

251

Blacks are to become white, and Whites black. Marafi even took the Christian Devil as his God.

In contrast to this hostility to the old order is the *fraternity* of the new cult, symbolized by the hand-shaking of the Taro enthusiasts. The believers also show their *dedication* to the new movement by actual withdrawal and separation from the unconverted (van Gennep's 'rites of segregation') and by setting up separate cult communities. They are the Chosen. If they do not actually physically withdraw, they adopt diacritical signs and symbols—songs, badges, dances, dress, ornaments, etc.—which emphasize their separateness and their dedication. By signs and symbols they also show that they have been *reborn*. One of the most appropriate and widespread symbols of rebirth is adult baptism, which gave its very name to the Anabaptist movement.

The snake is also a nigh-universal symbol of rebirth. Psychoanalytically-inclined writers often point out that the snake is a phallic symbol. It undoubtedly is a phallic symbol, because of its shape, but it has another equally important symbolic significance. It is the sloughing of the skin which has given rise to the universal association of the snake with resurrection and regeneration. The snake does not die, it is believed. Not only the snake, but other animals that shed their outer coverings or appendages and grow new ones are used as rebirth symbols. In Melanesia we find the crab, lobster, lizard and crawfish frequently used as well as the snake. A most striking example of snake symbolism occurs in the Mansren myth, where Mansren *is* the Snake. The story of his stepping into the fire (with its associations with sexual heat), the dropping off of his *scaly skin*, and his rebirth as a youth clearly equate him with the Snake. This is amply confirmed by comparative evidence from northern New Guinea, where the very details of the Mansren myth are found once more: the throwing of the fruit (an obvious fertility symbol), the shedding of the skin, the snake's travelling under water as Mansren was supposed to have done on his Creation Journey. Cowan has shown detailed etymological evidence of the close association between words meaning 'alive', 'living', 'reborn', 'revived', etc., and the words for 'lizard' and 'snake'.[1]

The snake is therefore commonly identified in New Guinea

---

[1] *Cowan, H. K. J.*, passim. *Malinowski* (1922) records similar myths for the Trobriand Islands at pp. 308-26; cf. also *Fortune*, pp. 218 ff.

with the Old Man or Old Woman,[1] the Demiurge who created men, animals, tools and social groups alike, and of whom Mansren is a typical example. The snake symbol has a further significance in representing the essence or soul, the continuing vital part of the organism which persists eternally while the outer husk of the body dies and is sloughed off. And, as we saw earlier, snakes and lizards frequent men's houses, which they enter unseen from the wild. They are thus friendly towards men, but at the same time potentially very dangerous. This makes them peculiarly suitable symbols for the ancestors who keep a close watch on the affairs of the living, and who are helpful if placated, but who are vengeful if mishandled. The symbol of the snake thus combines a number of symbolic ideas fused into one, and is particularly rich in its associations and overtones. It symbolizes human fertility because of its phallic implications, but it also symbolizes the fertility of non-human animal life and natural life in general. Because it never dies, it transcends all these narrow implications, and stands for the cycle of life itself, the continuity of the whole cosmos and the perpetuation of the soul. And in its friendliness towards the living, in its unpredictability and power to harm, the snake symbolizes the dead ancestors themselves, completing the cycle of life and death in yet another way.

It is this stress upon the life-cycle and upon rebirth that gives meaning to other actions of symbolic fertility: the elaborate display and consumption of food, the emphasis upon garden produce and upon magic to help the growth of the crops. This may appear to contradict the 'ascetic' destruction of crops we found elsewhere, but it should be noted that the use of garden magic occurs principally in the early, Taro-type cults where society was not so violently disturbed.

In the more advanced cults, all hope of happiness by purely human action is abandoned. Men look to the overthrow of existing society as the only hope, and it is in this setting that the 'ascetic' practices flourish. But as time passes, they find no hope in the limited prospects of improved crop fertility; only the rebirth of the whole cosmos can now save them. They must cut themselves off from the corrupted material world.

Clark suggests that the sects elevate necessities—'frugality, humility and industry—into moral virtues and regard as sins the

[1] *Held*, pp. 200-4; cf. also *Quinlivan*.

253

practices they are debarred from embracing. . . . [Puritan] morality is in considerable degree a corollary of their economic state, arrived at by a process of elevating the manners they cannot well escape into moral virtues established by the will of God. Vices are the practices of the rich, the very practices they themselves would be likely to follow if sufficiently affluent.'[1]

But moralities of plainness, simplicity, frugality and asceticism are not just the creations of poor men making a virtue of necessity and a creed out of sour grapes. They imply the rejection of a temporal order that makes the pleasures of the flesh the goals of human striving.

The First Stirrings of Nationalism

It is clear that pre-existing cultural and social divisions affect the extent of spread of the cults, especially in the early stages. We have stressed that the cults transcend ancient limits, but it is equally clear that they do not spread indefinitely. At first, the limits are generally set by linguistic and other cultural boundaries, as was largely the case in the Orokaiva Taro cult, for example. Sometimes cults spread along existing trade routes or other channels of social intercourse; sometimes they are confined to existing political divisions, geographical areas, and so on. But as the extension and intensification of European administration brings the different units of the various regions under a common political authority; as work on the plantations and in the mines brings together members of previously widely-scattered tribes; as the development of trade, transport, and other media of communication increases; as missions convert and bring into communion groups which were formerly discrete and often divided by cultural and political differences, so the area of spread of the cults grows accordingly.

It would be early yet to say just what cultural and social groupings are going to emerge from this highly fluid situation. We are, in fact, witnessing the early stages of formation of national groupings in Melanesia. These are likely to be conditioned both by the traditional cultural heritage and by the action of new political and economic forces on the societies of this region. Some tribes are breaking up, others are coalescing to form higher social formations. The process is obviously one, however, which will not be con-

[1] *Clark*, pp. 17, 220.

trolled by the limits of the arbitrary existing political boundaries, though these will affect the result. The new pressures shaping the future of the region will cut across these units as they cut across village, tribe and clan. As in India, and now in West Africa, ancient cultural ties may become factors of revived importance in shaping the ultimate political units of the region. If one can discern only the most tentative regional groupings, then, this is because the region is only giving birth to what I have called 'proto-national' formations of a transitional kind. M. Jean Guiart was therefore correct in referring to these movements as only 'forerunners of Melanesian nationalism'.

Future nationalist developments will probably be less and less under the aegis of millenarian cult leadership. We have seen how there is an eventual break away from this kind of political expression to that of a simple kind of political party. I believe, therefore, that the activist millenarian movement is typical only of a certain phase in the political and economic development of this region, and that it is destined to disappear or become a minor form of political expression among backward elements. It will not have escaped the reader that the movements have been absent in the towns of Melanesia. We may expect the principal leadership of more advanced, secular political movements to come from the towns, from the small entrepreneurs and the industrial, administrative and commercial employees, and from the educated, rather than from the small peasants of the rural areas. As Asia has shown us, such leaders will inevitably draw their mass support from the peasants in countries where the great bulk of the population lives on the land. Some rural areas which were formerly centres of Cargo activity have already taken to the cooperative and the Village Council as forms of political and economic expression of indigenous aspirations.

After the post-war efflorescence of Cargo ideas, largely conditioned by the hardships of reconstruction, there appears to have been a considerable slackening of enthusiasm, with the persistence of a period of high world prices for local products and plentiful employment. How far a reversion to the conditions of the late 'twenties would bring about a revival of Cargo activity it is difficult to say, but one suspects that discontent would take this particular form only in a limited number of backward areas in the future. As Shepperson has remarked of similar movements in Africa: 'after

255

1916, it might be said that the African independent churches of Nyasaland ceased to act in a genuine revolutionary capacity. Their function had become, perhaps, that of the safety-valve'.[1]

Though the movements in Melanesia have had a radical, anti-White and even communistic flavour in the past, they will probably follow the path of similar movements in the history of other regions and become passive sects in the future.

[1] *Shepperson*, p. 245.

Appendix

Appendix

A SHORT OUTLINE OF THE METHODOLOGY and wider theoretical setting of this book seems desirable, especially since the basic approach of the work differs in important respects from that of much contemporary British anthropology. The present study is not primarily concerned with morphological or institutional comparison. It is, rather, an attempt to define the conditions under which one particular social phenomenon, the millenarian cult, occurs. Such a study must be comparative and historical in approach.

Earlier essays at comparative analysis of these Melanesian cult movements* have been based on a limited selection of factual material. In this study I have attempted to bring together all the relevant available evidence before drawing general conclusions. Except for a handful of notes in obscure mission journals (whose contents I have at second hand), I believe that I have read everything published on these Melanesian cults, mainly in English, French, German and Dutch. I have tried to indicate how the selection has been made, and have given references so that the originals may be consulted. I believe that the reader will not fail to be impressed by the very close parallels in all these movements, and will conclude that these parallels are not the product of subjective interpretation.

I have also endeavoured to give at least a little factual material on each movement where possible. Certain typical and specially important movements receive greater attention, but the selection of material is unfortunately not controlled merely by choice. Much more practical limitations intervene: the material available on some movements is minimal; much of it is extremely poor and unreliable, consisting often of little more than scrappy and arbitary

* Notably those by Barber (1941), Firth (1950), Belshaw (1950), and Stanner (1953) amongst English-speaking anthropologists, and Lehmann (1934a and b), Eckert (1937 and 1941), Schlosser, Bodrogi (1951) and Guiart (1951c) amongst the continental writers.

selections from the facts written by biased and untrained observers who recorded what they knew poorly and with many lacunae. Those who have read the sources will know what they are like. But we have to work with the material available.

Since the movements are not solely products of the internal development of these small-scale societies, I have outlined the wider setting of the general political, economic and social development of the region, though the material available for such a background picture is often equally poor. It is to be hoped that official documents will become more generally available in the future. These will enable those historians, anthropologists and others who are already turning towards this field of research to write more detailed studies than I have been able to do. Both comparative and specific studies can contribute much of theoretical and practical value to our understanding of these movements and to the study of religion and political science generally.

Social Anthropology, A Comparative and Historical Science

This study, then, is a comparative work. During the last thirty years, British anthropologists have carried out a large number of intensive field studies. These studies, largely empirical in approach, are valuable both as detailed accounts of particular social groups and as analyses of problems within a single society. They also provide a basis for wider comparative work. Comparative studies, however, have been few in number. Those that have been done—notably the volumes on *African Political Systems, African Systems of Kinship and Marriage*, and *African Worlds*—whatever their undoubted merits, have been collections of essays by several hands on fortuitously 'available' societies, with a general introduction. They have not been comprehensive surveys even of these topics.

A growing number of studies * indicate that the time has now come to look at this accumulated mass of field material, together with the material collected by non-anthropologists, from a more general point of view. Many writers, in attempting to define the scope and nature of social anthropology, have tried to establish fixed, absolute, abstract criteria; little regard has been paid to the

---

* e.g. Forde, on the ecological background of human society; Fortes, on unilineal descent-group formation; Firth, Evans-Pritchard, and Nadel, in the field of general theory.

changing nature of the subject matter of the science, and equally little to the shifting frontier lines between it and other social sciences. But although sociology, social anthropology, history, etc., are all concerned with different aspects abstracted from human behaviour in general, there have been certain fields which have been the peculiar province of social anthropology. One of these fields has been the study of 'primitive' peoples.

This term is so often used merely as a value-loaded epithet that many anthropologists feel there is an implied judgment of superiority and inferiority necessarily contained in the use of words such as 'primitive'[1] or 'advanced'. I use them here, however, in recognition of objective differences between societies and not in any pejorative sense. Those who reject such words suggest that we cannot speak of more 'advanced' or more 'backward' societies, only of *different* societies. They consider that notions of 'higher' and 'lower', and especially of progress, are meaningless, unscientific prejudices. In this book, there is no suggestion that the individuals who compose any one society are in any way inferior to any others, either actually or potentially, but merely, to state the matter broadly, that development has been mono-directional from stateless into State societies. And objectively, some societies have achieved a more complex and richer technological, artistic and scientific development than others. We also have historical evidence that many societies have passed through various stages of development, and that these movements can be classified in more general evolutionary terms. Much more harm is done to relations between societies of different levels of complexity by relativists than by evolutionists, for relativism helps to keep backward societies backward in the name of preserving their cultural 'uniqueness'.*

Professor Fortes and Professor Evans-Pritchard, in their Introduction to *African Political Systems*, drew the distinction between stateless and State societies. The stateless type, to which alone I feel the label 'primitive' can legitimately be applied, has not been the unique subject matter of anthropology, for anthropologists have also studied societies which possessed State institutions. Hence attempts to define anthropology as *only* the study of primi-

---

* Margaret Mead, for example, once proposed keeping certain small island communities in the South Pacific as 'laboratories' (*Mead*, 1943).

[1] see, for example, *Dozier*, passim.

tive society or of 'non-literate' societies have broken down, for the great kingdoms of West Africa, and the ancient civilizations of the Orient, have long been the subject of anthropological study, though they are neither 'primitive', nor 'non-historic', nor 'preliterate', nor any of the other epithets that have been coined in unsuccessful attempts to avoid evolutionary implications.

But, on the whole, it is mainly in recent years that anthropologists have become greatly concerned with the more complex societies, and have even turned to study their own societies by anthropological methods. It has been largely true that anthropology has meant the study, not just of backward and primitive peoples, but rather of *colonial* peoples. The only common feature which States like those of the Barotse and the Baganda have shared with societies like those of the Bushmen and the Veddas has been their common position as peoples who have come under colonial rule.

Anthropology, then, has largely been the study of colonial peoples. Many anthropologists, seeing the limitations of earlier definitions, have preferred to speak of a common science of anthropology-sociology (which they call by a variety of names), the subject matter of which is human society. In fact, the complaint of colonial intellectuals, 'anthropology for us, sociology for you', though hotly contested by some anthropologists, has been largely true. There should be a special branch of the general science of society dealing with primitive social formations. We can call this anthropology. The sociology of colonies is an equally legitimate subject of study. But there is no justification for lumping colonial peoples, living in quite different kinds of society, together under the rubric 'primitive'. There can be no absolute division of spheres of influence between anthropology and sociology because the subject matter which they divide between them has not always been the same, and is still changing.

Interest in the study of the peoples of the newly opened up remote corners of the world originally stemmed from several sources. The powerful stimulus of the development of evolutionary theory in the natural sciences helped to turn men's attention to primitive societies, such as those of the Bushmen and the Australian aborigines. In addition, there was the interest of missions and their supporters in the peoples of the colonies whom they were evangelizing: much anthropological work has been done by missionaries. But, above all, the colonial Powers needed to know more about the people whom they were ruling. This became particularly urgent when the need for economies in administration, and the growing inadequacy of direct methods of rule under the changed circumstances of the *entre deux guerres*, brought about the introduction of Indirect Rule in many territories. It now became most important to find out how the indigenous systems of social control were organized. Anthropologists were obviously well qualified to help in finding this out and, since the 'thirties, a very great deal of anthropological research has been financed from colonial funds.

Anthropological research has now been extended, firstly to new regions of Asia, the Middle East, South America, etc., and also into the field which has traditionally belonged to sociology: modern industrial society and the classical historic civilizations.

Some scientists who have realized how important these changes have been and who recognize the inadequacy of definitions of the scope of the subject in terms of 'non-historicity', 'pre-literateness' or an undefined 'primitiveness', have always preferred to define anthropology more agnostically, not by its subject matter, but by its techniques. They believed that anthropology had no special province other than human society in general; what it did possess as a unique feature was a set of special techniques. Professor Firth, notably, sees anthropology as a kind of 'micro-sociology'.[1] Although some have sought to refute him by showing that sociology has always used some 'micro'-techniques (e.g., the interview), and that anthropology has equally used certain 'macro'-techniques (e.g., the survey), Firth's point remains true. Modern British anthropology can be distinguished by characteristic methods and techniques: direct participation in, and observation of, a society on the spot; intensive, detailed work in small social units, and so on. Sociology, on the other hand, has depended more upon such 'macro'-techniques as the survey and the sample.

Anthropological techniques were developed largely empirically in response to the special problems of studying small-scale groups, frequently without written records, without codified law or formal constitutions, with unfamiliar languages social usages, customs, etc. The techniques, then, were largely conditioned by the nature of the subject matter in the first place.

[1] *Firth*, 1945, p. 201, and 1951, pp. 17-18. In the latter work, he also refers to the holistic and comparative approach of anthropology as important characteristics of the subject.

By applying these techniques to the study of complex industrial societies, anthropologists have blurred the borderlines between the two branches of social science. At first anthropologists tentatively extended their investigations into rural communities, or ethnic groups (especially Negroes) within the main society. But we now have 'anthropological' studies of Hollywood and mental hospitals, and 'sociological' studies of the Copper Belt of Northern Rhodesia. Whether these studies are to be termed 'anthropological' or 'sociological' is largely determined by reference to the techniques employed.

This overlapping of fields and interchange of techniques is part of a process of ever-growing interaction between backward and advanced peoples, of the breakdown of colonial societies, their absorption into wider polities and of the growth of new national entities. It has been a process marked by heart-searchings about the adequacy of anti-evolutionary, particularly functionalist, anthropological theories formulated on the basis of the study of 'untouched' primitive societies and which later proved to be inadequate when applied to the phenomena of 'culture contact'. No one who has compared monographs written before and after the rise of the functionalist school can fail to appreciate the richness and vitality that the new approach brought to anthropology. But functionalism had its own weaknesses. Significantly, the first major criticism of Malinowskian functionalism was directed against Malinowski's attempt to analyse the rapidly changing society of southern Africa.[1] Other writers have sought to solve the problem by evolving a separate 'theory of change', but once attention had been drawn to the inadequacy of functionalist theory in one field, this led to a re-examination of its adequacy even when applied to relatively 'untouched' and 'stationary' societies. Such views have doubtless been partly conditioned by the technical limitations of anthropology, firstly, in that most field studies last only a year or two, and secondly, in that written historical records were frequently lacking. Field-workers were predisposed to accept the futility of historical analysis, and to cry 'guesswork' to interpretations some of which, indeed, were wild, formalistic and schematic guesses about the evolutionary development of society, but others of which contained a core of valid historical insight or even genuine historical evidence.

[1] *Malinowski*, 1945, and the critique by *Gluckman*, 1949.

Malinowski himself, however, found it difficult to exclude histori-cal analysis from his field studies. Where convenient, he even used myths, which he elsewhere describes in positivist terms as merely supplying a 'retrospective pattern of moral values', as valid historical data.[1]

This bias against history, however, was not just a mechanical function of technical conditions; it was fundamentally a question of theoretical preconceptions. Reacting against the old evolution-ism, anthropologists were attracted by the anti-historical tenets of certain continental sociologists, notably the positivists. Emile Durk-heim has probably exercised the most decisive influence of any one man, notably via the teachings of Professors Radcliffe-Brown and Malinowski in this country.

Anthropologists were also influenced by other theorists who asserted that neither anthropology nor sociology is an historical discipline. Weber's definition of history as 'the causal explanation of important individual events' was one which drew sympathetic assent from most anthropologists. In a modern re-statement of this position, Radcliffe-Brown has declared that history is concerned with factual description; it is explanatory only in the sense of arriving at the narrow, immediate causes of unique events. Sociology and anthropology, on the other hand, are theoretical studies aiming at a generalized and comparative understanding of social phenomena. The first type of study has been termed 'idiographic' and the second 'nomothetic'.[2]

Ethnography, in this view, is another idiographic study, only differing from history in some of its techniques. These views stem directly from nineteenth-century neo-Kantian sociologists and historians, many of whom went farther and declared that any study concerned with the human mind and spirit could not be a science.

That history is not science is a view still very widely held. Professor Nadel, who specifically acknowledges his debt to the writings of Rickert, Eduard Meyer, Collingwood and others, has

---

[1] A few examples from one volume (*Malinowski*, 1935): p. 69, f.n. 2, where he uses a myth as evidence of a 'more ancient cultural order'; p. 17, where a myth is adduced as 'correct' evidence that 'fishing was diffused into the Trobriands from the eastern archipelagos'; p. 145, where the importance of taro in garden magic is said to have arisen from times when 'taro was of greater importance than it is now'; cf. also p. 459,etc.,etc.

[2] *Radcliffe-Brown*, p. 1.

given the most forthright expression of this viewpoint: 'in the kind of inquiry which is not historical but *scientific*, we view events under the aspect of their repetitiveness and regularity, regardless of time and place, and use the observation of the individual and particular for the formation of universally valid laws . . . the main concern of history . . . is with the *uniqueness* and distinctiveness of events in the past.'[1]

Professor Evans-Pritchard, on the other hand, sees anthropology as a humanistic discipline, and definitely not a science: 'social anthropology is a kind of historiography, and therefore ultimately of philosophy or art . . . it studies societies as moral systems and not as natural systems . . . it therefore seeks patterns and not scientific laws.'[2]

These views are quite opposed in so far as Professor Nadel considers that anthropology is a science, and *therefore cannot be history*, while Professor Evans-Pritchard considers that social anthropology is not a science, *because it is a branch of history*. Yet there is a common term in both these sets of propositions: history is not science.

No more trenchant criticism of the inadequacy of defining history as the mere study of the unique and distinctive has been made than that by Professor Evans-Pritchard: 'The claim that one can understand the functioning of institutions at a certain point in time without knowing how they have come to be what they are, or what they were later to become, as well as a person who, in addition to having studied their constitution at a particular point in time, has also studied their past and future, seems to me an absurdity.'[3]

He goes on to show how many historians use those very procedures of abstraction, classification, comparison, the testing of hypotheses, etc., which the social anthropologist also uses. But, he says, by using these procedures one can only arrive at 'significant patterns', not laws. Yet from his own clear account of the procedures to be used for establishing and comparing these 'patterns', most of his readers have been convinced that his 'patterns' are what others would call scientific laws. Successive studies of a particular phenomenon, he says: '[reach], as our knowledge increases and new problems emerge, a deeper level of investigation and [teach] us the essential characteristics of the thing we are

[1] *Nadel*, pp. 10, 17.   [2] *Evans-Pritchard*, 1950, p. 123.
[3] *op. cit.*, p. 121.

inquiring into, so that particular studies are given a new meaning and perspective ... the conclusions of each study are clearly formulated in such a way that they not only test the conclusions reached by earlier studies but advance new hypotheses which can be broken down into field-work problems.'[1]

This rejection of the narrow definition of history as the study of the unique and distinctive is, to me, most convincing. But I believe, further, that the procedures outlined by Professor Evans-Pritchard are those of any science and that the use of methods like that of concomitant variation enables us to formulate scientific laws, and not merely 'patterns'. We can thus build up a body of theory which can be tested by application to the real world from which it was abstracted.

The second major theoretical inheritance from these nineteenth-century sociologists is the distinction between 'static' and 'dynamic' studies. In British anthropology, this has appeared most notably in Radcliffe-Brown's distinction between studies of changes in the 'form' of social life over a period ('diachronic' studies), and 'synchronic' studies which aim at abstracting society from time and change.[2]

All science involves abstraction, of course, whether the study be labelled 'synchronic' or 'diachronic', but time can no more be removed from the one than the other, as Nadel stresses.[3] Whether the anthropologist studies a society for a year, two years or a lifetime, he is still dealing with a society changing over time; he also utilizes the memories of his informants, written information, etc., and directly observes events over a certain period of time. It is a commonplace that a minimum of twelve months is desirable for a study of most societies, in order that the anthropologist may witness the different events of the whole seasonal cycle. Much of this continuous process of social life he observes is merely repetitive: it maintains, rather than modifies, existing patterns of behaviour. In a short-term study, changes in the form of a society will be difficult to observe and the evidence slight in quantity. But this technical limitation does not mean that structural changes are not taking place no matter how gradual they may be—and they may

---

[1] op. cit., p. 123.

[2] Radcliffe-Brown, p. 4; cf. Firth's distinction between 'social structure' and 'social organization': only in the latter sphere does time enter (Firth, 1950, p. 40). [3] Nadel, p. 17.

be extremely slow in a society like that, say, of an isolated Australian aboriginal tribe.

The high tide of anti-historicism has now passed. Professor Nadel recently declared that everyone recognizes that there is time-depth to all social action. We are all evolutionists, therefore, he suggests; we all recognize this 'cumulative process'.[1]

But this is no way of describing, say, the French Revolution or the opening of copper mines of Northern Rhodesia. *Dis*continuity and radical structural change are as much a part of evolutionary theory as 'continuity' or 'successiveness'. Though extreme functionalism is dying, its replacement by a dynamic theory which takes account of different kinds of change—repetitive, structural, gradual, radical—still remains to be carried out.

Professor Evans-Pritchard's reintroduction of the historical approach into British anthropology is, then, an important theoretical development: he has already given us a practical demonstration of its significance in his book *The Sanusi of Cyrenaica*. There is no doubt that there has been a general quickening of interest in the historical approach recently, especially amongst younger workers in this field.

But much remains to be done before social anthropology can resume its rightful place as a branch of historical science.

Ideal-Type Analyses of Millenarian Movements

(i) In 'Max Weber's Theory of Charisma' the re-introduction of an historical viewpoint into anthropology immediately raises the question as to what kind of analytical tools the historical anthropologist should use. The reader will have noted that I have made no use of Max Weber's celebrated theory of 'charisma': this is largely because the analytical tools used in this work are those forged by Marx, with whose ghost, it has rightly been said, Weber was engaged in a lifelong debate.

The debate has mainly been conducted on the subject of the 'Protestant Ethic'. It is Weber's theory of charisma, however, which is the most relevant part of his sociology for this book. Though the book itself constitutes a positive use of the approach of his opponent, this in itself is no criticism of Weber's own theories. To explain why I find Weber's theory of charisma unacceptable requires some consideration of his general theory.

[1] *Nadel*, pp. 104-6.

Weber bases his sociology on a classification of social action into four 'ideal types': firstly, a type of rational action in which action is oriented to the realization of an absolute value regardless of the cost, difficulty, etc., involved (*wertrationalität*); secondly, another type of rational action (*zweckrationalität*) in which the actor has several alternative ends in view, no one of them absolute; in achieving these ends, he considers the problems involved in carrying out any one of them, their possible results, effects on others, and so on; thirdly, 'affectual' action, in which action is guided principally by 'the specific affects and states of feeling of the actor'[1]; and fourthly, 'traditional' action, guided merely by habit and custom.

According to Weber, these four types of action are 'ideal' in that they are logically conceived 'pure' types of action which together will be found to make up specific concrete action. No one of them necessarily coincides with any concrete, particular action. This is most unlikely. At most, one might find concrete action which largely corresponds, though rarely completely, to any one type.

Weber then constructs different types of economic action and of political authority on the basis of this general classification. In the field of political authority, for example, he elaborates three types: a rational-legal type, a charismatic, and a traditional.

By rationality he meant the adoption of the means best suited to the achievement of an end or the fulfilment of a set of values. There are several important implications of this concept of rationality. Firstly, Weber leaves out of his scheme, as something extra-scientific, the analysis of the objectives or goals of action. He implies that we can say nothing meaningful about ends; we can merely take them as given, for science cannot help us when it comes to choosing between what are only matters of faith or arbitrary selection.[2] We have seen that the specific categories of affectual and traditional action within Weber's general scheme are treated as being non-rational; now we observe that irrationalism is built into the *whole* scheme, for the entire province of the ends of action is treated as beyond the reach of science.

These conclusions are entailed in Weber's subjectivist starting-point, for his classification of types of action is based upon the subjective meaning of the action to the actor. Again, as the jump-

---

[1] *Weber*, 1947, p. 105.   [2] cf. *Weber*, 1949, pp. 52, 54.

ing-off point for his analysis of economic action, he takes not the process of production but subjective utility and the operation of the market.

The problem of the objective significance of action is immediately raised. Weber, by limiting his definition of rationality to mere calculation of the relation of means to ends, excludes evaluation of the objective rationality of the ends.

His treatment of deviations from the rational types as non-rational foreshadowed the later elimination of even more social action from the sphere of rationality by Pareto. To Weber, 'objective possibility' means little more than 'logically conceivable', and has no connotation of existence in reality independently of human perception. But if we base our view of objectivity on the latter sense, then Weber's two types of rationality may encompass much irrational behaviour, and the affectual or traditional types may appear quite rational.*

'Traditional' action, for example, may not appear irrational if one examines its application in a particular situation; the extent to which the action is efficacious in practice will show how far it is based upon a correct theoretical understanding of reality. I do not imply that a short-run pragmatism is an adequate or exhaustive guide to objective correctness, for as well as the experimental proof practice provides, the conformity of action with general established theoretical knowledge and the procedures of science is a further important criterion. Thus racist doctrines and rule by force 'worked' to a degree in the short run of Nazidom, they failed in the (not very) long run; they also conflicted with the known findings of science from the very beginning. And in Melanesia, it is only when the 'rational' economic activity initiated by the Whites does not bring 'rational' results that the natives turn to magical solutions. But this non-rational action is itself conditioned by the failure of what Weber would call rational activity.

The limited knowledge at the disposal of the people prevents their reaching a correct estimation of reality, but within these limits they employ quite rational calculation. To evaluate the degree of rationality of the actions of Cargo adherents, one must

---

* I do not elaborate on my use of 'rationality' or of 'objective reality' here; I take it as given, just as Weber takes marginal utility theory as given in his scheme. The relative value of the two approaches may be judged when we come to apply them to the facts.

consider these objective limitations on the actors' knowledge. Cargo cult actions and notions are only non-rational in relation to non-available absolute standards of knowledge. Within the limits of available knowledge, however, they represent reasoned interpretations and hypotheses constructed from known facts, and actions taken to test these out in practice. We have seen many times, notably for the eastern Central Highlands of New Guinea, how hypotheses about the nature of White society were tested by applying them: they were then modified or rejected, and new hypotheses formulated which were again tested out. Invalid theory was progressively eliminated. The failure of magical action is thus a function of limitations of knowledge which are socially conditioned, not a failure to use rational procedures. But whether they are incorrect or not can only be established by objective criteria which Weber does not admit into his scheme.

The essential rationality of Melanesian thought and action is shown on a larger scale by the directional tendency of the movements, the transition from magical to political action.

'Traditional' action, then, is not necessarily non-rational, nor would modern psychology class 'affectual' action as irrational, since social action may be both rational and yet charged with affect. That Weber's 'traditional' category is either a weak form of value-orientated behaviour or else merely automatic habit has been pointed out by Nadel,[1] and even hinted at by Weber himself.[2]

In order to cope with the problem of change, Weber introduces a further irrationalist notion into his scheme. He looks for the source of change in social tensions which are the product of 'fundamental elements of irrationality in social life': the tendency of the office-holder to merge his personal interests with those of his office; the danger of resentment of disciplinary authority on the part of the disciplined; or the spill-over into irrational channels of affect which is not absorbed by the rational order (pp. 61-64). Especially important is the conflict between what he terms 'formal' and 'substantive' rationality. In the economic sphere, for example, this would mean a conflict of interest between the requirement of a rationally calculated economy (formal rationality) and those involved in complying with the given values of a society (substantive rationality). Thus, in a given situation, formal ration-

[1] *Nadel*, p. 31.   [2] *Weber*, 1947, pp. 101, 105.

ality might be said to entail the lowering of wages in the interests of general economic stability. Substantive rationality, however, requires the economist and politician to take account of the likelihood of the unpopularity of such cuts among wage earners—not merely out of self-interest, but also because people believe that they are 'entitled' to a certain level of wages. Weber implies that such beliefs and values are arbitrary and non-rational, and inhibit the rational operation of the economy. This theory is quite familiar to us today as Welfare State theory.

This way of posing the problem presumes that there is one agreed, rational, logical answer to a specific economic or political problem, an answer which can be determined by scientific analysis, and which may be arrived at without consideration of values or of partisan interests. The theory assumes that a common policy can be worked out by rulers and ruled, by management and worker, for the achievement of agreed and mutually beneficial objectives, on the basis of logical and rational assessment of the facts. It takes no account of fundamental antagonisms between ruler and ruled, employer and employee, lord and peasant, master and slave. For there *is* no agreed 'rational' interpretation of the situation, but rather two or more different interpretations, the practical implications of each being the advancement of the interests of each of the parties at the expense of the others. Such social strains, then, in our view, derive from the existence of opposed interests, not from sentimental interference with the working out of a 'scientific' social policy.

Weber's rational order, too, presumes the continuance of existing basic relationships. The status quo tends to be 'rational', and radical change non-rational. One of the irrational channels into which displaced social energy may flow, he suggests, is a traditionalist form of action; another, the charismatic. The charismatic leader is 'set apart from ordinary men and treated as endowed with supernatural, superhuman, or at least specifically exceptional powers or qualities'.[1] Weber notes that such leaders emerge in certain social situations: 'charisma', he says, 'is a phenomenon typical of prophetic religious movements or of expansive political movements in their early stages.'[2] But though he stresses the revolutionary nature of charismatic authority, and points out that conditions of social breakdown, anomie,

[1] p. 329.   [2] *op. cit.*, p. 340.

insecurity, etc., are favourable situations for its emergence, the genesis of these conditions is seen only in terms of formulas of 'strain'.

Thus, whilst stressing the revolutionary nature of charismatic authority, he contrasts it with the revolutionary force of reason. Reason alters the 'situations of action', whereas charisma alters rather the 'subjective or internal reorientation' (p. 333).

By using the word 'charisma' (the gift of grace), Weber emphasizes the inspirational, revelatory nature of this kind of authority. The followers of the charismatic leader show 'complete personal devotion' to him. His authority is based on a 'sign or proof, originally always a miracle'. The absence of a defined hierarchy is characteristic of charismatic authority. The 'staff' of the movement are recruited, not on the basis of rational requirements, but on the basis of an emotional experience open to all. The movement has no established administrative organs when it comes into existence; authority is merely 'based on an emotional form of communal relationship' (p. 331). Such movements are also irrational from the economic stand-point; they despise the 'attainment of a regular income by continued economic activity devoted to this end' (p. 333). They rely on loot, the spoliation of others' possessions, etc.

All these features may be found in Melanesian movements, but there is much in them, too, that Weber's theory cannot account for.

Firstly, there is often not one charismatic leader, but a division of leadership between an inspired prophet and 'political organizer'. The prophet is also often less important than the political leader. The prophet is frequently a retiring individual sometimes predisposed to dissociation phenomena, and claiming to be no more than the 'instrument' of higher powers, and is manipulated by the organizer. Secondly, there may be not one but several prophets, and not one but several organizers. Often each village or other social unit has its leader, and a 'federal' form of organization develops rather than a centralized movement united by loyalty to a particular leader. The mechanism of inspiration facilitates the emergence of numerous leaders and prophets, since anyone may become inspired; fissiparous tendencies are therefore constantly found.

Turning to the recruitment of 'staff', the evidence shows that while the mechanism of the 'call' appears to be an open form of recruitment, certain categories of people supply more leaders than others. The leaders usually derive their authority from the indigenous order (traditional 'big men', aristocrats, magicians,etc.), or from their special knowledge or experience of the new social order of the Whites, or from new-found wealth and power. Conversely, females are rarely leaders. The formally 'open' mechanism of selection, then, in fact selects individuals in certain social positions, not merely, as some writers suggest, the unscrupulous or the psychologically unstable.

By rejecting historical analysis and concentrating on the construction of 'ideal types', Weber only creates pigeon-holes into which fragments of social behaviour can be fitted. The formalism which Weber objected to in Simmel's work is therefore present in his own. We find such disparate individuals and movements as the shaman and the 'berserker', the Emperors of China and Kurt Eisner, Napoleon and John Smith, the Mormon leader, all classified together under the rubric 'charismatic'.

To sum up, non-rational action is seen here as a product of economic and political tensions within a particular social framework; i.e.,the 'irrationality' of the movement reflects the irrationality of a particular social structure, not any inherent limits of rationality common to all structures. The type of social action taken by millenarists, then, does not represent an affectual regression from rational action, but a questioning of the validity of this very 'rationality'. By considering objective limits of knowledge, by recognizing the existence of the opposed interests of different social groups within the one society, and by elucidating the processes of rational calculation involved in Cargo thought, we can reach a better understanding of the genesis and development of these movements. We cannot do this with the aid of the 'charisma' concept,whatever insights can be gained from Weber—and they are many; for this reason I have not used the term in this work.

*　　*　　*

(ii) *Ralph Linton.* A more recent attempt at using 'ideal-type' analysis in the study of millenarian and allied movements is that outlined by Linton. Linton calls these movements 'nativistic', a term which describes 'any conscious attempt on the part of a society's members to revive or perpetuate selected aspects of its culture'.[1] Such movements can be either revivalistic—stressing

---

[1] *Linton,* p. 230.

the readoption of customs fallen into desuetude—or perpetuative
—seeking to maintain the existing order.

Now it is true that there is a stress in these movements upon the
revival of the past, especially in the early movements. The White
man's goods are to be destroyed and the old native order restored.
But even in these early movements, there are expectations of benefits which were in no sense part of the traditional order. Thus the
validity of analysis in terms of revivalism (stress on the past) or
perpetuation (stress on the present) is limited; there is also a looking
forward to quite new prospects. Again, it is only certain of the features of the traditional order that are revived, and, since these are revived or perpetuated under changed social conditions, they may have
changed significance. The revival of polygamy, for example, may
represent a resistance to mission teaching on Christian marriage.

Dreams of reviving a past Golden Age are, of course, an implied
criticism of the present, and a hope for the future. As applied to
some of the early movements, there is much validity in Linton's
analysis. The millenarian vision of a return to the past reflects the
lack of real and close control over native society by the White in-
truders, and the growing extension of such control. It also shows
that the throwing off of White control was a real possibility for
many peoples in the early stages of colonial administration; the
revival of the old life of only yesterday seemed quite feasible to
natives who had only encountered one or two European officials
or missionaries. One strong effort, it appeared, and the Whites
could be expelled. But in the later movements, as evidence of
European power grows, as it becomes apparent that the foreigners
have come to stay and that they cannot easily be defeated, and as
wants for the Europeans' goods become ingrained, the natives no
longer strive for the mere rejection of the White man's civilization.
They now seek to take over the riches and power of the Europeans;
no longer do they desire merely to destroy his goods and revert to
the old ways. They want their independence, but only in order to
become more like the European. It is independence of political
control, not isolation from the cultural achievements and material
wealth of the Whites which the natives strive for.

Totally new elements, therefore, are always found in these
movements, and can be labelled neither 'traditional' nor 'Europeanisms'. Thus flagpoles become means of communication with
the agents of the millennium.

Linton goes on to distinguish 'rational' from 'magical' movements, thus necessitating four categories of movement: (*i*) Revivalistic-magical; (ii) Revivalistic-rational; (iii) Perpetuative-magical; (iv) Perpetuative-rational.

In magical 'nativistic' movements, he says, the society's members 'are attempting to recreate those aspects of the ancestral situation which appear desirable in retrospect' (p. 323). Rational movements, on the other hand, stress the past (revivalistic) or present (perpetuative) existence of the society 'as a unique entity'. Their 'usage is psychological, not magical'. Attempts to utilize these criteria, however, break down: 'It may well be questioned whether any sort of nativistic movement can be regarded as genuinely rational' (p. 232). 'In non-nativistic messianic movements, the millennial condition is represented as something new and unique . . . even in this respect the differences are not too clear.' Of the 'perpetuative-rational' type, this form is 'so rare that the writer has been unable to find any clear example of it' (p. 232).

It is thus clear that these four categories are not descriptions of real behaviour, but ideal types—'polar positions in a series' (p. 233).

When we turn to consider dominated groups, we are told that 'we stand on firmer ground' and that a clear analysis can be presented. The firmness of the ground disappears, however, when classification is attempted. A 'dominated-superior' group will 'normally' develop rationalistic nativism, but 'very often' such nativism 'will acquire a semi-magical quality'. The 'rational' movements may be either revivalistic or perpetuative but are most likely to be a combination of both. 'Fully-developed magical-revivalistic nativism is also very likely', but this may be 'somewhat mitigated'.

Thus, using the 'polar positions' cited above, we learn that a dominated group will develop types 2 and 4 nativism, though they may often acquire characteristics of types 1 and 3. A mixed type 2/4 is 'most likely', though this may be 'somewhat mitigated', and type 1 is also 'very likely'.

We may well ask how such confusion arises. Linton himself points out that 'the generalizations so far developed have been based upon the hypothesis that societies are homogeneous and react as wholes to contact situations'. He then observes: 'very frequently this is not the case, especially in societies which have a well-developed class organization'. His fundamental thesis thus ignores the existence of antagonistic groups bound together by a network of social relations; we have not two 'societies' in contact, but one divided society.

It might be objected that Linton means by 'society' the total configuration embracing both groups, for he cites the selection of European traits by some movements. In fact, he does use this concept in places, as his material obliges him to do so, but his basic concept is clearly that of 'societies' in 'contact'. Thus we read 'the society's members recreate the ancestral situation' (p. 232); selected symbols 'provide the society's members' with exclusive foci of interest and criteria of distinctiveness (p. 233). Or 'society' becomes 'group': 'symbols help to re-establish and maintain the self-respect of the group's members' (p. 233); 'the members of each group' (p. 234). In general, these terms are used interchangeably; 'each society considers itself superior' (i.e.,Mexicans and Whites in the South of the USA); 'the two groups are in close contact'; 'the life of each of the societies',etc.,etc.

Now it is obvious enough that these *are* groups. The essence of the mode of thinking displayed here, however, lies in the emphasis on the discreteness of the groups; in the Hegelian sense of the word, it is a metaphysical mode of thinking.* This attempt to separate out the component elements of the movements and place them in separate boxes ignores the fact that they are neither traditional nor European; they are part of a new social synthesis.

The movements are not therefore merely 'nativistic', nor are they focused on the past. Even less do they represent, as Linton tells us, 'frankly irrational flights from reality' (p. 233). To call these movements 'nativistic' and backward – looking, besides being theoretically incorrect, does not fit the facts.†

The concept of 'nativism' thus fails to account for many cult

* cf. Gluckman's criticism of Malinowski's 'stultifying scheme of three separate cultural phases' with its picture of the elements of a culture 'integrated into well-defined units'. Gluckman opposes to Malinowski's 'compartments', the conception of 'the Rand mines [and] the African tribe which supplies their labour [as] both part of a single social field' (*Gluckman*, 1949, p. 7; *Malinowski*, 1945, passim).

† Herskovits similarly calls the movements 'contra-acculturative . . . wherein a people come to stress the values in aboriginal ways of life, and to move aggressively, either actually or in fantasy, towards the restoration of these ways, even in the face of obvious coincidence of the irimpotence to throw off the power that restricts them' (*Herskovits*, 1948, p. 531; cf. also *Herskovits*, 1938, passim).

elements—rituals, modes of organization, doctrines, etc.—which are new, and quite foreign to the traditional order. Where old beliefs and practices are retained or revived, they have a new content: the ancestors are now given feasts in order to obtain the things of the White man. And there is little that is reversionary or perpetuative in the concept of expelling the Europeans, not in order to revert to the past, but in order to acquire their new goods, techniques, knowledge and power. The ancestors, too, are returning in order to build a new future in which Papuans will be as Whites. The movements are thus forward - looking, not regressive, the order of the future being the *inversion* of the present.

Bibliographies

Bibliography

Abel, Charles W. *Savage Life in New Guinea.* London: London Missionary Society, 1902.

Abel, Russell W. *Charles W. Abel of Kwato.* New York: Fleming H. Revell, 1934.

Allen, C. H. 'The Marching Rule Movement in the British Solomon Islands Protectorate.' Unpublished Dip. Anth. thesis, Haddon Library, Cambridge, 1950.

———. 'Marching Rule: A Nativistic Cult of the British Solomon Islands.' *Corona,* III, No. 3 (1951), 93–100.

Allen, Rev. L. W. 'The Purari Kompani,' *South Pacific Commission, Social Development Notes,* No. 7 (1952), 1–13.

Australia, Commonwealth Government. *British New Guinea, Annual Reports,* 1892–93 to 1905–6. Government Printer.

———. *Papua, Annual Reports,* 1906–7 onwards. Government Printer.

———. *Reports to the League of Nations on the Administration of New Guinea,* 1921–22 to 1939–40. Government Printer.

———. *Reports to the General Assembly of the United Nations on the Administration of New Guinea,* 1946–47 onwards.

Australian Board of Missions. 'Cults: Nationalism in the Pacific,' *Australian Board of Missions Review* (Field Survey No. 7), XL, No. 7 (1950), 101–3.

Baal, J. van. 'The Nimboran Development Project,' *South Pacific,* VI, No. 8 (1952), 492–98.

———. *The Nimboran Community Development Project.* (Technical Paper No. 45.) Sydney: South Pacific Commission, 1953.

Baar, W. van. 'Ein ganz eigentümlicher Vorgang,' *Steyler Missionsbote,* LIX (1931–32), 127–28.

Bader, Otto. 'Im Dunkel des Heidentums,' *Steyler Missionsbote,* LXIII (1935–36), 287–88.

Banton, Michael. 'Adaptation and Integration in the Social System of Temne Immigrants in Freetown,' *Africa,* XXVI (1956), 354–68.

Barber, Bernard. 'Acculturation and Messianic Movements,' *American Sociological Review*, VI (1941), 663–69.

Barrow, G. L. 'The Story of Jonfrum,' *Corona*, III, No. 10 (1951), 379–82.

Bax, E. Belfort. *The Social Side of the Reformation in Germany. (Rise and Fall of the Anabaptists*, Vol. III.) London, 1903; New York: American Scholar Publications.

Belshaw, C. S. 'Native Politics in the Solomon Islands,' *Pacific Affairs*, XX, No. 2 (1947), 187–93.

———. 'The Postwar Solomon Islands,' *Far Eastern Survey*, XVII, No. 8 (1948), 95–98.

———. *Island Administration in the South West Pacific*. London: Royal Institute of International Affairs, 1950a.

———. 'The Significance of Modern Cults in Melanesian Development,' *Australian Outlook*, IV, No. 2 (1950b), 116–25.

———. 'Recent History of Mekeo Society,' *Oceania*, XXII (1951), 1–23.

———. *Changing Melanesia*. Melbourne: Oxford University Press, 1954.

Berndt, R. M. 'A Cargo Movement in the East Central Highlands of New Guinea,' *Oceania*, XXIII, Nos. 1–3 (1952–53), 40–65, 137–58.

———. 'Reaction to Contact in the Eastern Highlands of New Guinea,' *Oceania*, XXIV, Nos. 3 and 4 (1954), 190–228, 255–75.

Bjerre, Jens. *The Last Cannibals*. London: Michael Joseph, 1956.

Blackwood, Beatrice. *Both Sides of Buka Passage*. Oxford: Clarendon Press, 1935.

Blood, N. B. Extract of report of patrol from Hagen to Ifitamin, in *ANGAU—Final Report on Activities*, Appendix A, 1946.

Bodrogi, Tibor. 'Colonization and Religious Movements in Melanesia, *Acta Etnografica Academiae Hungaricae*, II (1951), 259–92.

———. 'Some Notes on the Ethnography of New Guinea,' *Acta Etnografica Academiae Hungaricae*, III (1954), 91–184.

Bogesi, George. 'Santa Isabel, Solomon Islands,' *Oceania*, XVIII, Nos. 3–4 (1948), 208–32, 327–57.

Brenningmeyer, Leo. *Fünfzehn Jahre beim Bergvolke der Baininger*. Hiltrup: Herz-Jesu-Missionshaus, 1928.

Brewster, A. B. *The Hill Tribes of Fiji*. London: Seeley Service, 1922.

Bruijn, J. V. de. 'The Mansren Cult of Biak,' *South Pacific,* V, No. 1 (1951), 1–10.

Burridge, K. O. L. 'Cargo Cult Activity in Tangu,' *Oceania,* XXIV, No. 4 (1954a), 241–54.

———. 'Racial Tension in Manam,' *South Pacific,* VII, No. 15 (1954b), 932–38.

Cato, A. C. 'A New Religious Cult in Fiji,' *Oceania,* XVIII, No. 2 (1947), 146–56.

Central Office of Information. *Among Those Present—The Official Story of the Pacific Islands at War.* London: HMSO, 1946.

Chinnery, E. W. P., and Haddon, A. C. 'Five New Religious Cults in British New Guinea,' *The Hibbert Journal,* XV, No. 3 (1917), 448–63.

Clark, Elmer T. *The Small Sects in American Christianity.* New York: Abingdon-Cokesbury Press, 1949.

Colonial Office. *Reports on the British Solomon Islands Protectorate for 1948, 1949–50* and *1951–52.* London: HMSO, 1949, 1951, and 1953.

———. *Annual Report for the New Hebrides,* 1921–22, No. 1161, and 1923, No. 1216.

Conroy, W. R., and Bridgland, L. A. 'Native Agriculture in Papua-New Guinea,' in *Report of the New Guinea Nutrition Survey Expedition, 1947.* Sydney: Government Printer, 1947.

Cowan, H. K. J. 'Ethnolinguistics and Papuan Etymology,' *Oceania,* XXV, Nos. 1–2 (1954), 54–60.

Cranswick, George H., and Shevill, Ian W. A. *A New Deal in Papua.* Melbourne: F. W. Cheshire, 1949.

Deacon, A. Bernard. *Malekula, a Vanishing People in the New Hebrides.* London: Routledge & Kegan Paul, 1934.

Decker, J. A. *Labour Problems in the Pacific Mandates.* (Institute of Pacific Relations.) London: Oxford University Press, 1941.

Derrick, R. A. *A History of Fiji,* vol. 1. Suva: Printing and Stationery Dept., 1950.

Dozier, Edward P. 'The Concepts of "Primitive" and "Native" in Anthropology,' in *Year-book of Anthropology 1955.* New York: Wenner-Gren Foundation, 1955.

Du Bois, Cora. *The 1870 Ghost Dance.* (Anthropological Records, III, No. 1.) Berkeley: University of California Press, 1946.

Eckert, G. 'Prophetentum in Melanesien,' *Zeitschrift für Ethnologie,* LXIX (1937), 135–40.

———. 'Prophetentum und Kulturwandel in Melanesien,' *Bässler Archiv,* XXIII (1940), 26–41.

———. 'Das Prophetentum und sein Einfluss auf Geschichte und Kulturentwicklung der Naturvölker,' *Forschungen und Fortschritte,* XVII, No. 6 (1941), 59.

Elkin, A. P. *Social Anthropology in Melanesia.* London and New York: Oxford University Press, 1953.

Encyclopaedisch Bureau. *Schouten en Padaido-Eilanden,* Afl. XXI. The Hague: Martinus Nijhoff, 1920.

Engels, Friedrich. *The Peasant War in Germany.* New York: International Publishers, 1926.

Erskine, J. E. *Journal of a Cruise among the Islands of the Western Pacific including the Feejees.* London, 1853.

Evans-Pritchard, E. E. 'Some Collective Expressions of Obscenity in Africa,' *Journal of the Royal Anthropological Institute,* LIX (1929), 311–33.

———. 'Social Anthropology: Past and Present,' *Man,* L, No. 198 (1950). The Marett Lecture, 1950.

Fauset, Arthur Huff. *Black Gods of the Metropolis: Negro Religious Cults of the Urban North.* (Publications of the Philadelphia Anthropological Society, Vol. III.) London: Oxford University Press, 1944.

Firth, Raymond. *Human Types.* London: Thomas Nelson, 1945; New York: New American Library.

———. *Elements of Social Organization.* London: C. A. Watts; Gloucester, Mass.: Peter Smith, 1951.

———. 'Social Changes in the Western Pacific,' *Journal of the Royal Society of Arts,* CI, No. 4909 (1953), 803–19.

———. 'The Theory of "Cargo" Cults: A Note on Tikopia,' *Man,* LV, No. 142 (1955).

Flierl, J. *Gottes Wort in den Urwalden von Neuguinea.* Neuendettelsau, 1929.

Flierl, Leonhard. *Eemasang, die Erneuerungsbewegung in der Gemeinde Sattelberg (Neuguinea).* Gütersloh: Bertelsmann, 1931.

Fortes, Meyer. *The Dynamics of Clanship Among the Tallensi.* London: Oxford University Press, 1945.

Fortune, Reo. *Sorcerers of Dobu.* London: Routledge & Kegan Paul, 1932; New York: E. P. Dutton.

Freytag, W. *Spiritual Revolution in the East.* London: Lutterworth Press, 1940.

Gitlow, Abraham L. *Economics of the Mount Hagen Tribes, New Guinea.* (Monograph of the American Ethnological Society, XII.) New York: J. J. Augustin, 1947.

Gluckman, Max. *An Analysis of the Sociological Theories of Bronislaw Malinowski.* (Rhodes-Livingston Paper, No. 16.) London: Oxford University Press, 1949.

Goudswaard, A. *De Papoewa's van de Geelvinksbaai.* Schiedam: H. A. M. Roelants, 1863.

Guiart, Jean. '"Cargo Cults" and Political Evolution in Melanesia,' *South Pacific,* V, No. 7 (1951a), 128–29.

———. 'John Frum Movement in Tanna,' *Oceania,* XXII (1951b), 165–75.

———. 'Forerunners of Melanesian Nationalism,' *Oceania,* XXII, No. 2 (1951c), 81–90.

———. 'Report of Native Situation in the North of Ambrym (New Hebrides),' *South Pacific,* V, No. 12 (1952a), 256–67.

———. 'The Co-operative Called "The Malekula Native Company,"' A Borderline Type of Cargo Cult,' *South Pacific,* VI, No. 6 (1952b), 429–32.

———. 'Culture Contact and the "John Frum" Movement on Tanna, New Hebrides,' *Southwestern Journal of Anthropology,* XII, No. 1 (1956a), 105–16.

———. *Grands et petits hommes de la montagne, Espiritu Santo (Nouvelles-Hébrides).* New Caledonia: Institut Français d'Océanie, 1956b.

———. 'L'Organisation Sociale et Coutumière de la Population Autochthone de la Nouvelle-Calédonie,' in Jacques Barrau, *L'Agriculture Vivrière Autochthone de la Nouvelle-Calédonie.* Noumea: South Pacific Commission, 1956c.

———. *Mythe, Evolution et Histoire, un siècle et demi de contacts culturels à Tanna.* 1957.

Haaft, D. A. ten. 'De Betekenis van de Manseren-beweging 1940 voor het zendingswerk op de Noordkust van Nieuw Guinea,' *De Heerbaan,* I, No. 3 (1948a) 71–81.

———. 'De Manseren-beweging op Noord-Nieuw-Guinea, 1939–1943,' *Tijdschrift 'Nieuw-Guinea,'* 8th yr. (1948b), 161–65 and 9th yr., 1–8.

Haddon, A. C. (ed.). *Reports of the Cambridge Anthropological Expedition to the Torres Straits,* vol. i. Cambridge: Cambridge University Press, 1935.

Hanneman, Rev. E. F. 'Le culte de cargo en Nouvelle-Guinée,' *Le Monde Non-Chrétien,* No. 8 (1948), 937–62.

Harrisson, Tom. *Savage Civilization.* London: Victor Gollancz, 1937.

Hartweg, F. W. 'Das Lied von Manseren Mangundi (Biak-Sprache),' *Zeitschrift für Eingeborenen-Sprachen,* XXIII (1932), 46–58.

Hasselt, J. L. van. 'Eenige aanteekeningen aangaande de bewoners der Noord-Westkust van Nieuw-Guinea,' *Tijdschrift van het Bataviaasch Genootschap voor Kunsten en Wetenschappen,* XXXII, 1889.

Hasselt, P. J. F. van. 'De legende van Mansren Manggoendi,' *Bijdragen tot de Taal-, Land- en Volkenkunde,* LXIX (1914), 90–100.

Held, G. J. *De Papoea, Cultuurimprovisator.* The Hague: van Hoeve, 1951.

Herskovits, Melville J. *Acculturation.* New York: J. J. Augustin, 1938.

———. *Man and his Works.* New York: Alfred A. Knopf, 1948.

Hogbin, H. Ian. 'Trading Expeditions in Northern New Guinea,' *Oceania,* V, No. 4 (1935), 375–407.

———. *Experiments in Civilization.* London: Routledge & Kegan Paul, 1939.

———. 'Native Councils and Native Courts in the Solomon Islands,' *Oceania,* XIV, No. 4 (1944), 257–83.

———. 'Native Christianity in a New Guinea Village,' *Oceania,* XVIII, No. 1 (1947), 1–35.

———. *Transformation Scene.* London: Routledge & Kegan Paul; New York: Humanities Press, 1951.

Höltker, Rev. Georg. 'Die Mambu-Bewegung in Neuguinea: ein Beitrag zum Prophetentum in Melanesien,' *Annali Lateranensi,* V (1941), 181–219.

———. 'How "Cargo Cult" is Born: The Scientific Angle of an Old Subject,' *Pacific Islands Monthly,* XVII, No. 4 (1946), 16, 70. (Translated and condensed from 'Schwarmgeister in Neu–Guinea während des letzes Krieges,' *Zeitschrift für Missionswissenschaft,* 1946.)

Horst, D. W. *De Rum-Serams op Nieuw-Guinea, op het Hinduïsme in het Oosten van der Archipel.* Leiden: Brill, 1893.

Hurst, H. L. *Papuan Journey.* Sydney: Angus and Robertson, 1938.

Inselmann, Rev. Rudolf. 'Letub, the Cult of the Secret of Wealth.' Unpublished M.A. thesis, Kennedy School of Missions, Hartford Seminary Foundation, 1944.

———. ' "Cargo Cult" Not Caused by Missions,' *Pacific Islands Monthly*, XVI, No. 2 (1946), 44–45.

———. 'The Cargo Cult, a Hindrance to Missionary Work,' in 'Changing Missionary Methods in Lutmis New Guinea.' Unpublished B. Div. thesis, Faculty of Wartburg Seminary, Dubuque, Iowa, 1948.

Kamma, F. C. 'Messianic Movements in Western New Guinea,' *International Review of Missions*, XLI, No. 162 (1952), 148–60.

Keesing, Felix M. *The South Seas in the Modern World.* London: Allen and Unwin, 1942.

Kroef, Justus M. van der. 'The Messiah in Indonesia and Melanesia,' *Scientific Monthly*, LXXV (1952), 161–65.

Laufer, C. 'Religiöse Wahnideen unter Naturvölkern,' *Neue Zeitschrift für Missionswissenschaft* (1947), pp. 216–21.

Lawrence, P. 'Cargo Cult and Religious Beliefs among the Garia,' *International Archives of Anthropology*, XLVII, No. 1 (1954), 1–20.

———. 'The Madang District Cargo Cult,' *South Pacific*, VIII, No. 1 (1955), 6–13.

Lawry, W. *Visit to the Friendly and Feejee Islands.* London, 1850.

Leenhardt, Maurice. *Do Kamo.* Paris: Gallimard, 1947.

Leeson, Ida. *Bibliography of Cargo Cults and other Nativistic Movements in the South Pacific.* (South Pacific Commission Technical Paper, No. 30.) Sydney, 1952.

Lehmann, F. R. 'Prophetentum in der Südsee,' *Zeitschrift für Ethnologie*, LXVI (1934a), 261–65.

———. ' "Prophetentum in der Südsee,' *Christentum und Wissenschaft*, X (1934b), 56–58.

Lekahema, S. 'De "Manseren"-beweging,' *Tijdschrift 'Nieuw-Guinea,'* 8th yr. (1947), 97–102.

Lett, Mollie. ' "Vailala Madness": Wave of Religious Fanaticism that Swept Papua in 1919,' *Pacific Islands Monthly*, VI, No. 5 (1935), 25.

Linton, Ralph. 'Nativistic Movements,' *American Anthropologist*, XLV, No. 1 (1943), 230–40.

Lommel, Andreas. 'Der "Cargo-Kult" in Melanesien, Ein Beitrag zum Problem der "Europäisierung" der Primitiven,' *Zeitschrift für Ethnologie*, LXXVIII, No. 1 (1953), 17–63.

Luke, Sir Harry. *From a South Seas Diary, 1938–1942*. London: Nicholson and Watson, 1945.

McAuley, James. 'The Distance between the Government and the Governed,' *South Pacific*, VII, No. 8 (1954), 815–20.

McCarthy, F. D. ' "Trade" in Aboriginal Australia, and "Trade" Relationships with Torres Straits, New Guinea and Malaya,' *Oceania*, X (1939), 81–104, 173–95.

Macquarrie, Hector. *Vouza and the Solomon Islands*. London: Victor Gollancz, 1945.

Mair, L. P. *Australia in New Guinea*. London: Christophers; Mystic, Conn.: Verry, Lawrence, 1948.

Malinowski, Bronislaw. 'The Natives of Mailu,' *Transactions and Proceedings of the Royal Society of South Australia* (1915), pp. 494–706.

———. *Argonauts of the Western Pacific*. London: Routledge & Kegan Paul, 1922; New York: E. P. Dutton.

———. *Coral Gardens and their Magic*, vol i. London: Allen and Unwin, 1935; Bloomington: Indiana University Press, 1965.

———. *The Dynamics of Culture Change*. London, Oxford University Press; New Haven: Yale University Press, 1945.

Marwick, M. G. 'Another Modern Anti-Witchcraft Movement in East-Central Africa,' *Africa*, XX (1950), 100–112.

Marx, Karl, and Engels, Friedrich. *Selected Works*, vol. i. London: Lawrence and Wishart, 1950.

Mead, Margaret. *Sex and Temperament in Three Primitive Societies*. London: Routledge & Kegan Paul, 1935; Gloucester, Mass.: Peter Smith.

———. 'The Mountain Arapesh. I. An Importing Culture,' *Anthropological Papers of the American Museum of Natural History*, XXXVI, pt. 3 (1938).

———. *Growing Up in New Guinea*. Harmondsworth: Pelican Books, 1942; Gloucester, Mass.: Peter Smith.

———. 'The Role of Small South Sea Cultures in the Postwar World,' *American Anthropologist*, XLV, No. 2 (1943), 193–97.

———. *New Lives for Old*. New York: William Morrow, 1956.

Mikloukho-Maclay, N. N. *Sobranie Socheneniy*, vols. i and iii, pt. 1. Moscow: Academy of Sciences, 1950–51.

Miller, J. Graham. 'Naked Cult in Central West Santo,' *Journal of the Polynesian Society*, LVII, No. 4 (1948), 330–41.

M. L. (Maurice Lenormand). 'Le "cargo cult" à Bougainville,' *Etudes Melanésiennes,* No. 4 (1949), 82–83.

Monckton, C. A. W. *Last Days in New Guinea.* New York: Dodd, Mead, 1922.

Montauban, Paul. 'Schwärmgeister auf den Salomonen,' *Kreuz und Karitas,* 1934, pp. 137 ff.

———. 'Le grand rêve Buka depuis la guerre,' *Missions Mariste d'Océanie,* 2nd yr., No. 15 (1948), 135–39.

Moszkowski, Max. 'Die Volksstämme am Mamberamo in Holländisch-Neuguinea und auf den vorgelagerten Inseln,' *Zeitschrift für Ethnologie,* XLIII (1911), 315–46.

Murphy, Sir Hubert. *Papua of Today.* London: P. S. King and Sons, 1925.

———. 'Indirect Rule in Papua,' *Report of the 19th Meeting, Australasian Association for the Advancement of Science, Hobart,* 1928, pp. 329–36.

Murphy, John J. *The Book of Pidgin English.* Brisbane: W. R. Smith and Paterson, 1943; San Francisco: Tri-Ocean, 1962.

Nadel, S. F. *The Foundations of Social Anthropology.* London: Cohen and West, 1951; New York: Free Press, 1953.

Oliver, Douglas L. *The Pacific Islands.* Cambridge, Mass.: Harvard University Press, 1952.

O'Reilly, P. 'Les Chrétientés mélanésiennes et la guerre,' *Neue Zeitschrift für Missionswissenschaft,* 3rd yr., No. 2 (1947), 106–17.

———. 'Malaita (îles Salomon), un exemple de revendications indigènes,' *Missions Maristes d'Océanie,* 2nd yr., No. 15 (1948), 149–52.

———. 'Prophétisme aux Nouvelles-Hébrides: le mouvement Jonfrum à Tanna (1940–1947),' *Le Monde Non-Chrétien,* No. 10 (1949), pp. 192–208.

———. '"Jonfrum" is New Hebridean "Cargo Cult,"' *Pacific Islands Monthly,* XX, No. 6 (1950), 67, 69–70 and No. 7 (1950), 59–61, 63–65.

O'Reilly, Rev. P., and Sédès, Jean-Marie. *Jaunes, noirs et blancs.* Paris: Editions du Monde Nouveau, 1949.

Paton, W. F. 'The Native Situation in the North of Ambrym (New Hebrides),' *South Pacific,* VI, No. 5 (1952), 392–96.

Peel, Gerald. *Isles of the Torres Straits.* Sydney: Current Book Distributors, 1947.

Poirier, Jean. 'Les mouvements de libération mythique aux Nouvelles-Hébrides,' *Journal de la Société des Océanistes*, V, No. 5 (1949), 97–103.

Pos, Hugo. 'The Revolt of "Manseren",' *American Anthropologist*, LII, No. 4 (1950), 561–64.

Powell, H. A. 'Cricket in Kiriwina,' *Listener*, XLVIII, No. 1227 (1952).

Quinlivan, P. J. 'Afek of Telefolmin,' *Oceania*, XXV, Nos. 1-2 (1954), 17–22.

Radcliffe-Brown, A. R. *Structure and Function in Primitive Society*. London: Cohen and West; New York: Free Press, 1952.

Read, M. K. E. 'Effects of the Pacific War in the Markham Valley, New Guinea,' *Oceania*, XVIII, No. 2 (1947), 95–116.

———. 'Missionary Activities and Social Change in the Central Highlands of Papua and New Guinea,' *South Pacific*, V, No. 11 (1952), 229–38.

Reed, S. W. *The Making of Modern New Guinea*. (Memoirs of the American Philosophical Society, Vol. XVIII.) Philadelphia, 1943.

Rhys, Lloyd. *Jungle Pimpernel: The Story of a District Officer in Central Netherlands New Guinea*. London: Hodder and Stoughton, 1947.

Richards, A. I. 'A Modern Movement of Witch-Finders,' *Africa*, VIII (1935), 448–61.

Riley, E. Baxter. *Among Papuan Headhunters*. Philadelphia: J. B. Lippincott, 1925.

Rivers, W. H. R. *Essays on the Depopulation of Melanesia*. Cambridge: Cambridge University Press, 1922.

Romilly, H. H. *The Western Pacific and New Guinea*. London: John Murray, 1886..

Rousseau, Madeleine (ed.). *L'Art Océanien, sa présence*. Paris: Le Musée Vivant, 1951.

Roy, Sarat Chandra. *The Mundas and Their Country*. Calcutta: Kuntaline Press, 1912.

Sayers, G. F. (ed.). *Handbook of Tanganyika*. London: Macmillan, 1930.

Schlosser, Katesa. 'Der Prophetismus in niederen Kulturen,' *Zeitschrift für Ethnologie*, LXXV (1950), 60–72.

Seligman, C. G. *The Melanesians of British New Guinea*. Cambridge: Cambridge University Press, 1910.

——. 'Temperament, Conflict and Psychosis in a Stone-Age Population,' *British Journal of Medical Psychology,* IX (1929), 187–202.

Shepperson, George. 'The Politics of African Church Separatist Movements in British Central Africa, 1892–1916,' *Africa,* XXIV (1954), 233–45.

Simpson, Colin. *Adam in Plumes.* Melbourne: Angus and Robertson, 1954.

——. *Islands of Men.* Sydney: Angus and Robertson, 1955.

South Pacific Commission. *The Purari Delta—Background and Progress of Community Development.* (Technical Paper No. 35.) Sydney, 1952.

Spier, Leslie. *The Ghost Dance of 1870 Among the Klamath of Oregon.* (University of Washington Publications in Anthropology, No. 2.) Seattle: University of Washington, 1927.

——. *The Prophet Dance of the Northwest and its Derivatives: The Source of the Ghost Dance.* (General Series in Anthropology, No. 1.) Menasha: University of Wisconsin Press, 1935.

Stanner, W. E. H. *The South Seas in Transition.* London: Australasian Publishing Co., 1953.

Sundkler, Bengt G. M. *Bantu Prophets in South Africa.* (Missionary Research Series, No. 14.) London: Lutterworth Press, 1948; New York: Oxford University Press, 1961.

Sutherland, W. 'The "Tuka" Religion,' *Transactions of the Fijian Society, 1908–10,* 1910, pp. 51–57.

Teutscher, H. J. 'Some Mission Problems in Post-war Indonesia: Experiences in Dutch New Guinea,' *International Review of Missions,* XXXVII, No. 148 (1948), 410–20.

Thompson, Laura. *Fijian Frontier.* New York: Institute of Pacific Relations, 1940a.

——. *Southern Lau, Fiji.* Hawaii: Bernice P. Bishop Museum, 1940b.

Thomson, Basil. *Diversions of a Prime Minister.* London: Blackwood, 1894.

——. 'The Kalou-Vu (ancestor-gods) of the Fijians' and 'A New Religion: The Tuka Cult,' *Journal of the Anthropological Institute of Great Britain and Ireland,* XXIV (1895), 340–59.

Thomson, J. P. *British New Guinea.* London: George Philip and Sons, 1892.

Tjideman, E. 'De legende van Meok Woendi,' *Mededeelingen van het Bureau voor Bestuurszaken der Buitengezittengen, bewerkt door het*

Encyclopaedisch Bureau, vol. ii. The Hague: Martinus Nijhoff, 1912, pp. 253–56.

Tueting, L. *Native Trade in Southeast New Guinea. (Bishop Museum Occasional Papers,* II, No. 15). Hawaii: Bernice P. Bishop Museum, 1935.

United Nations. *Report of Committee on New Guinea (Irian),* Part III, 1950.

———. *Report of U.N. Visiting Mission to Trust Territories in the Pacific, Reports on New Guinea,* 8th and 12th Sessions. New York, 1951, 1953.

———. *Information from Non-Self-Governing Territories, Papua,* 9th Session. New York, 1954.

Wallace, Anthony F. C. 'Revitalization Movements,' *American Anthropologist,* LVIII, No. 2 (1956), 264–81.

Warner, W. Lloyd. *A Black Civilization.* London: Harper, 1937; New York: Harper & Row, 1958.

Weber, Max. *The Theory of Social and Economic Organization.* London: Hodge, 1947; New York: Free Press, 1957.

———. *The Methodology of the Social Sciences.* New York: Free Press, 1949.

Westermann, D. *Die heutigen Naturvölker im Ausgleich mit der Neuen Zeit.* Stuttgart: Ferdinand Enke, 1940.

White, Bishop G. *Thirty Years in Tropical Australia.* London: Society for Promoting Christian Knowledge, 1919.

Williams, F. E. *The Vailala Madness and the Destruction of Native Ceremonies in the Gulf Division.* (Papuan Anthropology Reports, No. 4.) Port Moresby, 1923.

———. *Orokaiva Magic.* London: Oxford University Press, 1928.

———. 'The Vailala Madness in Retrospect,' in *Essays Presented to C. G. Seligman.* London: Routledge & Kegan Paul, 1934.

———. 'Some Effects of European Influence on the Natives of Papua,' *Report of the 22nd Meeting, Australian and New Zealand Association for the Advancement of Science,* Melbourne, 1935, pp. 215–22.

———. 'The Creed of a Government Anthropologist,' *Australian and New Zealand Association for the Advancement of Science,* Report 24, Sydney, 1939, 145-59.

Wolferstan, Bertram. *The Catholic Church in China from 1860 to 1907.* London: Sands, 1909.

Supplementary Bibliography of Literature on Melanesian Cargo Cults 1957–67

Compiled by D. A. Heathcote

Attenborough, David. 'The Cargo Cult and the Great God Frum,' *Sunday Times* (London), April 24, 1960, p. 5.

Baal, J. van. 'Erring Acculturation,' *American Anthropologist*, LXII, No. 1 (1960), 108–21.

Bureau for Native Affairs, Netherlands New Guinea. 'Anthropological Research in Netherlands New Guinea since 1950,' *Oceania*, XXIX, No. 2 (1956), 132–63.

Burridge, Kenelm O. L. 'The Cargo Cult,' *Discovery*, XXIII (February, 1962), 22–27.

———. *Mambu: A Melanesian Millennium.* London: Methuen; New York: Humanities Press, 1960.

Clemhout, Simone. 'Typology of Nativistic Movements,' *Man*, LXIV, No. 1 (1964), 14–15.

Devereux, G. 'An Ethno-Psychiatric Note on Property Destruction in Cargo Cults,' *Man*, LXIV (November–December, 1964), 184–185.

Eliade, M. 'Dimensions religieuses du renouvellement cosmique,' *Evanos Jahrbuch*, XXVIII (1959), 241–76.

Ellenberger, H. P. 'Les mouvements de libération mythique,' *Critique*, XV, No. 190 (1963), 248–67.

Fabian, J. 'Führer und Führung in den prophetisch-messianischen Bewegungen der (ehemaligen) Kolonialvölker,' *Anthropos*, LVIII, No. 5–6 (1963), 773–809.

Fischer, H. 'Cargo-Kulte und die "Amerikaner," ' *Sociologus*, XIV, No. 1 (1964), 17–29.

Gott, K. D. 'Cargo Cult in New Guinea,' *Eastern World*, IX, No. 8 (1955), 6–13; No. 10 (1955), 20–21.

Guariglia, Guglielmo. 'I movimenti profetico-salvifici e le missioni,' *Missioni cattolici*, LXXXIX, Nos. 8–9 (1960), 258–69.

—————. 'Pour une nouvelle typologie des "mouvements prophetiques" au niveau ethnologique,' *Sixth International Congress of Anthropological and Ethnological Sciences, 1964,* II, No. 2, 393–97.

—————. 'Prophetismus und Heilserwartungsbewegungen bei den niedrigen Kulturen,' *Numen,* V, No. 3 (1958), 180–98.

—————. *Prophetismus und Heilserwartungs-Bewegungen als völkerkundliches und religion-geschichtliches Problem.* (*Wiener Beiträge zur Kulturgeschichte und Linguistik,* Vol. XIII.) Horn and Vienna: Verlag Ferdinand Berger, 1959.

—————, and Lanternari, Vittorio. 'Oceania. Movimenti profetico-salvifici a livello etnologico,' *Studi e materiali di Storia delle Religione,* XXXII, No. 2 (1961), 247–308.

Guiart, Jean. 'Conférences sur les millénarismes, Université de Chicago, April, 1960, *Archives de Sociologie des Religions,* IX, 105–9.

—————. 'Culture Contact and the "John Frum" Movement on Tanna, New Hebrides,' *Southwestern Journal of Anthropology,* XII, No. 1 (1956), 105–16.

—————. 'Institutions religieuses traditionelles et messianismes modernes à Fiji,' *Archives de Sociologie des Religions,* II, No. 4 (1957), 3–30.

—————. "Le mouvement coopératif aux Nouvelles-Hébrides,' *Journal de la Société des Océanistes,* XII (1956), 326–34.

—————. 'Naissance et avortement d'un messianisme: Colonisation et décolonisation en Nouvelle Calédonie,' *Archives de Sociologie des Religions,* IV, No. 7 (1959), 3–44.

—————. *Un siècle et demi des contacts culturels à Tanna, Nouvelles-Hébrides.* Paris: Musée de l'Homme, 1956.

—————, and Worsley, Peter. 'La répartition des mouvements millénaristes en Mélanésie,' *Archives de Sociologie des Religions,* III, No. 5 (1958), 38–47.

Hogbin, H. Ian. *Social Change.* London: C. A. Watts; New York: Humanities Press, 1958.

Höltker, Rev. Georg. 'Der Cargo-Kult in Neuguinea lebt noch,' *Nouvelle Révue de Science Missionaire,* XVIII (1963), 223–26.

Inder, S. 'On the Trail of the Cargo Cultists, with a Short Biography of Anton Hinina Kearei,' *Pacific Islands Monthly,* XXXI, No. 2 (1960) 57–58.

Inglis, Judy. 'Cargo Cults: the Problem of Explanation,' *Oceania,* XXVII, No. 4 (1957), 249–63.

⟶ ———. 'Interpretation of Cargo Cults—Comments,' *Oceania*, XXX, No. 2 (1959), 155–58.

⟶ Jarvie, I. C. *The Revolution in Anthropology.* London: Routledge & Kegan Paul; New York: Humanities Press, 1964.

⟶ ———. 'Theories of Cargo Cults: A Critical Analysis,' *Oceania*, XXXIV, No. 1 (1963), 1–31; No. 2 (1963), 108–36.

Julius, C. 'Cargo Cults in Papua and New Guinea,' *Australian Territories*, II, No. 4 (1962), 14–20.

Kabel, J. P. 'De Kesjep-beweging in Nimboran,' *De Heerbaan*, VI (1953), 106–24, 148–71.

Kamma, F. C. *De Messiaanse Koreri-bewegingen in het Biaks-Numfoorse culturgebied.* The Hague: J. N. Voorhoeve, 1954.

Köbben, A. J. F. 'Prophetic Movements as an Expression of Social Unrest,' *Internationales Archiv für Ethnologie*, XLIX (1960), 117–64.

Kooijman, S. 'Die messianischen Koreri-Bewegungen auf Neuguinea,' *Evangelisches Missions-Magazin* (Basel) (November, 1955), pp. 180–88.

Koppers, W. 'Prophetism and Messianic Beliefs as a Problem of Ethnology and World History,' *Proceedings of the IXth International Congress for the History of Religions, Tokyo and Kyoto, 1958.* Tokyo, 1960, pp. 39–50.

———. 'Prophetismus und Messianismus als völkerkundliches und universalgeschichtliches Problem,' *Saeculum*, X, No. 1 (1959), 38–47.

Kouwenhoven, W. J. H. 'Nimboran, A Study of Social Change and Economic Development in a New Guinea Society.' Thesis, The Hague, 1956. Pp. 240.

Kroef, Justus M. van der. 'Culture Contact and Culture Conflict in Western New Guinea,' *Anthropological Quarterly*, XXXII, No. 1 (1959), 134–60.

Lanternari, Vittorio. 'Fermenti religiosi e profezie di libertà fra i popolo coloniali,' *Nuovo Argomenti*, XXXVII (March-April, 1959), 54–92.

⟶ ———. 'Messianism: Its Historical Origin and Morphology,' *History of Religions*, II, No. 1 (1962), 52–72.

———. 'Origini storiche dei culti profetici melanesiani,' *Studi e Materiali di Storia delle Religione*, XXVII (1956), 36–86.

————. *The Religions of the Oppressed: A Study of Modern Messianic Cults.* London: MacGibbon and Kee; New York: Alfred A. Knopf, 1963.

Lawrence, Peter. *Road Belong Cargo: A Study of the Cargo Movement in the Southern Madang District, New Guinea.* Manchester: Manchester University Press; New York: Humanities Press, 1964.

Luck, G. C. 'The Problems of the Sepik: Progress vs. Cargo Cultism,' *Pacific Islands Monthly,* XXIX, No. 8 (1959), 69.

Maahs, A. M. *A Sociological Interpretation of the Cargo Cult of New Guinea and Selected Comparable Phenomena in Other Areas of the World.* Ann Arbor, Michigan: University Microfilms, 1956.

Maher, Robert F. *New Men of Papua: A Study in Culture Change.* Madison: University of Wisconsin Press, 1961.

————. 'Tommy Kabu Movement of the Purari Delta,' *Oceania,* XXIX, No. 2 (1958), 75–90.

Mair, Lucy P. 'Independent Religious Movements in Three Continents,' *Comparative Studies in Society and History,* I, No. 2 (1958–59), 113–36.

————. 'The Pursuit of the Millennium in Melanesia,' *British Journal of Sociology,* IX, No. 2 (1958), 175–82.

Martin, P. 'Les mouvements de John Frum et de Tieka. Deux faits sociaux totaux aux Nouvelles-Hébrides,' *Monde non-chrétien* (July–December, 1957), pp. 43–44, 225–65.

Mead, Margaret. 'Independent Religious Movements,' *Comparative Studies in Society and History,* I, No. 4 (1959), 324–29.

————. *New Lives for Old: Cultural Transformation, Manus, 1923–1953.* London: Victor Gollancz; New York: William Morrow, 1956.

————, and Schwartz, Theodore. 'The Cult as a Condensed Social Process.' *Transactions of the 5th Conference of the Joseph Macy, Jr. Foundation.* New York, 1960.

Mühlmann, W. E., *et al. Chiliasmus und Nativismus: Studien zur Psychologie, Soziologie und historischen Kasuistik der Umsturzbewegungen.* Berlin: Reimer, 1961. (Includes Müller, E. W., 'Die Koreri-Bewegungen auf den Schouten-Inseln, West Neuguinea'; and Uplegger, H., and Mühlmann, W. E., 'Die Cargo-Kulte in Neuguinea und Insel-Melanesien.')

Oosterwal, G. 'A Cargo Cult in the Mamberamo Area,' *Ethnology,* II, No. 1 (1963), 1–14.

O'Reilly, Patrick. 'Mouvements messianiques en Océanie,' *Vie intellectuelle* (December, 1956), pp. 22–30.

Pouwer, J. 'Cargo Cults (in the Biak Numfoor Culture Area),' *Oceania*, XXVIII, No. 3 (1958), 247–52.

Read, K. A. 'A "Cargo" Situation in the Markham Valley, New Guinea,' *Southwestern Journal of Anthropology*, XIV, No. 3 (1958), 273–94.

Russo, A. 'Profetismo e movimenti salvifico-messianici,' *Revista di Etnografia*, XIV (1960), 78–85.

Salisbury, Richard F. 'An "Indigenous" New Guinea Cult,' *Kroeber Anthropological Society Papers*, No. 18 (1958), 67–78.

Schaffner, B. 'Group Processes.' *Transactions of the 5th Conference of the Joseph Macy, Jr., Foundation*. New York, 1960.

Schwartz, Theodore. *The Paliau Movement in the Admiralty Islands, 1946–1954. (Anthropological Papers*, XXXXIX, No. 2.) New York: American Museum of Natural History, 1962.

Sierksma, F. *Een nieuwe hemel en een nieuwe aarde: Messianistiche en eschatologische bewegingen en voorstellingen bij primitieve volken*. The Hague: Mouton, 1961.

Smith, Marian W. 'Towards a Classification of Cult Movements,' *Man*, LIX (January, 1959), 8–12.

Stanner, W. E. H. 'On the Interpretation of Cargo Cults,' *Oceania*, XXIX, No. 1 (1958), 1–25.

Suzuki, M. 'Higashi New Guinea no Paliau Undo,' *Kaigai Jijo*, XII, No. 10 (1964), 33–41.

Thrupp, Sylvia L. (ed.) *Millennial Dreams in Action: Essays in Comparative Study. (Comparative Studies in Society and History*, Supplement 2.) The Hague: Mouton; New York: Humanities Press, 1962.

Tichelman, G. L. 'Papoese Leilsverwachtingen,' *Studium Generale*, VI, No. 2 (1960), 41–44.

Valentine, C. A. 'Uses of Ethnohistory in Acculturation,' *Ethnohistory*, VII (1960), 1–15.

Watters, R. F. 'Cargo Cults and Social Change in Melanesia,' *Pacific Viewpoint*, I (1960), 104–7.

Worsley, Peter M. 'Cargo Cults,' *Scientific American*, CC, No. 5 (1959), 117–28.

———. 'Millenarian Movements in Melanesia,' *Rhodes-Livingstone Journal*, XXI (1957), 18–31.

Wouters, A. 'Le "marching rule." Aspects sociologiques d'un mouvement politique et social aux Salomons meridionaux,' *Sociaal Kompas*, VI, No. 2 (1961), 45–55.

Index

Index